The Secret Trauma

Other Books by the Author

Rebellion, Revolution, and Armed Force

The Politics of Rape: The Victim's Perspective

Crimes Against Women: The Proceedings of the International Tribunal
(with Nicole Van de Ven)

Rape in Marriage

Against Sadomasochism: A Radical Feminist Analysis
(with Robin Linden, Darlene Pagano, and Leigh Star)

*Sexual Exploitation: Rape, Child Sexual
Abuse, and Workplace Harassment*

THE SECRET TRAUMA

Incest in the Lives of Girls and Women

Diana E. H. Russell

Basic Books, Inc., Publishers / New York

Table 4–3, "Extrapolation from the Kinsey Study's Data on Child Sexual Abuse by Adult Males," is here adapted by permission of the Kinsey Institute for Research in Sex, Gender, and Reproduction. The data originally appeared in an unnumbered table in Kinsey, A. C., Pomeroy, W. B., Martin, C. E. and Gebhard, P. H., *Sexual Behavior in the Human Female* (Philadelphia: W. B. Saunders, 1953), p. 117.

Library of Congress Cataloging-in-Publication Data

Russell, Diana E. H.
  The secret trauma.

  References: p. 413
  Includes index.
    1. Incest—United States. 2. Incest victims—United
States—Psychology. I. Title. [DNLM: 1. Incest.
2. Women—psychology. WM 610 R962s]
HQ72.U53R87 1986   306.7'77   85–43107
ISBN 0–465–07595–9

Printed in the United States of America
Copyright © 1986 by Diana E. H. Russell
Designed by Vincent Torre
86 87 88 89 90 HC 9 8 7 6 5 4 3 2 1

To those who have contributed

to the new perspective on incest victimization,

to those who are working

toward ending incestuous abuse,

and to the incest victims

who have been willing to talk about

their pain

PART FOUR
THE PERPETRATORS

PART FIVE
THE FAMILIES

List of Tables

List of Figures

Acknowledgments

The study on which this book is based began in April 1977. Eight years later, hundreds of people have helped in widely varying capacities. Many have already been thanked in my first book to come from this study—*Rape in Marriage* (1982), as well as in my second—*Sexual Exploitation* (1984). While I will remain ever grateful to them, I will mention by name here only those who have assisted me with *The Secret Trauma*.

The data-gathering phase of my research on incest was funded by the National Institute of Mental Health (Grant R01MH28960). Analysis of the interviews on child sexual abuse was partially funded by the National Center on Child Abuse and Neglect (Grant 90–CA–813/01). I am grateful to both agencies for recognizing the merits of this research and for funding it. Without their support this ambitious undertaking would have been impossible. I am also grateful to those responsible for obtaining generous speaking honoraria for me; my research depended on these sources when my funding from NCCAN ran out. A small faculty grant from Mills College also helped pay for the preparation of the final manuscript.

Karen Trocki, Ph.D., has been the research analyst for this project since 1979. She has played an indispensable role in all phases and aspects of the quantitative analysis. She plotted the graphs included in this book and conducted the analysis of the changes in incestuous abuse over time as well as the regression analyses and all the other more routine runs. In addition, she wrote first drafts of a section of the methodology chapter and of the interpretation of one regression analysis. I am deeply grateful to her for her commitment to this ongoing research project despite the sometimes inconvenient timing, as well as for her skill and understanding of my complex data base.

I am also indebted to Nancy Howell for her assistance with the cohort analysis of incestuous abuse and extrafamilial child sexual abuse, to Bill Wells for his contribution to the computer programming in the early phases of this research, and to Eda Regan, the reference librarian at Mills College, for her help.

The coding of the qualitative data was done with great care and competence by Jan Dennie and Chantal Rohlfing. Jan Dennie also did an excellent job of keying into the word processor many drafts of this manuscript. Her patience with all the changes, as well as her willingness to work long hours when deadlines loomed, is much appreciated.

For critical evaluation of earlier drafts of this manuscript I am very much indebted to my good friend and colleague David Finkelhor. His bold and valuable criticisms of more than one version of most of the manuscript resulted in many quite radical and significant changes. My indebtedness to his intellectual contributions to the field will be apparent in my many discussions of his work throughout this book.

Sandy Butler, another very good friend and colleague, brought her extraordinary editorial skills to her reading and evaluation of the entire manuscript, plus a second reading of some of it. I owe her a great deal for her excellent and timely assistance.

Rachel Schurman also read the whole manuscript with great care and offered very useful and detailed criticisms and suggestions. The evaluations of Sandy, David, and Rachel have reminded me that the hardest criticisms to hear at first often become the greatest spur for improvement.

Judith Herman was the only person—aside from the editors at Basic Books—to read the final draft of the manuscript. I am extremely grateful to her for her comments and suggestions. Her approval of my treatment of this—her special area of expertise—reassures me that this book is ready to be launched into the world. I am also greatly indebted to Nancy Howell and Jeffrey Masson for reading the entire manuscript in galley form. Both made numerous valuable suggestions and helped me through this final stage of publishing this book.

Others who have given me useful feedback on portions of the manuscript include Lucy Berliner, Sue Saperstein, Pat Phelan, Constance Backhouse, Kathleen Coulborn Faller, Gail Wyatt, Stephanie Peters, Lenore Walker, Barbara Rosenblum, Abby Abinanti, Richard Sullivan, Mary Williams, and Denah Griffiths.

In the three years since I started to write this book, Cheryl Colopy, Laura Tow, and Meredith Maran Graham have all provided me with editorial assistance. I am particularly grateful to Meredith for her excellent efforts to make the manuscript more accessible to the general reader in a very short space of time.

Many others have helped me with the research, sometimes by discussing important incest-related issues with me, sometimes by offering encouragement and emotional support. For this, I'd like to thank Sandy Butler, David Finkelhor, Kee MacFarlane, Florence Rush, Marny Hall, Pat Phelan, Maryel Norris, and Lidia Hermida for their assistance. Michelle Morris, Roland Summit, and Judith Herman also helped at a crucial point in my search for a publisher, and my agent, Jonathan Dolger, has assisted at all stages of the publication process in whatever way he could with a promptness and patience that is all too rare.

A few pages of an article coauthored by Judith Herman, Karen Trocki, and myself have been rewritten and included in chapter 13. The last segment of chapter 19 is a slightly changed version of a piece from a previously published chapter coauthored by David Finkelhor and myself. Constance Backhouse and Diana Majury undertook a great deal of work on a chapter intended for this book about incest laws and the reforms that are needed. Unfortunately, it seemed to be too difficult to integrate into this book. But I want to thank them for their efforts and to express the hope that their good ideas will find another home.

Finally, I'd like to thank my Basic Books editor, Jo Ann Miller, for wanting to publish *The Secret Trauma* and for her many important and valuable suggestions in revising it and shepherding it through the publication process, and Sabrina Soares for her contribution to the editing.

—DIANA E. H. RUSSELL
July 1985

The Secret Trauma

All names, locations, and other identifying characteristics of the respondents mentioned and/or quoted in this book have been changed.

1

Introduction:
The Problem
and Its History

For those who aspire to an image of free womanhood, incest is as destructive to women as genital mutilation or the binding of feet.
—Judith Herman, 1981

When we examine a cross-section of the population, as we did in the Kinsey Report, . . . we find many beautiful and mutually satisfying relationships between fathers and daughters. These may be transient or ongoing, but they have no harmful effects.
—Wardell Pomeroy, 1976

Contradictory views, such as those expressed in the quotations from psychiatrist and author Judith Herman and Kinsey researcher and author Wardell Pomeroy, are as common in the incest literature as they are in the culture at large. Nevertheless, 1978 marked the beginning of a new look at incest from a more victim-oriented perspective. In that year Sandra Butler's *Conspiracy of Silence* and Louise Armstrong's *Kiss Daddy Goodnight* gave us the first feminist analyses of incest ever published in book form—building on feminist author Florence Rush's earlier groundbreaking work (1974; 1977). The proliferation of scholarly and popular books and articles since then reflects the tremendous upsurge in public awareness and concern about incest. (For two excellent and thorough annotated bibliographies on incest, see Bagley 1985 and de Young 1985.) As sociologist Wini Breines and historian Linda Gordon point out: "Incest, a heretofore unmentionable subject, is now part of popular consciousness, explored often in Ann Landers' columns, television talk shows, and movies, to say nothing of its explosion in pornography of all types" (1983, p. 523).

What accounts for this new and growing interest?

The answer is not that incestuous abuse is a new phenomenon. Although I will show that incestuous abuse has been increasing over the past few decades, the increase is not so great as to account for the new willingness to confront this issue. The answer is a sad one indeed. While it is reasonable to expect that clinicians—who are privy to the anguish and impact of incestuous abuse on the lives of some of their clients—would have been the ones to break the silence, in fact few of them have done so. On the contrary, it appears that the higher the status of the mental health professionals, the more unwilling they have been to question their old assumptions about the rarity of incestuous abuse and about their favorite scapegoats—the seductive child and the collusive mother (Herman 1981). For example, Canadian psychiatrist James Henderson argues as recently as 1983 that

the all-pervasive anguish to which incestuous behavior is a dysfunctional solution is the same anguish which we later identify in the subsequent adult life of the little girl who was the alleged victim of this interaction—that the intense personal pain preceded the incestuous interaction and was in part its motive rather than its consequence. (P. 34)

Just as Freud's oedipal theory focused on the child's motivation to engage sexually with the adult, so Henderson emphasizes the motivation of "the alleged victim" to ease her intense personal pain by having sex with her father.

One has only to read some of the venomous and outrageously personal attacks by psychoanalysts and their defenders on Jeffrey Masson for daring to criticize Freud for his dismissal of incest as a female fantasy to realize how deep and serious their resistance is (see, e.g., Cole 1984; Kendrick 1984; Malcolm 1984; Robinson 1984; and Rycroft 1984).

There have probably always been some sensitive, nonsexist clinicians who believed their female clients' reports of incest and other child sexual abuse, recognized the resulting trauma, and tried to help them to heal. But many women—some perhaps anticipating a response like Henderson's—have never told anyone, particularly not a therapist.

Scientists—who are supposed to be unbiased and dedicated to discovering the truth—were also unwilling for the most part to recognize and expose the problem of incest. Instead, it was feminists (some of whom were also researchers and clinicians) together with incest victims who were willing to speak out, who broke what Butler has so aptly called the conspiracy of silence about this formerly secret trauma (1978). As a result of feminists' efforts, this new awareness about the reality of incestuous abuse is also occurring outside the United States (see, e.g., Nelson 1982; Renvoize 1982; Ward 1985).

Aside from incest, the feminist movement has also been responsible for raising public awareness about rape and wife abuse as well as the woman-hating nature of pornography (Breines and Gordon 1983). It is a terrible indictment of both researchers and clinicians that credit for the public attention now focused on these serious and longstanding societal problems must be given not to themselves but to a political movement that was willing to provide validation and support for victims with the courage to tell the truth about their experiences.

Incest Denied: The Legacies of Freud and Kinsey

Discounting the experiences of incest victims has a long history. Sigmund Freud and Alfred Kinsey are two of the major figures implicated in this cover up.

Florence Rush (1977, 1980), Judith Herman (1981), and Jeffrey Masson (1984) have provided excellent but disturbing accounts of how Freud came to argue that his patients' descriptions of incestuous abuse were fantasy, not fact. Disturbed by his own incestuous desires toward his daughter and by suspicions of his father's incestuous wishes, Freud expressed enormous relief and even a feeling of triumph when he decided that "it was hardly credible that perverted acts against children were so general" (Herman 1981, p. 10). Instead, he concluded that his patients' accounts were figments of their imaginations based on their own sexual desires for their fathers.

Freud's theory of the Oedipus complex—the notion that every child between three and six years of age goes through a stage during which she or he sexually desires the parent of the opposite sex—also makes it very easy to shift the responsibility for incestuous acts onto the child. This theory seems to be a projection onto children of the sexual desires of adult males (Masson 1984; Miller 1984).*

Just as the notion that women secretly want to be raped serves the needs of those who would secretly—or not so secretly—desire to rape them, so

---

*Psychoanalyst Alice Miller, however, fails to make a gender analysis of the problem and instead accuses adults and parents—rather than just male adults and fathers—of projecting their desires onto children. Considerable empirical data show that very few adult women sexually abuse children—their own or anyone else's.

the notion that children desire sex with adults serves the needs of adults who desire sex with children as well as those who want to *protect* adults who have such desires.

The Freudian legacy, then, is to discount the reality of incestuous abuse and, where discounting is impossible, to blame the child for being the one who wanted the sexual contact in the first place.

But all the blame for the mistreatment of incest victims in this century cannot rightly be heaped on Freud. Responsibility should also be placed on those clinicians who, following in his footsteps, have refused to take seriously the experiences of incestuous abuse reported by their clients.

Incest researchers have a comparable—though briefer—tradition of discounting the experiences of incest victims. Judith Herman points out that Alfred Kinsey, "though he never denied the reality of child sexual abuse, did as much as he could to minimize its importance" (1981, p. 16). Despite the fact that the majority of the cases of incest disclosed to the Kinsey researchers were cross-generational and involved perpetrators who were uncles, fathers, and grandfathers rather than brothers, they saw fit to write the following commentary on their incest data:

Heterosexual incest occurs more frequently in the thinking of clinicians and social workers than it does in actual performance. There may be a good many males who have thought of the possibilities of sexual relations with sisters or mothers or with other close female relatives, but even this is by no means universal, and is usually confined to limited periods in the boy's younger years. . . . The most frequent incestuous contacts are between pre-adolescent children, but the number of such cases among adolescent or older males is very small. (1948, p. 558)

Why, one wonders, did the Kinsey study never provide any data to substantiate its conclusion that most incest occurs among preadolescent children? As Herman has suggested, the answer seems to be that its authors had little respect for the personal integrity of children. "By contrast," Herman writes, "this group demonstrated a keen sensitivity toward the adult offender. As scientists and leaders in the struggle for enlightened sexual attitudes, they felt it incumbent upon themselves to plead the offender's case" (1981, p. 16).

In support of Herman's conclusion, consider the following quote from the Kinsey team's classic text on females, in which they place the responsibility for the repetition of incestuous sexual contacts on the young victims.

Repetition [of preadolescent contacts with adults] had most frequently occurred when the children were having their contacts with relatives who lived in the same household. In many instances, *the experiences were repeated because the children had become interested in the sexual activity and had more or less actively sought repetitions of their experience.* (1953, p. 118; emphasis added)

While acknowledging that 80 percent of the girls who had "sexual contacts" with adults both within and outside the family reported being "emotionally upset or frightened," the Kinsey study argued that this was due to adverse conditioning and not a sign of having been sexually abused. This is how they expressed this idea:

It is difficult to understand why a child, except for its cultural conditioning, should be disturbed at having its genitalia touched, or disturbed at seeing the genitalia of other persons, or disturbed at even more specific sexual contacts. When children are constantly warned by parents and teachers against contacts with adults, and when they receive no explanation of the exact nature of the forbidden contacts, they are ready to become hysterical as soon as any older person approaches, or stops and speaks to them in the street, or fondles them, or proposes to do something for them, even though the adults may have had no sexual objective in mind. Some of the more experienced students of juvenile problems have come to believe that the emotional reactions of parents, police officers, and other adults who discover that the child has had such a contact, may disturb the child more seriously than the sexual contacts themselves. The current hysteria over sex offenders may very well have serious effects on the ability of many of these children to work out sexual adjustments some years later in their marriages. (1953, p. 121)

Kinsey and his colleagues failed to distinguish between what Herman refers to as " 'nuisance' acts such as exhibitionism, and frankly exploitive acts such as the prostitution of women and the molestation of children. Ignoring issues of dominance and power," Herman continues, "they took a position that amounted to little more than advocacy of greater sexual license for men" (1981, p. 17).

The fact that child sexual abuse frequently results in no physical harm was another justification used by Kinsey and his colleagues to discount the seriousness of its consequences. While acknowledging instances of adults physically damaging children with whom they have attempted sexual contacts, they nevertheless commented: "But these cases are in the minority, and the public should learn to distinguish such serious contacts from other adult contacts which are not likely to do the child any appreciable harm if the child's parents do not become disturbed" (1953, p. 122). In those cases where physical harm resulted, they chose to minimize these injuries as well. They maintained that "we have only one clear-cut case of serious injury done to the child, and a very few instances of vaginal bleeding which, however, did not appear to do any appreciable damage" (1953, p. 122).

Why, one wonders, did Kinsey and his colleagues have the courage and honesty to inform the scientific community and the public at large about the prevalence of homosexuality, masturbation, premarital and extramarital sexual relations, sexual contacts with animals, and some women's ca-

pacity for multiple orgasms, when they were so unwilling to address the
problem of child sexual abuse?

Later statements by two of the authors of the Kinsey studies, Wardell
Pomeroy and Paul Gebhard, indicate that their relative silence on the
subject in 1948 and 1953 may have been no accident. Herman has speculated that these men may have thought the public was not yet ready to hear
about incest (1981, p. 18). Perhaps there is another explanation: that the
authors' reports were distorted by their own benign attitudes toward it.

In 1976 Wardell Pomeroy wrote the following passage—as well as the
one cited at the beginning of this chapter—in Penthouse's *Forum*:

Incest between adults and younger children can also prove to be a satisfying and enriching
experience, although difficulties can certainly arise. (In any case, I want to emphasize
that in no case would I condone incest—be it between adults or between children
and adults—when force, violence, or coercion are involved.) (P. 10; emphasis
added)

To point out that parentheses are rarely used for emphasis is a rather trivial
point. Far more serious is Pomeroy's euphemistic understatement that
"difficulties can certainly arise" in incestuous relations between adults and
children. He overlooks the whole issue of children's powerlessness in
relation to adults who want to have sex with them.

Paul Gebhard was quoted in 1977 as saying that only a tiny percentage
of the incest cases disclosed to the Kinsey researchers were ever reported
to police or psychologists, and "in the ones that were not reported, I'm
having a hard time recalling any traumatic effects at all. I certainly can't
recall any from among the brother-sister participants, and I can't put my
finger on any among the parent-child participants" (Nobile 1977, p. 118).

These comments suggest that regardless of whether the public was ready
to hear about incest when the Kinsey reports were published, the researchers may have been unwilling at that time to reveal the extent of their own
positive bias toward it.

Other researchers have been as guilty as the Kinsey team of discounting
the problem of incestuous abuse and blaming the victims. (The statements
of some of these people will be discussed in later chapters.) Most social
anthropologists, for example, continue to focus their attention on why
there is an incest taboo, rather than on the prevalence and effects of its
breach and the factors that are associated with its occurrence. Although
there are notable exceptions (e.g., Phelan 1981), they almost invariably
assume that when incest does occur, it is a mutual act by consenting
partners (e.g., Fox 1980). The unequal power relationship that is characteristic of incestuous abuse is usually ignored. It seems curiously inconsistent

that social anthropologists don't seem to find it important to consider why there is a murder taboo or a taboo against theft in most societies. These taboos are presumably accepted as to be expected and hence of little interest. Personally, it doesn't strike me as odd that most societies would outlaw sex between adults and children. It seems as readily understandable as the taboo against parents abandoning their children or imprisoning them in the basement.

The point here is that there are long histories in both the clinical and research fields of deeply discrediting and denigrating views of incest victims. In addition, two of the giants in each of these fields—Freud and Kinsey—are implicated. This legacy is the backdrop to the new feminist research and thinking on incest victimization that finally started to surface in 1978.

Recent Research on Incest

Groundbreaking as some of the recent writings on incest have been, the generality of most studies' findings has been unclear due to the unrepresentativeness of the samples on which they were based. For example, in her book *Incest* psychologist Karin Meiselman attempted to list all studies of incest with samples larger than five published in this country (1978, pp. 45–49). Many of the studies were based on cases obtained by referrals from therapists, psychiatric hospitals, courts, social agencies, and private practices; some of the studies had been conducted on incarcerated offenders. The samples used in all thirty-six studies were highly selective in one way or another. Almost all studies conducted since Meiselman published her analysis have been equally unrepresentative. This means that it is not scientifically sound to generalize any of their findings to a larger population.

A few total samples of students have been questioned about their experiences of child sexual abuse, including incest (e.g., Finkelhor 1979). ("Total sample" means that efforts were made to get *all* members of particular classes of students at particular schools to complete questionnaires.) This methodology has many important advantages over clinical or prison samples. However, students are themselves a select group in terms of age, social class, and race as well as such other possible characteristics as mental health. Hence findings obtained from student samples can also not be generalized to the nonstudent population.

Our survey is the first to study incest victims identified through interviews with a large representative sample of women.* Although this study was limited to 930 residents of San Francisco, it still provides the first scientifically sound basis for generalizing findings about incestuous abuse to the population of adult women in a major U.S. city. Another comparable though smaller-scale study based on interviews with 248 women between the ages of eighteen and thirty-six was conducted more recently by psychologist Gail Wyatt in Los Angeles (1985). The findings of these two studies on the prevalence of incest and extrafamilial child sexual abuse are astonishingly similar and mutually validating (as will be discussed in chapter 4).

A national sample would, of course, be preferable to these two local ones. But most other studies have been local, unrepresentative, and based on small numbers of incest victims.† Our study is based on the accounts of 187 incest experiences reported by 152 incest victims obtained from interviews with a probability sample of 930 women. This study therefore provides the soundest data base yet available for making tentative national estimates about such issues as the prevalence of incestuous abuse, whether or not father-daughter incest is more common than brother-sister or uncle-niece incest, how often incestuous abuse is repeated and over what period of time, and so on. In addition, it provides us with the first opportunity to evaluate some of the contemporary controversies surrounding incest on the basis of a scientifically selected, nonclinical population. This opportunity constitutes an important breakthrough.

One of the most shocking findings of our probability sample is that 16 percent of the 930 women had been sexually abused by a relative before the age of eighteen, and 4.5 percent had been sexually abused by their fathers before this age. If we extrapolate from this 16-percent figure to the population at large, it means that 160,000 women per million in this country may have been incestuously abused before the age of eighteen, and 45,000 per million may have been victimized by their fathers. These prevalence figures are much higher than those obtained by any previous study (but not higher than Wyatt's more recent one). The best estimate of father-daughter incest prior to our survey was 1 percent, and prevalence figures for incestuous abuse in general ranged from 4 to 12 percent (Herman 1981, p. 12).

*Although I was the principal investigator of this study, many people participated and contributed at all levels, including the decision making. For this reason, except when a decision or idea was clearly my own, I will often refer to "our study."

†The three national studies that include data on incestuous abuse and extrafamilial child sexual abuse are the Kinsey survey (1953), the National Study on Child Neglect and Abuse Reporting (1980, 1981), and the National Incidence Study sponsored by the National Center on Child Abuse and Neglect (1981). These studies are severely flawed, particularly with regard to their data on incestuous abuse. (See Finkelhor and Hotaling for a detailed critique of the National Incidence Study [1984].) In addition, as studies of incidence, their findings are difficult to compare with those obtained from studies of prevalence.

This research discovery—along with many of the others to be presented in this book—has important implications for theory, prevention, and treatment. It suggests that incestuous abuse can no longer be viewed as a problem that involves but a few sick or disturbed sex offenders. Particularly when considered along with wife rape, wife beating, and nonsexual child abuse, it reveals an intensely troubled contemporary American family. And the fact that the vast majority of this abuse is being perpetrated by males suggests that a full understanding of this problem requires seeing it within the context of severe gender and generational inequality.

It is difficult to solve a problem, or to ascertain its causes, until we know its magnitude and some of its true characteristics. For example, if incestuous abuse, when it occurs, is something that is usually repeated many times (as contemporary clinical knowledge suggests), it is not surprising that theorists have applied addiction models in an attempt to understand it (e.g., Carnes 1983). But our study found that incestuous abuse occurred only once in 43 percent of the cases, including 36 percent of the cases of father-daughter incest. These are the cases, presumably, that rarely come to the attention of clinicians.

To date, nearly all the incest literature has focused on father-daughter incest.*Although our study confirms that this form of incest is usually more traumatic than incestuous abuse by other relatives, it is nevertheless important to extend our knowledge to include brother-sister, grandfather-granddaughter, and uncle-niece incest as well. Twelve percent of the women in our sample were sexually abused by some relative other than their father.

Why Incestuous Abuse Is an Important Issue

That incestuous abuse is getting a great deal of public attention right now is beyond dispute. But attention aside, why is it an important issue?

Incestuous abuse is an important social problem because of the intense suffering and sometimes destructive long-term effects that result from it. Here are a few examples of what victims in our probability sample had to say about their experiences.

*Father-daughter incest has been the subject of autobiographical accounts by Armstrong (1978), Brady (1979), Allen (1980), McNaron and Morgan, eds. (1982), Hill (1985); a novel by Morris (1982); treatment-oriented books by Sgroi, ed. (1982) and Giaretto (1982); of some recent more scholarly works as well as popular and semipopular books by Forward and Buck (1978), Butler (1978), Justice and Justice (1979), Herman (1981), Renvoize (1982), Thorman (1983), Ward (1985); and of scholarly books published before 1978 by Weinberg (1955), DeFrancis (1969), and Maisch (1972).

"I went completely inside myself. I'm only now beginning to come out after five years of intensive therapy. There probably isn't one area it hasn't touched because without a solid family foundation you don't have anything." —Victim of father-daughter incest at age fifteen

"I can't seem to get over it. It's so deep-seated, even now at forty-three I'm still affected." —Victim of attempted rape by brother-in-law at age sixteen

"It had an extremely great effect. . . . Everything that's happened to me since in my life has been a result somehow of that experience." —Victim of stepfather-daughter incest at age fourteen

"It changed my way of thinking. I think now that all men are out there for what they can get. You can't even trust your own brother." —Victim of brother-sister incest at age sixteen

"Sexually I was very messed up for a long time. I feel that I could have ended up in a mental hospital from the experiences. I'm lucky I didn't, but it will affect me forever." —Victim of stepfather-daughter incest at age nine

That incestuous abuse is not always so traumatic, and in some cases no long-term effects were reported, is salutary information. It does not diminish the fact that incestuous abuse often causes a great deal of pain at the time, besides having severely deleterious effects for years to follow.

Two of our survey findings—that incestuous abuse is so much more widespread than heretofore thought possible and that there is a strong relationship between experiences of such abuse in childhood and adolescence and later experiences of victimization—suggest that millions of American girls are being socialized into victim roles. Other research suggests a connection between incest victimization and drug abuse, prostitution, suicide, mental illness, self-mutilation, alcoholism, running away from home (which greatly increases the risk of sexual victimization by other perpetrators), and later becoming a mother who is less able to protect her daughters from incest victimization (see, e.g., Benward and Densen-Gerber 1975; James and Meyerding 1977; Densen-Gerber and Hutchinson 1978; Herman 1981; Silbert and Pines 1981; and Kubler-Ross 1984). Concern about any of these other problems leads us right back to a concern about incestuous abuse. We have only recently begun to uncover the extent to which child sexual abuse in general appears to be at least one of the causative factors in many serious manifestations of self-destructive behavior in female adolescents and adults.

Progressive people who believe in women's and children's rights will not need to be persuaded that there can be no equality between the sexes as long as girl children are being sexually violated in such massive numbers.

But this is an adult women's issue as well as a girls' issue because millions of adult women still carry the scars of incest victimization. The fact that this commonplace but deeply distressing abuse has been hidden for so long is as horrifying as the fact that it occurs in the first place. As feminist author Susan Brownmiller (1975) has pointed out:

> The unholy silence that shrouds the interfamily sexual abuse of children and prevents a realistic appraisal of its true incidence and meaning is rooted in the same patriarchal philosophy of sexual private property that shaped and determined historic male attitudes toward rape. For if woman was man's original corporal property, then children were, and are, a wholly owned subsidiary. (P. 281)

Particularly female children.

It is crucial that we as a society stop participating in the conspiracy of silence that has kept incest one of the best-kept secrets for so long.

The Organization of This Book

Because the methodology of our survey is one of the things that sets it apart from all previous studies and makes it uniquely significant, chapter 2 describes it in some detail. Using case material from our survey to illustrate the points made, chapter 3 tackles the question of exactly what incest is, how it differs from incestuous abuse, and how, in turn, incestuous abuse differs from sexual trauma.

In chapter 4 our findings on the prevalence of incestuous abuse are presented and compared with those reported in other studies. Chapter 5 addresses the question of whether or not incestuous abuse has been increasing in this century in the United States. The few cases of incestuous abuse that were reported to the police in our study are quoted and discussed in chapter 6. Chapter 7 presents some of our basic findings about incestuous abuse—for example, its frequency and duration, the degree of physical force employed by the perpetrators, the severity of the abuse in terms of the sex acts involved, and so on. And in chapter 8 the relationship between the occurrence of incestuous abuse and social factors such as race and ethnicity, social class, religious upbringing, and type of family background are explored.

Chapter 9 focuses on the victims of incest: how they differed at the time of the interview from women who had never been incestuously abused in terms of their employment status and history, their marital and maternal status, their social class and religious preference. Data are also presented on how the victims handled their victimization, their resistance strategies, and what ended the sexual abuse.

The trauma as perceived by the victims is the subject of chapter 10, while chapter 13 focuses on how victims who reported extreme trauma differed from those who felt less traumatized by their incest experiences.

Data showing the relationship between incestuous abuse and later experiences of rape, marital abuse, and other sexual victimization are presented in chapter 11, and a theory to explain this controversial phenomenon of revictimization is offered.

Chapters 12 and 14 provide detailed case histories of four women whose experiences illustrate many of the points made in part 3.

In part 4 an overview chapter on the incest perpetrators is followed by chapters on fathers, brothers, female relatives, grandfathers, uncles, and other male relatives. Because so few female perpetrators were identified by our survey, it was impossible to undertake an analysis by type of female relative comparable to the analysis done on male incest perpetrators.

Part 5 uses case material to illustrate the various roles played by relatives in response to incestuous abuse in their families. Chapter 24 provides the rare opportunity to find out more about two mothers of incest victims.*

Terminology

The term "incest victim" is used here in lieu of the now more popular term "incest survivor" because of the wide range of incestuous abuse experiences that were the subject of this study. The extremely severe connotation of the word "survivor" suggests that merely to have survived incestuous abuse is a remarkable achievement. I do not in any way wish to belittle the seriousness of incest, but I prefer to use a word with which victims of less severe forms of abuse are able to identify. A girl who has once been touched on the breast by an uncle or a brother might well feel alienated by the term "survivor." I choose to use a term that all incest victims can embrace, not only those who suffered the most extreme experiences. For the same reason, I use the term "wife beating" rather than "wife battering" (Russell 1982).

The dictionary definition of "victim" is someone destroyed, injured, or otherwise harmed by some act or circumstance; the definition of "survivor" is a person who survives. It seems to me that another advantage of using the word "victim" over "survivor" is that it better conveys that the

---

*A chapter on the causes of incestuous abuse is not included in this book because I dealt quite extensively with this topic in my most recent book, *Sexual Exploitation* (1984b).

responsibility for the injury or destruction lies outside the victim (cf. Janoff-Bulman and Frieze 1983, p. 13, for the same argument).

Case Material

In presenting case material I had to choose between selecting appropriate passages to quote as illustrative material for different topics and keeping the entire experience intact. For the most part I chose the latter course, since it better allows the reader to get an overall sense of the girl's whole experience. It also offers the reader valuable "raw data" on incestuous abuse. Quoting a girl's experience in full allows the reader to draw her or his own conclusions, apart from those I offer.

Some people believe it is only necessary to quote one example to illustrate a point. This seems often to be a wise policy. However, there are two reasons why I feel more than one example is sometimes appropriate. First, because these cases come from a nonclinical probability sample, their value goes beyond merely illustrating a point. The experiences described by the victims provide us for the first time with a picture of what incestuous abuse in the general population looks like—not just the more extreme cases that clinicians, child protective service workers, and police tend to see, nor what we read about in our newspapers. Just reading the cases can teach us things about incestuous abuse and the way victims process their experiences that cannot be conveyed by statistics or sociological analysis.

In addition, although we now have quite a rich literature of first-person accounts of father-daughter incest, there is still very little about incest with other kinds of perpetrators. This is a second reason for the central place given in this book to the victims' accounts of their sexual abuse. However, there are many chapters, particularly in the first half of the book, without them. The chapters that include a considerable amount of case material are chapters 3, 6, and 16 to 23. Chapters 12, 14, and 24 consist almost entirely of victims' experiences.

I made another choice about the format of the interview material. Some people advised that the interviewer's questions be "edited out" because they were distracting and intrusive; others suggested that the questions be fully written out and that each question appear on a separate line like the dialogue in a play. I chose a middle course between these two options. The interview was an interactive process; few women simply held forth with a lengthy monologue. The interviewer's questions clearly affected what the women said. So the questions are included, but in a paraphrased, parenthetical form to render them less distracting and obtrusive.

Anonymity

Respondents' anonymity is of course a crucial issue in a study of this kind. All of their names have been changed as well as other information that might identify them. Pseudonyms were obtained by random selection from a dictionary. Names that are exclusively associated with a particular ethnic group were omitted. Each respondent is referred to by the same name throughout this book (as well as in my other books: 1982, 1984). First names only were used because it is customary to refer to children by their first names. Although the respondents were adult women, it seemed awkward to introduce case material by referring to Mrs. Mary Nelson, and then describing an experience that occurred to her at five years of age.

Book Title and Goal

Our study suggests that a minimum of one in every six women in this country has been incestuously abused. Yet most victims suffer this often devastating experience in silence. Some keep the secret all of their lives. Hence my title.

Sociologist James Ramey argues that incest "usually involves only a small portion of the childhood years" (1979, p. 6). The material on the impact of incestuous abuse presented in this book indicates, on the contrary, that incest often involves the rest of the victim's life. That is why the subtitle of this book is *Incest in the Lives of Girls and Women.*

This common female experience has been taking its toll on the lives of girls and women, no doubt for centuries. For the most part, neither society nor the perpetrators have yet been held accountable for the occurrence and continuation of this secret trauma. This book has been written with the hope that it may contribute to breaking the vicious incest cycle of betrayal, secrecy, unaccountability, repetition, and damaged lives.

PART ONE

THE STUDY

study focused on all experiences of completed or attempted sexual assault. Only twenty-six cases of incestuous abuse were disclosed to their team of female interviewers. Given their sample size of 2,004, twenty-six cases constitutes a prevalence rate for incest—age unspecified—of *only 1 percent* (1984, p. 20). This extremely low figure contrasts with our finding of a *16 percent* prevalence rate for incestuous abuse obtained from face-to-face interviews with a probability sample of 930 women. And when we make our prevalence figure more comparable to Kilpatrick and Amick's by not limiting it to women under 18 years of age, it increases to *19 percent.*

Clearly, an enormous difference exists between a problem that directly affects only one woman in a hundred and one that affects one woman in five. What can possibly explain such a sizable discrepancy in the prevalence of incestuous abuse found by these two surveys? And which findings are closer to the truth?

In explaining why I believe the findings of my study are more valid than Kilpatrick and Amick's, I will also provide the reader with an inside view of how we approached the challenging task of getting women to share some of their best-kept secrets with interviewers who were total strangers to them.

I have been doing research on sexual assault since 1971, so when I began the current study, I had already recognized some of the connections between rape and incest and was well acquainted with the literature on both forms of sexual assault (Russell 1975). The advantage of being well informed about a subject before undertaking a large-scale quantitative survey about it is that one is likely to have a better sense of what kinds of questions encourage disclosure, what types of resistance to expect, and what needs respondents will have when talking about the subject.

The objective of the present survey was to discover the true magnitude of incestuous abuse, extrafamilial child sexual abuse, rape, and other forms of sexual assault of adult women as well as to answer a host of other questions about sexual exploitation in the lives of girls and women in this country. The challenging question was: How can potential respondents, chosen on a random basis, be approached so that they will be willing to answer intimate questions about experiences of sexual abuse they might have had, including experiences with their fathers, mothers, brothers, sisters, or husbands?

One of the most basic tenets of survey research is that interviewers need not be informed about the subject under investigation. This tenet was inappropriate to our study for two reasons: the taboo nature of the topics being inquired about and the victim-blaming attitudes most people have about sexual assault. Few women are likely to be willing to disclose experiences about which there is frequently a great deal of self-blame to a strange interviewer who might convey in one way or another that victims are responsible for what happens to them. It would have been foolish to send *supposedly* unbiased interviewers into the field without first educating them about the issues involved.

Hence included in the interviewers' sixty-five hours of intensive training for our survey were at least ten hours of education about rape and incest. In addition, half a day was spent on defining and desensitizing them to words about sexual acts and parts of the body so that they would be as relaxed as possible with whatever vocabulary respondents might choose to use.

Ten hours of education, however, cannot transform a bigot into an unprejudiced person. Hence interviewers were carefully selected not only for their interviewing skills but also for their nonblaming attitudes toward sexual assault victims.

Since our survey was limited to female respondents, we assumed that female interviewers would be more likely to elicit honest disclosure about experiences of sexual assault. A serious attempt was made to hire interviewers from all class backgrounds as well as all age groups. In addition, sixteen of the thirty interviewers were women of color: six Asian, five Afro-American, and five Latina women. Interviews were held in private and, whenever possible, race and ethnicity of interviewer and respondent were matched. Each respondent was paid ten dollars for her participation.

Interviewers were paid by the hour, not the interview, in recognition of the fact that the more successful the interviewers were in eliciting honest disclosures, the longer the interviews would tend to be.

An important decision to be made was whether to use self-administered questionnaires, telephone interviews, or face-to-face interviews. The latter was chosen for several reasons. First, the goal of the study was to reach women from all social classes, and self-administered questionnaires are suitable mainly for middle-class, educated people. Second, it was felt that empathetic, well-trained interviewers would be more successful in eliciting honest disclosures than an impersonal questionnaire. Third, telephone interviews would have limited our interviews to people with telephones, another bias we wished to avoid. Also it might have resulted in respondents hanging up midinterview, leaving the respondent isolated and the interviewer with an incomplete interview. Fourth, anticipating the distress that the subject matter to be covered would elicit in some subjects, it was believed that the actual presence of an interviewer would both encourage frankness and provide the subjects with someone to be with them if they became very upset or needed a referral to a therapist, a rape crisis center, a women's shelter, or other source of help. Fifth, an in-person interviewer would be better able than a telephone interviewer to ensure that the privacy necessary for these kinds of interviews would be successfully arranged and maintained.

Having made this decision, the next task was to design an interview schedule that would help the interviewer develop sufficient trust and rapport with respondents so that they would be willing to talk freely and honestly.

A preliminary interview schedule was drafted incorporating suggestions made by consultants. The interview schedule was then administered to acquaintances and friends. This led to more revisions. As the following example indicates, a well-designed interview schedule is vital.

There were thirty-nine questions on different kinds of experiences of sexual assault. When respondents who had been subjected to many sexual assault experiences—as a substantial percentage of them had been—realized that a separate questionnaire was to be completed for each of the more serious experiences they disclosed, some of them would stop disclosing experiences to save themselves the effort and stress of having to complete further questionnaires. To remedy this, the final version of the interview schedule required that the interviewer ask all thirty-nine questions. Then, for each serious incident of sexual assault disclosed, she would ask the respondent for an "identifier"—something that would remind her of the experience. When all thirty-nine questions had been completed, the interviewer returned to those with identifiers and proceeded to complete a separate questionnaire for each incident. This strategy succeeded in preventing some respondents from stopping their disclosure of sexual assault experiences.

Each revised draft of the interview schedule was tested by administering it to, and getting feedback from, volunteer respondents. Later drafts were administered to paid volunteers. This process of revision went on for eight months before the pilot study was undertaken.

The Pilot Study

A pilot study is customarily done in survey research to determine whether the methods chosen (sampling techniques, manner of locating respondents, interviewer training and instructions, and the usability of the interview schedule) are workable and sound. Eleven interviewers, after appropriate training, completed ninety-two interviews over a period of three weeks with randomly selected women. The results were then analyzed and our methods evaluated. Further changes were made in the interview schedule as a result of the pilot study. In general it also demonstrated that despite the extreme difficulty of conducting interviews on these taboo subjects, an excellent and workable methodology had been developed.

This extensive pretesting revealed that when a number of different questions are asked in a variety of ways, the chance of tapping memories stored under many different categories is greatly facilitated. The following questions were used to elicit memories of child sexual abuse experiences in particular:

1. Before you turned fourteen, were you ever upset by anyone exposing their genitals?
2. Did anyone ever try or succeed in having any kind of sexual intercourse with you against your wishes before you turned fourteen?
3. In those years, did anyone ever try or succeed in getting you to touch their genitals against your wishes (besides anyone you've already mentioned)?*
4. Did anyone ever try or succeed in touching your breasts or genitals against your wishes before you turned fourteen (besides anyone you've already mentioned)?
5. Before you turned fourteen, did anyone ever feel you, grab you, or kiss you in a way you felt was sexually threatening (besides anyone you've already mentioned)?
6. Before you turned fourteen, did you have any (other) upsetting sexual experiences that you haven't mentioned yet?

The following questions did not stipulate an age limit, but nevertheless yielded many experiences of child sexual abuse.

7. At *any* time in your life, have you ever had an unwanted sexual experience with a girl or a woman?
8. At any time in your life, have you ever been the victim of a rape or attempted rape?
9. Some people have experienced unwanted sexual advances by someone who had authority over them, such as a doctor, teacher, employer, minister, therapist, policeman, or much older person. Did *you ever* have *any* kind of unwanted sexual experience with someone who had authority over you, at *any* time in your life?
10. People often don't think about their relatives when thinking about sexual experiences, so the next two questions are about relatives. At *any* time in your life, has an uncle, brother, father, grandfather, or female relative ever had *any kind* of sexual contact with you?
11. At any time in your life has anyone less closely related to you, such as a stepparent, stepbrother, or stepsister, in-law, or first cousin, had *any* kind of sexual contact with you?
12. In general, have you ever *narrowly missed* being sexually assaulted by someone at any time in your life (*other* than what you have already mentioned)?
13. And have you *ever* been in any situation where there was violence or threat

---

*Despite its grammatical incorrectness, the word "their" was used in order to be gender neutral. The sections in parentheses were read by the interviewer only if the respondent had already mentioned a childhood sexual experience.

of violence, where you were also afraid of being *sexually* assaulted—again, *other* than what you (might) have already mentioned?

14.   Can you think of any (other) unwanted sexual experience (that you haven't mentioned yet)?

The word "rape" was only used once in these fourteen questions, and words like "incest" and "molestation" were not used at all. We believed that many respondents might be unable to accept that such value-laden words might apply to their experiences. The respondents' responses to the questions on rape strongly support this hypothesis. Twenty-two percent of them answered yes to the one question that used the word "rape" directly. But another 22 percent described experiences that met the legal definition of rape used in our survey in answer to other questions. Hence the direct question yielded only half of the actual rape experiences reported by our respondents.

Before these fourteen questions were asked, there were a number of "warmup" questions about more minor experiences of sexual abuse, such as receiving obscene phone calls, being upset by men's sexual advances on the street, and being upset by a peeping Tom.

In addition, several questions were phrased to impart a nonvictim-blaming attitude on the part of the study personnel and to convey that sexual assault happens frequently. Such questions were included primarily as a device to encourage honest disclosure rather than just to assess the respondents' attitudes.

Separate sexual assault questionnaires were administered for each of the more serious cases of sexual abuse. Interviewers were instructed to obtain descriptions of the sexual contact(s) sufficiently detailed to ensure that the level of intimacy violated could be precisely coded.

Since some of the women had been sexually assaulted many times in their lives while others had never been assaulted, several survey research experts advised that questions should focus on the most recent two or three experiences, or the most traumatic, or the earliest, or the most serious. This way the data would be more manageable, easier to analyze, and the length of the interviews would be more uniform. This advice was resisted because all such methods of selection would have undercut the study's ability to get an accurate understanding of the true incidence and prevalence of all kinds of sexual assault.*

*For example, if the study had been limited to the three most traumatic experiences, and no incest experiences were included, it wouldn't have revealed whether this was because the woman had never been subjected to such an experience or because she didn't regard it as sufficiently traumatic. The findings would have depended on the respondent's assessment of trauma. It is for just this reason that Finkelhor's student study (1979)—which is widely quoted for its prevalence figures—is really not a complete prevalence study. He instructed the student respondents to pick the most important sexual experiences—or however many

In summary: Some of the main methodological features that may explain why our survey obtained a 19-percent prevalence rate for incestuous abuse of women of all ages (compared to Kilpatrick and Amick's prevalence rate of only 1 percent) include use of face-to-face interviews (Kilpatrick and Amick used telephone interviews); use of a range of questions that helped to tap women's memories of experiences, some of them long repressed (Kilpatrick and Amick used only three questions); avoidance of words like "incest," "molest," "rape" (used only once) (Kilpatrick and Amick used the word "rape" in one of their three questions and "molest" in another); careful selection of interviewers who did not subscribe to the usual myths about sexual assault (Harris Poll interviewers are usually not screened and selected for their attitudes to the survey topic); and rigorous training of interviewers in both the administration of the interview schedule and education about rape and incest (since Harris Poll interviewers are not educated in this fashion, they can therefore be assumed to subscribe to common myths about women who are sexually abused).

City Selected

San Francisco was selected as the locale for this survey rather than Oakland or Berkeley or other communities near where I live because it is by far the best known of these cities. We believed that the results were more likely to be taken as seriously as they deserve to be if the study were based in this large and prominent community. While every city is unique in certain ways, and none can be assumed to be representative, San Francisco is known in particular for its large population of homosexual people. What impact this fact might have on our findings about incestuous abuse is unknown. Since we interviewed only women, the relatively high proportion of homosexual men is probably irrelevant. Whether or not lesbians have higher or lower rates of incestuous abuse has not yet been established.

San Francisco also has an unusually high number of elderly residents.

---

up to three—before the age of twelve with other children, then three that occurred before the age of twelve with an adult over sixteen, then three that occurred after the age of twelve with a family member or relative, then three that occurred after the age of twelve that they did not consent to. No guidance was offered regarding the criteria to be used for evaluating importance; nor was an attempt made to find out what criteria the respondents had used. Despite the fact that these guidelines allow for up to twelve different experiences, they indicate that Finkelhor's study did not obtain a complete picture of the experiences of his respondents.

Since our survey found some increase in the incidence of incestuous abuse over time, this means that our overall prevalence rates for incestuous abuse are likely to be slightly lower than in cities with a younger population of women.

The Sample

Field Research Corporation, a well-known and highly reputable marketing and public opinion research firm in San Francisco, was hired to draw the sample for the survey. The firm used its customary procedure of first selecting "key addresses" from the San Francisco telephone directory. Each address served as a starting point for obtaining a cluster of household listings. Enumerators used these key addresses as starting points for listing all the addresses on the entire side of that block. Another systematic random procedure was then applied to obtain the number of addresses in each block that was in proportion to the density of the block.*

A "Dear Resident" letter in English, Spanish, and/or Cantonese, depending on the ethnic makeup of that particular block, was mailed to each address drawn in the sample. No mention was made of the fact that it was a survey about rape and incestuous abuse. The word "crime" was used instead to minimize the possibility that some husbands, fathers, and boyfriends might object on behalf of a potential respondent.

An interviewer followed up the letter with a visit to the address. Her first task was to obtain a list of all household members, their ages, relationships with each other, and their marital and employment status. If there was more than one woman eighteen years or over in a given household, a random procedure was applied to select one of them. It was only upon speaking with the respondent herself that the interviewer divulged the subject matter of the interview. Respondents signed consent forms before the interview commenced. Anonymity and confidentiality were stressed.

Our probability sample of 930 women residents of San Francisco were interviewed during the summer of 1978. The length of the interviews varied from twenty minutes to just over eight hours. The average length of time was one hour twenty minutes. Usually only one visit was necessary once the interview had been arranged.

*Normally, Field Research instructs the enumerators to list a fixed number of addresses in the same block as each key address. We were advised, however, that this would likely result in a bias against higher-density blocks (i.e., poor and minority neighborhoods). Since we wanted to interview at least the percentages of Afro-American, Latina, Asian, and other women of color residing in San Francisco, we felt it necessary to ask Field Research to make this small change in its methodology.

Refusal Rate and Representativeness of Sample

There are several ways to calculate a refusal rate. The proportion of respondents who, knowing that the study was about sexual abuse, refused to participate was 19 percent. If men as well as women who declined even to give a listing of those in the household are included in the refusal rate, it increases to 36 percent. The final category of refusals includes the following: households in which no one was ever at home; households made inaccessible to the interviewer by locked gates or other physical deterrents; women who had agreed to be interviewed but were unavailable because of logistics, or because their husbands or some other person would not give the interviewer access to them. If this final category is included, the refusal rate rises to 50 percent.

Many of the households that were inaccessible or where no one was at home might have been households in which no eligible woman lived (e.g., there are a large number of all-male households in San Francisco). Therefore, the 36 percent refusal rate seems to be the most valid of the three presented.

One major factor affecting the refusal rate stemmed from the concern of the staff of the Rape Center at the National Institute of Mental Health (which funded the research) for the protection of human subjects. Because of this concern, they forbade any attempts to change refuser's minds by sending back to that household a second interviewer who was particularly adept at this task or who was better matched in age and social class to the person who refused.

One method of assessing the adequacy of a sample is to compare the characteristics of those who were interviewed with the characteristics of the population from which the sample was drawn—in this case, female residents of San Francisco. The 1980 census was used for this comparison since it was taken only two years after the survey interviews were conducted in 1978.

Three demographic characteristics were chosen from the 1980 census to check for biases in our San Francisco sample: age, ethnicity, and marital status. Comparison of the marital status of our 1978 sample of women with the 1980 census data for women eighteen years and older in San Francisco reveals a remarkably similar distribution (see table 2–1).*

On race and ethnic distribution, our sample had proportionately the same number of Afro-American women and those of "Other" ethnicities

---

*Comparison of a fourth variable, household composition, was problematic since the 1980 census changed its previous methods of gathering data on this factor. Hence our survey lacked the information necessary to make household composition exactly comparable with the census.

TABLE 2–1

Comparison of Marital Status of Respondents in Russell's Sample
and 1980 Census Data for Women 18 Years and Older in
San Francisco

	Russell Sample %	1980 Census %
Single	31	33
Married	39	38
Separated	4	3
Widowed	12	15
Divorced	14	11
Total	100	100

(see table 2–2). However, there were proportionately more white women and fewer Asian and Latina women.

Two factors make the underrepresentation of Asians in our sample less serious than the 7-percent difference suggests. First, there has been a tremendous influx of Asians into San Francisco in the past few years, so that the 1980 figures are probably less comparable to 1978 for Asians than is the case for the other comparisons being made. More specifically, the percentage of Asian people has increased from 13 percent in 1970 to 20 percent in 1980.

Second, our survey was limited to English- or Spanish-speaking people because several Asian female consultants advised us that non-English-speaking Asian women were likely to be extremely unwilling to talk honestly about their experiences of sexual assault. A significant number of Asians living in San Francisco do not speak English and hence were not eligible for our survey. Thus our sample of Asians was not as unrepresentative of the number of English-speaking Asians in the San Francisco population in 1978 as table 2–2 suggests.

Comparison of the age distribution shows that our 1978 sample of

TABLE 2–2

Comparison of Race/Ethnicity of Respondents in Russell's Sample and
1980 Census Data for Women 18 Years and Older in San Francisco

	Russell Sample %	1980 Census %
White	67.4	57.2
Latina	7.1	10.8
Afro-American	9.6	10.8
Asian	13.1	20.1
Other	2.7	1.1
Total	99.9	100.0

TABLE 2–3

Comparison of Age of Respondents in Russell's Sample and
1980 Census Data for San Francisco

Age	Russell Sample %	1980 Census %
18–19	3	3
20–24	13	11
25–29	17	13
30–34	14	12
35–39	8	7
40–44	4	6
45–49	6	6
50–54	5	7
55–59	6	7
60–64	6	6
65–69	6	6
70–74	6	6
75–79	3	4
80–84	2	3
85+	1	2
Total	100	99

women was somewhat younger on the whole than women in San Francisco in 1980. As can be seen in table 2–3, in the three age groupings between twenty and thirty-four, there were 2 percent more in our sample in the group between twenty and twenty-four, 4 percent more in the middle group, and 3 percent more in the thirty to thirty-four age group. Our sample had proportionally fewer women over forty in several age groups. However, the figures rarely varied by more than one percentage point.

A significant relationship exists between age and the number of experiences of incestuous abuse reported by women in our sample (with the younger women reporting more experiences). Hence the small over-representation of younger women in this sample has slightly raised the prevalence rates found in our study from what they would have been had the age distributions been identical to those reported in the 1980 census. The difference is small, however.*

*Before the results of the 1980 census were published, we attempted to assess the bias introduced by refusals by comparing the characteristics of those about whom basic household information was obtained but who refused to be interviewed with the characteristics of those who cooperated. This comparison revealed few differences between the race or ethnicity of these two groups, the number of persons living in each household, and the employment status of those who refused (i.e., the percentages who were working full-time, part-time, were laid off or looking for work, or were retired). However, women who refused to participate in the study were more likely to be older and married than those who agreed to be interviewed.

The problem with these data is that basic household information was frequently not ascertainable for refusals, particularly in the large number of cases where no one was ever found at home. For this reason the comparison of our sample with the 1980 census data has greater validity than our comparison of refusals with interviewees.

The refusal rate in our survey was higher than we had hoped. However, given the immense difficulties of tackling a probability sample survey on this subject, the data obtained are quite remarkable. Previous researchers such as Alfred Kinsey and his colleagues (1948, 1953), William Masters and Virginia Johnson (1966), and Shere Hite (1976, 1981) all based their studies on volunteers, presumably because they considered a representative sample too difficult to accomplish.

Validity of Data

In their classic studies of male and female sexual behavior, Alfred Kinsey and his collaborators also used the interview method to obtain data about people's sexual feelings, preferences, and practices. Their questions also spanned people's entire lifetimes. Hence there is considerable similarity between some of the problems each study faced. Some of the limitations of their methodology apply to our study as well. As they observed:

Throughout research of the sort involved here, one needs to be continuously conscious . . . that it is impossible to get more than approximations of the fact on the incidences and frequencies of various types of human sexual behavior. Memory cannot be wholly accepted as a source of information on what has actually happened in an individual's history. There is both deliberate and unconscious coverup, especially of the more taboo items; and in dealing with people of diverse mental levels and educational backgrounds, there are differences in their ability to comprehend and to answer questions with any precision in an interview. (1948, p. 120)

Several factors affected the validity of our data. First, how willing were respondents to disclose their experiences of incestuous abuse and how honest were they willing to be about all the details? Second, even when willing to disclose, what was their *capacity* to cooperate? For example, could they hear adequately? Could they understand the questions? Would they necessarily remember if they had had such experiences, and how accurate would their memories be? Third, how accurate and honest were the interviewers in recording the data?

Willingness to Disclose

Each interview concluded with a section on interviewer observations. Two questions in this section probed the interviewer's assessment of the respondent's willingness to disclose and her overall confidence in the validity of the data.

In answer to the question, "How willing do you think the respondent was to disclose experiences of sexual assault she might have had?" the interviewers answered as follows for the 152 victims of incestuous abuse: 64 percent, "very willing"; 33 percent, "willing"; and 3 percent, "unwilling." In answer to the even more important question "In general, how confident are you about the validity of the data the respondents gave you?" 85 percent of the interviewers answered "completely confident"; 12 percent, "very confident"; and 3 percent, "somewhat confident" or "not very confident." It should be remembered that these questions did not only apply to the incest data but to the entire interview.

Although interviewers were instructed to emphasize the importance of privacy during the interview, and even to insist on it, a few respondents were unable to control the situation. Of the 152 victims of incest, in the interviewer's estimation, only five respondents were affected "some" by the presence of others, and for one, "much" effect was reported.

Respondents were also given a very brief self-administered questionnaire at the end of the interview. One of the questions was "How comfortable have you felt about answering the questions on unwanted sexual experiences?" Fifty-one percent of the victims of incest answered "very comfortable," 27 percent answered "somewhat comfortable," 17 percent answered "somewhat uncomfortable," and 6 percent answered "very uncomfortable."

Another question was "How frank were you able to be during this interview about any unwanted sexual experiences you may have had?" Eighty-eight percent circled the answer that read "I felt comfortable enough to answer *all* the questions as accurately as I could"; 10 percent admitted that they didn't feel comfortable enough to answer one or two of the questions accurately; and 2 percent admitted they had not answered "a few" or "some" questions accurately. (Again, these questions didn't necessarily relate to the incest experiences per se, since many respondents had many other sexual assault experiences.)

Respondents were also asked to describe which questions they had felt unable to answer accurately. These answers provide unambiguous evidence that several women were unwilling to admit experiences of incestuous abuse.

For example, Yvonne specifically told the interviewer that she felt it was very important for women to talk about experiences of sexual abuse and that she thought we were doing important work, but she admitted that she felt too uncomfortable to answer one or two "relative-related questions" accurately. In addition to an incident with a female cousin, Yvonne was extremely upset by her stepfather propositioning her and trying to kiss her when she was eleven. There is, of course, no way of knowing which of these experiences Yvonne was not completely frank about, or whether her lack of frankness applied to an experience she didn't mention.

Peggy explained why she chose not to answer accurately one particular question about a sexual experience with a relative: "I don't feel comfortable talking to too many people about this incident. It is a very touchy subject. I have discussed it with a few prominent psychiatrists and I've worked the situation out in my head. I feel better about it, but I prefer not bringing it up to strangers."

Lena explained her unwillingness to disclose as follows: "Due to the people involved being friends or relatives, I was hesitant about revealing too much of the personal contacts made sexually." Rona admitted that what she had said about an incestuous relationship with her brother "was not complete." She had told the interviewer that she had not been at all upset by it and that it had had no effect on her, but on the self-administered questionnaire she wrote that the incident had affected her relationship with her brother.

Admitting to an experience of incestuous abuse by an uncle, Dawn said that she had also had sexual contact with a more distant relative. However, she refused to talk about it further.

While Mabel was willing to disclose her victimization by a stepfather, she said that she felt too uncomfortable to answer "details of how my stepfather did it all." Fifty-eight-year-old Mabel added that "it's been so long ago, I don't know why it upset me, but it did." (In fact, the perpetrator was Mabel's adoptive father, not her stepfather.)

A few respondents were willing to describe their experience of incestuous abuse but were very reluctant to divulge their relationship with the perpetrator. Vivian explained that the relative in question was dead, but his family was not. After the interviewer explained the importance of knowing the relationship, she admitted he was her grandfather. Sharon, however, refused to divulge her relationship with the perpetrator. She described the experience as extremely upsetting and having had a great effect on her life. The interviewer also noted that Sharon was very upset during the interview when talking about it. To add to the confusion, Sharon started out describing the relative in question as a male, but then insisted the perpetrator was a female. (The interviewer remained unconvinced, for reasons that will be described in chapter 19 on female perpetrators.)

Sonia also refused to say what male relative had sexually abused her at the age of six, although she was willing to say that he was eleven and to provide other quite detailed information about the incident aside from this. This is how she described the experience.

He was a relative who was only a few years older than me. I was home sick in bed; my mother had gone to the store. Sam came into the room and asked to play doctor, which sounded like fun. I said okay to his game, but I had no idea what he meant by it. He pulled down the covers of my bed and grabbed me. Then he started playing around with my genital area. He said, "Let's take your temperature" and he took out a thermometer and tried to put it in my rear end. I got scared, pushed him away, and started crying. Then he took his fingers and tried to put them in my rear. I was crying hard at this point. When he put his finger in my vagina I started screaming and kicking. He left the room but came back a little later after I had calmed down to try again. I told him to get out, then I started crying and screaming again. He left, then my mother came home. (Upset?) Extremely upset. (Effect on your life?) A little effect.

The rest of the interview provides no insight into why Sonia would not disclose her relationship with this relative. She completed six other separate sexual assault questionnaires on other incidents of sexual abuse and was described by the interviewer as friendly and eager both initially and during the interview. Given that the perpetrator was only eleven years old and that she mentioned the experience in response to the first question on relatives ("At *any* time in your life, has an uncle, brother, father, grandfather, or female relative ever had *any kind* of sexual contact with you?"), it would seem that this perpetrator was probably a brother.*

If any conclusion can be drawn from these few cases, it seems that unwillingness to disclose information about incestuous abuse reveals unresolved trauma rather than the desire to suppress a positive incest experience. Several of these women were cooperative respondents who willingly disclosed many other experiences of sexual assault by people unrelated to them.

Capacity to Disclose

Willingness to disclose is one problem; capacity to disclose is another. After each interview the interviewer was asked whether the respondent had appeared to have any difficulty understanding the questions. Of the 152 victims of incestuous abuse, 80 percent were judged to have no difficulty; 19 percent, some difficulty; and only 1 percent, great difficulty. The

*However, he was classified with "other male relatives," not brothers.

difficulties referred to may in part be due to unfamiliarity with English. While all but 3 of these 152 interviews were conducted in English, 22 percent of our respondents mentioned that a language other than English was spoken in their home at the time of the interview.

Five victims of incest were judged by the interviewer to have difficulty hearing the questions, and five had some difficulty reading (a few answers were broken down into categories and handed to respondents on a card, so that they could simply give the number of the category that applied to them). But repression was almost certainly a far more important problem than the respondents' capacity to read, hear, and comprehend the questions.

Repression is a common protective mechanism employed by victims of all ages, but particularly victims of childhood traumas. In addition, unlike some other traumas, like major medical illnesses, accidents, or loss of a loved one, the incest trauma is often kept a total secret. Even when incest is known to others, it is rarely reminisced about or shared with others. Deliberate silence on the part of the victim and all who know about this trauma is more common. This silence makes repression all the more likely to occur.

Many people cannot remember any childhood experiences before the ages of three or four or even five. How often incestuous abuse occurs with small babies, infants, and three-, four-, and five-year-olds is unknown.* Difficult as it is to conduct research on incestuous abuse of older children, research on the effects on babies is infinitely more difficult. Our study was necessarily limited to experiences of incestuous abuse that were remembered. Unfortunately, this is a serious though unavoidable limitation. In a recent study of fifty-three female outpatients who participated in short-term therapy groups for incest victims, Judith Herman and Emily Schatzow (1985) found that patients "who were abused early in childhood and/or who suffered violent abuse" were the most likely to engage in what they referred to as "massive repression" (p. 19). Several victims were only able to recall their experiences after group therapy with other incest victims. It is important, therefore, to bear in mind that our study findings likely underrepresent the very young and severely abused incest victims, as well as the overall prevalence of the problem.

The question of whether some respondents might have fabricated incest

---

*With the increased awareness about child sexual abuse that exists today, numbers of such cases are coming to the attention of some child protective workers or other professionals. One such recent case involved a father who self-disclosed that he had orally copulated his two-week-old daughter. Most of these very young victims will never remember the incestuous abuse—a fact that some perpetrators are likely taking advantage of. They can even tell themselves that what cannot be remembered cannot have an effect. This is very unlikely to be the case, however.

experiences will now be addressed. The training of interviewers emphasized that the contribution of respondents with no experiences was every
bit as valuable as those who had been sexually victimized, and interviewers were instructed to convey this to the respondent whenever it seemed
appropriate. In general, while the percentage of women who think incest
victims are responsible for their victimization has probably decreased in
the last few years, few women are likely to believe that being an incest
victim would enhance their status and worth in the eyes of others. Hence
a motive for fabricating such experiences to a strange interviewer is likely
to be rare indeed.

Nevertheless, interviewers, interviewer supervisors, and coders were
asked to try to assess the honesty and reliability of the respondents' answers. The consensus among these people was that *underdisclosure* was a
significant problem in the case of some respondents, not fabrication of
experiences. As already mentioned, a few respondents admitted on the
self-administered questionnaire completed at the end of the interview that
they were unwilling to disclose or talk about some of their experiences. No
one admitted to fabricating or embellishing an experience.

Given the common Freudian belief that many self-proclaimed incest
victims fantasize their experiences, it is relevant to note that Herman and
Schatzow found—in the study referred to earlier—that "the large majority
of patients who recalled experiences of sexual abuse in childhood were
able to validate their memories from other information sources" (p. 19).
These researchers conclude that there was no positive evidence that "any
of the patients' reports were fantasized" (p. 19).

In summary: There is no reason to believe our study suffers from the
problem of women inventing or remembering experiences of incestuous
abuse that they never really had. The study undoubtedly suffers from
women forgetting and being unwilling to divulge experiences. Of course,
it shares this problem with all other studies.

Accuracy and Honesty of Interviewers

Twenty-two percent of the interviews were verified, which is an unusually
high verification rate (about 10 percent is average). This means that interviewer supervisors checked that the interviews had indeed been conducted
in 22 percent of the 930 cases, and the accuracy of two sample questions
was also checked. All 22 percent of the respondents recalled the interview
and said the interviewer had been polite. And there were very high correla-

tions between the answers to both questions reported by the interviewer and then reported to the interviewer supervisors (these correlations were 0.91 and 0.99). All but twenty-two of these verifications were done by telephone, the remainder being done by postcard. At least half of the verified interviews were drawn at random.

Basic Demographic Information on Survey Respondents

Information about the age, marital status, race, and ethnicity of our respondents has already been presented. To fill out this picture of our 930 respondents a little further: Only 50 percent of the women interviewed had ever raised a child (they were not specifically asked whether they had borne a child, but whether they had raised one). Just over one-third (34 percent) had raised one or two children, and 16 percent had raised three or more.

Fifty-six percent of the women were working full or part time at the time of the interview; 18 percent had retired, 13 percent were keeping house, and 14 percent had some other status, including looking for work (6 percent), being a student (3 percent), disabled (2 percent), and on welfare (1 percent).

Sixty-two percent of our respondents had worked in the labor force most of the time since leaving school, 17 percent had worked almost half the time, and only 22 percent had worked less than half the time. Of the 884 respondents who had worked in the labor force, 29 percent had upper-middle-class occupations, 46 percent had middle-class occupations, and 25 percent had lower-class occupations.

Sociologists commonly assess a woman's social class by her husband's occupational status because women's own occupational status often doesn't reflect their class very accurately. Of the 344 respondents who were married at the time of the interview and about whom such information was available, 41 percent had husbands with upper-middle-class occupations, 35 percent had husbands with middle-class occupations, and 24 percent had husbands with lower-class occupations.

Sixteen percent of the 930 respondents had never graduated from high school, 25 percent were high-school graduates, 28 percent had some college education, 17 percent were college graduates, and 14 percent had some postgraduate education.

The total household income of our respondents in 1977 is presented in table 2–4.

TABLE 2–4

Respondents' Total Household Income in 1977

	Percent	N
Less than $5,000	21	198
$5,000–$9,999	22	207
$10,000–$14,999	20	187
$15,000–$24,999	21	194
$25,000 and more	11	100
Don't know/refused	5	44
Total	100	930

In answer to a question about their religious preference, 28 percent of our respondents mentioned Catholicism; 26 percent, a Protestant religion; 5 percent, Judaism; 9 percent, some other religion; and 33 percent said they had no religious preference.

In conclusion, our aim was to combine the most rigorous and scientifically sound methods of gathering and analyzing data on incestuous abuse and other forms of sexual assault with a sophisticated and empathetic understanding of the experience of sexual victimization. Despite certain flaws—such as a 36 percent refusal rate, a slight underrepresentation of Latina and Asian women and an overrepresentation of white women, and a sample of women that was slightly younger than the general population of adult women in San Francisco—I believe we obtained the most valid and reliable material on incest and other forms of sexual assault, both quantitative and qualitative, heretofore available.

3

Can Incest Be
Nonabusive?

In their classic work *Patterns of Sexual Behavior* (1951), Clellan Ford and Frank Beach point out that "among all peoples both partners in a mateship are forbidden to form sexual liaisons with their own offspring. This prohibition characterizes every human culture" (p. 112). In addition, they maintain that "strict regulations against intercourse between brothers and sisters are nearly as universal as those prohibiting parent-offspring relations" (p. 112). While Ford and Beach acknowledge that sexual intercourse between siblings does of course occur in this and many other societies, they contend that "it is always condemned and is believed to be relatively uncommon" (p. 112).

Patterns of Sexual Behavior was published in 1951, and it can no longer be said that brother-sister or even father-daughter incest is always condemned in the United States. For example, the René Guyon Society, with its slogan of "sex by age eight or else it's too late," doesn't appear to be concerned about whether the participants are related or not (Rush 1980). Dr. Alayne Yates, in her book *Sex Without Shame* (1978), argues more specifically that "incest between prepubertal children commonly follows a pattern of normal sex play, leading eventually to heterosexual intercourse with no particular emotional damage" (p. 114).

In his keynote address to the first national conference on the sexual abuse of children, held in 1979, LeRoy Schultz, a well-known expert on child sexual abuse, startled his audience by declaring that some incest "may be either a positive, healthy experience or at worst, neutral and dull" (Janus 1981, p. 126). He is also quoted as saying that "there is no research to support the belief that the trauma of incest often results in neurotic or psychotic behavior" (Janus 1981, p. 126). On the other hand, Dr. Suzanne Sgroi—also a well-known expert in the field—maintains that she has "never knowingly talked to a happy, well-adjusted, unconcerned incest victim" (Janus 1981, p. 126). Many researchers and other students of incest subscribe to one or other of these polar opposite views.

While much of this book will address the larger issue of the trauma of incest, we will start here by focusing on the more preliminary question: Can incest be nonabusive?

The answer to this question is yes. When brothers and sisters or cousins who are peers engage in mutually desired sex play, it is not abusive.

Nonabusive Incest

Consider the following three examples of nonabusive incest that were recounted to our survey interviewers.

Emily was six years old and her brother eight when the following experience took place.

My brother was basically experimental. He asked me to french kiss him, and we did it, and I said, "Yuk!" He said, "If you don't like it, I won't do it." (Did anything else sexual happen with him?) No, nothing. (Was it wanted or unwanted?) I was indifferent. (Upset?) Not at all upset. (Effect on your life?)* No effect.

Kathy was sixteen or seventeen years old when she had the following experience with her sister.

It was an experimental thing. I'd left home, and we were dating guys who were brothers. It was a matter of sexual curiosity. It was not forced at all. We were talking about the pleasures that our boyfriends got from kissing our breasts. We hadn't experienced this, and we wondered what it would feel like, so we kissed each other's breasts. I never felt any secret guilty thing about it. I was close to her so it was a good person to find out with, but we never repeated the experience.

Cheryl was eight years old the one time her eleven-year-old brother initiated her into sexual experimentation.

He said he knew this thing to do and that he wanted to experiment. I was in bed and he tried to insert his penis into me. I guess my feeling wasn't one of fear; I just let him do it for a little bit. I don't know if I quit or he quit, but nothing came of it. There was no emotion; there was no passion involved. He tried to get his penis

---

*The reader may be confused by the frequency with which the respondents reply to the questions on upset and effects with the same cryptic answers. The reason is that these replies were included in the questions. For example: "Overall, how upset were you by this experience —extremely upset, very upset, somewhat upset, not very upset, or not at all upset?"

in, but it didn't work; he didn't have an erection. It was strictly a mechanical thing. He was on top, but he was not holding me down. My parents were gone, so he came into the room and said, "Let's try this . . ." hemming and hawing as a young boy would do, not sure of the approach. You know how boys talk about things like that when they get together. Probably the older boys told him about sex, so he wanted to try it. I don't think he had reached puberty yet because he didn't get an erection at all, and he wasn't excited.

(Upset?) Not at all upset. (Effect on your life?) No effect. Well, maybe it had an effect. I think that sex should be taught in school or there should be classes on sex that you can send your child to, so they wouldn't have to do things like that to find out about it. (Personal effect on you?) No.

What Is Abusive Incest?

Probably most people would agree that these three cases were nonabusive and nonexploitive. Homophobic individuals might consider the sexual experimentation of the two girls problematic. Others might point out that six-year-old Emily expressed the negative emotion of disgust in response to her brother's french kiss. Some might also argue that Cheryl's brother's attempt to insert his penis in her vagina goes beyond "healthy" sex play. Most people, however, would probably agree that the terms "victim" and "perpetrator" are inappropriate in these cases.

But what if Cheryl had felt devastated by her brother's attempt to insert his penis? What if she had felt used by his unemotional mechanical approach and violated by his touching her vagina? Would such reactions make what her brother did to her abusive? Most researchers would answer no, since most ignore sexual experiences between children who are peers (children whose ages are less than five years apart are commonly considered peers) (e.g., Finkelhor 1979; Mrazek and Kempe 1981, p. 12).

Clinicians, on the other hand, would likely answer yes. Most clinicians would take into account the victim's feelings, believing that they play a crucial role in the impact of the experience on her, both at the time and later. Indeed, it *is* extremely important to recognize that peers, even when they are children, can sexually abuse each other. Consider how unacceptable it would be for an age disparity to be used as the criterion for determining whether or not an adult had been sexually assaulted. What if cases of forcible intercourse occurring between adults less than five years apart in age were not considered rape! As ridiculous as this seems, it is equally discounting of many painful victimization experiences, as well as destructive victimizing behavior, to ignore the reality of child sexual abuse by peers.

The importance of distinguishing between abusive and nonabusive incestuous experiences is both more complicated and more essential when dealing with siblings and cousins than when dealing with cross-generational incest. Because some cases of sibling and cousin incest are experienced by their participants as positive or neutral, some people have been diverted from the fact that many are negative—often extremely so.

Definition of Incestuous Abuse

The definition of incestuous abuse used in our survey was *any kind of exploitive sexual contact or attempted contact that occurred between relatives, no matter how distant the relationship, before the victim turned eighteen years old. Experiences involving sexual contact with a relative that were wanted and with a peer were regarded as nonexploitive and hence nonabusive.*

One of the reasons some researchers may ignore sexual abuse by peers is that it is sometimes extremely difficult to determine. Just how upset must one party be in order for it to qualify as exploitive? And what if the distress is not due to the sexual contact but to adults' responses to it? Here are two such examples from our survey. Freda reported the following experience with her brother.

> When I was real young I played pre-sex games with my brother and sister. Our mother came in and yelled at us. It was real confusing to me. I knew that what we were doing seemed wrong to my mother, and I knew that I would keep my feelings and experiences from her from then on.

Denise was twelve years old and her brother eleven when they began their mutual sexual exploration. The sexual incidents occurred from six to ten times over a period of one year.

> It wasn't forced. We were just curious. We were experimenting. We used to make a game out of it. I showed him my breasts, and he got an erection. He would pester me to go in the cellar with him to play strip poker. (Was there any kind of sexual intercourse?) No. (Petting breasts and genitals?) Yes, but it was more like a game until we found out it was considered dirty. (How did it end?) We figured out what incest was. (We?) I guess it was me. We were Catholic, and I learned about it in school.
>
> (Upset?) Not at all upset. (Effect on your life?) Some effect. After we found out

it was wrong, I felt guilty until I found out that it happened in lots of families, and then I felt all right. (When was that?) When I was about nineteen or twenty.

Both cases were classified as nonexploitive since the distress clearly did not result from the sexual contact per se, but from others' response to it. These experiences may have been traumatic in the lives of these women, but sexual trauma should not be confused with sexual abuse. Sexual abuse is often traumatic, but not always. Trauma should not be used as the sole defining criterion for sexual abuse.*

The researcher's emphasis on the importance of an age disparity as a criterion for determining exploitiveness or abuse has considerable merit, as long as it is not the only criterion. In general, the greater the age disparity between children, the greater the power disparity between them and the more difficult for the less powerful child to assert her or his feelings. Age and power go hand in hand. Usually when there is a significant age dispar- ity—five years or more—sexual contact between children is likely to be distressing for the younger child. The possibility of true consent recedes as the age gap increases.

We have followed the tradition of many researchers in using the five- year age difference as *one* of the criteria for deciding whether or not sexual abuse occurred and in considering the experience exploitive, even if the respondent who was the younger child insisted that it was a positive experience. There were only four such cases out of the 187 experiences of incestuous abuse reported by the women in the sample. This constitutes only 2 percent—a figure that will surely come as a surprise to those who argue that positive incest experiences are very common, even for the younger party (see, e.g., Pomeroy 1976; Nobile 1977; DeMott 1980). Three of these cases will be cited here (the fourth is included in chapter 18 on brother-sister incest).

Exploitive Experiences That Were Wanted

Helen reported that she was eight years old when her sexual experiences with her brother began. He was fifteen—seven years older. The sexual incidents occurred more than twenty times over a period of four or five years.

*Finkelhor (1979) specifically argues against using a person's own feelings of victimization as a criterion for whether sexual abuse has occurred. "Many people," he observes, "react strongly against the idea of seeing themselves as victims under any circumstances. Others readily embrace the label. Whether they do or not seems related to how they like to view themselves in general, and not to the objective circumstances of their childhood sexual experiences" (p. 51).

It was not actually unwanted. It was a long, continuing thing. He was seven years older than I. He went away to school and came back when I was about eight years old. He was always fondling me. I didn't resist; I rather liked it. (Fondling?) My breasts and genitals; and one time he asked me to masturbate him. I didn't know what I was doing. (Pause.) I did it. He joined the navy at seventeen. He came back when I was twelve or thirteen and again he was always fondling me. (How did it happen?) We'd be alone in the house together and he'd come up to me and start to touch my breasts and then my genitals. (Upsetting?) No, never. There was never a question of force. (How did it end?) He went away to school and got a girlfriend. (Upset?) Not at all upset. (Effect on your life?) No effect.

Only one out of the forty-eight cases of uncle-niece incest was described by the niece as wholly positive. Cecilia was sixteen years old the one time her forty-year-old uncle touched her breast.

My aunt was out shopping. He came closer to me. He was just playing around, but he didn't try to put his hand down there (indicated genitals). (Playing around?) It was beautiful; he put his hand on my breast. I was young and I just laughed. We were so happy together. He just touched it a little. (How old was he?) In his menopause maybe. There was no inserting or anything. (Else?) No, it never happened again and I never thought about it again. He is still a strong and wonderful man. My aunt was terrible. (Upset?) Not at all upset. (Effect on your life?) No effect.

Norma was five or six years old when her thirteen- or fourteen-year-old cousin started fondling her. These incidents occurred from two to five times over a period of six months.

He lived next door and I wanted to sleep with him. We were in a bed together and he started rubbing my genitals and breasts. He would place his penis on my legs and suddenly he would ejaculate. One time he showed me the sperm under the microscope. (Did you feel threatened?) No, except knowing I shouldn't do it. (Did you feel coerced?) No. If I hadn't wanted to do it, he would have stopped. (Did he try to have intercourse?) No. (Did he use force?) No, there was no force. (What ended it?) My mother finally said I couldn't sleep with him any longer. (Upset?) Not at all upset. (Effect on your life?) No effect.

In defending our survey's inclusion of such experiences as Helen's, Cecilia's, and Norma's as cases of incestuous abuse, it is useful to compare them with other situations in which power is used to accomplish sexual abuse. A therapist, for example, who has sexual relations with his or her client has abused his or her authority and trust, whether or not a particular client believes that it was unharmful.

It may be both erroneous and question-begging to assume that when the younger parties in incestuous relationships report them as positive or neutral, they are invariably engaging in denial. Nevertheless, denial is clearly operative in some cases. Many examples of discounting and denial will be evident in the case material quoted in this book.

Age differences of even two or three years are extremely salient to children, particularly to siblings. For this reason, the five-year age difference criterion errs, if at all, in the direction of discounting valid cases of sexual abuse. Neutral or positive experiences like those of Helen, Cecilia, and Norma were rare in our probability sample survey, even for siblings who were closer in age.

Positive Feelings and Incestuous Abuse by Fathers

As mentioned, the 930 women we interviewed were asked to report all experiences involving sexual contact with relatives, not just unwanted or negative experiences. Interviewers were instructed to complete additional separate sexual assault questionnaires for *every* case of parent-child sexual contact no matter how enjoyable the respondent reported it to be. *Not a single case of father-daughter incest was reported to be positive in its entirety.* However, there were four cases in which some positive elements were present. One involved Barbara, whose father used to "poke around" her genitals when he bathed her. She described this as feeling good. Other sexual things he did to her distressed her greatly.

Carmen's experience with her biological father was one of the few that involved actual sexual intercourse.

Carmen's father started to sexualize his contact with her when she was twelve. These experiences occurred more than twenty times over a period of five years.

All my life as a child I sat on his lap. After I was twelve, I felt a difference in his holding. He would come up behind me, hug me, and hold my breasts. It was very confusing. I didn't know how to take it. I knew it was different, but it felt nice. There was also a strong thing about obedience, like I had to obey him. It went on as an unspoken game. But as I became more aware, it became very frightening to me. At the same time I felt responsible because I sort of knew what was happening. It was very hard to handle. I became angry at my mother because I was aware that she and my father didn't have a good sexual relationship. I felt sorry for him and that I was going to help him. I also felt sorry for my mother, but she was remote. It would have been impossible to talk about it with her. She seemed really innocent and couldn't conceive of what was happening.

When I was seventeen I went to college. I fell in love and started making love with the man, but I didn't know what to do about my father. I asked someone I *thought* was wise what I should do. He said I should entice him; my mother and I look alike. I believed him, so I did it. It really shocked my father, but he complied. He expressed his disappointment that I wasn't a virgin, which was heavy for me. Shortly thereafter I thought I was pregnant by him, which I told him. He got really angry and said it must be my boyfriend and that it couldn't be him. It was the biggest rejection I ever faced. I was so frightened. I had heard all these things about incest—about deformed kids and so on—otherwise I wouldn't have told him. It turned out I wasn't pregnant. But the feelings about what had happened were never resolved. I left home.

(Upset?) Extremely upset. (Effect on your life?) A great effect. The rejection was the thing more than the sex. I felt totally unloved and worthless. It made me feel like I was just a body. Also, not being able to trust; being deserted like that. I mean, if not your parents, who can you possibly trust? I had a sense of guilt because of following the advice of that guy. I felt that I really seduced him. It brought to mind archetypes about Eve, the fall of man, and that sort of thing.

(Who or what was most helpful in dealing with the experience?) Nothing. Myself. I never told anyone for years and years. (What advice would you give someone in the same situation?) Wow! (Laughs.) What can you tell someone in that state of ignorance? I don't know. It's hard to talk about this kind of thing to children. I guess that your body is private. (Carmen stopped and shook her head.) I don't know. It did please me at first. I don't have an answer. (Which of all your experiences was the most upsetting?) The one with my father.

The other experiences that were less upsetting to Carmen than the experience with her father include an attempted rape by a fellow student when she was twenty-three, unwanted sexual intercourse with her therapist when she was twenty-nine, and sexual abuse by an employer when she was in her mid-twenties and by a policeman when she was twenty-eight.

Carmen mentioned that she felt she had seduced her father. But her "seduction" occurred after years of his physically seductive behavior toward her, to say nothing of the fact that fathers might be expected to resist such behavior from their daughters. Carmen's account demonstrates that the sexual aspect of sexual abuse can be relatively insignificant compared to other aspects of the experience (in this case, her father's disappointment that she wasn't a virgin and his anger and rejection when she thought she had become pregnant by him). Just as some women have found that men are appalled when they initiate sexual contact, so Carmen's father appears to have been shocked when she stopped merely submitting to his advances and took the initiative—even in the passive form of "enticing" him.

While Carmen expressed some positive feelings about her sexual relationship with her father, she also reported negative feelings of confusion, fear, guilt, and rejection in relation to her father as well as anger toward her mother. From the considerable number of experiences of sexual abuse by authority figures that she reported in the following years, it also seems that at the age of thirty-five Carmen was still far from having resolved her traumatic experience with her father. This is not to say that she is responsible for these subsequent experiences, but rather that her vulnerability and need for approval from authority figures appears to have been exploited.

Dora described having one sexual incident with her father when she was ten or eleven years old.

We were on vacation and my mother could not sleep in the bed with my father, so she came into my room and told me to go to the other room in the cabin. My father called me by my mother's name and started to make advances. I responded because I was asleep. I was very young, ten or eleven. (What kind of sexual advances did he make?) He probably fingered me enough to make my legs cross over him. (Did he touch your breasts or genitals?) Genitals, yes. I had no breasts. (Petting or more?) More than that. He fingered me under my pants. He probably wanted to have intercourse if he had not realized that I was his daughter, not my mother. When he realized I was not my mother he got mad at me and gave me a big lecture because I had responded. Then we both went to sleep. (Do you think he was conscious of what he was doing?) No, I think that what he did to me he did routinely to my mother. (Was he asleep?) Yes, but he obviously was not sleeping well. He gave me a warning: "Don't ever do it before you are married."

(Upset?) Very upset. (Effect on your life?) A great effect. I am afraid of saying no. I'm scared of men. It's easier to give in than to say no because it won't hurt me that way. If somebody tried to rape me in Union Square I'd rather give in than give up my life. I figure that it's not worth fighting back.

Although it is not clear how the long-term effects described by Dora related to her experience with her father, it does seem clear that her feelings about the total experience were very negative, even though she "responded" to her father's fondling in her state of semisleep.

Edna is the fourth case in which there was at least some positive element in the experience. She was eleven years old when her father started fondling her. These incidents occurred about twenty times over a period of about a year.

He would come and get in my bed at two or three in the morning. He would fondle, kiss, and suck on my breasts. The breast fondling was pleasant but he would also fondle my genitals, which was not pleasant. He'd have an erection; I could feel it against me and it hurt. I don't remember how long it went on for, maybe a year. (How exactly did it happen?) I would wake when he came into my room. I enjoyed the breast fondling so I went along with it. One time I was going to bed and he kissed me good night full on the mouth. After he did these things with me, he'd do the same things with my sister. He had had an operation for a head injury—a lobotomy. Then some kind of mental illness followed.

(How did it end?) I ended it by rolling over on my stomach and stopping him, conveying that I no longer wanted it. My mother found out at about the same time. She told us she knew about it and that we should tell her if anything else happened and that she would stop it. My sister says she had intercourse with him.

(Upset?) Very upset. (Effect on your life?) A great effect. For a long time I didn't trust men much or rely on them. When I was younger, I thought that was why I never married. I saw a psychiatrist in graduate school. He said one experience cannot totally scar a life, so there were other reasons why I didn't marry.

We were a country family. My socialization with boys was very limited, so he [father] was a big taste of men for me. It was the major incident in the drama of growing up for me. (Right now?) Right now, I hold it as a blessing. I've had an interesting life. If it had not happened, I might have been married out of high school. In my relationships with men, I really don't support them. I mean, I'm not the kind of woman that devotes time to supporting the man rather than herself, and I know that's rooted in my mistrust of men's motives.

Right now, my relationship with my parents is fine.

Edna said that in addition to fondling her and having sexual intercourse with another sister, her father had also attempted to sexually abuse a third sister but had not succeeded. At the end of the interview Edna mentioned that she and her father barely spoke for ten years, and that only after going through EST was she able to speak with him about his abusive behavior.

Although the father-daughter incest experiences of Carmen, Dora, and Edna seem clearly negative and abusive, they each included at least one positive or neutral element. These experiences are the ones that come closest to having been perceived by the daughters as positive in our representative sample.

Feelings About Incest and Trauma

After careful evaluation by the research staff of the degree to which each experience of incestuous abuse was wanted or unwanted, 85 percent were judged completely unwanted and 7 percent, mostly unwanted; ambivalence was apparent in 7 percent of the cases, and 2 percent were judged mostly or completely wanted.*

The following two survey findings confirm the unreliability of basing a

---

*Finkelhor (1979) reported that almost a third of the students who had participated in sex with their siblings in his sample of 796 undergraduates said that it had been a positive experience (p. 178). This high percentage may be partly due to his very broad definition of incest, which included many noncontact experiences, such as the display of genitals and verbal propositions that were never acted upon. (See chapter 4 for a more thorough discussion of the methodology of Finkelhor's survey.) Finkelhor also did not differentiate between the perspectives of the brothers and the sisters, or the younger and the older siblings. Because older males are the most likely initiators of sibling incest, it seems likely that far fewer than a third of the sisters in his survey would have reported positive experiences had he separated the responses of the males and females.

Finkelhor quite rightly did not use the fact that almost a third of those who had engaged in sex with their siblings felt positive about it as an argument for not being concerned about sibling incest; instead he analyzed what differentiated positive from negative experiences, for example, the age difference between the siblings and the degree of force or violence involved (p. 178). He also pointed out that regardless of the fact that some of the experiences were reported as positive, the negative experiences deserve attention and intervention (p. 192).

definition of incestuous abuse on whether or not it was wanted. Most people would probably assume that the more unwanted the experience of incestuous abuse, the more traumatic it would be. Yet the experiences judged to involve ambivalence on the incest victims' part were, on average, more traumatic than those judged to be unwanted. More specifically, 54 percent of the experiences that were considered unwanted were reported to be considerably or extremely traumatic, compared with 83 percent of the experiences considered ambivalent (statistically significant at < 0.05 level).

Perhaps victims who experience some positive feelings are more apt to blame themselves for what happened. This in turn might mute their anger and make them feel at least partially responsible for their own pain.

Most people would probably also expect that the more severe the incestuous abuse in terms of the degree of violation involved, the more likely that it would be judged unwanted. This expectation was also not confirmed. When the four "wanted" experiences were combined with the twelve where ambivalence was evident, there was a statistically significant relationship between severity and the respondents' feelings. Forty-five percent of the experiences that were completely unwanted were at the more severe level, compared to 69 percent of the mostly unwanted experiences and 88 percent of the experiences that were wanted or in which ambivalence was involved.

Differential Perception of Incest

Another important fact to recognize is that the two parties involved in sexual encounters will often perceive the experience very differently. Although the perception of both has equal validity from a phenomenological point of view, the perception of the younger and less powerful person is the more relevant one for determining whether or not sexual abuse occurred. For example, there is no way of knowing whether Betty's younger brother felt distressed by what she defined as sex games in the following account.

Betty was seven years old when she and her five-year-old brother first started their sexual games. These games occurred from two to five times over a period of four years.

We used to play doctor. We'd pull each other's pants down, play with each other's butts, and giggle. (Where touch?) Inside buttocks. (Else?) Thighs, stomachs. (Genitals?) I really don't remember.
Once a girlfriend and I paid my brother and a friend 25 cents to show their

wieners. They were overpaid and underworked! They barely flashed. They were too squeamish. (How did these experiences end?) We grew out of it.

(Upset?) Not at all upset. I wanted to do it more than he did. It was very enjoyable. (Effect on your life?) A great effect. It made sex desirable to me because it was not easily granted. (Like your brother barely showing his genitals?) Yes.

Even had we known that Betty's younger brother was upset by these experiences, they would not have qualified as sexual abuse for our purposes because our survey was designed to study respondents' experiences of victimization, not their experiences as victimizers.

Although our respondents were asked to describe all experiences involving sexual contact with any relative whatsoever—not just upsetting ones —few experiences between older sisters and their younger brothers were mentioned. And *no* case was reported in which a sister sexually abused a brother seven or more years younger than herself. In cases of sibling incest, it was usually older brothers who initiated sexual contact.

It may be that even nonexploitive sexual play between relative peers is usually initiated by older brothers. No case of a younger brother initiating sexual contact with an older sister (before she turned eighteen) was reported in our survey, although it seems unlikely that this never occurs. Nor were there any cases of younger sisters initiating sex with older brothers.

Since gender differences as well as age differences involve power differences in our society, we must be wary that sexual abuse by males of females does not sometimes—or perhaps often—masquerade as sex play.

Of course power differences based on age also exist between two sisters and between two brothers. Perhaps the absence of gender-related power differences in such relationships makes age differences less significant when sexual contact occurs. Yet in both cases of nonabusive sister-sister incest cited next, it is the older sisters who described the experiences in glowing terms. It would be interesting to know what the younger sisters would have to say about what happened.

Iris was twelve years old when she and her ten-year-old sister started to relate sexually. There were more than twenty incidents over a period of six years. This is how Iris described what happened.

I am rather unclear about how it started. We were lying in bed next to each other, talking. I think we just started touching each other. (Where?) Our genitals. It was a marvelous experience. We would lie there and caress each other. (Ever any force?) No, there was no force. (How old were you?) I was maybe about twelve years old; it lasted until I met my husband when I was about eighteen. (Any unwanted sexual experience with her?) Oh, no, it was all wanted. We enjoyed it tremendously. (How did it end?) I got engaged and outgrew it. (Upset?) Not at all upset. (Effect on your life?) No effect.

Iris reported that she had never had a problem with guilt or shame, and that she and her sister have remained close.

Joy was also twelve years old and her sister ten or eleven when their sexual contact began. She said the experiences occurred from six to ten times over several years.

It was petting. Exploration is the word that comes to mind, and it probably happened all through our childhood. (Was it wanted or unwanted?) Wanted. (Upset?) Not at all upset. (Effect on your life?) Some effect. As far as an initiation, they were all positive experiences. (Other effects?) Not really. In terms of learning about my own body and feeling good about it and learning to exchange affection, they were really good experiences.

Neither of these cases of sister-sister incest qualified as sexual abuse.

Contact/Attempted Contact a Criterion for Sexual Abuse

Although actual contact or attempted contact was one of our criteria for defining incest as abusive, this is not to deny the fact that verbal proposals can sometimes be more violating than some contact experiences. For example, seven-year-old Veronica was very upset when her second cousin propositioned her. He was under fifteen at the time. The incidents occurred from two to five times over a period of one to two weeks.

He offered me toys. He said that if I wanted the toys, I'd have to show him my breasts. I didn't want to do this, so I left. (Did anything else sexual occur with him?) No, nothing. (What ended it?) I told his parents and they also moved away. (Upset?) Extremely upset. I was very scared. (Effect on your life?) A great effect. I didn't understand why he would do that. I was very afraid of him. It affected me because I was very young.

Gladys provides another example of a noncontact experience that was quite traumatic. Her father propositioned her once when she was eleven or twelve years old.

As I remember it, he and I were home alone. I had started to grow pubic hair. It was summer and I had shorts on and he said he wanted to see how I was developing. He said I should pull down my pants. I remember thinking, "Why do you want to see what I look like? No!" It seemed that leaving the house was the best way out of an uncomfortable situation, so I left. He didn't say it in any kind of a harsh voice, it was more everyday. (Did anything else sexual ever happen with him?) No, I don't remember anything else.

(Upset?) Not very upset. I remember avoiding being alone with him for a few days. (Effect on your life?) A great effect. I feel protective of my younger sisters. I don't know him very well now, and I don't know if he's ever done anything or said anything to them, but if he did, they are different people and I don't know how they'd react. I didn't tell my mother at the time, but a few years ago I did.

It had an effect in that I've become more aware that that happens to women and children. I've talked with my friends and my husband about the problem of sexual abuse of children. I haven't had anything else happen to me or known if my friends have had that happen.

Why, then, were distressing noncontact experiences excluded from our analysis of incestuous abuse? The answer is that a definition that would include all such experiences would also include many incidents of little or no significance in the girls' lives. It would therefore serve to dilute our findings about incestuous abuse. It might also be used to trivilialize the problem.

The following examples of verbal propositions or genital exposure were also disqualified as cases of sexual abuse.

Helga reported that her uncle made comments to her like: "Why don't you come up and sleep with me? Your aunt never does anymore." Janet described an incident when her uncle was taking her home in his car. "He stopped the car and said, 'Let's you and me make a date.' I said, 'No, Uncle. You're my father's baby brother!' "

Wanda's uncle propositioned her when she was fifteen years old.

It was a verbal thing. I was living with my grandfather, and my aunt and uncle and their kids were there on vacation. We [she and her uncle] were watching TV when he asked me if I wanted to have sex with him. I told him he was nuts, packed my clothes, and left. I moved in with friends. (Was there any physical contact?) No.

Gay was thirteen when her uncle started talking suggestively to her.

I had an uncle who made sexual comments to me while babysitting. He never did anything but I felt his remarks were inappropriate to a thirteen-year-old girl. They would have been better said to his wife. (What sort of remarks?) He talked about what men and women do together. "Is that exciting?" he asked. "Would you like to do that?" I told my aunt but she didn't believe me. (Did he ever touch you?) No, never. I was afraid to be alone in the house with him. He also left a heterosexual porno book for me to see. I never told him that I looked at it, and I felt guilty I even wanted to see it.

Ilona described the following incident with her uncle.

We lived together and I was asking him questions about sex. He was upset that I was growing up and he showed himself to me. (What did he show you?) His genitals, his penis. It happened once. Nothing else happened again. It was embarrassing. (Was there any physical contact?) No, not in a sexual way.

While all these experiences were disqualified as cases of incestuous abuse, it is clear that some of them were quite distressing. Gay was afraid to be alone with her uncle after his suggestive conversations, and Wanda moved out of her grandfather's home after her uncle's verbal sexual advance toward her.

Perhaps we might have included as cases of incestuous abuse only those noncontact experiences that were reported to be distressing. Of course, this would have put a great deal of weight on the respondents' subjective evaluations. We don't know if some of our respondents exaggerated the stress they felt as a result of sexual abuse. We are certain, however, that many respondents discounted the trauma. The case of Irene provides one of many such examples.

Irene was unwilling to refer to the perpetrator as her father throughout her description of what happened. She identified him only when directly asked how he was related to her. Sexual contact with her father had started when Irene was about six years old and had occurred four times over a period of two years.

I was a young child—six or eight—and it was oral sex, but not to completion on the male's part. It happened four times. I think I was young enough that I was not traumatized by it. I don't think about it now. I feel pity for the male and have an understanding of what generated the situation. I was distressed because I did not like it, rather than feeling threatened or abused or frightened. I felt more disgusted, if disgusted is a feeling a six-year-old can have. I felt most of all that it was not right, and that something was wrong with the person. But there was no threat or force involved in the situation.

(What happened?) Basically it involved touching my genitals, and his creating an oral situation where I was the recipient. Also, I had to fondle his genitals with my mouth. (He performed oral sex on you and you on him?) Yes, but as I said, he didn't achieve completion, so I'm sure it was not as dramatic as it would have been if he had had an orgasm. (Was there any one time that was different or more upsetting?) No. (Did you ever report it?) No, I never told anyone.

(How did it end?) I think it was a combination of things. I was no longer quite such a vulnerable child and I also think the person became aware of what he was doing. Because I loved him and he loved me very much, it was not malicious, which is why it has not affected me. I think it was an unsure time in his life. As I got older I would not have been as willing a participant, and I think he knew that.

(Upset?) Somewhat upset, but I was so young, it didn't have any reality to me. It didn't infringe on my daily life while it was occurring. It bothered me, but I'd wake up in the morning and not think of it. (Effect on your life?) A little effect. It gave me an awareness that it can happen to anyone regardless of what that person is really like. As a future wife and mother, I have a sense that you can't be blind to such things. I'm not suspicious, though. I'm not aware of any feelings of guilt or other effect on my development as a person.

Although Irene described herself as being only "somewhat upset" by these experiences, she also mentioned that they distressed and disgusted her, that she felt they were wrong, that she thought something must be wrong with her father to be doing this, that she wouldn't have cooperated had she been older, and that she had never told anyone, which is to say, she had kept it a secret for twenty-two years. In addition, she was very reluctant to identify her relationship with the perpetrator to the interviewer. These facts and feelings suggest that these experiences may well have been more traumatic to Irene than she is yet aware of.

In the study as a whole, considerable attention was given to the women's subjective evaluation of what happened to them (chapter 10 is devoted to trauma as perceived by the victims). But it is also true that women are often not aware of the full effects, and that less subjective measures are equally important. With this in mind, perhaps we should have included distressing noncontact experiences as cases of incestuous abuse. But we did not.

Sexual Trauma Versus Sexual Abuse

As already mentioned, it is also important to distinguish between sexual trauma and sexual abuse. These terms are not synonymous. Sometimes sexual trauma does not involve sexual abuse. For example, a child may be traumatized because she witnesses her parents engaged in sex. Such an incident would not be a case of sexual abuse.

Also, as we have seen, some cases of sexual abuse do not appear to cause distress. For example, Fay described the following incident with her biological father when she was sixteen years old.

I was in bed and my father came over to kiss me good night and started to feel my breasts through the blanket. I asked him, "What are you doing?" so he stopped. He was just frustrated. My mother didn't believe in sex. (Did anything else sexual ever happen with him?) No. (Upset?) Not very upset. (Effect on your life?) A little effect.

While Fay did not perceive her experience with her father as traumatic, it was nevertheless abusive.

Applying Our Definition

Whatever definitional criteria are used for determining sexual abuse, there will always be borderline cases. For example, does the person have to choose the categories "not at all upset" and "no effect" for an experience with a peer to be considered "wanted"? What if she chooses "not very upset" instead, revealing that there was at least some distress? And what if she said that she was not upset at the time, but she became upset about it later? Or if she said she was not upset and there were no long-term effects, but in her description of what happened she provided contrary evidence of distress and trauma? And what exactly is contact or attempted contact? Does a verbal sexual proposition count as an attempt at sexual contact? If not, how are propositions and attempts to be distinguished?

Here is how some of these difficult issues were handled.

- When a respondent reported physical sexual contact or attempted contact of any kind by a relative five years or more older than herself, the experience was defined as incestuous abuse.
- In the case of relatives who were peers, an experience was defined as incestuous abuse if the respondent was not the initiator and if she reported at least some distress or long-term effects as a result of the experience—*not* as a result of an adult's reaction to it. It was not essential that she felt this distress at the time; retrospective distress or negative consequences long after the abuse was over could qualify an experience as sexual abuse.
- It was not enough that a verbal proposition be made. Some gesture had to be made by the perpetrator to act on the proposition. Even if the child was successful in escaping or avoiding the sexual contact, if contact had been attempted, the experience qualified as sexual abuse.

At least two members of the research staff carefully read the descriptions of each experience, weighed these different criteria, then made a judgment about the abusive nature of the experience. Any differences in judgment were discussed by three, and sometimes four, of the research staff until consensus was reached.

Following this procedure, seven experiences with brothers and three with sisters were found to be nonabusive, and twenty-five experiences with brothers and three with sisters were found to be abusive. This means that 78 percent of the experiences with brothers and 50 percent of the experiences with sisters were considered to meet our definition of incestuous abuse.

Summary

We used the following criteria to determine whether or not incest was abusive:

1. The respondent had to be less than eighteen years of age at the onset of the sexual contact or attempted contact.
2. Sexual contact of a physical nature had to have occurred or been attempted by the relative; exhibitionism and verbal propositions did not qualify as incestuous abuse.
3. Incest included sexual contact with all relatives, no matter how distant the relationship, no matter whether they were related consanguineally or not.
4. If the relative with whom the respondent had sexual contact or who attempted sexual contact was five years or more older than the respondent, the experience qualified as abusive regardless of whether or not she considered it to be a neutral or positive experience.
5. If the relative was less than five years older than the respondent, the experience qualified as abusive if there was evidence that it was unwanted, for example, if it was initiated by the relative and caused the respondent some degree of distress or some long-term effects, either at the time or in retrospect.

In general, only a small minority of the cases of incestuous abuse in our sample of 930 women were judged to be wanted. Of those that met our definition of incestuous abuse, four were completely or mostly wanted by the victims, and in twelve cases the victims responded ambivalently. Contrary to conventional wisdom, the experiences considered ambivalent were more likely to be both traumatic and serious—in terms of the sex acts involved—than experiences that were judged unwanted.

Children frequently consent to behavior—sexual and otherwise—regardless of their own wishes, particularly when the request or command comes from an adult or a much older child. Obedience and deference to family members are generally both expected and rewarded. Hence consent by children to sexual encounters with persons older than themselves cannot be seen as indicative of the child's desires. Therefore consent should never be used as a criterion for whether incest is abusive or not, at least not when there is a power relationship between the parties involved.

PART TWO

THE PROBLEM

4

The Prevalence of Incestuous Abuse in Contemporary America

The percentage of women who have ever been sexually abused by a relative in this country—or any other country—is unknown. Kirson Weinberg, in his classic study originally published in 1955, estimated that there were 1.1 cases of incest per million persons in 1930 in the United States (1976, p. 39). Franco Ferracuti (1972) estimated that between one and five cases of incest per million persons occurs every year throughout the world.

Most other estimates have focused on the prevalence of incest and/or other child sexual abuse, rather than the incidence. (*Prevalence* refers to the percentage of girls who were victimized by incest at some time in their lives. *Incidence* refers to the number of cases that occurred within a specified period of time—usually one year.) Our study was specifically designed to try to ascertain the *prevalence* of all kinds of sexual assault, including incestuous abuse. Our definition of incestuous abuse was narrower than many others, since it excluded verbal propositions and exhibitionism. Since the precise definition used is so crucial to any discussion of prevalence, it will be repeated here.

Incestuous abuse includes any kind of exploitive sexual contact or attempted sexual contact that occurred between relatives, no matter how distant the relationship, before the victim turned eighteen years old.

Experiences involving sexual contact with a relative that were wanted *and* with a peer were regarded as nonexploitive. (For example, sex play between cousins or siblings of proximate ages.) A peer relationship was defined as one in which the age difference between the participants was less than five years.

TABLE 4–1

Different Measures of the Prevalence of Incestuous and Extrafamilial Child Sexual Abuse
(Separated)

	Women Who Had at Least One Experience (N = 930)		Number of Experiences of Sexual Abuse with Different Perpetrators*
	%	N	N
Incestuous abuse of females involving sexual contact (under 18 years)	16	152	187
Incestuous abuse of females involving sexual contact (under 14 years)	12	108	134
Extrafamilial sexual abuse of females involving petting or genital sex (under 18 years)	31	290	461
Extrafamilial sexual abuse of females involving petting or genital sex (under 14 years)	20	189	255

*Multiple attacks by the same perpetrator are only counted once; abuse involving multiple perpetrators is also counted as only one experience.

Table 4–1 shows that *16 percent of the sample of 930 women reported at least one experience of incestuous abuse before the age of eighteen years.* These 152 women reported a total of 187 experiences with different perpetrators. *Of these women, 12 percent (108) had been sexually abused by a relative before reaching fourteen years of age.* *

Nineteen percent of the sample of 930 women reported at least one experience of incestuous abuse at some time in their lives. Because the focus of this book is on the incestuous abuse of children, the forty cases of exploitive sexual contact by a relative beginning after the respondent was eighteen years or older have been excluded from all the quantitative analyses.

The old myth used to be that most child sexual abuse was perpetrated by strangers. It is now frequently stated that sexual abuse by a relative is the most common form of child molestation. What light do our data shed on this issue?

Our definition of extrafamilial child sexual abuse was narrower than our definition of incestuous abuse.

*These prevalence figures exclude eight cases of incestuous abuse in which information on the respondent's age at the time was missing. The figures also exclude two cases in which the interviewer failed to determine whether actual sexual contact had occurred—or been attempted—between the respondent and her relative. Hence even in the unlikely event that all respondents were willing to disclose their experiences of incestuous abuse, these figures err on the side of underestimation.

Extrafamilial child sexual abuse involves unwanted sexual experiences with persons unrelated by blood or marriage, ranging from attempted petting (touching of breasts or genitals or attempts at such touching) to rape, before the victim turned fourteen years, and completed or attempted forcible rape experiences from the ages of fourteen to seventeen years (inclusive).

Extrafamilial child sexual abuse was defined more narrowly than incestuous abuse, particularly for the ages of fourteen to seventeen years, to avoid inclusion in our survey of teenage girls' common experiences of unwanted petting and intercourse in dating situations. This does not mean that these experiences are necessarily nonabusive, but the study was focused on more severe cases of extrafamilial child sexual abuse. In contrast, the experiences of unwanted petting and intercourse with *relatives* reported by fourteen- to seventeen-year-old girls were included in the definition of incestuous abuse, since sex between relatives is taboo behavior in this culture.

Using this more stringent definition of extrafamilial child sexual abuse, *31 percent of the sample of 930 women reported at least one experience of sexual abuse by a nonrelative before reaching the age of eighteen years. Twenty percent (189) of these women had been sexually abused by a nonrelative before reaching fourteen years of age* (see table 4–1).

As might be expected, there is some overlap between the respondents who have experienced incestuous child abuse and those who have experienced extrafamilial child sexual abuse. When these two categories of child sexual abuse are combined, *38 percent (357) of the 930 women reported at least one experience of incestuous and/or extrafamilial sexual abuse before reaching the age of eighteen years; 28 percent (258) reported at least one such experience before reaching fourteen years of age* (see table 4–2).

Shockingly high as these prevalence figures for child sexual abuse are, they would have been still higher had we used definitions of incestuous and extrafamilial child sexual abuse as broad as those used in some other studies. For example, Kinsey and associates (1953), Landis (1956), Gagnon (1965), Finkelhor (1979), and Wyatt (1985) included in their definitions of adult-child sex or sexual abuse exhibitionism and sexual advances or propositions that did not involve actual sexual contact or attempted contact with the child.

Some respondents in our survey replied to the two questions on incest —which specifically asked about experiences involving sexual contact—by describing incidents that did not involve actual physical contact or attempted contact. It is probable that many other respondents would also have revealed such experiences had they been asked about them. Despite their incompleteness, these inadvertently obtained data help to derive a prevalence figure based on a broader definition than the one that guided

TABLE 4–2

*Different Measures of the Prevalence of Incestuous and Extrafamilial Child
Sexual Abuse of Females (Combined)*

	Women Who Had at Least One Experience (*N* = 930)	
	%	N
Incestuous and/or extrafamilial sexual abuse of females under 18 years	38	357
Incestuous and/or extrafamilial sexual abuse of females under 14 years	28	258
Incestuous and/or extrafamilial sexual abuse of females under 18 years—broad definition (includes noncontact experiences—exhibitionism, sexual advances not acted upon, etc.)	54	504
Incestuous and/or extrafamilial sexual abuse of females under 14 years—broad definition (as above)	48	450

our research. Quantitative data were also obtained about other noncontact experiences in childhood, such as being upset by witnessing someone exposing his or her genitals. Additional quantitative data were also obtained on some of the less severe experiences of extrafamilial child sexual abuse that did not meet our definition—for example, unwanted kisses, hugs, and other nongenital touching.

These broader definitions of incestuous and extrafamilial child sexual abuse (including experiences with exhibitionists as well as other unwanted noncontact sexual experiences) were then applied to our data. *Of the 930 women, 54 percent (504) reported at least one experience of incestuous and/or extrafamilial sexual abuse before they reached eighteen years of age, and 48 percent (450) reported at least one such experience before they reached fourteen years of age* (see table 4–2).

Detailed information was routinely obtained for only those experiences of child sexual abuse that met our narrower definitions of incestuous and extrafamilial child sexual abuse. For this reason and various others, the analysis and discussion of our survey data on both forms of child sexual abuse in this book will focus on our less inclusive definitions.

Comparisons with Other Studies

THE KINSEY STUDY

Although the samples studied by Alfred Kinsey and his colleagues were not representative, their scope and influence have been such that an effort will be made to reconstruct their findings on incest in order to compare them with ours.

Only 6 of the 761 text pages of *Sexual Behavior in the Human Female* (1953) were devoted to the subject of adult-child sexual contacts (pp. 116–22). (The phrase "sexual contact" appears to be preferred over "sexual abuse.") The words "incest" and "child molestation" do not appear in the index; nor are they used in the 6 pages of text.

The actual number of incest cases reported by the Kinsey study is difficult to reconstruct, since their data are reported in percentages that add to 107 percent instead of 100 percent (1953, p. 118). Table 4–3 shows our extrapolation from Kinsey and his colleagues' table on adult males (referred to as "partners") who had "approached" preadolescent girls—that is, girls under the age of fourteen years.

The percentages of cases of sexual abuse by relatives in the table add to only 3.1 percent (see column C). This figure is actually inflated because (1) columns B and C represent slightly inflated figures due to the fact that the

TABLE 4–3

Extrapolation from the Kinsey Study's Data on Child Sexual Abuse by Adult Males

Adult Partners	A % of Active Sample[a] (N = 609)	B Recalculated Numbers[b]	C % of Total Sample[c] (N = 4441)
Strangers	52	317	7.1
Friends and acquaintances	32	195	4.4
Uncles	9	55	1.2
Fathers	4	24	0.5
Brothers	3	18	0.4
Grandfathers	2	12	0.3
Other relatives	5	30	0.7
Total	107	651	

SOURCE: A. C. Kinsey, W. B. Pomeroy, C. E. Martin, and P. H. Gebhard, *Sexual behavior in the human female* (Philadelphia: W. B. Saunders, 1953), p. 117.

[a]The term "active sample" refers to the number of girls sexually abused by males who were at least fifteen years of age, and who were at least five years older than the female.

[b]The percentages in column A were converted into numbers by using the formula $X = (609) \times$ the percentage in column A/100.

[c]The percentages in column C were obtained by calculating the numbers in column B as a percentage of the 4,441 female subjects that the Kinsey study mentioned as their basis for determining the incidence of preadolescent sexual contacts with girls by adult males.

percentages in column A add to 107 percent instead of 100 percent and (2) 15 percent of the girls who were sexually abused by an "adult" male were sexually abused by more than one adult male. Hence there were significantly more male perpetrators than there were sexually abused girls, whereas the 3.1 percent figure assumes that each perpetrator sexually abused a different girl.

Furthermore, almost exactly half of the incidents of sexual abuse include acts that did not meet our definition of incestuous abuse because no sexual contact was involved or attempted (1953, p. 119). Most of these cases included males exhibiting their genitals, and a few included "approaches" only.*

In summary: Extrapolating from the data provided by the Kinsey study, it appears that *from 2 to 3 percent of the females in their classic study were sexually abused by a male relative before the age of fourteen.* † They reported no female incest perpetrators in this context.

The Kinsey team claimed that too few incest experiences—approximately 139—were disclosed to them to warrant any analysis beyond commenting on the very low frequency. Since it is so patently absurd to dismiss 139 cases as too few to analyze, this stance suggests that the Kinsey team was unwilling to deal with incest. As Judith Herman (1981) stated so succinctly: "On the subject of incest, apparently, they felt the less said the better" (p. 17). Other evidence of their extremely unsympathetic and victim-blaming attitudes regarding incest was presented in chapter 1. Although the 3-percent prevalence figure for incestuous abuse of females before the age of fourteen years extrapolated from the Kinsey team's data is remarkably low in comparison to our 12-percent figure, it still represents a sizable number: 30,000 girls per million.

One possible explanation for both the low prevalence of incestuous abuse disclosed to the Kinsey researchers and their discounting of the cases they did obtain is their bias against recognizing the abusiveness of incest. This bias may have been so strong that only a minority of incest victims

---

*There is an even more serious error in the Kinsey study's table on the *type* of sexual contact involved in these incidents. Here the percent column adds to 125 instead of 100 (p. 119). Furthermore, in this table the number of cases in which adult males approached preadolescent girls is given as 1,075—466 more than the 609 given in the previous table as the total for this same group of people (see column A of table 4–3). The figures in yet another table on ages of females having adult contacts are also different—adding to 1,039. No explanation of these large differences is offered. This section of the Kinsey team's analysis is shockingly sloppy and inaccurate.

†Judith Herman (1981, p. 118) also attempted to extrapolate from the Kinsey study's tables the number of cases of incestuous abuse. By her calculation, 40 women reported incestuous relations with their fathers and an additional 200 women reported other incestuous experiences. This compares with our calculations of 24 cases of father-daughter incest and 115 cases of other incestuous abuse (see table 4–3). It appears that Herman, for reasons unknown, used the figure 1,039—the number of cases mentioned in a previous table—rather than 609 as the basis for her recalculation.

may have been willing to reveal their experiences to them. It is pertinent here to point out that all the interviewers were male; Kinsey himself did over half of the interviewing (58 percent) and Pomeroy did 31 percent (1948, p. 11). The Kinsey researchers themselves grant that in a study like theirs, in which "the forms of the question are not standardized," greater responsibility is placed on the interviewer to try to avoid bias (p. 52). As far as the data on incest and extrafamilial child sexual abuse are concerned, they appear to have seriously failed in this undertaking.

FINKELHOR'S STUDIES

Although David Finkelhor's student survey of child sexual abuse was not based on a random sample, it shares with the Kinsey study the advantage of being based on a nonclinical population. While his analysis does not focus on incestuous abuse, it is possible to calculate a prevalence figure from the data Finkelhor provides (1979, p. 58).

The crucial criterion in Finkelhor's definition of child sexual victimization—including incestuous abuse—was a substantial age difference between the parties involved. More specifically, he included sexual experiences between children twelve years and under with adults or adolescents at least five years older than the child, and young adolescents thirteen to sixteen years of age with an adult at least ten years older (1979, p. 55).

Finkelhor (1979) defined incest as sexual experiences between family members, including sexual propositions, exhibition, sexual fondling, hand-genital or oral-genital contact, mutual masturbation, and intercourse (p. 84). Family members included steprelations as well as cousins and in-laws.

Of the 530 female students in social science classes at six New England colleges and universities who completed self-administered questionnaires in 1978, approximately 10 percent had been sexually victimized by a relative.* While this figure is substantially lower than our 16 percent prevalence rate, the difference is smaller than the difference between our rate and the prevalence rate reported in most other studies. On the other hand, it must be remembered that Finkelhor's definition of incestuous abuse was much broader than ours. For example, he included "an invitation to do something sexual"; "other person showing his/her sexual organs to you"; and "you showing your sex organs to other person" (1979, p. 178). None of these experiences qualify as incestuous abuse in our study since only experiences that involved some direct physical contact or attempted

*This figure was obtained by recalculating Finkelhor's figures (p. 58). Since 43 percent of 119 girls were victimized by a relative, approximately 51 girls were incest victims, by Finkelhor's definition. Since there were 530 female college students, 51 constitutes 9.6 percent of Finkelhor's sample of females.

contact were included. However, our definition included incestuous abuse by peers, while Finkelhor's did not.

Finkelhor also provides data on the prevalence of *incest*—including but not limited to experiences of *incestuous abuse.* The same broad range of experiences qualified as incest as for child sexual abuse in general, but experiences between peers were included, and no age limit was applied. As so defined, 28 percent of Finkelhor's sample of 530 female college students described a sexual experience with a family member (1979, p. 83).

Although the two questions we asked our respondents about sexual contact with relatives included both wanted and unwanted experiences, the ratio of abusive to nonabusive experiences that were reported to us was quite the opposite of the approximately 18-percent nonabusive to 10-percent abusive experiences reported by Finkelhor. While we did not keep count of the number of nonabusive experiences outside of the nuclear family, the ratio of abusive to nonabusive sibling experiences was approximately three to one in our study compared to Finkelhor's one to two ratio of abusive to nonabusive experiences with relatives in general. I believe that the ratio for relatives outside of the nuclear family in our San Francisco survey would have been much the same as the ratio within the nuclear family had we kept comparable records on them. What might explain this considerable difference in our findings on the prevalence of incest as distinct from incestuous abuse?

Again, the fact that Finkelhor included noncontact experiences in his definition, while ours was limited to contact or attempted contact, is probably relevant. Milder experiences that do not involve actual sexual contact are much more likely not to be distressing, particularly when they occur between peers.*

Also, the introduction to Finkelhor's questionnaire likely encouraged the reporting of innocuous experiences. This is how it reads: "We would like you to try to remember the sexual experiences you had while growing up. By 'sexual,' we mean a broad range of things, anything from playing 'doctor' to sexual intercourse—in fact, anything that might have seemed 'sexual' to you" (1979, p. 168).

In Finkelhor's more recent random sample of 521 parents in Boston, 15 percent of the women interviewed reported having been sexually abused before the age of sixteen, approximately 5 percent by a relative (1984, p. 72).†

*Unfortunately, Finkelhor did not include an analysis of the relationship between the trauma scores reported and the degree of sexual violation involved. Nor did he provide information on the frequency of incestuous experiences at the ten different levels ranging from "an invitation or request to do something sexual" to "intercourse."

†Personal communication, 1985. Once again it is possible to calculate a prevalence figure for incestuous abuse from the data provided by Finkelhor, but not for females separate from males (1984, p. 83).

Finkelhor's figures for both child sexual abuse and incestuous abuse are so low probably because they were obtained from questions included in a study basically designed to explore other issues, such as parents' opinions of child sexual abuse. As discussed previously, the fact that we asked a number of questions in different ways was a major factor in our obtaining a high disclosure rate.

In addition, Finkelhor confined his interviews to parents with children aged six to fourteen years, thereby excluding all childless, elderly, and young women. Data from our study show that some incest victims are less likely to ever marry. Hence Finkelhor's sample does not provide a good basis for arriving at prevalence rates of child sexual abuse for women in general.

A final problem with Finkelhor's Boston study for our purposes is that he did not distinguish between incestuous and extrafamilial child sexual abuse.

THREE TEXAS STUDIES

In an unpublished study conducted in the late 1970s, G. Riede, T. Capron, P. Ivey, R. Lawrence, and C. Somolo sent a questionnaire on pornography and child sexual abuse to a random sample of 2,000 licensed drivers in the state of Texas. Fifty-five percent of these questionnaires were returned. Of those who returned questionnaires, 4.3 percent reported a sexual experience with someone in their family and 11.8 percent reported a sexual experience with someone outside their family (Kercher and McShane 1984, p. 496).*

One of the problems with Riede and associates' study—as researchers Glen Kercher and Marilyn McShane point out—is that the questions were asked about sexual *experiences* rather than sexual *abuse.*

A. Sapp and D. Carter followed Riede and coworkers' methodology, mailing questionnaires to a random probability sample of 2,000 names from the list of people holding valid drivers' licenses in Texas. The return rate was 66 percent. Of those returning questionnaires, 5.4 percent ($N = 72$) reported having been sexually abused by a parent or other adult before the age of fifteen (1978, p. 13). No breakdown was given for sexual abuse by relatives and nonrelatives. Nor did Sapp and Carter calculate different prevalence rates for male and female respondents.

These researchers provide very little information on their methodology —for example, what questions were asked. Presumably their prevalence figure is so low for many of the same reasons that apply to Kilpatrick and Amick's random sample survey in South Carolina (see chapter 2).

*Information about this study was obtained from Kercher and McShane's article, since it is not available for distribution even in unpublished form.

Kercher and McShane (1984) replicated Sapp and Carter's sampling procedure but expanded the definition of child sexual abuse to include abuse perpetrated by an older child or adolescent (p. 496). More specifically, they defined child sexual abuse as:

Contacts or interactions between a child and an adult when the child is being used for the sexual stimulation of the perpetrator or another person. Sexual abuse may be committed by a person under 18 when that person is significantly older than the victim or when the perpetrator is in the position of power or control over another child.

In addition, the term sexual abuse was said to include the obscene or pornographic photographing, filming or depiction of children for commercial or personal purposes, or the rape, molestation (fondling), incest, prostitution or other such forms of sexual exploitation of children under circumstances which indicate that the child's health or welfare is harmed or threatened thereby. (P. 497)

Presumably this definition includes noncontact experiences such as being subjected to an exhibitionist or peeping Tom or verbal propositions that were not acted out.

Of the 2,000 addresses to which questionnaires were mailed, there was a 56-percent return rate for female respondents, 11 percent of whom reported having been victims of child sexual abuse as just defined. This compares with our prevalence figure of 38 percent for both extrafamilial and intrafamilial child sexual abuse. Unfortunately, Kercher and McShane did not provide information on the prevalence of incestuous abuse as distinct from other child sexual abuse.

These researchers used a definition of child sexual abuse that was complicated and, therefore, difficult for a random sample of women from all educational backgrounds to understand and apply. After reading the definition in their survey booklets, respondents were asked but one question: "As a child—were you ever sexually abused?" As was previously emphasized, one question simply isn't enough to obtain even a moderate disclosure rate.

KILPATRICK AND AMICK'S STUDY

Kilpatrick and Amick's random sample survey (1984) that found a 1-percent prevalence rate for incestuous abuse was discussed in chapter 2. It was concluded that the poor methodology used accounted for this extremely low figure.

WYATT'S STUDY

Psychologist Gail Wyatt's prevalence figures were obtained from lengthy interviews with a sample of 248 Afro-American and white women, eighteen to thirty-six years old, in Los Angeles County. The respondents were obtained by random-digit dialing of telephone prefixes in Los Angeles County combined with four randomly generated numbers to obtain a stratified probability sample with quotas to recruit comparable samples of white and Afro-American women (1985, p. 509). Three hundred thirty-five women terminated the telephone conversation before their eligibility for the survey could be determined. Twenty-seven percent of the women in the other 1,013 households contacted refused to participate. Of the 709 women who agreed to participate, 248—or 35 percent—were interviewed. Their selection was based on whether or not they met the demographic criteria needed to complete the various quotas required by the study, such as social class, age, and race. One hundred twenty-six of them were Afro-American and 122 were white (p. 509).

Wyatt defined child sexual abuse as "contact of a sexual nature, ranging from those involving non-body contact such as solicitation to engage in sexual behavior and exhibitionism, to those involving body contact such as fondling, intercourse and oral sex" (1985, p. 510). Her definition also required that such behavior had occurred before the age of eighteen, with a perpetrator five years older than the victim. In cases where the age difference was less than five years, "only situations which were not wanted by the subject and which involved some degree of coercion were included" (p. 511).

Sixty-two percent of Wyatt's sample of 248 women reported at least one experience of sexual abuse prior to age eighteen (p. 513). When Wyatt distinguished between sexual abuse that involved body contact of some kind and noncontact abuse, she obtained the following prevalence rates: 21 percent of her respondents reported at least one experience of incestuous abuse; 32 percent reported at least one experience of extrafamilial child sexual abuse; and 45 percent reported at least one experience of incestuous *or* extrafamilial child sexual abuse (Wyatt and Peters, 1986*b*).

In order to make our figures more comparable with Wyatt's, we recalculated our prevalence rates for the same eighteen to thirty-six-year-old age group that she studied. As can be seen in table 4–4, the prevalence rates for these two studies are astonishingly close.*

The similarity of the prevalence rates found by these two studies is all the more remarkable since Wyatt did not set out to replicate the methodology used in this study. While we used a probability sample obtained by drawing key addresses from the San Francisco telephone directory, she used random-digit dialing to obtain a stratified probability sample from

*Wyatt and Peters include a further recalculation of their data to make their definition of extrafamilial child sexual abuse more comparable to ours, but have not included my recalculation to adjust to their eighteen to thirty-six-year-old age group. Hence our comparisons do not yield identical results (Wyatt and Peters, 1986*b*, table 5).

TABLE 4–4

*The Prevalence of Incestuous and Extrafamilial Child Sexual Abuse Reported by Women 18 to
36 Years of Age: The Russell and Wyatt Findings Compared*

	Russell Survey		Wyatt Survey*	
	%	N (470)	%	N (248)
Incestuous abuse of females involving sexual contact	19	91	21	51
Extrafamilial sexual abuse of females involving sexual contact	35	164	32	80
Incestuous and/or extrafamilial sexual abuse of females involving sexual contact	43	200	45	112
Incestuous and/or extrafamilial sexual abuse of females—broad definition (includes noncontact experiences—exhibitionism, sexual advances not acted upon, etc.)	59	276	62	154

*Source: Wyatt and Peters, 1986*b*.

which she then selected two comparable subsamples of white and Afro-American women. In addition, Wyatt's interviews were much longer than ours (three to eight hours compared to our average one hour twenty minutes), and her four interviewers underwent an intensive three-month training program compared to our ten-day program for thirty interviewers. Finally, her study was in Los Angeles County while ours was in San Francisco. Yet the differences between our four prevalence rates reported in table 4–4 never exceed 3 percent. This similarity in our findings is quite extraordinary.

Some people have argued that the high prevalence rates for child sexual abuse found by our study and Wyatt's may be due to the fact that they were both conducted in California.* Wyatt obtained data that contradict such a conclusion. Of the women who had grown up in California, 43 percent reported child sexual abuse involving sexual contact before the age of eighteen compared to 48 percent of the women who had grown up elsewhere in the United States. Furthermore, Wyatt and collaborator Stephanie Peters point out that: "a more detailed examination of the prevalence rates in Wyatt's sample using the nine regional designations developed by the U.S. Census Bureau also failed to show evidence of regional variations" (1986*a*).†

*D. Finkelhor. Personal communications, 1984. D. Kilpatrick. Public statement at the second National Family Violence Research Conference, Durham, New Hampshire, August 1984.
†In July 1985 after this work had already been completed, the first national random-sample study of the prevalence of child sexual abuse was conducted. A *Los Angeles Times* poll of 2,627

CANADIAN STUDIES

Under the chairmanship of Robin Badgley, an ambitious national survey of child sexual abuse in Canada was commissioned by the Minister of Justice and Attorney General of Canada (1984). Unfortunately, the figures for incestuous abuse are difficult to extrapolate from the data on child sexual abuse in general. Not only are the findings reported in percentages without information being provided on the numbers from which they were calculated, but the four categories of incestuous abuse used include sexual abuse by nonrelatives, that is, employers or work supervisors of female employees under twenty-one years of age (p. 216). As the latter cases of sexual abuse are combined with sexual abuse by stepfathers and foster fathers, meaningful comparison with the U.S. studies described above is impossible.

It is also impossible to extrapolate prevalence figures for incestuous abuse from the data on child sexual abuse obtained by a probability sample of 387 women in Calgary, Canada (Bagley and Ramsay 1985).

SUMMARY OF PREVALENCE RATES OBTAINED IN DIFFERENT STUDIES

The findings of the studies discussed in this chapter on the prevalence of incestuous abuse, the prevalence of extrafamilial child sexual abuse and incestuous abuse combined, and the prevalence of father-daughter incest are presented in table 4–5.

Of all these studies, Wyatt's prevalence findings are the most comparable to ours. This is probably because both our surveys involved personal interviews by well-trained interviewers who were knowledgable about sexual abuse and were relatively free of victim-blaming attitudes. Both our methodologies also required the asking of numerous questions about child sexual abuse experiences.

In general, both our survey and Wyatt's suggest that when studies are designed with knowledge and sensitivity to the issue of child sexual abuse, high disclosure rates can be obtained. When they are not so designed, or when a strong unsympathetic bias is present, as with the Kinsey researchers, disclosure rates are very low.*

---

adults, directed by journalist I.A. Lewis, found that 27 percent of the women interviewed by telephone reported having been sexually abused as children (*San Francisco Chronicle*, August 26, 1985, p. 51). Unfortunately, it is not possible to extrapolate the prevalence of incestuous abuse from these data because people were only asked questions about one experience of child sexual abuse. If they happened to describe an extrafamilial experience, there is no way of knowing whether or not they had also had an incestuous experience, and vice versa (Lewis, 1985).

Although Lewis's 27 percent prevalence rate for child sexual abuse falls well below our 38 percent figure—particularly since he includes noncontact experiences in his definition—it is still remarkably high given the use of telephone interviews.

*For excellent discussions of methodological issues relating to child sexual abuse prevalence studies see Peters, Wyatt, and Finkelhor, in press, 1986 and Wyatt and Peters, 1986*a, b*.

TABLE 4–5

Sexual Abuse of Female Children: A Comparison of Major Studies

Study	Publication Date	Number of Female Respondents	Type of Sample	Population	Definition of Abuse	Incestuous Abuse (%)	Abused by Father (%)	Child Sexual Abuse (%)	Abuse Before Age
Kinsey et al.	1953	4,441	Volunteer	Largely middle-class women in the U.S. (white only)	Includes noncontact experiences	3	0.5	24	14
Finkelhor	1979	530	Total	College students in New England (largely white)	Includes noncontact experiences	10	1.3	19	17
Sapp and Carter	1978	2,000 (males & females)	Random	Licensed drivers in Texas (all races)	Unclear	—	—	5	18
Russell	1983	930	Probability	Household sample in San Francisco (all races)	Excludes noncontact experiences	12 16 19	— 4.5 —	28 38	14 18 no age limit
Kercher and McShane	1984	2,000 (males & females)	Random	Licensed drivers in Texas (all races)	Includes noncontact experiences	—	—	11	18
Kilpatrick and Amick	1984	2,004	Random	Household sample in North Carolina (all races)	Excludes noncontact experiences	1	0.4	—	no age limit
Wyatt	1985	248 (18–36-year-olds)	Probability	Household sample in Los Angeles (white and Afro-American)	Excluding noncontact experiences Including noncontact experiences	17 21 18* 23*	— 8.1* — 8.1*	36 45 47 62	14 18 14 18

*Wyatt. Personal Communication, 1985. The 8.1 figure on fathers includes mother's live-in boyfriends.

Conclusion

As with all survey research relying upon retrospective memory, there are limitations to our study too. Some of the shortcomings were discussed in chapter 2, including its limitation to the city of San Francisco. Since San Francisco is a cosmopolitan city, might it be that the high prevalence figure of 16 percent for incestuous abuse before the age of eighteen is disproportionately accounted for by foreign-born residents?

The answer is no. In fact almost one-fifth (18 percent) of the women in our sample who were born in the United States reported being incestuously abused before the age of eighteen, compared with only 11 percent of foreign-born women (this difference is statistically significant at <0.05 level). Since almost one-quarter of our sample was foreign-born, and a wide variety of countries were represented, this finding is difficult to interpret. At the very least, though, it means we cannot attribute the high rate of incestuous abuse to the large number of foreigners who live in San Francisco.

Of far more significance, however, is the remarkable agreement between our findings and Wyatt's on the prevalence of incestuous and extrafamilial child sexual abuse. In addition, Wyatt's finding that 5 percent fewer of the women in her sample who had grown up in California reported experiences of child sexual abuse than women who had grown up elsewhere in the United States should discourage attempts to discount our high rates by attributing them entirely to any real or imagined characteristics of California. It may be tempting for some researchers to hypothesize about regional differences rather than to examine possible weaknesses in their own methodologies that might account for low disclosure on this sensitive subject, but this temptation must be resisted.

Of all the studies reviewed in our discussion of the prevalence of incestuous and/or child sexual abuse in general, only the Kinsey study had the advantage of being national in scope. However, it had the disadvantage of being based on a sample of volunteers rather than a random sample, to say nothing of the extreme bias of the research team against recognizing abusive sexual experiences.

Until a well-designed national probability sample survey is conducted, our estimates of the prevalence of incestuous and other child sexual abuse must be based on regional studies.* I believe our survey findings plus Wyatt's offer the soundest prevalence figures at this time from which to make national estimates.

*The National Center on Child Abuse and Neglect's National Incidence Study (1981) is so fraught with methodological problems that many of its findings—including the findings on the incidence of child sexual abuse—are of doubtful validity. For a well-deserved critique of this study, see Finkelhor and Hotaling (1984).

Finkelhor (1979) commented on his estimate of a 1-percent prevalence rate of father-daughter incest as follows: "One percent may seem to be a small figure, but if it is an accurate estimate, it means that approximately three-quarters of a million women eighteen and over in the general population have had such an experience, and that another 16,000 cases are added each year from among the group of girls aged five to seventeen" (p. 88). In fact, the rate of father-daughter incestuous abuse reported in our survey is close to five times higher than Finkelhor's estimate (see chapter 15). The rate of other incestuous and nonincestuous child sexual abuse is similarly very much higher than any prior study had led us to believe: 16 percent of our sample reported at least one experience of incestuous abuse before the age of eighteen years.

If our findings are indicative of the prevalence of child sexual abuse in areas other than San Francisco, it means that approximately one in six women are incestuously abused before the age of eighteen and one in approximately eight are so abused before the age of fourteen. It means in addition that over one-quarter of the population of female children have experienced sexual abuse before the age of fourteen, and well over one-third have had such an experience by the age of eighteen years.

It is imperative that a problem of this magnitude in the United States be addressed, and it is urgent that more effective preventive strategies be developed and implemented.

In the next chapter we will consider whether or not the prevalence of incestuous abuse has been increasing in the United States over the last several decades.

5

Has Incestuous Abuse Increased in the United States?

It is clear that the *reporting* of all types of child abuse and neglect has increased greatly in the past few years. The *National Study of the Incidence and Severity of Child Abuse and Neglect* reports that the incidence of child sexual abuse reported to Child Protective Service agencies, the police, and other social service or treatment facilities is increasing each year (NCCAN 1981). Specifically, "in 1976, the first year for which data from all 50 states were available, 416,033 reports were documented; by 1979, the number had jumped to 711,142, an apparent increase of 71 percent over a three year period" (p. 2). The stated assumption is that this increase is due to "growing public awareness" and "trends toward broadening and publicizing of report laws," not to an increase in the incidence of child sexual abuse (p. 2).

Parents United in Santa Clara County, California, was one of the first and is perhaps the best-known facility for the treatment of incest in the country. Parents United reports that since its inception in 1971, each year has been marked by a dramatic increase in the number of cases of incest brought to its attention (Giarretto 1982). Other facilities, including the Sexual Assault Center at the Harborview Medical Center in Seattle, Washington,* report a similar increase.

Dr. Michael Durfee circulated information gathered by the Los Angeles County Department of Health Services showing a considerable increase in suspected cases of child sexual abuse in Los Angeles County from 1983 to 1984, most particularly in the two year and younger age group (Durfee 1984). Indeed, more suspected cases of sexual abuse were reported for babies of two years old than children of any other age up to sixteen years old, followed by three- and then four-year-olds.

*L. Berliner. Personal communication, 1983.

Most Child Protective Service workers at these and other treatment centers attribute the escalating use of their services to the growing public awareness of their existence, not to an increase in the occurrence of child sexual abuse (Finkelhor 1979, pp. 131–32). According to Finkelhor, most observers believe that "what we are witnessing is a revolution in consciousness, a situation where, because of changed mores, professionals are more sensitive to identifying instances of sexual abuse and victims and their families are more willing than before to seek help" (p. 132).

After a detailed comparison of data gathered in three studies—that of Alfred Kinsey and associates (analyzed by John Gagnon 1965), Judson Landis (1956), and his own (1979)—Finkelhor (1979) concluded that the incidence of adults physically molesting girls has probably stayed about the same in the last thirty years, while the incidence of exhibitionism toward girls has probably declined (p. 134).

Since we interviewed adult women of all ages about their experiences of child sexual abuse and other sexual assault, it is possible to plot changes in the incidence of different forms of abuse reported by our respondents from the beginning of this century until 1974.

Of the 187 incidents of incestuous abuse, there was exact information about the age of the victim at the time the abuse began in 182 cases. Since these incidents occurred over a period of approximately seventy-four years we grouped all the incidents that occurred (or began, in the case of repeated sexual abuse) into three-year blocks of time. To prevent the multiple experiences of incestuous abuse reported by some women from unduly affecting the incidence in any three-year period, only one experience of incestuous abuse per woman was counted in any three-year block of time. This data analysis stopped in 1974 rather than in 1977, the year prior to the interviews, because there were only thirty-nine women in the sample who had been at risk of incestuous abuse in the 1975 to 1977 period, and none of them had been so abused. Because women had to be eighteen years old to be eligible for our survey, the women at risk from 1975 to 1977 were aged fifteen to seventeen—not a peak age for incestuous abuse.

We calculated the number of girls in our sample who had been at risk of incestuous abuse in each three-year period. The number of girls who experienced incestuous abuse for the first time with a particular perpetrator in each period was then calculated as a percentage of the total number of girls at risk during that period. Figure 5–1 shows the fluctuations over time in the incidence of incestuous abuse before the age of eighteen and extrafamilial child sexual abuse before the age of fourteen.* (The data from

*Period rates for both incestuous abuse that occurred by the ages of five, ten, fifteen, and eighteen and for extrafamilial sexual abuse by the ages of five, ten, and fourteen were included in my book *Sexual Exploitation* (1984*b*). Some of the years in which there were peaks

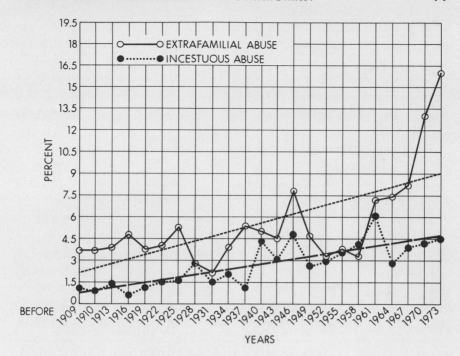

FIGURE 5–1

Period Rates for Incestuous Abuse Under 18 and Extrafamilial Sexual Abuse Under 14 for Three-year Age Groupings—with Regression Lines

which this graph was plotted may be found in the appendix.) For the sake of simplicity, the years appearing on the horizontal axis of figure 5–1 represent the midpoints of each three-year period.

Figure 5–1 shows that incestuous abuse before the age of eighteen has roughly quadrupled from the early 1900s to 1973. More specifically, it increased from 1.1 percent of the 88 girls at risk prior to 1909 to 4.5 percent of the 110 girls at risk in 1973. The graph reveals that there was little change in the incidence of incestuous abuse prior to 1937: It fluctuated between a low of 0.6 percent in 1916 to a high of 2.7 percent in 1928. In

and declines for incestuous abuse in the period rate analysis in that book differ from those that emerge in our analysis here because of two crucial methodological differences. First, following common demographic practice for period rate analysis, only the first incest experience was included in *Sexual Exploitation.* Once a girl had been incestuously abused, she was removed from the total number of at-risk girls in the age group. Second, five-year periods were used rather than the three-year periods used here.

This method of doing period rate analyses was originally devised for calculating morbidity rates—an event that can, after all, only occur once in a person's life. Since many women are victimized by sexual assault more than once, this analytical method is less suitable for our data than many other catastrophes. Hence, we decided here to forego this type of analysis.

1940, however, the incidence increased quite sharply to 4.3 percent. After this period, the incidence fluctuated between a low of 2.6 percent in 1949, to a high of 6.1 percent in 1961. When the incidence figures for the first three three-year periods are averaged (i.e., from before 1909 to 1913) as well as those for the last three three-year periods (i.e., from 1967 to 1973), the increase in the rates of incestuous abuse evident in figure 5–1 is significant at < 0.05 level.

These percentages are so much lower than the overall prevalence figure of 16 percent because they refer to the proportion of girls at risk over periods of three years who were sexually abused, rather than the percentage who were ever sexually abused during all their childhood years.

The increase in incestuous abuse is visually somewhat dwarfed in figure 5–1 by the increase in extrafamilial child sexual abuse before fourteen, but in fact both forms of child sexual abuse quadrupled since the early 1900s. Starting with an incidence of 3.7 percent before 1909, the incidence of extrafamilial child sexual abuse dipped to a low of 2.1 percent during the depression in 1931, peaked at 7.8 percent after the second world war in 1946, then dipped again from 1949 to 1958. Since 1961, child sexual abuse by nonrelatives more than doubled from 7.2 percent in that year to 16 percent in 1973—a period of only twelve years. When the incidence figures for extrafamilial abuse are averaged for the years before 1913 and for the years from 1967 to 1973, the increase evident in figure 5–1 is significant at < 0.05 level.

Figure 5–1 also reveals that while 4.5 percent of the girls at risk before eighteen were incestuously abused in the three-year period of which 1973 is the midpoint, *nearly four times* that percentage of girls were abused by a nonrelative during that same three-year period, i.e., 16 percent of the girls at risk before fourteen. This is consistent with the finding reported earlier that there is considerably more extrafamilial child sexual abuse than incestuous abuse* (see chapter 4).

Cohort Rates for Incestuous Abuse†

Figure 5–2 shows the cumulative proportion of women who disclosed one or more experiences of incestuous abuse before the age of eighteen for five age groups of women. Cohort 1 refers to those women born in 1918 and

---

*However, it must be remembered that a respondent can only be included once in the prevalence figures cited in chapter 4, whereas in the incidence analysis undertaken here, victims of multiple abuse can be included in more than one three-year period.

†An analysis of cohort rates for extrafamilial child sexual abuse is available in *Sexual Exploitation* (Russell 1984*b*)

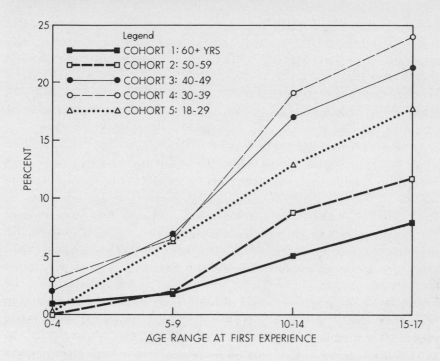

FIGURE 5–2

Cumulative Proportion of Women Experiencing Incestuous Abuse for Five Cohorts of San Francisco Women

---

earlier who were sixty and older at the time of the interview; Cohort 2, to those born between 1919 and 1928 who were in their fifties; Cohort 3, to those born between 1929 and 1938 who were in their forties; Cohort 4, to those born between 1939 and 1948 who were in their thirties; and Cohort 5, to those born between 1949 and 1960 who were from eighteen to twenty-nine years of age when interviewed.

Of those women who disclosed more than one experience of incestuous abuse, only their first experiences are tabulated here.

Figure 5–2 shows that with the exception of the youngest cohort of women, the older the cohort the less incestuous abuse was reported. Only 8.0 percent of the women who were sixty and older reported having been incestuously abused compared to 12.0 percent of women in their fifties, 22.5 percent of women in their forties, and 24 percent of women in their thirties. This linear pattern of increasing incestuous abuse for the younger cohorts is broken by the eighteen- to twenty-nine-year-olds, 17.7 percent of whom reported an experience of incestuous abuse.

However, since the prevalence of incestuous abuse for the 930 women sampled was 16 percent before age eighteen, we see that the percentage of incestuous abuse reported by the youngest group of women is still slightly higher than the overall prevalence rate. Furthermore, it is also more than twice as high as the 8.0 percent of incestuous abuse reported by the oldest cohort of women.

While the overall prevalence of 16 percent seems astonishingly high to some people, this cohort analysis reveals that fully a quarter (24 percent) of the Cohort 4 women who were in their thirties had been sexually abused by a relative before the age of eighteen.

Similarly, incestuous abuse before the age of fourteen was least often reported by women sixty years and older: 5.1 percent compared with 8.8 percent of the women in their fifties, 17.7 percent of the women in their forties, and 19.6 percent of the women in their thirties. As with incestuous abuse before eighteen years of age, the percentage of women reporting an experience of incestuous abuse before fourteen in the eighteen to twenty-nine-year age group broke this linear trend: only 13.3 percent reported such an experience.

Our findings cannot be compared with those of other studies because comparable analyses have not been made. The only partial exception is provided by Gail Wyatt's probability sample of 248 women in Los Angeles. Although her analysis differs from ours in not being based on the numbers of women at risk during particular periods, and in combining intrafamilial and extrafamilial child sexual abuse, it is nevertheless of interest that she found that fewer of the younger women—aged from eighteen to twenty-six years—reported experiences of child sexual abuse than women aged twenty-seven to thirty-six (Wyatt and Peters 1986a). For abuse that involved some kind of sexual contact, the difference was 41 percent and 48 percent, respectively; and for abuse that also included noncontact experiences, the difference was 60 percent and 64 percent, respectively.*

*Whether or not these differences are statistically significant is not reported by Wyatt and Peters (1986a).

Despite the differences in our methods of analyzing this question, our data and Wyatt's suggest that the youngest cohort (the eighteen to twenty-nine year olds for our study and the eighteen to twenty-seven year olds for hers) were subjected to less incestuous abuse than women aged thirty to thirty-nine years in our study, and less child sexual abuse in general for women aged twenty-eight to thirty-six years in Wyatt's study (Wyatt and Peters 1986a).

While this finding about the youngest cohort of women is of interest, it is less significant than the overall trends of increasing child sexual abuse over time.

Why Has Child Sexual Abuse Increased?

According to our survey, both incestuous abuse before eighteen and extrafamilial child sexual abuse before fourteen have quadrupled between the early 1900s and 1973. What might account for this increase? Could it be that younger women are simply more willing than older women to report experiences of sexual abuse?

The cohort analysis showing that the youngest group of women reported less incestuous abuse than two other older cohorts contradicts this explanation. This evidence is strengthened by a similar finding for extrafamilial child sexual abuse: once again the second and third youngest groups of women reported more of this form of sexual abuse than the youngest women (Russell 1984*b*, p. 204).

There are a number of factors that may have contributed to the increase in child sexual abuse prior to 1973.

CHILD PORNOGRAPHY AND THE SEXUALIZATION OF CHILDREN

Although the use of children as pornography models finally became a criminal offense in the United States in 1982, it was flourishing in the period before 1973. This was particularly true after the Government Commission on Obscenity and Pornography concluded in 1970 that all pornography is harmless (*The Report,* 1970). Nor did the outlawing of the use of children in pornography stop the illegal use of children for this purpose. The McMartin Preschool case in Manhattan Beach, California, is one particularly shocking recent example that appears to have involved hundreds of children over a period of several years. In addition, there is easy access to an endless supply of books that condone and justify child sexual abuse in most so-called adult bookstores. The following are some of the titles on incest available in one pornographic bookstore in downtown Berkeley, California: *Incest Sinners: Daddy's Slave Girl, Docile Daughters, Seduced by Mom, Incest: Taking His Sister's Ass, Daddy's Hot Girl, Eager for Mom, Joanie's Lust for Dad, Incest Discipline: Trained Daughters, Raped Mom: Degraded Daughter, Incest: Abused Innocence, Mom's Incest Urges, Family Sex Trip, The Nympho Stepmom, Raped Daughter.*

Considerable research has been conducted in recent years on the effects of pornography (see, e.g., Malamuth and Donnerstein 1984). This research demonstrates a connection between exposure to violent pornography and violent behavior toward women (Malamuth 1984; Donnerstein 1984). It also shows an association between both violent and nonviolent pornography and violence-condoning attitudes (e.g., Zillmann and Bryant 1984). Even before such research was conducted, the simple application of the laws of learning suggested that pornography, like other media, conditions attitudes and behavior.

Child pornography may create a predisposition to sexually abuse children in some adults who view it. Because child pornography commonly portrays children as enjoying sexual contact with adults, it seems even more likely that it may undermine some viewers' internal inhibitions against acting out their desires to have sex with children. And when pornography makes it appear that child sexual abuse is something that adults can do without much risk of being caught and punished—a message pornography commonly conveys—it likely undermines viewers' social inhibitions against acting out their desires (Russell 1984b).

It seems likely, then, that the increasing availability of child pornography in the period under consideration, along with the concomitant increase in the sexualization of children in advertising and other mass media, has contributed to an increase in child sexual abuse. Figure 5–1 reveals that extrafamilial child sexual abuse in particular accelerated sharply from 1967 until 1973, the year our analysis ends. (For a more fully developed theory of how pornography may be causally related to rape and child sexual abuse, see Russell and Trocki 1985.)

SEXUAL REVOLUTION

The so-called sexual revolution may have also contributed to the rise in child sexual abuse. Its nondiscriminating all-sex-is-okay philosophy appears to have resulted in a more accepting attitude in certain segments of the population toward adult-child sex. "Sex by age eight or else it's too late"—the slogan of the René Guyon Society—is but one of many examples of blatantly pro-child sexual abuse groups that have sprung up since the 1960s. The North American Man/Boy Love Association (NAMBLA) is another example. These groups commonly rationalize their self-interested desires to have sex with children by pleading the cause of children's rights to have sex with whomever they please.

Figure 5–1 shows a dramatic increase in extrafamilial child sexual abuse from 1961 to 1973, roughly coinciding with the time when the sexual revolution began. In contrast, incestuous abuse actually declined from 1961 to 1964, then increased somewhat from 1964 to 1973. Before expending great efforts to try to explain these divergencies between intrafamilial and extrafamilial child sexual abuse during this period, it would be useful to see if future research replicates these findings.

BACKLASH AGAINST SEXUAL EQUALITY

A third factor that may play a causative role in increasing the prevalence of child sexual abuse is the growing number of men who, terrified of dealing with adult women as equals or near equals, may turn to children for the sense of power and adoration that they were raised to expect from women. Gloria Steinem (1977) offered this explanation for the fact that younger and younger females are being held up as ideal sex objects for men of all ages in this country. If twelve-year-old Brooke Shields could be perceived by so many men as one of America's most glamorous and sexually desirable females, then the probability is high that many men will find themselves sexually attracted to some other twelve-year-old girls. While it is important not to equate sexual attraction with sexual abuse, attraction can be one important motivating factor in child sexual abuse.

UNTREATED CHILD SEXUAL ABUSE

There is growing evidence that a significant number of the perpetrators of incestuous abuse were themselves sexually abused as children. For example, Nicholas Groth (1979) reports that 46 percent of the sexual offenders who showed a persistent and exclusive preference for children reported being sexually victimized as children. This is double the percentage (23 percent) of those whose involvements with a child was a clear stress-precipitated departure from their preferred sexual relationships with adult women (p. 101).

Although I believe that some experts, including Groth, are now exaggerating the causative role of early-childhood sexual abuse in the lives of adult sex offenders, there is little doubt that it is a significant factor. Since effective intervention in cases of child sexual abuse is still relatively rare, and since many perpetrators sexually abuse a number of children—sometimes literally thousands—child sexual abuse is likely to grow geometrically on the basis of this one causative factor alone. For example, let us speculate that 20 percent of males who are sexually abused as children will grow up to be adult sex offenders against children. Let us further speculate that each of these men, on average, sexually abuses ten children. The result would be that for every adult sex offender in this generation, there will be double the number in the next generation.

STEPFAMILIES

The final factor to be discussed here relates to incestuous abuse, not extrafamilial child sexual abuse. Data will be presented in chapter 16 showing that 17 percent of the women in our probability sample who were reared by a stepfather were sexually abused by him before the age of fourteen. In contrast, only 2 percent of the women raised by a biological father were sexually abused by him before that age.

Extrapolating from these findings, it would seem that as the number of stepfamilies increases, the rate of incestuous abuse will likely increase as well.

Conclusion

Except for the fact that it has become illegal for children to be used as pornography models in this country, resulting in changes in the form of child pornography in recent years,* all the other factors discussed here are as relevant for the period after 1973 as they were for the period on which this analysis has focused. Hence, if they have merit, it suggests that the real incidence of child sexual abuse—as distinct from the incidence of reported cases—may have continued to increase during the last decade.

---

*For example, young-looking models of eighteen or nineteen years old are used to pose as children, and millions of books and articles are written describing young girls engaged in sex with adults. In addition, there is a flourishing—though illegal—cottage industry in pornographic photographs of young children (Florence Rush. Personal communication, 1985).

6

The Tip of the Iceberg: Reported Cases

This chapter focuses on cases of child sexual abuse that were reported to the police—not to parents, other adults, or peers.

In our probability sample of 930 women, 648 cases of child sexual abuse before the age of eighteen were disclosed to our interviewers. Of these, only 30 cases—or 5 percent—were ever reported to the police: 4 cases of incestuous abuse and 26 cases of extrafamilial child sexual abuse. This represents 2 percent of all incest cases and 6 percent of all cases of extrafamilial child sexual abuse. These extremely low figures provide powerful evidence that reported cases are only the very tip of the iceberg.

These findings are all the more alarming since in 32 percent of the cases of incestuous child abuse, the respondent reported knowing that the perpetrator had also sexually abused one or more other relatives.*

The fact that the report rate for incestuous abuse is even lower than that for extrafamilial child sexual abuse may be due in part to our more stringent definition of the latter (i.e., more serious cases are presumably more *likely* to be reported).† On the other hand, it would not be surprising if incestuous abuse were even more rarely reported to the police than extrafamilial child sexual abuse, given what is known about power relationships within the family, the secrecy that commonly surrounds the breaking of the incest taboo, and the realistic fear that reporting the incest could result in the breakup of the family unit.

Of the thirty reported cases, all of which involved male perpetrators, only seven were known to result in convictions. In two additional cases,

---

*Sixteen percent of the respondents said they did not know if the perpetrator had sexually abused another relative, and 53 percent said that another relative had *not* been sexually abused by the person who abused them.

†As mentioned, our definition of incestuous abuse included any kind of exploitive sexual contact that occurred between relatives, but extrafamilial child sexual abuse was limited to unwanted sexual experiences with persons unrelated by blood or marriage, ranging from petting to rape before the victim turned fourteen years, and completed or attempted forcible rape experiences from the ages of fourteen to seventeen years.

the respondents knew that the perpetrators were arrested but did not know if convictions were obtained. It seems unlikely that successful convictions would not be known to the victim.

If the conviction rates are calculated on the basis of reported cases only, the rates for incestuous abuse and extrafamilial child sexual abuse are very similar: 25 percent and 23 percent, respectively. If the conviction rates are calculated on the basis of the total number of experiences disclosed to the interviewers, they are 0.5 percent for incestuous abuse and 1.3 percent for extrafamilial child sexual abuse. And the combined conviction rate for the total number of both forms of child sexual abuse is 1 percent.

These figures are shockingly low. However, our data on child sexual abuse predates the legislation that has made the reporting of such cases mandatory. It also predates increased public awareness of the problem. Hence it is safe to assume that the reporting rate for child sexual abuse has increased in the last few years. Whether or not conviction rates have also increased is unknown.

How does this minuscule conviction rate compare with the conviction rate for rape found in our survey?

Of the sixty-six rape or attempted rapes that were reported to the police, only six cases resulted in convictions. If the conviction rate for rape and attempted rape is calculated on the basis of reported cases only, it is 9 percent, a rate significantly lower than the 23 percent conviction rate for extrafamilial child sexual abuse and the 25 percent rate for incestuous abuse.

But if the conviction rate is calculated on the basis of the total number of experiences of rape and attempted rape disclosed to the interviewers, it is only 1 percent. This is identical to the conviction rate for both incestuous and extrafamilial child sexual abuse combined.

Of the four cases of incestuous abuse that were reported to the police, one involved a biological father; two, stepfathers; and one, an uncle. While four perpetrators were reported, only three girls did the reporting. One of them reported to the police sexual abuse by both her biological father and her stepfather. Her biological father was the only incest perpetrator known to have been convicted.

All four of the incest victims who reported their abuse to the police were women of color (two Latina, one Afro-American, and one Native American woman). The perpetrators were white, Latino, Afro-American, and Native American. In three of these cases the victim and perpetrator were of the same race or ethnicity; one case of stepfather-stepdaughter sexual abuse involved a white perpetrator and a Latina victim. The only incest perpetrator who was convicted was Latino.

When considering all cases of child sexual abuse together, of the thirty cases reported to the police in our survey, sixteen perpetrators were white, ten were Afro-American, two were Latino, and two were categorized as "other." Of the seven cases that ended in convictions, three perpetrators were Afro-American, two were Latino, and two were white. This means that the conviction rate for reported cases of child sexual abuse was 100 percent for Latino perpetrators, 30 percent for Afro-American perpetrators, and only 13 percent for white perpetrators.

Despite the fact that these numbers are small—and it is therefore not permissible to generalize these rates to the population of San Francisco at large—it nevertheless seems clear that the perpetrators' race or ethnicity is a major determinant in child sexual abuse convictions. These findings also reveal how extremely unrepresentative incarcerated sex offenders are likely to be of sex offenders in general in terms of race and ethnicity. It is reasonable to assume that incarcerated sex offenders are equally unrepresentative by other criteria, particularly social class.

Comparison of Reported and Unreported Cases

Aside from the perpetrator's race or ethnicity, how do reported cases compare with the vast majority that are never reported? Examination of the four cases of incestuous abuse that were reported to the police may shed some light on this question.

Ida was one of two respondents to have been sexually assaulted by both her biological father and her stepfather. She was twelve years old the first time her stepfather forced her to perform fellatio on him. Her stepfather sexually abused Ida from eleven to twenty times over a period of three years until she ran away at the age of fifteen. In answer to the question about which incident was the most upsetting, Ida answered as follows.

Probably, the first time, because I was so shocked although he had threatened me with it for three years. I went out to feed the cows. My stepfather was in the barn, and he made me have oral copulation with him. I was just twelve, and I was scared, but he pulled me to him and made me do it. He tried to do it on several other occasions. He would also touch my breasts, even though I was still flat. I went to the police about it but they didn't believe me, and he kept doing it after that. It was horrible.

He was working on a vacant plot of land. He'd have me come over there and when I was alone with him, he would try something. (Did he use verbal threats?) He said he would fix it so that my grandmother would keep me and I couldn't see my mother. (How did it end?) I ran away. I told the police why I had run away and they took my stepfather to jail, then released him on bail. He and my mom came to H. [the name of the youth authority where Ida was held] and said that if I wanted to come home, I must say I was lying. So I did.

(Upset?) Extremely upset. (Effect on your life?) A great effect. When I was first with my husband I was terrified. Certain things would make me hysterical. I couldn't stand the thought of oral copulation. Sex was for having babies, not for fun, and that was it.

Incest victims' decisions not to press charges against their perpetrators are frequently assumed to be an indication that they were lying in the first place, or that they willingly participated in the experience. A far more common reason for lying about incest is illustrated by Ida's account: In order to be released from the youth authority, she was required to lie.

It should also be noted that Ida actually reported her stepfather's sexual abuse on two different occasions. Apparently the police simply disbelieved her the first time.

Of all twenty-seven cases of biological father–daughter incest, only Ida's experience was reported to the police—a report rate of approximately 4 percent. This compares with a 12-percent report rate for adoptive, foster, and stepfathers, since two out of the seventeen of them who were incest perpetrators were reported to the police.

Ida's biological father attempted to rape her on one occasion when she was sixteen years old.

I was going to spend the summer with my father. He had just been released from prison. He was acting crazy. He started talking to me like I was my mother and telling me to put the kids to bed. I said, "Daddy, what do you mean?" Then he beat me up real bad with a log from the fireplace. I had a broken jaw and a concussion. He knocked me out. (Did he have sexual intercourse?) He was on top of me, trying to penetrate me, but he couldn't. Then the police ambulance came. (What was the result of the police report?) My father was sent to a medical facility, then back to jail.

(Upset?) Extremely upset. (Effect on your life?) A great effect. For a long time I was unable to trust anyone. If I had a problem I kept it to myself. After that, I had psychiatric care for a year. (Which of your experiences was the most upsetting?) The one with my [biological] father.

Ida had also been raped by a stranger when she was twenty-four, the same year she was interviewed. The interviewer noted at the end of the interview that Ida and her husband seemed somewhat distrustful and uncooperative at first. When the interviewer returned for the interview she noted that "both apologized and said that they didn't trust people because people seemed so apathetic in San Francisco and because Ida had had a very traumatic rape experience." As traumatic as the recent rape was, Ida felt the attempted rape by her biological father was the most traumatic of all her experiences of sexual assault.

The conviction of Ida's father was probably a result of several factors: the fact that he was so violent toward her, that her injuries were so evident, that he was so blatantly psychotic, that he was Latino, and that he was an ex-convict.

Chapter 14 is devoted to Jacqueline's experiences of sexual abuse, since her history provides such an eloquent example of why some girls run away from home and what often happens to them when they do. Like Ida, Jacqueline was raped by her biological father at the age of fifteen after she had run away from her stepfather. She described both fathers as alcoholics. However, she reported only the experience with her stepfather—which occurred when she was fourteen years old—to the police. Jacqueline said that her stepfather insisted on having intercourse with her more than twenty times over a period of six months. She described the most upsetting time first.

It was when he actually penetrated me the first time. He'd been working up to it for two months by petting, sitting close, feeling my leg, and finally he got me. It was in the front seat of his car. He was determined to do it. He took his pants off, then took my pants off and told me how all right it was going to be. I was looking up at the full moon crying: "Please! I don't want this to happen," because I was a virgin then. But there was nothing I could do to stop it. He got down on his knees on the floor of the car in front of me and started to penetrate me. I kept crying and saying no. He kept saying, "Relax" and that there was no danger of pregnancy because he was sterile. He wasn't sensitive to anything but his own horniness. It really hurt a lot, and I kept telling him that. He said, "Relax, it won't hurt," but how could I? Besides, he was about forty and I was only fourteen. So he got his rocks off and we went home.

Every Friday night for about six months that happened. Finally I ran away. (Did he ever use physical force?) No, he forced me mentally. I was very scared of him. He said: "I've been your father since you were three. I've been a good father. You owe it to me." But I knew it was wrong. (Did he use verbal threats?) The only form of fun I had was to go skating, so he bribed me with that. He said if I didn't do it, I couldn't go skating. (How did it end?) I ran away from home.

(Were these experiences reported to the police?) Yes. I had to tell the court why I ran away, so I told them about it. They interrogated me for three hours, then they set a court date. But I saw my mother and stepfather before that date, and I decided not to go to court.

(Upset?) Extremely upset. (Effect on your life?) It had an extremely great effect. It was the main source of my problems with my family. We're still having run-ins about it. They refuse to believe that it really happened. My mother says it's because I'm an incorrigible liar and that I'm just trying to hurt them. She really thinks I'm psychotic. Everything that's happened since in my life has been a result of that experience.

The interviewer reported that Jacqueline was very upset when talking about this experience. When asked which of all her experiences of sexual abuse she found the most upsetting, she selected the experience with her stepfather.

As mentioned, only one case of sexual abuse by an uncle was reported to the police. Since there were forty-eight incest perpetrators who were uncles, this represents a report rate of 2 percent. Stephanie's uncle tried to rape her once when he was in his forties and she was seventeen years old.

I was pregnant and my uncle was staying in the house with me and my father. My father was not at home at the time and my uncle got drunk. I was in bed and he came in and got on top of me. I pushed him off and hit him with the phone. He started coming toward me again and I ran to the kitchen and got a butcher knife. He was behind me and I told him that I would kill him if he didn't leave me alone. He kept talking crazy and then started after me again, but then he stopped. I called my mother and she called the police. (Did he touch your breasts or genitals?) I pushed him off so fast he didn't have time. He was really drunk and he didn't even remember doing it. He never tried anything again.
(What resulted from the police report?) They took him to jail. He did a little time there for warrants. I didn't press charges because he was my uncle. (Upset?) Extremely upset. (Effect on your life?) A little effect.

Stephanie's violent resistance—including her threat to kill her uncle—is an exceptional feature of this case as well as the fact that she sought the help of the police. Despite her determination, however, Stephanie was not willing to press charges "because he was my uncle." She felt loyal toward him as a relative, though he appears to have felt no such sentiment toward her.

Stephanie described herself as extremely upset, yet she said that the attempted rape by her uncle had only a little long-term effect on her. The fact that she was seventeen years old and not younger may be one relevant factor. In addition, Stephanie appears to have similarly assessed two other experiences of rape; the first was a violent gang-rape when she was in her teens. She said this experience was "very upsetting" but had only "a little effect." The gang-rape was also reported to the police. One of the men was arrested, but there was no conviction because one of his relatives was willing to substantiate his claim that Stephanie had not been raped.

The other experience was a violent attempted rape by an acquaintance when she was in her early teens. He beat her up with a gun and threatened to sell her to a pimp, but when he discovered she was menstruating, he lost interest in completing the rape. Although Stephanie described herself as "extremely upset" and "scared to death," once again she said this attack only had a little effect on her subsequent life.

Unfortunately, we know little about Stephanie's background. If she had already experienced a great deal of violence, this might explain why she might downplay the effect of all three of these very violent experiences. Stephanie's evaluations of the impact of these assaults on her life illustrate the inherent difficulty of interpreting people's subjective reports of trauma.

Although Stephanie's uncle ended up in jail, it wasn't because of the sexual attack on her. Hence this case does not qualify as resulting in a conviction. But along with the cases of Ida and Jacqueline, it does remind us that the conviction rate for incestuous abuse is so low not just because perpetrators are not found guilty but because victims are so often reluctant to press charges. This reluctance was seen in three out of the four reported cases in our survey.

Conclusion

Out of 187 cases of incestuous abuse, the only conviction obtained involved an apparently psychotic and very violent biological father—a Latino ex-convict who knocked his daughter unconscious and who may even have been caught in the act of attempting to penetrate her. Who called the police and why we do not know. In such an extreme case as this, the police and other law enforcement personnel probably identify less than when the offender is apparently of sound mind, nonviolent, and without a criminal record.

It is not a new insight to point out that incarcerated sex offenders are not representative of sex offenders in the population who are never incarcerated. However, our 1-percent conviction rate emphasizes the importance of this insight. Since it is so difficult to conduct research on undetected perpetrators of incestuous abuse—or of any other kind of sexual abuse, for that matter—who are neither incarcerated nor in a treatment program, there has been a tendency to lean too heavily on studies based on these highly unrepresentative offenders for our development of theory as well as empirical knowledge (e.g., Groth 1979).

Louise Armstrong (1978) has argued that it is not incest that is taboo—it's *talking* about incest. If talking about incest is taboo, it is evident from our survey that reporting it to the police and pressing charges against the perpetrators are even more taboo.

7

What Actually
Happened?
The Characteristics of
Incestuous Abuse

Chapter 3 was devoted to elaborating on the differences between incest and incestuous abuse. Now we will examine some of the factors that differentiate one experience of incestuous abuse from another. Did it occur only once, or many times? Was it accompanied by violence? How severe were the sexual acts involved? How old was the victim when it started? What was the age of the perpetrator? How big an age difference was there between the participants? And perhaps most important of all, *who* was the perpetrator: the victim's father, mother, grandfather, brother, sister, uncle, or cousin?

Of all these factors, the relationship between the perpetrator and victim is usually considered the most salient. And our study confirms its importance. Hence part 4 will focus on the differences—as well as the similarities—between sexual abuse perpetrated by different relatives. In this chapter sexual abuse by different relatives will be combined so that we can examine the characteristics of *all* these forms of incestuous abuse.

It is important to remember that although our interviews were conducted in 1978, most of the cases of incest occurred well before that date.*

*In 31 percent of the cases the onset of the incestuous abuse was over thirty years prior to the 1978 interview date; in 20 percent of the cases, from twenty-one to thirty years before; in 36 percent of the cases, from eleven to twenty years ago; in 9 percent of the cases, from six to ten years ago; and in only 3 percent of the cases had the incestuous abuse started less than five years before the interview was conducted.

Multiple Incest Victimization

While 16 percent of our probability sample of women reported being incestuously abused before the age of eighteen, twenty-four, or 2.6 percent, of them had been victimized by more than one relative. Seventeen of these women were incestuously abused by two relatives, four by three relatives, two by four relatives, and one by five relatives.

Frequency and Duration of Incest Victimization

The belief that incestuous abuse tends to occur over a period of many years has become quite entrenched in contemporary thinking. Consequently, in cases where a victim reports that a relative sexually abused her only once, some clinicians believe she must be repressing other experiences.

In our probability sample survey *43 percent of the cases of incestuous abuse were described as having occurred only once.* Since knowledge of incest has been so influenced by data from clinical samples, the common assumption of multiple experiences must be questioned. While acknowledging that repression plays a significant role in whether or not women remember experiences of incest—a subject discussed in chapter 2—it seems seriously premature to maintain that in 43 percent of the cases, repression of additional experiences of sexual abuse must have occurred. These women were, after all, sufficiently unrepressed to remember one experience.

Thirty-one percent of the experiences of incestuous abuse were reported to have occurred from two to five times; 17 percent, from six to twenty times; and 10 percent, over twenty times. It is important to note that these frequency categories were precoded, so over twenty times was the maximum frequency that could be recorded.

With regard to the time period over which the multiple incidents of incestuous abuse occurred, 35 percent occurred over a period of less than six months, 31 percent occurred over a period of more than six months but less than two years; 28 percent occurred over a period of more than two years but less than ten years; and 6 percent occurred over a period of more than ten years.

Solitary Versus Pair or Group Incestuous Abuse

Many cases of child sexual abuse involving the abuse of many children simultaneously have come to public attention in recent years. The term "sex rings" has been coined to refer to cases in which numerous children are involved (Burgess, et al. 1978). Most of the children in these rings have been unrelated to the perpetrators, although the perpetrators' own children are also involved in some cases.

Surprisingly, then, in our probability sample survey, only three cases (2 percent) of incestuous abuse involved two or more female victims being sexually abused together, and there was only one case in which a female victim was incestuously abused together with two male victims. What might account for this very low number of cases of children being incestuously abused simultaneously?

It is possible that there has in fact been an increase in such cases over the past decade. Because much of our study data reflects abuse that occurred many years ago, our findings on group and pair incestuous victimization are more relevant to the past than the present.

There were five cases in our survey in which a respondent was sexually abused before the age of eighteen by two or more perpetrators acting together, at least one of whom was a relative. In two cases, both involving first cousins, the attacks were committed exclusively by relatives. The other three attacks also involved nonrelatives.

Illustrative Cases of Pair or Group Attacks

The first case involves first cousins only. Amanda was twelve years old when two of her first cousins, one fourteen and the other fifteen, fondled her. This was the only sexual incident with these relatives.

I was spending a weekend with their family. The ladies had gone shopping and we were alone in the house. I had been bathing and I came out with just my robe on. They [two cousins] followed me and started fondling me. (Where?) My breasts mostly, and one put his hands on my genitals. One of them grabbed my hand and put it on his genitals. I slapped one of them. I was both scared and mad. I told them I'd tell my father, but I didn't. (Did they use physical force?) No, but there were two of them and only one of me. (Upset?) Extremely upset. (Effect on your life?) A little effect.

Valerie was only nine years old when a first cousin and three of his friends tried to rape her. Her cousin was fifteen years old at the time, and his friends were all fifteen or younger. Valerie said these incidents happened twice over a period of three years.

L. [cousin] and some friends took me to a barn. L. tried to have intercourse with me while his friends watched. He pulled my pants down and tried to put his penis in me. (Did he use force?) Yes. Not violence, but it was force. He pushed me down and had me feel his dick; he took my hand down there. The second time they all touched my breasts and genitals. (What ended these incidents?) I quit going near them.

(Upset?) Somewhat upset. (Effect on your life?) Some effect. It made me afraid of men and unable to have satisfactory sexual experiences with them because of my fear of them. I get paranoid when I'm the only woman in a room full of men.

Angela was fifteen years old the one time a first cousin and a friend of her family's sexually abused her. They were in their thirties at the time.

I babysat for Larry a lot. One night when I was babysitting he and his wife and another couple went out. I lived half a mile up the road and Larry and his friend Bob would usually drive me home. Bob would always make advances; Larry never did. This time Larry said, "Come on, I'll drive you home." Larry drove, I was in the middle, and Bob was on my right. There were two ways to get to my house: one was down a dirt alleyway, the other was on a main street. They turned down the alley and went by a field. Halfway home Larry stopped the car and turned the lights off and Bob laughed and said, "What are you going to do, Larry?" Larry put his hand on my leg and squeezed it and put his other arm around me and said, "You're the prettiest thing I ever saw." Then he said, "How about a kiss?" Bob was laughing and had his arm around me too. I didn't know what to do. Larry then took his hand off my leg and put it on my chin to kiss me. I took his hand off and said, "Take me home." He said, "Okay, but promise you won't tell your mother." I said no, but I did tell her. He took me home and as I got out of the car he said, "I still think you're the prettiest thing I've ever seen."

(Did he touch your breasts or genitals?) No, just my leg. (Did he kiss you?) Just on my cheek. I wouldn't let him kiss me on my lips. (What do you think he wanted?) He was just after a kiss. I don't know if he had thoughts of intercourse; I don't think that was his intention. He was drunk and horny. Before that time it was just verbal stuff. When I babysat or if he saw me somewhere else, he'd always say, "You're really growing up there." But there had been no physical contact before. (What did Bob do?) He just laughed and had his arm around my shoulders, nothing else. (Upset?) Somewhat upset. (Effect on your life?) No effect.

Although two men twice her age were flirting with her and touching her, Angela did not appear to have felt threatened or afraid. Her statements show a sense of being in control, which sheds some light on the relatively low level of trauma that she reported.

Another case in which a female first cousin and an acquaintance were the perpetrators will be cited in chapter 19.

Violence and Physical Force

It is becoming increasingly well known that child sexual abuse often involves no force or violence. Is this new insight confirmed or refuted by our probability sample survey?

Verbal threats of physical harm were only used in 3 percent of the incidents of incestuous abuse, and verbal threats that did not involve physical harm were used in an additional 4 percent of the cases. In two cases the perpetrator specifically threatened to kill the victim. It is important to point out that there was no question in our survey on covert threats, nor on the extent to which respondents had felt scared or threatened by the perpetrator. Verbal threats were the only form of threat investigated.

In answer to a question on weapons, only one perpetrator was mentioned as having, but not using, a gun, two as having but not using a knife, one as having another kind of weapon, and one as using some other kind of weapon. Hence a weapon was involved in only 2 percent of all the incidents of incestuous abuse.

With regard to the use of physical force or violence, not including the use of threats or weapons, just over two-thirds of the cases (68 percent) involved no physical force; 29 percent involved physical force at the mildest level of pushing or pinning the victim; 2 percent involved more serious physical force at the level of hitting or slapping; and only 1 percent involved violence at the level of beating or slugging.

A violence scale was developed that combined the use of verbal threats, weapons, and other physical force or violence by the perpetrator into one measure. (See table 7–1.)

Application of this violence scale revealed that 65 percent of the cases of incestuous abuse were completely nonforceful, 31 percent involved some force or violence, and only 3 percent involved substantial violence.

Although incest victims were not asked about physical injuries, only two of them mentioned suffering from them. One respondent, who was raped by her brother-in-law when she was thirteen, said that the entrance to her vagina was damaged. Ida, the respondent discussed in chapter 6, was the victim of an attempted rape by her biological father who beat her unconscious with a fireplace log in the course of his attack. She was hospitalized with a concussion and a broken jaw.

TABLE 7–1

Violence Scale

	Score*
1. *Verbal Threats*	
Extreme verbal threat of bodily harm	3
Other verbal threat of bodily harm	2
Other verbal threat, but not of bodily harm	1
No verbal threat	0
2. *Weapon*	
Used a gun or knife	3
Had gun or knife, but didn't use/or used other weapon	2
Had other weapon, but didn't use	1
No weapon	0
3. *Physical Force or Violence*	
Beat, slugged, kicked, choked, etc.	3
Hit, slapped, etc.	2
Pushed, pinned, etc.	1
No physical force	0

*A total score of 0 = *Nonforceful,* 1–3 = *Forceful,* more than 3 = *Violent.*
  Where there was a missing value on one or two dimensions, the score was calculated only on the dimension(s) for which there were scores. When two dimensions were missing, the available score was multiplied by 3. When one was missing, the sum of the remaining 2 was multiplied by 1.5.

Despite these two cases, our survey strongly substantiates the view that incestuous abuse rarely involves much physical violence. This finding is consistent with the view that child sexual abuse and the nonsexual physical abuse of children are separate phenomena affected by different dynamics. So, while the sexual abuse of children is certainly a form of child abuse, it is sufficiently different from nonsexual physical abuse that merging the two would be a serious mistake.

Severity of Incestuous Abuse

Legal definitions of incest have traditionally been limited to penile-vaginal sexual intercourse. Although there is no consensus on a more meaningful definition, researchers and clinicians recognize that this definition is far too restricted. Perhaps this history partially accounts for the extraordinary inattention in much of the contemporary literature to exactly what the incest perpetrator did to his or her victim. In rejecting the normative preoccupation with traditional sexual intercourse, some researchers have ignored the possibility that the sex acts involved in the incestuous abuse may affect the impact on the victims in important ways (e.g., Herman 1981). In later chapters it will become evident that the severity of incestuous abuse was highly related to the amount of trauma reported by victims in our survey.

Eighteen different degrees of sexual abuse were differentiated in our survey according to whether or not force was used as well as the degree of sexual violation involved. The frequency with which these different degrees of sexual abuse occurred is presented in table 7–2. In cases of multiple abuse, interviewers asked about the most upsetting episode and attempted to document the most severe experience of sexual abuse.

The table reveals that there were only twenty-six cases of forcible rape or attempted rape, constituting 14 percent of the total number of sexual abuse experiences. When nonforceful penile-vaginal intercourse or attempts at such acts (i.e., statutory rapes) are combined with the forcible rapes and attempted rapes, the percentage of the total number of sexual abuse incidents that qualify as rape rises from 14 to 20 percent*—that is, one-fifth of the total.

It is now widely recognized that most child sexual abuse involves sexual fondling rather than intercourse (see, e.g., Finkelhor 1979). But the fact that approximately one in seven cases involved forcible penile-vaginal rape or attempted rape (or one in five if statutory rape is included) shows the danger of underestimating incestuous child rape.

In addition, although our definition of forcible rape (like the legal definition) includes intercourse or attempted intercourse by physical force, threat of force, or inability to consent because of being drugged, unconscious, asleep, or in some other way totally physically helpless, all but one of the twenty-six cases of forcible rape involved physical force. The one exception involved inability to consent.

This eighteen-category typology of sexual abuse was collapsed into three: sex acts in the first eight categories were considered cases of very severe sexual abuse; sex acts in the next eight categories were considered severe cases; and sex acts in the last two categories were considered least severe cases. When this simplified typology was applied to our survey data, almost one-quarter (23 percent) of the cases of incestuous abuse qualified as very severe, 41 percent as severe, and 36 percent as least severe.

When differentiating between forceful and nonforceful incestuous abuse, 41 percent of the cases involved force and 59 percent involved no force. (Note that force here includes the threat of force as well as the inability to consent.)

*This percentage was recalculated from the *N*'s for completed and attempted genital intercourse to avoid inaccuracy due to rounding to the nearest whole number.

TABLE 7–2

Severity of Incestuous Abuse

Type of Sexual Abuse	%	N
I. *Very Severe Sexual Abuse*		
1. Rape—forcible genital intercourse*	6	11
2. Nonforcible genital intercourse	3	5
3. Attempted rape	8	15
4. Nonforcible attempted genital intercourse	4	7
5. Forcible fellatio, cunnilingus, analingus, anal intercourse	1	2
6. Nonforcible fellatio, cunnilingus, analingus, anal intercourse	2	3
7. Forcible attempted fellatio, cunnilingus, analingus, anal intercourse	0	0
8. Nonforcible attempted fellatio, cunnilingus, analingus, anal intercourse	0	0
II. *Severe Sexual Abuse*		
9. Forcible genital contact (unclothed) including manual touching or penetration	11	20
10. Nonforcible genital contact (unclothed) including manual touching or penetration	17	31
11. Forcible attempted genital contact (unclothed) including manual touching or penetration	1	2
12. Nonforcible attempted genital contact (unclothed) including manual touching or penetration	3	5
13. Forcible breast contact (unclothed) or simulated intercourse	4	8
14. Nonforcible breast contact (unclothed) or simulated intercourse	3	6
15. Forcible attempted breast contact (unclothed) or simulated intercourse	0	0
16. Nonforcible attempted breast contact (unclothed) or simulated intercourse	2	4
III. *Least Severe Sexual Abuse*		
17. Forcible sexual kissing, intentional sexual touching of buttocks, thigh, leg, or clothed breasts or genitals	10	19
18. Nonforcible sexual kissing, intentional sexual touching of buttocks, thigh, leg, or clothed breasts or genitals	26	48
Total	101	186

Force includes physical force, threat of force, or assault when the victim is unable to consent because she is unconscious, severely drugged, or in some other way totally helpless. Note: It does *not* include the inability of a child to consent to sexual contact with an adult.
Missing observations: 1.

Age of Victims

In 11 percent of the cases of incestuous abuse, our respondents reported being victimized for the first time before the age of five; in 19 percent of the cases, such abuse started between the ages of six and nine; in 41 percent, it started between the ages of ten and thirteen; and in 29 percent, it started between the ages of fourteen and seventeen. The two youngest victims were two years old.

Thus we see that in only one out of every nine cases were the victims of incest five years or younger. It is likely that these figures are biased toward the older ages because of memory difficulties. For example, we noted in chapter 5 that more suspected cases of sexual abuse were reported for children of two years than for children of any other age up to sixteen years old in Los Angeles County in 1984 (Durfee 1984). Further research is needed to inform us whether or not there has been a real increase in the incestuous victimization of children at this young age.

Our survey data show that girls at the ages of ten to thirteen are the most vulnerable for incestuous abuse; approximately two-fifths of the cases occurred in this age group.

The mean age for incestuous abuse in our study was 11.15 years. This is higher than the mean ages reported for child victims of both incestuous and nonincestuous abuse by many other researchers (e.g., Landis [1956] reports 10.4 years; Benward and Densen-Gerber [1975], 10.3 years; Finkelhor [1979], 10.2 years; and Gagnon [1965], 9.9 years [Finkelhor 1979, p. 154]). However, the differences may be due to different definitions of what constitutes child sexual abuse, particularly the upper age limit used.

Although our average age of 11.15 years is higher than the average age reported in other studies, it is still sufficiently young to contradict the view that men are merely succumbing to the charms of sexually attractive adolescent girls.

Age Disparity Between Incest Perpetrators and Victims

The age disparities between the incest perpetrators and their victims in our survey were as follows: 16 percent of the perpetrators were forty years or more older than their victims; 39 percent were twenty to thirty-nine years older; 30 percent were five to nineteen years older; 13 percent were less than five years older; and 2 percent were the same age or younger than their victims.

As mentioned in chapter 3, the 2 percent of incest perpetrators who were the same age as their victims or younger and the 13 percent who were less than five years older would be disqualified by most researchers as cases of sexual abuse. This amounts to discounting one out of approximately every seven cases.

Where Incestuous Abuse Occurred

Ninety-five percent of the incest victims said that they were living with their parents when they were sexually abused. Although respondents were not specifically asked about the location of the incestuous abuse, in most cases their descriptions of what happened revealed the locale. It is hardly surprising to learn that most perpetrators lived under the same roof as their victims. In 38 percent of the cases the incestuous abuse occurred in their shared home. In 18 percent of the cases the main location mentioned was the incest victim's home; in 12 percent it was the perpetrator's home; in 7 percent, a car; and in 25 percent of the cases some other place was mentioned. Hence, in over two-thirds (68 percent) of the cases where the location was mentioned, the sexual abuse occurred in the home of either the victim or the perpetrator or both.

In thirty-six cases the victim mentioned that the incestuous abuse occurred in her own bed, in eight cases the perpetrator's bed was mentioned, and in nine cases, another person's bed.

In part 4 we will examine how some of these characteristics of incestuous abuse varied for different perpetrators.

8

Social Factors in
the Occurrence of
Incestuous Abuse

Historically, most researchers and other writers on incest have been psychologists. Hence most previous attempts to understand the causes of incest have focused on family dynamics and psychopathology rather than social factors (e.g., Forward and Buck 1978; Meiselman 1978; Groth 1979; Mrazek and Kempe 1981; Giaretto 1982). With the exception of David Finkelhor, sociologists have, for the most part, ignored the subject altogether. Feminist scholars, on the other hand, share a perspective inherently more attentive to social factors—particularly those related to patriarchal institutions (e.g., Armstrong 1978; Butler 1978; Rush 1980; Herman 1981; Nelson 1982).

This chapter examines the relevance of social factors to the occurrence of incestuous abuse. Emphasis is on those factors about which others have theorized: the victim's family of origin, urban versus rural upbringing, social class, race and ethnicity, and religious upbringing. Along with evaluation of existing theories, some of the risk factors for incest victimization are explored.

The most startling finding to emerge from our survey data on social factors is that *girls reared in high-income families were more frequently victimized by incest than girls in lower-income families.* To my knowledge, this is the first study to report such a finding; it contradicts prevalent prejudices as well as previous research. The fact that it is based on the first large-scale probability household sample gives it particular validity and credibility.

Our other findings are less dramatic than this one; but it is important to bear in mind that discovering an absence of associations between background variables and incestuous abuse can be as significant and useful as discovering positive associations. One example is our finding that for the most part, race and ethnicity have little to do with the prevalence of incestuous abuse. Not only does such a finding help to destroy prevalent stereotypes, but it may also be helpful in providing better services for incest victims. For example, this finding may help service organizations that are unintentionally attracting disproportionate numbers of incest referrals from only one race or ethnic group to search for the reason and rectify any problems rather than to assume that differential prevalence rates are responsible.

Incest Victims' Family Background

When the analysis of our survey data was confined to father-daughter incestuous abuse, we found an enormous difference between the vulnerability of girls raised by stepfathers and those raised by biological fathers. More specifically, 17 percent of the women in our sample who had been raised by a stepfather in the first fourteen years of their life were sexually abused by him before the age of fourteen. In contrast, only 2 percent of the women who had been raised by a biological father were so abused by him before that age. Thus stepdaughters are over eight times more at risk of sexual abuse by the stepfathers who reared them than are daughters reared by their biological fathers. There is reason to believe this disparity in the vulnerability of stepdaughters and biological daughters may be even greater when less permanent stepfathers are included in the analysis. (This issue will be further discussed in chapter 16.)

Table 8–1 reveals that women who were reared by both of their biological or adoptive parents were the least likely to be incestuously abused (15 percent were so victimized). Those reared by biological mothers only were a close second in avoiding incestuous abuse (18 percent became victims). In contrast, over a quarter (28 percent) of the women who were reared by a stepfather and biological mother were incestuously abused. And although the numbers are unreliably small, women reared by both grandparents proved to be slightly more vulnerable yet to incestuous abuse (30 percent). However, these associations did not reach statistical significance at <0.05 level.

One of the shortcomings of this analysis is its failure to reflect the multiple experiences of incestuous abuse reported by some victims. It assumes instead that each incest victim was sexually abused by only one

TABLE 8–1

Parent/Parent Substitutes in Childhood Years and Girls Incestuously Abused Before 18 Years

Parent/Parent Substitutes	Girls Incestuously Abused		Girls Never Incestuously Abused		
	%	N	%	N	Total
Both biological or adoptive parents	15	114	85	629	743
Biological mother only	18	17	82	79	96
Stepfather and biological mother	28	8	72	21	29
Both grandparents	30	3	70	7	10
Other	19	10	81	42	52
Total		152		778	930

Not significant at < 0.05 level.

relative. When we distinguish between victims who were only incestuously abused once from those who were abused more than once, there is a highly significant association between the type of family background and multiple incest victimization (at < 0.001 level).

As can be seen in table 8–2, 2 percent of those girls who were reared by both their biological parents were incestuously abused by more than one relative, compared to 2 percent of the girls who were reared by their biological mother only and 17 percent of the girls who were reared by their stepfather and biological mother.

In contrast, the differences in the percentages of girls who were sexually abused by only one relative show little relationship to family background. Indeed, of the girls reared by a stepfather and biological mother, a slightly

TABLE 8–2

Parent/Parent Substitutes in Childhood Years and Multiple Incest Victimization Before 18 Years

Parent/Parent Substitutes	Victim of Multiple Relatives		Victim of Only One Relative		Girls Never Incestuously Abused	
	%	N	%	N	%	N
Both biological or adoptive parents	2	14	14	100	85	629
Biological mother only	2	2	16	15	82	79
Stepfather and biological mother	17	5	10	3	72	21
Other	5	3	16	10	79	49
Total		24		128		778

Significant at < 0.001 level.

lower percentage (10 percent) were the victims of one incest experience than girls from other types of family backgrounds.

Our finding that being reared by a stepfather increases a girl's vulnerability to incestuous abuse is consistent with those reported in Finkelhor's student survey. He concluded that having a stepfather was one of the strongest of forty different risk factors evaluated. "Virtually *half* the girls with stepfathers were victimized by someone (not necessarily their stepfather)," he wrote. "Moreover, this risk factor remained the strongest correlate of victimization, even when all other variables were statistically controlled" (1984, p. 25).

The girls with stepfathers in Finkelhor's study were more likely than other girls to be victimized by other men as well as their stepfathers. "In particular," he reported, "they are five times more likely to be victimized by a friend of their parents" (1984, p. 25). The latter finding is not confirmed by our survey data. Girls with stepfathers were not significantly more subject to victimization by nonrelatives than other girls.

Social Class

It is commonly believed by both researchers and laypeople that incestuous abuse is more prevalent among people from the lower socioeconomic classes (see, e.g., Lukianowicz 1972; Weinberg 1976; Mrazek 1981; Finkelhor 1984). The studies of most researchers who have arrived at this conclusion have been based on very selective samples without control groups; they therefore provide a poor basis for evaluating the distribution of incest cases by social class. Finkelhor's student survey is one of the few useful studies on this issue.

Finkelhor found that two different measures of social class were significantly related to the sexual victimization of girls. (His analysis includes incest victimization as well as extrafamilial child sexual abuse.) Thirty-three percent of the girls from families with incomes of less than $10,000 were sexually victimized, compared to 19 percent for his sample as a whole (1980, p. 4). "In other words," Finkelhor concluded, "lower-income girls were two-thirds more likely to be victimized than the average girl. No one should be surprised at this finding," Finkelhor comments. "Reported cases of sexual abuse come predominantly from lower-socioeconomic-strata families. . . . Moreover, this association with lower social class status has been confirmed in studies of family violence and child abuse in nonclinical populations" (1984, p. 24).

Finkelhor (1984) reported that girls whose fathers had blue-collar occupations were also significantly more likely to be victims of child sexual abuse (p. 31). Bearing in mind that, in contrast to Finkelhor's study, our analysis focuses on incestuous abuse only, what are our findings on this important question?

FATHER'S OCCUPATION AND EDUCATION

Following the standard methods of coding occupations used by the United States Census, the twelve groups of occupations differentiated were collapsed into three classes: upper middle class (professional, technical, and managerial occupations), middle class (sales, clerical, and crafts), and lower class (operatives, laborers, service and transportation workers). As so measured, there was no statistically significant association between the respondents' fathers' occupation and the rate of incest victimization.

Nor was there a significant relationship between the respondents' fathers' education and the rate of incest victimization. By these two measures of social class, then, the hypothesis that incestuous abuse occurs more frequently in the lower class is not confirmed.

Are our findings on social class so different from Finkelhor's because of our focus on incestuous abuse and his inclusion of extrafamilial child sexual abuse? The answer is no. According to our survey, there is no relationship—nor a significant trend—between these two measures of social class and the occurrence of either incestuous abuse or extrafamilial child sexual abuse. This important finding is confirmed by Gail Wyatt's more recent study of 248 Afro-American and white women in Los Angeles (Peters, Wyatt, and Finkelhor, 1986).

TOTAL HOUSEHOLD INCOME AT TIME OF
(FIRST) INCESTUOUS ABUSE

Another measurable indicator of social class is total household income at the time of the incestuous abuse. For every instance of sexual abuse inquired about, the respondent was asked, "Can you tell me about what was your total yearly family income, from all sources, before taxes at that time?" A card with various income ranges was then handed to her to help her arrive at an answer. The figures on income thus obtained were then converted into 1978 dollars for comparability.

Income information on two different comparison groups were used for this analysis: first, the total household income of the victims of sexual assault other than incest. This information also applies to the time the assault occurred and was also converted into 1978 dollars. Included here are victims of adult rape, sexual abuse by authority figures, and victims of extrafamilial child sexual abuse. The second comparison was made with the total household income of women in our sample who had never been incestuously abused.

As can be seen in table 8–3, only 18 percent of the incest victims came from families with incomes of $7,500 or less. In comparison, just over twice as many of the victims of other sexual assault (38 percent) came from families with a total household income of $7,500 or less, and just under twice as many (34 percent) of the women who had never been incestuously abused reported incomes of $7,500 or less when interviewed.

Similarly, well over half of the victims of incest (56 percent) came from families with a total household income of $15,000 or more, compared with 35 percent and 33 percent of the other two groups.

Our survey data indicate exactly the opposite of Finkelhor's finding that incest victims from lower-income families were overrepresented among incest victims. In our survey incest victims were underrepresented in lower-income families and overrepresented in the highest-income families. How might this crucial difference in our findings be explained?

As Finkelhor (1984, p. 24) himself points out, his survey was limited to college students, and college students—including those from lower-income backgrounds—are obviously a special group. He speculates that students are probably psychologically healthier than people who never go to college and that individuals who were very traumatized by child sexual abuse may consequently not have attended college. He concludes that his data may therefore underestimate the real risk of child sexual abuse for lower-class children. Our data, which are not limited to a particular group like students and which therefore more accurately represent the social class composition of an urban community, do not support Finkelhor's reasoning on this matter.

TABLE 8–3

Comparison of Household Income at Time of (First) Victimization for Incest, Other Sexual Assault (Converted into 1978 Dollars), and Household Income for Women Never Victimized by Incest

Household Income	Incest Victimization		Other Sexual Assault Victimization		Women Never Incestuously Abused	
	%	N	%	N	%	N
Less than $7,500	18	19	38	356	34	250
$7,500–$14,999	26	28	26	243	33	247
$15,000 or more	56	61	35	330	33	246
Total	100	108	99	929	100	743

Missing observations: 78 on incest victimization; 35 on women who were never incestuously abused.
Significant at <0.001 level.

TABLE 8–4

Comparison of Household Income at Time of (First) Victimization for Incest, Extrafamilial Child Sexual Abuse (Converted into 1978 Dollars), and Household Income for Women Never Incestuously Abused

Household Income	Incestuous Abuse Before 14		Extrafamilial Sexual Abuse Before 14		Women Never Incestuously Abused	
	%	N	%	N	%	N
Less than $7,500	19	15	26	45	34	250
$7,500–$14,999	29	23	19	32	33	247
$15,000 and More	53	42	55	95	33	246
Total	101	80	100	172	100	743

Missing observations: 172.
Significant at < 0.001 level.

Could it be that the focus of our analysis on incestuous abuse, in contrast to Finkelhor's on all child sexual abuse (both incestuous and extrafamilial), explains our contradictory findings on socioeconomic status at the time of the abuse? In order to answer this question we will consider only sexual abuse that occurred before the victim turned fourteen years old, since our definitions of incestuous and extrafamilial sexual abuse are more comparable for these years.*

Table 8–4 reveals that the percentages of victims of both extrafamilial sexual abuse and incestuous abuse before the age of fourteen who came from families in the highest income group were significantly higher than the percentage of women from high-income families who were never incestuously abused. And while the victims of incest were indeed even more underrepresented in the lower-income group than were the victims of extrafamilial child sexual abuse, the victims of extrafamilial child sexual abuse were also underrepresented in the lower-income group when compared with women who had never been victimized by incest.

RESPONDENT'S EDUCATION

Since the average age of our respondents at the time of the interview was forty-three years, the level of education they achieved is probably more of a reflection of their social class background than of their current social class status. Contrary to expectations, slightly *more* incest victims than nonincest victims had received at least some college education (66 percent compared to 57 percent, respectively), and fewer incest victims had not

*This comparison remained essentially the same when the milder incidents of child sexual abuse were excluded to make the data on incestuous and extrafamilial child sexual abuse even more comparable.

graduated from high school (10 percent compared to 17 percent for nonincest victims). (This relationship is significant at <0.05 level.)

This finding is surprising, since it is common to hear about cases in which incest victims' school grades decline as a result of their distress about incestuous abuse. However, it is consistent with the fact that incest victims in our survey were more likely to come from higher-income homes than women who had no history of incestuous abuse.

Mother's Status

Finkelhor (1984) notes that his study "suggests a connection between the oppression of wives and the victimization of daughters" (p. 26). Arguing that education is an important power resource, Finkelhor found that girls whose mothers had never finished high school were significantly more likely to be sexually victimized as children (p. 31).

Finkelhor (1984) also surmised that a wife who "has substantially less education than her husband is much more likely to be subordinate to and dependent on him" (p. 26). This was confirmed by his study: "The most dangerous parental combination for a daughter," Finkelhor wrote, "is not when her mother and father are both poorly educated, but when her father is well educated and her mother is not. . . . Here is very concrete testimony of how inequality between the sexes may be dangerous to the health and well-being of children" (p. 27).

This same argument could be extended to disparities in occupational status between husbands and wives, and the wife's employment history. We will start by looking at these variables for mothers independently of their husbands.

MOTHER'S OCCUPATION, EDUCATION,
AND EMPLOYMENT HISTORY

We found no statistically significant relationship between the occupational status of mothers who had worked in the labor force and their daughter's incest victimization. And all three questions asked about the mothers' employment history were also not significantly related to incest victimization.*

Since many mothers didn't have occupations but all of them had an

---

*Respondents were asked whether or not their mothers worked in the labor force during their daughter's first fourteen years; if yes, what percentage of time they had worked; and whether or not they had worked after their daughters turned fifteen.

education, the latter variable is of particular interest. It turned out to be significantly related to incest victimization, although the relationship was curvilinear rather than linear. More specifically, 13 percent of the respondents whose mothers had attended college were victimized by incest, compared to 21 percent of those whose mothers had graduated from high school and 13 percent of those whose mothers had an eighth-grade education or less (significant at < 0.05 level).

Thus our survey data on incestuous abuse do not confirm Finkelhor's finding that girls whose mothers had never finished high school were significantly more likely to be sexually victimized as children. Instead, according to our data, girls whose mothers were high-school graduates were most at risk of incestuous abuse—more so than girls whose mothers had never finished high school and girls whose mothers had attended college.

DISPARITIES IN PARENTAL EDUCATION AND
OCCUPATIONAL STATUS

When we examine the discrepancies between the education and occupational status of the parents of our respondents, we find no statistically significant association between these variables and incest victimization. Once again, then, our survey data do not support Finkelhor's findings that daughters are particularly vulnerable to incest victimization when their fathers are well educated and their mothers are poorly educated.

Race and Ethnicity

Very little research has been undertaken on race and ethnic differences in the occurrence and characteristics of incestuous abuse. According to Kirson Weinberg's classic study of 200 cases of incest that came to the attention of authorities in Illinois, Afro-Americans, Mexicans, Poles, and Scots were among the groups that were overrepresented (1976, pp. 43–44).

However, as already mentioned, data based on cases that come to the attention of authorities are likely to be extremely unrepresentative. We have seen how different our findings on social class were from other studies. Is this also the case with race and ethnicity?

Our survey found that the percentage of women in each race or ethnic group who were incestuously abused was quite similar, except for Asians. Only 8 percent of the Asian and Filipina respondents reported incest victimization, a significantly smaller percentage than all the other groups in our survey. Latinas reported the highest rate of incestuous abuse (20 percent), then women from "Other" race or ethnic groups (19 percent), followed by white women (17 percent), then Afro-American women (16 percent). However, these differences are small and not statistically significant (see table 8–5). Once again we see that distorted samples have led to distorted findings. (Data on Jewish women will be presented in the section on religious upbringing.)

Why incestuous abuse was so much lower among Asian and Filipina women is unknown. As mentioned earlier, several consultants had warned us before we went into the field that many Asian women would find it extremely difficult to talk about experiences of incest and other sexual abuse. Were Asian women less willing to talk to us honestly? Or is there really less incestuous abuse among Asians? Future research will have to address these questions.

Although Wyatt's analysis includes extrafamilial child sexual abuse as well as incestuous abuse, she too found no significant difference in its prevalence among Afro-American and white women in her Los Angeles study (1985, p. 513). Since her study was specifically designed to compare the sexual abuse experiences of these two groups, her findings are particularly significant.

No study comparable to Wyatt's has been undertaken for Latina or Asian women. However, Kercher and McShane (1984) did examine the victimization rates for both incestuous and extrafamilial child sexual abuse in their random sample of 2,000 adult Texas residents. They found the victimization rate for Latina women was 21.7—substantially higher than the 9.8 rate for white females (p. 498). (The rate for Afro-American females was statistically unreliable.) Although our rate of incestuous abuse for Latina women was slightly higher than our rate for white women, this

TABLE 8–5

Race/Ethnicity and Rates of Incest
Victimization Before 18 Years

Race/ Ethnicity	Incest Victims (N)	Survey Participants (N)	Victimization Rate/100
White	108	627	17
Afro-American	14	90	16
Latina	13	66	20
Asian and Filipina	9	111	8
Other	7	36	19
Total	151	930	16

Missing observation: 1.
Not significant at <0.05 level.

difference is not statistically significant. It is clear that further research on racial and ethnic differences in the prevalence of incestuous abuse as well as almost all other aspects of the incest experience is urgently needed. This has been a seriously neglected area in the field.

Religious Upbringing

Some clinical accounts have suggested that men who are highly religious, with rigid or conservative views about sex and the family, are among those most prone to sexually abuse children. While our survey data only obtained information on religious upbringing, not the intensity of religious commitment or practice on the part of parents, we will examine our findings for some insight into this question.

Table 8–6 shows that 18 percent of the women in our sample who were brought up with a Protestant religion were incestuously abused, followed closely by 17 percent of the women who were raised Catholic, 14 percent who were raised with no religion, 13 percent who were raised with some "other" religion, and 10 percent who were raised as Jews.

By definition, women who were raised with no religious preference did not come from families that were highly religious. However, the difference between a 14-percent prevalence rate for these women and the 17- and 18-percent rates for women raised Catholic or Protestant, respectively, is small. The only really noteworthy difference revealed by the table is that women raised as Jews were incestuously abused less often than those raised Catholic or Protestant.

TABLE 8–6

Religious Upbringing and Rates of Incest
Victimization Before 18 Years

Religious Upbringing	Incest Victims (N)	Survey Participants (N)	Victimization Rate/100
Catholic	60	358	17
Protestant	67	380	18
Jewish	6	59	10
None	10	69	14
Other	8	61	13
Total	151	927	16

Missing observations: 1 on incest victims; 3 on survey participants.
Not significant at < 0.05 level.

Religious background was also not significantly related to child sexual abuse in Finkelhor's student survey (1984, p. 31).

Rural Background

It is commonly believed that incestuous abuse occurs more frequently in rural areas. A substantial amount of research confirms this belief (e.g., Lukianowicz 1972; Katz and Mazur 1979, p. 257; Finkelhor 1980, p. 5). For example, in his student survey Finkelhor found that a significantly larger percentage of children who grew up on farms were sexually victimized as children (1984, p. 31).

Our study does not confirm that a rural background constitutes a risk factor in the occurrence of incestuous abuse. It could be argued that people who move out of rural areas into cities are different from those who remain in rural areas. But this possibility does not explain why a rural background turned out to be a significant risk factor in Finkelhor's study but not ours.

Conclusion

In their exhaustive review of the literature, Sedelle Katz and Mary Ann Mazur (1979) observed that "empirical research has confirmed the fact that most incest families are from the lower socioeconomic levels" (p. 256). When we focused on household income at the time of the incestuous abuse as the measure of social class, we found quite the opposite: *Fewer* of the incest victims came from low-income backgrounds, and more of them came from high-income backgrounds than was the case for women who had never been incestuously abused. Similarly, the incest victims were slightly better educated than women with no incest history. However, when the respondents' fathers' education and occupation were used as the measures of social class, there was no relationship between incest victimization and social class background. Despite these inconsistencies, these findings are perhaps the most significant of all those reported in this chapter. It will be difficult for people to give up the notion that incest is more prevalent in the lower class, and even more difficult still to accept that it is most prevalent in the highest of the income groups compared, but as our study was a probability sample survey with a built-in control group, these findings cannot be dismissed.

The social variables that our survey found to be high-risk factors for incest victimization were: high-income background, having a mother with a high-school education (rather than some college education or an eighth-grade education or less), and being raised by a stepfather.* Chapters 16 and 17 explore further differences between incestuous abuse by biological fathers and stepfathers and why stepfathers are so much more likely to sexually abuse their daughters than biological fathers are.

Of the variables considered in this chapter, our survey found three that may be regarded as low-risk factors: being reared by both biological or adoptive parents, a low-income background, and a Jewish religious upbringing. Asian ethnicity is a fourth low-risk factor, assuming that the low percentage of Asian women who reported incestuous abuse is not due to their being less willing to disclose these experiences than women from other race and ethnic groups. Also significant was the finding that a rural background and having a mother who worked during her daughter's childhood years were not high-risk factors for incestuous abuse.

*For an excellent review of risk factors for both incestuous abuse and extrafamilial sexual abuse combined for female children, see Finkelhor and Baron (1985).

PART THREE

THE VICTIMS

9

The Incest Victims:
Who They Are
and How They Coped

How do incest victims differ from women who were never victimized by incest? In chapter 8 we explored some of the differences in their backgrounds as well as some of the similarities. Here we will look at some of their social characteristics at the time of the interview—for example, their social class, their employment status and history, their marital and maternal status, and their religious preference. All of these are variables that might have been affected by their incest victimization. For example, an experience of incestuous abuse may retard a girl's educational achievement, make her less inclined to marry, discourage her from having children of her own, and so on. By examining these variables we can measure the extent to which the lives of incest victims as a group may have been affected in these particular areas, if at all.

In the second half of the chapter we will address the following questions: How do incest victims handle their victimization? What ended the sexual abuse? What resistance strategies did they find effective? Why do some victims resist more assertively than others? What were the victims' perceptions of why the sexual abuse occurred?

Victims' Social Characteristics

The entire sample of 930 women was divided into those who reported one or more experiences of incestuous abuse before the age of eighteen years and those who reported no such experience before this age. The fact that we can compare the incest group with a nonincest group drawn from the same sample means that we have a built-in control group. Positive correlation, however, does not prove causation; even it if turns out that incest victims have ten times more children than nonincest victims, we cannot be sure that their reproductive histories were in response to their incest experience. Nevertheless, it does suggest that a causative relationship is a distinct possibility.

AGE AT TIME OF INTERVIEW

At the time of the interview the average age of women who had been incestuously abused was thirty-eight years—significantly younger than women who had never been incestuously abused, whose average age was forty-four years. This is consistent with the fact that the two older cohorts of women reported significantly less incestuous abuse than the three younger ones (see chapter 5 for a detailed discussion of trends over time).

Only one of the women who had been incestuously abused was under twenty years old; 34 percent were between twenty and twenty-nine; 31 percent, between thirty and thirty-nine; 22 percent, between forty and fifty-nine; and 13 percent, sixty years or older.

AGE AT FIRST CHILDBEARING AND INCEST VICTIMIZATION

Many clinicians have observed that victims of incest often marry at a young age in order to escape their abusive home situations. Consequently, they are also more apt to become mothers at an early age.* This clinical observation was supported by our survey data. The average age of victims of incest when they first gave birth was 22.5 years compared to 24.2 years for women who had never been incestuously abused (this relationship is significant at < 0.05 level).

However, incest victims were not significantly more likely to have been mothers than women who had never been incest victims, and the mean number of children raised by these two groups of women was also not significantly different.

MARITAL STATUS AND INCEST VICTIMIZATION

Another significant finding is that more of the incest victims than women who had never been incest victims were separated or divorced at the time of the interview—28 percent and 16 percent, respectively (see table 9–1). While in no way wishing to support the view that it is necessarily healthier to marry or stay married than to separate, get divorced, or never marry, it is nevertheless noteworthy that incest victims' marital

*I am indebted to psychiatrist Judith Herman for suggesting we investigate the relationship between the age at first childbearing and incest victimization.

status is different from nonincest victims as far as divorce and separation are concerned.

However, this table also shows that there was virtually no difference in the percentages of incest victims and nonincest victims who never married. Nor was there a significant difference in the number of marriages women in these two groups had contracted.

DEFECTION FROM RELIGIOUS UPBRINGING AND INCEST VICTIMIZATION

Although there was no significant relationship between religious upbringing and incest victimization (see chapter 8), table 9–2 reveals that there is a statistically significant relationship between such victimization and religious preference at the time of the interview. The most striking finding is that 42 percent of the incest victims reported no religious preference compared to 31 percent of the women who had never been incest victims.

When those who had rejected their religious upbringing were taken as a percentage of the total number who had been raised with that particular religion, table 9–3 reveals a defection rate for incest victims of 53 percent compared with only 32 percent for women with no incest history (significant at < 0.001 level). Both Catholic and Protestant incest victims had equally high defection rates—56 percent (significant at < 0.001 and < 0.05 levels, respectively). However, the defection rate for Catholics who had not been incestuously abused was much lower than for Protestant nonvictims—28 percent and 43 percent, respectively. Indeed, Catholic incest victims were twice as likely to defect than Catholics who were never victimized by incest.

In contrast, only one of the seven Jewish incest victims rejected Judaism. This 14 percent defection rate is actually *lower* than the defection from

TABLE 9–1

Marital Status and Incest
Victimization Before 18 Years

Marital Status	Incest Victimization		No Incest Victimization	
	%	N	%	N
Married	36	54	40	312
Widowed	7	10	13	99
Divorced or separated	28	42	16	127
Never married	30	45	31	240
Total	101	151	100	778

Missing observation: 1.
Significant at < 0.01 level.

TABLE 9–2

Religious Preference at Time of Interview and Incest Victimization Before 18 Years

Religious Preference	Incest Victimization		No Incest Victimization	
	%	N	%	N
Protestant	23	34	27	207
Catholic	21	31	29	226
Jewish	4	6	5	38
Other	11	17	8	63
None	42	64	31	241
Total	101	152	100	775

Missing observations: 3.
Significant at < 0.05 level.

Judaism of women who had never been incest victims. While this difference is not significant at < 0.05 level, the low defection rate for Jewish incest victims was significantly different from the defection rate for Catholic and Protestant incest victims combined (at < 0.02 level).

The defection rate from other religions was almost the same for both incest victims and women who had never been incest victims.

What is the explanation for the high defection rates for Catholic and Protestant incest victims? And why did more Catholic than Protestant incest victims reject their religion of upbringing than the comparable groups of women who had never been incestuously abused?

One possible answer is that incestuous abuse is very disillusioning. It may be more difficult to accept the notion of a just and loving God after such an experience. And perhaps Catholicism has a more blaming attitude

TABLE 9–3

Religious Defection and Incest Victimization Before 18 Years

Religion of Upbringing	Defection Rate for Incest Victims (%)	Defection Rate for Nonincest Victims (%)
Protestant[a]	56	43
Catholic[b]	56	28
Jewish[c]	14	25
Other[c]	38	40
Total[b]	53	32

Missing observations: 4; and 69 respondents were raised without a religion.
[a]Significant at < 0.05 level.
[b]Significant at < 0.001 level.
[c]Not significant at < 0.05 level.

toward incest victims. The latter explanation is suggested by Cynthia, one of the incest victims in our survey who defected from Catholicism. Here is her account of what happened to her and her response to it.

Cynthia was thirteen, and her uncle was in his thirties, the one time he sexually abused her.

I was thirteen, and not very sophisticated. He had always liked me, and he reached back and stroked my leg when we were riding in a car one day. This preceded the sexual thing. What happened was that I wanted to learn how to drive, and my uncle offered to take me out. He said, "All you have to do is drive," and we went out on the road. Then he started moving closer to me while I was driving. First he put his arm around me. Then he started feeling between my legs. I drove off the road on to a field. He kept his hand between my legs, but after I drove off the road I jumped up and got out of the car and said, "I don't want to learn how to drive." I was very upset. He drove back and he kept saying, "Now calm down." (Did he touch your genitals?) Yes, it was very pronounced. He was trying to get me aroused. This was my first time driving, and both my hands were on the wheel. I couldn't fight him off until I turned off the road. (Did anything else sexual occur with him?) No, I stayed clear of him after that.

(Upset?) Extremely upset. (Effect on your life?) Some effect. I was upset and I felt guilty and I wondered if I had done something to cause it. But I realized that wasn't so, and that it wasn't my fault. I was raised Catholic, and at that time the responsibility was put on the woman for what happened to her. It was always believed that the girl is bad while the boys are just acting out their natural impulses. That was drummed into my head so much at the time, I thought something was wrong with me.

Despite all Cynthia's efforts to stop the abuse (she drove off the road, jumped up and got out of the car, told her uncle she didn't wish to learn how to drive after all, and avoided him from then on), she felt guilty.

Besides having a victim-blaming attitude, the Catholic tradition of confession may be particularly guilt inducing for incest victims so many of whom have been manipulated into silence by the perpetrator.

And what is it about Judaism that might explain why the defection rate was so much lower for Jewish than for Protestant and Catholic incest victims? One possible explanation is that identifying as Jewish involves far more than a religious belief system; it involves an ethnic identification as well.

I believe our finding of a significant relationship between incest victimization and religious defection is a new one. Hopefully, other researchers will start to investigate it, and if it is replicated, to explain it.

We analyzed other sociological factors that might have been related to incest victimization but that turned out not to be, such as social class at the time of the interview, employment history, and how traditional the respondent was in terms of economic dependence on a husband. Though sociology rarely pays as much attention to negative findings as to positive ones, they can be just as important.

TRADITIONALITY OF WOMEN AND INCEST VICTIMIZATION

An index of traditionality was developed on the basis of three factors: Whether at the time of the interview the woman supported herself in whole or in part or whether she was supported by a husband; whether she had raised one child, more than one, or no children; and whether she had worked most of the time, about half the time, or less than half the time in her adult life. (See table 9–4.)

The mean traditionality score for incest victims was 3.08 compared to 3.24 for women who had never been incestuously abused. By this measure of traditionality, then, the incest victims were no more or less traditional than women with no incest history.

RESPONDENTS' EMPLOYMENT STATUS AND HISTORY AND INCEST VICTIMIZATION

All the respondents in our sample about whom we had information (i.e., 922) said they had worked for pay outside the home at some time in their lives, although there was no significant relationship between incest victimization and the percentage of time they had worked in the labor force. There was a significant relationship between incest victimization and employment status at the time of the interview, however. In particular, twice as many incest victims as nonvictims were unemployed, half as many were keeping house, and notably fewer were retired. The

TABLE 9–4

Traditionality Scale

	Score*
Motherhood	
Raised no children	2
Raised 1 child	1
Raised 2 or more children	0
Work History	
Worked most of the time during adult life	2
Worked about half the time during adult life	1
Worked less than half the time during adult life	0
Main Provider	
Herself	2
Herself plus some other person	1
Other(s)—(not including herself)	0.5
Husband	0

*A total score of 0 = the extreme in traditionality, while 6 = the extreme in nontraditionality.

TABLE 9–5

Women's Employment Status at the Time of the Interview and Incest Victimization Before 18 Years

Employment Status	Incest Victimization		No Incest Victimization	
	%	N	%	N
Full-time work	49	74	43	336
Part-time work	11	17	10	79
Unemployed	11	17	5	41
Retired	11	17	18	143
Student	6	9	5	38
Keeping house	7	11	14	108
On welfare	1	1	1	6
Disabled	2	3	2	14
Other	2	3	2	13
Total	100	152	100	778

Missing observation: 1.
Significant at < 0.05 level.

latter finding reflects the underrepresentation of incest victims in the older cohorts (see chapter 5).

RESPONDENTS' SOCIAL CLASS AND INCEST VICTIMIZATION

Because there is no consensus among sociologists about how best to measure social class, we used several different measures: the respondent's occupation (the Census Bureau categories were applied to all the occupational data), and job prestige (as measured by the widely used scale developed by the National Opinion Research Center in which occupations were rank-ordered by a large random sample of people); the respondent's husband's occupation and education; and the respondent's total household income in the year prior to being interviewed.*

By all these measures, no significant relationship was found between incest victimization and social class at the time of the interview. This suggests that incestuous abuse in our study does not appear to have resulted in downward social mobility for the victims as a group.

However, it was reported in chapter 8 that incest victims were more likely to come from higher income homes and to be significantly better educated than women who had no history of incestuous abuse. These differences might lead one to expect that incest victims—other things being equal—would have a higher social class at the time of the interview than nonincest victims. The fact that they did not may have been affected

*When the prestige of these women's occupations was measured, the mean score for the incest victims was 42.67 compared with a 41.27 for the women who had never been incestuously abused. This small difference is not statistically different.

by their victimization. Clearly, these issues need to be further explored by other researchers.

Conclusion

Our survey found that incest victims were more inclined than women who had never been incestuously abused to be divorced or separated at the time of the interview. Also, more incest victims than nonincest victims were unemployed, and fewer were keeping house or retired. In addition, the average age of incest victims when they first gave birth was 22.5 years compared to 24.2 years for women who had never been incest victims. Finally, incest victims who had been raised Catholic or Protestant were much more inclined to defect from their religion of origin than Jewish women or women who had never been incestuously abused.

None of the other sociological variables examined in this chapter—social class at the time of interview, employment history, and traditionality—were significantly related to incest victimization.

The fact that several of these variables turned out to be unrelated to incest victimization suggests that researchers must develop more subtle measures of the effects of incestuous abuse. It is simply not legitimate to presume that because an incest victim completes an education, marries, has children, and holds down a job as readily as women who were never incestuously abused, she was not traumatized by the experience. The next five chapters will show some of the other ways in which incest victims in our survey were affected.

How the Incest Started and Ended

The widely held notion of the child taking the initiative in sexual liaisons with adults is a classic case of the victim blaming so common in sexual abuse mythology. How can children initiate acts of which they have little or no understanding? To avoid propagating this myth, we did not specifically ask who took the initiative. But two members of our research staff carefully read through each case to see if the initiator could be identified from the victim's account. There was one case—discussed in chapter 3—in which a woman, confused by her father's touching her sexually over a period of many years, decided to initiate intercourse with him some years later. But in no case, including this one, was there evidence that the victim perceived herself as having initiated the first sexual contact.

It is often assumed that incest perpetrators do as they please with their victims. If intercourse did not occur, it is assumed that the perpetrator did not wish it, or that he had some moral or other compunction about proceeding to this more severe act of violation.

In those cases in our survey where sexual intercourse (including penile-vaginal, oral, or anal intercourse) did not occur, two members of the research staff attempted to ascertain from the descriptions of the abuse why the perpetrator had stopped. In as many as 66 percent of the cases where information was available, the researchers concluded that the sexual encounter did not proceed to a more serious degree of violation because of the strategy employed by the victim. In only 4 percent of the cases did the intervention of a third party prevent the incident from becoming more serious, and in 30 percent of the cases some other factor was considered responsible.

Examples of these other factors include the victim's mother coming home, other people's presence in the next room, a sister walking in while the sexual abuse was occurring, the perpetrator's fear that the victim would tell her mother or that the mother would wake up (when all three were in the same bed). Inadvertent interruptions were one of the most frequently mentioned reasons the sexual abuse did not proceed to a more severe level. However, in several cases the abuse did not become more serious because the perpetrator appeared to be content with what he was doing. "I think he just got sexual satisfaction from doing that" (genital fondling), one victim said. In another case the perpetrator stopped when he discovered he couldn't insert his penis in the victim because her vagina was too small.

In those cases where the respondent was incestuously abused more than once, she was asked, "What finally brought it to an end?" The answers to this question and the entire account of the experience were used to try to ascertain what terminated the sexual abuse. In 44 percent of the cases the abuse appeared to end because of some action taken by the victim, particularly avoidance of the perpetrator. In 27 percent of the experiences someone other than the victim was primarily responsible for ending the abuse, for example, when the victim's mother or other relative intervened or when the perpetrator moved out of town or appeared to stop of his own volition. In 7 percent of the cases, it wasn't ascertainable who was primarily responsible for ending the abuse. And in 21 percent, the victim believed the abuse ended for a combination of reasons. For example, Irene said that one cause of the termination was her growing up and no longer being the vulnerable child she had been; another was her father's realization that what he was doing was wrong.

The sexual relationship ended for Carmen when she told her father—the perpetrator—that she thought she was pregnant. He angrily denied that the child was his and rejected her. Marriage ended the sexual abuse for other respondents.

PRIMARY RESISTANCE STRATEGY OF INCEST VICTIMS

Incest victims were not specifically asked about their resistance strategies, but we attempted to ascertain this information from their accounts. Since many respondents reported multiple incidents of sexual abuse, we coded the most assertive strategy that the victim ever mentioned using against her perpetrator. The strategies are listed in table 9–6 from the most assertive to the least assertive.

This table reveals that the majority of victims about whom information was available used an assertive strategy to try to stop the sexual abuse from continuing or escalating. Almost three-quarters (74 percent) of the victims used one of the five most assertive strategies. In four cases the victim mentioned having or using a weapon in the course of her resistance. Abby —at ten years old—hit her stepfather with a hammer when he was trying to rape her. A seventeen-year-old niece, Stephanie, hit her uncle with a telephone in self-defense and brandished a kitchen knife while she threatened to kill him. Evelyn, a twelve-year-old victim of a distant male relative, picked up a flower pot and threw it at him. A sixteen-year-old victim, Dorothy, let her brother-in-law get on top of her and then cut him in the back with a razor.

Just over one-fifth (21 percent) of the primary strategies of the incest victims didn't fit into any of the categories listed in the table and so were

TABLE 9–6

Primary Resistance Strategies of Incest Victims Under 18 Years

Primary Resistance Strategy	%	N
Used physical resistance, force, or violence	21	27
Fled or tried to flee	22	28
Screamed, refused assertively, or protested vigorously	11	14
Employed other verbal measures (e.g., pleas, threats, requests to stop)	13	17
Sought assistance from a third person	7	9
Cried or showed other distress signals to perpetrator	3	4
Passive resistance techniques (e.g., pretending to be asleep)	1	1
Other resistance strategy	21	26
Total	99	126

Missing observations: 26.

classified as "other." Many of the "other" strategies included avoidance: "We stayed out of his way, so didn't give him the opportunity"; "I never was alone with him again"; "I jumped out the window"; "I avoided visiting him when I could." Another victim said, "I finally mustered enough courage to squirm out of situations." Sometimes this avoidance behavior had to be kept up for years.

One granddaughter embarrassed her grandfather in front of a group of people by turning around when he touched her buttocks and asking him very loudly what he was doing. Another granddaughter would try to kiss her grandfather hello or good-bye as quickly as possible so that he wouldn't have a chance to feel her breasts.

Some strategies were classified in the "other" category because it was impossible to determine which one was primary. For example, one fourteen-year-old girl pleaded with her stepfather to stop what he was doing, cried, and after six months of continual sexual abuse by him, ran away.

Two members of the research staff also tried to ascertain from the accounts whether or not the victims' strategies were ever in any way successful. In nearly two-thirds of the cases (63 percent) there was consensus that the victim's strategy was successful to some degree. Some examples of successful strategies will be presented next, from the most assertive to the least assertive as listed in table 9–6.

SUCCESSFUL RESISTANCE STRATEGIES

The use of physical force proved an effective or partially effective strategy for some incest victims. For example, seven-year-old Marjorie said she was furious with her eleven-year-old first cousin. She bit his hand and "let him know he'd have to force me." When fourteen-year-old Faith's stepfather touched her buttocks, she slapped him and he never tried anything again. Ten-year-old Libby escaped intercourse with her uncle by fighting to free herself, then fleeing into the backyard.

When Holly was thirteen, her stepuncle pulled off the road and started kissing and grabbing her. She slapped him hard and told him she would tell her aunt. He stopped and never tried it again. Twelve-year-old Amanda slapped one of her fifteen-year-old first cousins, two of whom were bothering her, and told them she would tell her father. This strategy was totally successful.

Fleeing from the perpetrator worked for some victims such as thirteen-year-old Cynthia, just discussed. Jacqueline ran away from home and got herself admitted to a child's shelter when she was fifteen, after one and a half years of sexual abuse by her father. Ten-year-old Theodora jumped off her uncle's lap and out of the car. After disappearing into the bushes

—presumably to masturbate—her uncle drove home. When six-year-old Zelda was old enough to know that her uncle's caresses were sexual, she would flee from the room when he tried to touch her, and go into the room where her mother and aunt were.

When thirteen-year-old Debra screamed at her father to get out of her room, he left. Dorothy, who was also thirteen years old, screamed when her brother-in-law tried to rape her, and he stopped. The second time he stopped raping her only when he saw that she was bleeding from a broken hymen. When seventeen-year-old Florence's father pushed her down on the couch to try to kiss her, she "screamed bloody murder" and he stopped immediately.

In some cases, intervention occurred only because the respondent told someone. Sometimes the chain of relatives involved was very complicated. For example, Dorothy told her brother that her brother-in-law had sexually abused her. He told their mother who told their father, who threatened to kill his son-in-law. Dorothy's sister divorced her husband after she was told about his rape of her sister.

Threatening to tell their mothers is one of the most frequently mentioned effective strategies; sometimes the threat was carried out but sometimes the threat alone was effective. For example, Camille was raped by her stepfather for six years. The rapes stopped when she threatened to tell her mother. Thirteen-year-old Joan's sexual abuse by her first cousin ended after she jumped up and said, "I'll tell my mother if you don't stop." Abby, also thirteen years of age, told her father that if he bothered her again she would tell her mother and the police.

Threats to tell other relatives were also often successful. Seven-year-old Karla told her mother after two years of sexual abuse by her uncle, and that ended it. When Jennifer was thirteen, her uncle tried to get her to touch his penis. She called for her aunt, and it never happened again. Many other examples of this strategy will be cited in chapter 23. As might be expected, it wasn't always successful.

Nor can tears be counted on to move the perpetrator to stop his abusive behavior. But crying worked for seven-year-old Natalie when she woke to find her cousin's husband touching her all over. The next day she pretended she was sick so she could return to her parents' house.

When seven-year-old Ingrid's fifteen-year-old brother grabbed and squeezed her, then threw her down on a pile of clothes, she started crying. He backed off, then left her alone. He had raped her three-year-old sister before this incident.

MULTIPLE STRATEGIES

The first and second time twelve-year-old Winifred's grandfather tried to touch her breasts or genitals, she got up and left. Next he propositioned her sister while Winifred was in the room. The two of them decided never to leave each other alone and kept a chair propped in front of their bedroom door. When it happened again, Winifred and her sister told their aunt, whose husband spoke to their grandfather. That ended the abuse.

Until recently, people assumed that if the child did not actively resist the sexual abuse, she or he must have been complicit in it. It is now understood that this view fails to take into consideration both the power imbalance that exists in most cases of sexual abuse and the physical superiority of the adult, as well as the child's dependency and training to obey adults. Despite this imbalance, many children are extraordinarily brave and resourceful in implementing strategies to end the abuse, as the sample of quotes just given shows.

REASONS WHY SOME VICTIMS DIDN'T RESIST MORE

Although victims were not asked why they didn't resist more, the research staff ascertained many reasons from the case material. Some did not resist more *because of the perpetrator's use of physical force.* Vicki, for example, resisted by trying to get up and leave but her brother forced her to sit down. She then touched his genitals as he demanded because she was frightened. When thirteen-year-old Winifred was attacked by her sixteen-year-old first cousin, she said she "couldn't scream because he had me pinned down. I tried to fight him off but he was stronger than I was."

Other victims were *too afraid of physical force to resist more.* For example, Jacqueline didn't resist her father when she was fifteen years old because he was a very violent, alcoholic man with a bad temper who didn't take no for an answer. Olga resisted her father to some extent when she was thirteen years old, but when he insisted, she submitted out of fear of being slapped.

Some victims *never had a chance to resist* because they were asleep when their relative took advantage of them. Leila woke up to find her six-year-old first cousin feeling her genitals when she was nine. And eight-year-old Violet was asleep when her uncle started fingering her genitals.

Others mentioned *economic dependence* as a factor in their inability to resist more. When Sarah was sixteen, her foster father threatened that she would have to leave home if she didn't comply with his sexual demands. She said she submitted because "I didn't have anywhere else to go." Gloria said that she put up with the sexual abuse by her grandfather "because he was the sole financial support of my family and I didn't want to make him mad." She was fifteen when it started.

Some victims were *disarmed by nonphysical threats.* For example, Ida's stepfather threatened when she was twelve that if she didn't cooperate, he'd see to it that she lived with her grandmother and never saw her mother. At fifteen, Jacqueline was afraid that her foster uncle would tell her father that she'd been shoplifting if she didn't submit to sexual intercourse with him. Eileen's uncle threatened that he would make up things about her mother so that her father would beat her mother up—as he often did.

Other victims were *disarmed by deception.* When she was eight years old, Marcia's eighteen-year-old first cousin got her to play a game in which whoever won got to touch the other. Marcia didn't understand the sexual nature of the "game" she had agreed to play.

Many children didn't resist more because they were *too naïve to understand what was happening.* Barbara said that she didn't know what was going on when, at four years old, her father put his penis in her mouth. Jill was only six and did not know what her fifteen-year-old first cousin was doing to her when he touched her sexually, until she saw her other cousin give him a disapproving look.

The first time her twenty-six-year-old cousin rubbed her "prepuberty chest" when she was eleven years old, Adele said she didn't consider it sexual and it felt good. The second time she resisted and he stopped "because he knew I was old enough to understand." Diane's uncle started to molest her when she was two years old. She said that for a long time she didn't know it was wrong. "It was just something that he did that I didn't like; only later did I realize it was not supposed to be done."

The sexual abuse by her uncle started when Zelda was six. She didn't realize it was sexual until she was about nine and heard about sex from girls at school; she then resisted successfully.

Some victims mentioned being unable to resist more *because of the perpetrator's authority.* Mabel said that she had intercourse with her adoptive father when she was thirteen because "he was my parent and telling me what to do, naturally you don't argue with parents." He also threatened to beat her up if she didn't acquiesce.

Fifteen-year-old Sylvia was sexually abused by her twenty-eight-year-old first cousin. His attack on her was interrupted by a family member returning home, so he did not proceed to have intercourse with her. Had he tried, Sylvia believed "Being scared, I would have submitted. He had authority. He was the man of the house."

Zelda didn't resist the first incident of sexual abuse by her stepfather when she was twelve because she was in bed with him and her mother. Had she left the bed, she would have had to explain her departure to her mother. She was *afraid of her mother* finding out what had happened. The next time her stepfather tried to make her feel his genitals, she got out of the bed. Her mother wasn't in bed with them on this second occasion.

When Kitty was sexually abused by her uncle at the age of ten, she said she was too afraid to tell anyone for *fear of being blamed.*

Wilma said that she was only ten years old and *was afraid* to do anything when her brother touched her breasts and genitals, so she pretended to be asleep. Bonnie's brother would sneak under the bed and feel her breasts when she was twelve. "This experience scared me and I froze," she said.

At thirteen years old, Theresa said that she was too scared to resist when her uncle pinched her and felt her breasts. "I was scared of him," Jacqueline said of her stepfather. "He was about forty and I was only fourteen."

Other victims were *disarmed by their feelings for the perpetrator.* Sixteen-year-old Ruth said that she was fond of her twenty-four-year-old first cousin and didn't want to hurt him by refusing to do something that he wanted to do. Of the sexual contact with her thirteen-year-old brother, Audrey said she couldn't get herself to say no because "I looked up to him. I admired him. I didn't have the nerve to stand up to him" and "I didn't want to get him in trouble." She was ten at the time.

Yvette was sexually abused by her twenty-five-year-old sister when she was fifteen. She said she allowed her sister to touch her sexually because she loved her very much.

Some victims didn't resist more because they *felt needy or craved attention.* For example, thirteen-year-old Rachel said that she loved her stepfather, and if she could have earned some approval by sleeping with him, she would have. She therefore submitted to his relatively mild acts of sexual abuse. Ethel said she craved affection and consequently sometimes initiated contact with her uncle. She also mentioned that he was supporting her that year (when she was fifteen) and that she had very low self-esteem and was confused about how to get attention.

Others were *disarmed by feelings of powerlessness.* Karla said she didn't like the sexual abuse but at five years old she was so young that she felt she didn't have much choice. Sharon said that she didn't tell her forty-year-old female relative—whose relationship with her she refused to disclose—that she didn't want the sexual contact because she "was older" and "I didn't know what to do about it."

Finally, there were a few victims who didn't resist more because *the sexual abuse was pleasurable, wanted by them to some degree, or not stressful to them.* When Bernadette was seventeen years old she "kissed and petted" with her twenty-three-year-old brother-in-law. She didn't resist because "I enjoyed it." However, she later felt resentful and taken advantage of. Lorna was six when her eight-year-old brother initiated sexual contact with her. She said this was "partially wanted. Even when I said no, I yielded, so I can't say he forced me." However, she also said it was unwanted because "I knew I shouldn't."

When Yvette was thirteen, she was molested by her forty-six-year-old half brother. She said that because he had been in prison for seven years, he didn't seem like a brother. In other words, the incest taboo was not operating normally for her.

TELLING OR NOT TELLING ABOUT THE INCESTUOUS ABUSE

Although not directly asked whom, if anyone, they told about the incestuous abuse, 17 percent of the victims volunteered that they had told someone else about it at the time of the first incident or soon afterward. An additional 10 percent said that they told someone at some later point. In 19 percent of the cases the victims mentioned that they hadn't themselves told anyone, but that someone knew about it anyway. In only 5 percent of the cases did the victims specifically mention that they hadn't told anyone. (In 49 percent of the cases there was no information on this question.) Hence where information was available, slightly more of the incest victims volunteered that they had told someone (27 percent)—sometimes long after the abuse had occurred—than that they had not told anyone (24 percent). Thus at least 46 percent of these incest experiences were known to someone, even if years after the abuse had ended.

If all the cases where no relevant data were volunteered on this issue were to be excluded from the analysis, then nine out of ten cases were known to at least one other person at the time the interview was conducted. This suggests that incestuous abuse is not quite as well kept a secret as it is now believed to be.

In those cases where the victim did not tell anyone, we tried to ascertain the primary reason for secrecy. For these forty-four incest victims, the two most common reasons were fear of punishment by the perpetrator and/or someone else, including abandonment or rejection and a desire to protect the perpetrator, or fear of hurting someone else. For other victims self-blame made them feel too ashamed or guilty to tell. Some expressed fear of being blamed or of not being believed.

The category "other reasons" was the largest of all. What were some of these other reasons?

Since telling others can be a method of coping with the sexual abuse, some of the reasons victims didn't tell are the same as the reasons they didn't resist more. The few who enjoyed the sexual contact, for example, clearly had no motivation to tell. Nor did the victims who didn't realize it was sexual, or that it was wrong, or what it meant at the time.

Some of those who were too afraid to resist more were also too afraid to tell anyone. They didn't necessarily specify that they were afraid of punishment or afraid of not being believed or being blamed. They just said things like "I was afraid to tell my mother," or "I was afraid because he said, 'I'll tell on you,' " or "I was scared shitless." The last respondent said it took years of seeing a psychiatrist to even get her to think about the sexual abuse.

Other victims mentioned being terrified of the perpetrator, or taking seriously whatever threat he had made, or feeling they had no one to turn to, or that their mother or father knew about the sexual abuse but closed her or his eyes to it.

One five-year-old victim—Eileen—was afraid to tell her father because she believed he would kill the perpetrator (her uncle) and that her father would then be sent to prison. Beverly didn't tell because there was nothing her uncle did that couldn't be classified as play or as uncle-like affection, even though she couldn't stand him and believed that his demonstrations of affection were really done "to get off." Zelda said she didn't tell her parents or aunt "because to them sex is dirty," while Cindy explained she hadn't told her mother because "we never talked about these things."

Pamela's abusive brother told her that their mother knew and didn't disapprove of his behavior because "it couldn't harm anything since I wasn't menstruating yet." Although her brother may well have been lying, Pamela never knew if what he had said was true or not. Trudy didn't tell her mother at the time because her mother had blamed her when told about an assault three years earlier.

Incest Victim's Perception of the Reason for Sexual Abuse

Although incest victims were not specifically asked, 20 percent of them indicated that they perceived what happened as taboo because it involved a relative. In 11 percent of the cases of incestuous abuse, there was evidence that the victim did not understand the sexual nature of the abuse at the time. We have already cited several examples of this phenomenon in explaining why some victims didn't resist more assertively. It appears from the victims' accounts that in at least 16 percent of the cases, the situation evolved from one that was nonsexual into one that was sexual.

Our research staff also tried to ascertain from the case material the victim's perception of the reasons—apart from sexual motivation—that the sexual assault occurred. In the vast majority of cases the victim attributed it to some characteristic of the incest perpetrator, rather than to some characteristic in herself, or to her parents' marital relationship, or to situational factors. Alcohol was also mentioned as a causal factor quite frequently.

INCEST PERPETRATOR BLAMED

A few respondents considered the perpetrator to be mentally ill. For example, Edna said that her father's head injury and subsequent lobotomy caused "some kind of mental illness" that in turn caused him to sexually abuse her. Ida reported that her father started talking to her as if she were her mother, and in general was "acting crazy" when he knocked her out and tried to rape her. Her description of the attack suggests that he was indeed psychotic.

Carol believed that her uncle assaulted her because he was mentally deficient and "he thought it was a game" to try to insert his penis into her when she was nine years old. According to Natalie, her cousin's husband who sexually abused her was "a pervert" who had also sexually abused two other cousins. Holly believed that her grandfather had molested her because "he was a dirty old man."

Lenore said of her father: "I think he did have sexual problems." In support of her view she cited the fact that he had also made sexual advances to other relatives. According to Maria, when her father sexually abused her he seemed to regress to childlike behavior. Kitty said that her uncle felt her breasts only when others were present, and that it was the danger of risking discovery that seemed to excite him.

Lorna considered her brother's sexual abuse to be motivated by the desire for sexual exploration: "He lacked knowledge of sex and he was trying to get educated." Shirley said of her father's sexual behavior toward her: "That is the way he taught me about sex." According to Jacqueline, her father seemed to be motivated by curiosity. She said he was constantly comparing her with her mother in sexual ways, including their genitals.

Olive described her sexually abusive seventeen-year-old brother as being in a transitional stage. She said his attention was focused on her before it was channeled toward his peers. Sylvia seemed to think her first cousin, being "the only man of the house" and having authority, felt he had the right to have sexual contact with her.

Dora believed that her father licked her genitals to prepare her for future intercourse or because he couldn't get an erection. Paula said her uncle-in-law thought she didn't know what he was up to and "just wanted to see what he could get away with." In other words, he tried to exploit her naïveté.

Irene attributed her father's sexually abusive behavior toward her to his insecurity: "It was an unsure time of his life," she said. Irma said her uncle touched her breasts "like it was okay because it was all in the family." According to Janet her father was not molesting her, but just "keeping tabs on my development."

Heidi explained her uncle's behavior toward her as being a case of "older men being curious about young girls." Similarly, Yvette said that she was very young at the time (twelve) and her older stepbrother had a fantasy about young girls.

PARENTAL RELATIONSHIP BLAMED

The most frequently mentioned explanation of the perpetrator's motivation was that he was frustrated because his wife "didn't believe in sex." For example, Edith's father told her that her mother was sexually inhibited, and he wanted to teach her and her sister not to be the same. Gloria said her grandfather complained that his wife was frigid and that he had an unhappy marriage. Elaine's father told her that her mother "wasn't much to make love to." Winifred's grandfather told her that his wife wouldn't let him share her bedroom any more.

A few of the respondents were at least somewhat understanding of this reasoning. For example, Vera said her mother was sick, so she could understand that her father would want another woman. However, she did not understand that he would turn to his daughter.

SITUATIONAL FACTORS

Daisy said she came upon her brother when he was preparing to have sex with a calf, and he decided to substitute her for the calf.

VICTIM'S SELF-BLAME

Although not specifically asked whether or not they blamed themselves, 12 percent of the incest victims said things that suggested self-blame. For example, in response to her uncle's feeling her between her legs at the age of thirteen, Cynthia said: "I was upset and I felt guilty. I wondered if I had done something." Another respondent—Barbara—appeared to feel guilty that she didn't enjoy her uncle's sexualizing contact with her when she was twelve. "My experience of it was that here were these middle-aged guys who just wanted a little excitement; young girls turned them on. It was an accepted thing and I had the feeling I was supposed to like it. But I never did."

In response to being sexually abused by her first cousin at the age of seven, Rachel said: "It probably reinforced that I was a whore and a slut." Both her mother and her brother had treated her as such when she was sexually abused by a babysitter before this experience. Of her brother's sexual abuse of her, Rachel said: "He was contemptuous of me as a sexually permissive person."

Ann blamed her insecurity for "inviting" the sexual abuse by her grandfather. "I think men can smell insecurities," she said. "I was always in situations with him when I was alone. I just think I was so afraid it shined through."

Of the sexual abuse by one of her brothers, Ingrid said: "For the longest time I thought I was the only one it ever happened to. Like it was my fault."

SUBSTANCE ABUSE

Victims frequently cited alcohol consumption by the perpetrator as playing a role in the occurrence of incestuous abuse. For example, by way of explanation of how the sexual abuse happened, Stephanie said, "My father was not home and my uncle got drunk." Dolores's explanation for her brother-in-law's behavior was: "I think it happened because he was drunk and my sister was pregnant and he thought he'd try something."

Conclusion

Many people have come to understand that children's passive behavior in response to sexual abuse is common for some of the reasons discussed in this chapter: their socialized obedience to adults; their fear—of being hurt, of losing affection and love, of their parents finding out, of being blamed; their naïveté about what is going on. But the accounts of incestuous abuse obtained by our study and quoted in this book also reveal that many children are remarkably assertive in their handling of their perpetrators. Indeed, a considerable percentage of the incestuous experiences ended only through the efforts of the victims. Unequal as the power balance is between children and most of their perpetrators, for the most part they have had to draw on their own resources to try to prevent, deescalate, or stop the sexual abuse. Some of the excellent new child abuse prevention programs that have recently been introduced in the elementary schools in some states will likely provide children with additional strategies for coping with this distressing and prevalent violation of their bodies and minds.

10

Trauma Through
the Eyes
of the Victims

The question of how traumatic incestuous abuse is remains a controversial one. Others before me—such as Florence Rush (1980) and Judith Herman (1981)—hoped to settle this question. Perhaps the findings from our probability sample survey—presented in this and the chapters that follow—will provide the best opportunity yet to implement this hope.

David Finkelhor (1984) points out that both scholars and ideologues tend to focus on the long-term effects of childhood sexual abuse rather than the initial effects. Does it or does it not cause later psychopathology, marital instability, sexual problems, homosexuality, criminal behavior, and so on? (Homosexuality is invariably included as if it were a serious illness.) Finkelhor describes this preoccupation as betraying an adultocentric bias. He points out that "the impact of an event on childhood itself is treated as less important. It is only 'childhood,' a stage which, after all, everyone outgrows" (p. 198). Finkelhor argues that traumatic experiences in adulthood are not responded to in this manner. "Does the seriousness of rape depend on whether it has a disruptive effect on old age?" he asks. He answers his own question in this way:

No. In fact, rape is treated as a serious life event whether or not it causes long-term effects. Research demonstrating that the negative effects of rape attenuate after a year or two . . . is greeted with relief by everybody, rape activists included. Few people would try to conclude from such research that rape is really a less traumatic experience than was previously thought. . . . Rape is traumatic because adults consider it so. Adults can speak eloquently about their experience and communicate its pain. Child sexual abuse should be similarly viewed . . . especially because children cannot speak for themselves. It is a noxious event of childhood, serious for its immediate unpleasantness, if nothing else, not necessarily for its long-term effects. (P. 198)

Measures of Trauma

The analysis in this chapter will focus on the effects of incestuous abuse as they were perceived and reported by the victims. Since twenty-four of the incest victims reported experiences of sexual abuse by more than one relative, we will focus on the 187 different experiences rather than the 152 victims. The following two multiple-choice questions on the impact of all forms of sexual abuse, including incestuous abuse, were asked of all respondents who reported such an experience.

1.   Overall, how upset were you by this experience—extremely upset, somewhat upset, (or) not very upset, (or not at all upset)?*
2.   Looking back on it now, how much effect would you say this experience has (these experiences have) had on your life—a *great* effect, *some* effect, a *little* effect, or *no* effect?

Exactly one-third (33 percent) of the experiences of incestuous abuse were described by the victims as extremely upsetting, 20 percent as very upsetting, 27 percent as somewhat upsetting, 12 percent as not very upsetting, and 9 percent as not at all upsetting.

How can we interpret the fact that victims reported 9 percent of the incidents of incestuous abuse to be not at all upsetting? First, it must be remembered that our definition of incestuous abuse is quite broad; it includes relatively mild experiences such as sexual kisses or touching of nongenital areas that, moreover, might have occurred on one occasion only. It also includes abusive sexual experiences with relatives no matter how distantly related they were.

Second, the case material presented throughout this book provides evidence that many victims' responses were muted by the psychological defenses of denial and repression. For example, some victims who described themselves as only slightly upset, or not upset at all, nevertheless gave accounts of the sexual abuse that suggested they had indeed been negatively affected.

*The reason the final choice was put in parentheses is to prevent the respondent from experiencing this part of the question as insulting or insensitive. For example, if a woman has described being devastated by a sexual assault by her father when she was ten years old, to ask her if she was "not at all upset" by the experience could be very alienating. It was therefore left to the discretion of the interviewers to decide when to read the parenthetical segments of the questions.

Third, a few victims appeared not to be upset because they were success-ful in preventing an incident from becoming more serious. Because of their successful handling of the situation, some of these women instead reported a sense of competence and a confirmation of their coping skills.

The victims reported a quarter (25 percent) of the experiences to have had great long-term effects, 26 percent to have had some effect, 27 per-cent to have had a little effect, and 22 percent to have had no long-term effect.

A measure of trauma was obtained by combining the answers to the two questions, but giving twice as much weight to the long-term effects as to the degree of upset. This will be referred to as our subjective trauma variable. By this measure, just over one-third (34 percent) of the incest victims reported extreme trauma, just under one-quarter (23 percent) re-ported considerable trauma, exactly a quarter (25 percent) reported some trauma, and 18 percent reported no trauma.

Respondents who said that the experience had had some or a great effect were then asked to explain how it had affected their lives. Some women reported many different effects whereas others reported only one or two. Others were not asked because they had reported that the experience had only a little or no long-term effects. The numbers of women reporting specific long-term effects would undoubtedly have been much higher had the victims been asked whether or not they had experienced each of them, instead of being left to volunteer the ways in which the incestuous abuse had affected their lives.

Long-Term Effects Mentioned by Incest Victims

The most frequently mentioned long-term effects of incestuous abuse were:

- Increased negative feelings, attitudes, or beliefs about men in general: 38 percent.
- Increased negative feelings, attitudes, or beliefs about the perpetrator of the incestuous abuse: 20 percent.
- Increased negative feelings, attitudes, or beliefs about herself, for example, a lowered sense of self-worth, self-blame, self-hatred, shame, guilt, negative feelings about her body: 20 percent.
- Increased negative feelings in general such as fear, anxiety, depression, mis-trust: 17 percent.
- Negative impact on the victim's sexual feelings in general or on her percep-tion of her sexuality: 14 percent.
- Increased upset or worry about the safety of others: 12 percent.

- Negative impact on relationships with others besides the perpetrator: 12 percent.
- Changed behavior associated with the assault, for example, stopped showing physical affection, avoided being alone with certain relatives: 11 percent.

Other effects of incestuous abuse volunteered by the victims included: increased general anger, vengeance, desire to hurt; negative feelings about specific sexual acts, such as fellatio, breast fondling, certain sexual positions, or whatever was reminiscent of the incest experience; deterioration of marriage, including divorce; negative feelings about physical closeness; fearing that men's behavior or attitudes had changed or would change toward them if the sexual abuse were known about; feeling emotionally cold, callous, hard, or frigid as a result of the sexual abuse; becoming more passive; becoming generally more cautious; becoming preoccupied with the incest experience(s); having nightmares or other sleep problems; requiring therapy as a result of the sexual abuse; suffering from physical health problems as a result of the experience; having an unwanted pregnancy or child; increased negative feelings, attitudes, or beliefs about people of a specific age, nationality, race or ethnicity, or profession associated with the perpetrator; increased negative feelings, attitudes, or beliefs about other relatives.

Interestingly, a few incest victims reported positive long-term effects as a result of the recovery process. Some mentioned developing greater awareness of the problem of sexual assault or sexism in general; developing greater sympathy for sexual assault victims; becoming motivated to take action against sexual assault; getting their life in order; taking better care of themselves; feeling like a stronger person; improving their relations with men by seeking more equal relationships, becoming more in charge of, or more independent in relationships.

In addition to the measure of trauma just described, two staff researchers read the interviews of every victim of incestuous abuse in an effort to evaluate the victim's overall feelings about the abuse. As mentioned in chapter 3, they concluded that the experience was completely unwanted in 85 percent of the cases, mostly unwanted in 7 percent, in another 7 percent some ambivalence was revealed, and in only 2 percent of the cases were the experiences mostly or completely wanted.

We see, then, that there was a considerable range in the degree of subjective trauma reported by incest victims. This comes as no surprise. Common sense suggests that many factors would likely influence the degree of trauma experienced: who the perpetrator was, the severity of the sexual abuse involved, its frequency and duration, whether or not force or violence was involved, and so on. The next section considers which of these and other factors were significantly associated with the victim's reported level of trauma. But first, a word is in order about the pros and cons of our subjective measure of trauma.

Limitations of Trauma Measures

There is no one perfect measure of trauma. We have already noted that as a protective mechanism, some women appear to discount the pain caused by sexual abuse. In addition, people have different notions of what constitutes being "very upset" or "greatly affected" by an experience. In some cases when women said an incident of sexual abuse only had a little effect on their subsequent life, the interviewer asked them to describe that effect. Some of these women described what appeared to be considerable effects. For example, Faith said that she became pregnant at the age of sixteen in order to escape her stepfather's sexual advances, yet she described these experiences as having no effect on her life. It is regrettable that we didn't routinely ask all respondents what, if any, the long-term effects had been, rather than reserving this open-ended question for those who answered that the abuse had had "some" or a "great" effect.

In chapter 13 we will explore the extent to which our subjective measure of trauma correlates with nonsubjective measures of long-term effects.

Although the trauma variable was differentiated into four categories—extreme, considerable, some, and none—for some purposes it is preferable to collapse it into two—extreme or considerable (57 percent of the experiences) and some or none (43 percent of the experiences)—to avoid having too few cases in each cell and for ease of interpretation. The data were analyzed using the four categories and the two categories of trauma separately, so wherever the dichotomy conceals a finding that emerged only with the more complex typology, it will be reported. Otherwise it can be assumed that little has been lost by using the dichotomized version of this variable.

Time Elapsed Since Incestuous Abuse Occurred and Trauma

Let us begin with a question that has important methodological implications. Is there any relationship between how long ago the sexual abuse occurred and the degree of trauma reported? It might be expected that the longer the time that had elapsed, the less trauma would be reported. However, there was only a slight statistically insignificant trend in this direction.* This finding is important methodologically because it means that when significant relationships emerge between trauma and other variables, it will not be because our measure of trauma is affected by the amount of time that has elapsed since the abuse occurred.

We will now consider whether or not the severity of the sexual abuse is related to the degree of trauma.

Severity of Incestuous Abuse and Degree of Trauma

The experiences of incestuous abuse included in our survey range from unwanted but nonforceful kissing to forcible rape. In chapter 7 we described how acts of sexual abuse were collapsed into the three categories referred to as very severe, severe, and least severe incestuous abuse.

Table 10–1 indicates that, according to our survey, there is a statistically significant relationship between the severity of incestuous abuse and the degree of trauma reported. For example, 54 percent of very severe incestuous abuse was reported to be extremely traumatic, compared with 35 percent of severe abuse and only 19 percent of the least severe abuse. Similarly, only 2 percent of very severe incestuous abuse resulted in no trauma, compared with 19 percent of severe abuse and 27 percent of the least severe abuse.†

While this finding seems to fit a commonsense expectation, Browne and Finkelhor (1985) point out that some studies have not found a significant relationship between the degrees of severity of sexual abuse and trauma. Indeed, in Finkelhor's own groundbreaking survey of 796 college students he concluded that "the seriousness of sexual activity as it is usually understood does not seem related to greater trauma in children. Children who have been involved in intercourse do not seem more negative about their experiences than those who only have their genitals touched" (1979, p. 103).

*For example, 52 percent of the women who were incestuously abused over thirty years ago described the experience as extremely or considerably traumatic compared to 62 percent of the women who were incestuously abused from one to ten years ago.

†As table 10–1 would lead one to expect, there is also a statistically significant difference between the mean trauma scores associated with the three categories of severity. Specifically, on a one- to four-point scale the mean trauma score for very severe incestuous abuse was 3.05; for severe incestuous abuse, 2.58; and for least severe incestuous abuse, 2.31 (significant at < 0.001 level).

TABLE 10–1

Severity of Incestuous Abuse Before 18 Years and Degree of Trauma Reported

Degree of Trauma	Very Severe Incestuous Abuse		Severe Incestuous Abuse		Least Severe Incestuous Abuse	
	%	N	%	N	%	N
Extreme	54	23	35	26	19	12
Considerable	26	11	24	18	20	13
Some	19	8	22	16	34	22
None	2	1	19	14	27	17
Total	101	43	100	74	100	64

Missing observations: 6.
Significant at < 0.001 level.

This finding is surprising, given the fact that this culture defines female virginity in terms of vaginal intercourse and the purity and good character of young females in terms of virginity. It is also surprising because the physical act of penile-vaginal intercourse between an adult male and a young girl (Finkelhor did not include sexual abuse by peers) is likely to be physically traumatic for the young girl, even if the act was devoid of social and moral connotations. In addition, older girls and young women suffer the fear of pregnancy.

How can Finkelhor's findings be explained? Unfortunately, the only frequency distribution of the different degrees of severity of abuse he reports is that no more than 4 percent of the experiences reported by girls involved intercourse (1979, p. 62). Since the total number of incidents was 119, 4 percent represents about five cases of sexual abuse in which sexual intercourse occurred. This is a very small number on which to base the conclusion that sexual intercourse between a male adult and a female child is no more traumatic than genital fondling.

Browne and Finkelhor (1985) point out that other studies have confirmed Finkelhor's finding of no clear differentiation between the effects of genital fondling and intercourse (e.g., Anderson, Bach, and Griffith 1981; Fromuth 1983; and Tufts New England Medical Center 1984). On the other hand, they cite four studies that show less trauma from the least severe forms of contact (Landis 1956; Peters 1984; Seidner and Calhoun 1984; and Tufts New England Medical Center 1984). However, one important study conducted in Calgary, Canada—important because it was a random-sample survey of 387 women—found that child sexual abuse involving vaginal, anal, or oral penetration was highly related to mental health problems in adulthood (Bagley and Ramsay 1985, table 16).

We were moved by all this inconsistent evidence to examine our findings on the relationship between the severity of incestuous abuse and trauma even more closely. A most remarkable fact emerged from our examination. When we differentiated between extreme trauma and the other three degrees of trauma, and when we made finer distinctions between the different degrees of severity of sexual abuse, an almost perfect linear relationship was evident between trauma and severity, despite the small number in some cells. (See table 10–2.)

The notion that there is no difference in the trauma experienced by female children between genital fondling and intercourse is—if untrue—a dangerous one because it could disinhibit men who sexually abuse children from engaging in intercourse. The results of our study are very clear on this issue: the distinction between intercourse and genital fondling was important in predicting the degree of trauma reported by incest victims.

While tables 10–1 and 10–2 reveal a strong relationship between trauma and severity of incestuous abuse, they also reveal that the correlation is far from perfect. For example, 21 percent of incestuous abuse that was defined as very severe was rated by the victims as causing only some or no trauma, while 19 percent of the experiences that fell into the least severe category were rated as extremely traumatic. Hence it is apparent that factors other than the degree of sexual violation affect the degree of trauma experienced.

TABLE 10–2

Type of Incestuous Abuse Before 18 Years and Degree of Trauma Reported

Type of Sexual Abuse	Extreme Trauma		Considerable, Some, and No Trauma	
	%	N	%	N
1. Genital intercourse	63	10	38	6
2. Attempted genital intercourse	50	11	50	11
3. Fellatio, cunnilingus, analingus, anal intercourse—completed and attempted	40	2	60	3
4. Genital contact (unclothed) including manual touching or penetration—completed or attempted	35	20	65	37
5. Breast contact (unclothed) or simulated intercourse—completed or attempted	35	6	65	11
6. Sexual kissing, intentional sexual touching of buttocks, thigh, leg, or clothed breasts or genitals—completed or attempted	19	12	81	52
Total		61		120

Missing observations: 6.
Statistically significant at <0.05 level.

Frequency and Duration of Sexual Abuse
and Degree of Trauma

Along with Finkelhor's conclusion that sexual intercourse is no more distressing to the female child than genital fondling, he also found that the
duration and repetition of sexual abuse were unrelated to the trauma. "Just
because the experience runs on for some time and occurs with some frequency," he wrote, "does not necessarily imply that it is going to have a
more negative impact. . . . If anything, the shorter, one-time experiences
were reported as more negative" (1979, p. 104).

Literally interpreted, Finkelhor's findings imply that a father who
touches his daughter's genitals once may cause more trauma to her than
if he were to have intercourse with her regularly for ten years. This does
not make sense intuitively, yet in their recent review of the research on this
issue, Browne and Finkelhor (1985) conclude:

Although many clinicians take for granted that the longer an experience goes on,
the more traumatic it is, this conclusion is not clearly supported by the available
studies. Of nine studies, only four find duration associated with greater trauma.
(We are treating duration and frequency synonymously here, since they tend to
be so highly correlated.) Four find no relationship, and two even find some evidence
that longer duration is associated with less trauma. (P. 23)

What, then, are the findings from our survey on the relationship between reported trauma and the frequency and duration of the incestuous
abuse?

As can be seen in table 10–3, there is a statistically significant relationship between the frequency with which the incestuous abuse occurred in
our survey and the degree of trauma that resulted. While 46 percent of the
incidents of incestuous abuse that occurred only once were described as
considerably or extremely traumatic, 61 percent of the experiences that
occurred from two to twenty times and 78 percent of the experiences that
occurred more than twenty times were so described.

However, when finer distinctions were made between the numbers of
experiences of sexual abuse, the relationship between frequency and
trauma was not quite as linear as it appears in the table. For example,
incestuous abuse that occurred from two to five times was considered more
traumatic than abuse that occurred six to ten times or eleven to twenty
times. Hence it is evident that while frequency of abuse is a significant
factor in predicting the degree of trauma in our study, one cannot simply
infer the degree of trauma from the number of incidents.

There was also a significant relationship between the very gross categor-

TABLE 10–3

Frequency of Incestuous Abuse Before 18 Years and Degree of Trauma Reported

Frequency of Incestuous Abuse	Extreme or Considerable Trauma		Some or No Trauma	
	%	N	%	N
One time only	46	33	54	39
2–20 times	61	54	39	34
Over 20 times	78	14	22	4
Total		101		77

Missing observations: 9.
Significant at < 0.01 level.

ization of the duration of incestuous abuse presented in table 10–4 and the degree of trauma reported by the victims. For example, 73 percent of the incestuous abuse that occurred over a period of more than five years was reported to be considerably or extremely traumatic compared with 62 percent of the experiences of sexual abuse that occurred over a period of one week to five years and 46 percent of the experiences in which the sexual abuse occurred on one occasion only.

However, once again when finer distinctions were made, the relationship between these variables turned out not to be so simple. For example, 73 percent ($N = 8$) of the incestuous abuse experiences that occurred over a period of from one week to less than one month were reported to have caused considerable or extreme trauma—exactly the same percentage ($N = 15$) as for experiences that occurred over more than five years. However, when these finer distinctions are made the numbers in some cells are unreliably small.

So, despite the significant relationship we found between our very broad

TABLE 10–4

Duration of Incestuous Abuse Before 18 Years and Degree of Trauma Reported

Duration	Extreme or Considerable Trauma		Some or No Trauma	
	%	N	%	N
One time only	46	33	54	39
One week to 5 years	62	56	39	35
More than 5 years	73	11	27	4
Total		100		78

Missing observations: 9.
Significant at < 0.06 level.

measure of duration and trauma, the relationship was not a totally linear one when more discriminating measures were used. It may be that the impact of duration is muted by other factors. For example, we will see in chapter 15 that there is a significant relationship between duration and the type of incest perpetrator.

Intuitively, it seems likely that, other things being equal, the longer the duration of the incestuous abuse, the more traumatic it is. However, because of the intricate and not yet fully understood interrelationships between this and other significant variables, the duration effect can be lost. This is a complicated way of saying that other things are rarely equal.

Physical Force and Other Violence and Degree of Trauma

A composite measure of the degree of physical force or violence that accompanied the incestuous abuse was developed that took into account the degree of physical force used and the use of verbal threats and weapons (see chapter 7 for more precise information on how the violence scale was developed). There was a statistically significant relationship between this measure of force or violence and the degree of trauma reported.

As can be seen in table 10–5, the seven cases of incestuous abuse that were violent were all reported to be extremely or considerably traumatic; 74 percent of the cases involving forceful incestuous abuse were similarly evaluated, compared with 46 percent of the nonforceful cases.*

Surprisingly, Browne and Finkelhor (1985) found four studies in which force or coercion were not related to trauma. However, five other studies found significant relationships between these two variables. In Finkelhor's student survey *"use of force* by an abuser explained more of a victim's negative reactions than any other variable, and this finding held up in multivariate analysis" (Browne and Finkelhor 1985, p. 26).

Browne and Finkelhor (1985) conclude their review of the research on the significance of force by saying that they are "inclined to give credence to the studies finding force to be a major traumagenic influence" (p. 27). This seems a sound conclusion.

*When force was defined as physical coercion, threat of physical coercion, or the inability of the victim to consent because she was unconscious, drugged, asleep, or in some other way totally physically helpless, a statistically significant relationship (at < 0.01 level) was also found between the use of force and the degree of trauma reported by incest victims. Seventy-one percent of forceful incestuous abuse was reported to be extremely or considerably traumatic compared with 47 percent of nonforceful incestuous abuse.

TABLE 10–5

Force and Violence of Incestuous Abuse and Degree of Trauma Reported

Force/Violence	Extreme or Considerable Trauma		Some or No Trauma	
	%	N	%	N
Violent	100	7	0	0
Forceful	74	42	26	15
Nonforceful	46	54	54	63
Total		103		78

Missing observations: 6.
Significant at < 0.001 level.

Type of Relative and Degree of Trauma

The recent literature has tended to ignore any differences between biological father–daughter and stepfather-daughter incest. However, most researchers and nonresearchers, if pressed, would likely predict that other things being equal, sexual abuse by a biological father is more traumatic than sexual abuse by a stepfather. Yet table 10–6 reveals that sexual abuse by stepfathers (plus one adoptive and one foster father) was reported to be just as traumatic as sexual abuse by biological fathers. Indeed, when we examine the upset and long-term effect variables separately and in their uncollapsed forms, more victims of stepfathers than biological fathers reported being very or extremely upset, and more reported great long-term effects. However, because 42 percent of the victims of biological fathers reported "some effect" compared to only 18 percent of the victims of stepfathers, the difference between them was obliterated by the composite, weighted measure of trauma used in this chapter.

Once again, it might well be that other things being equal, sexual abuse of daughters by biological fathers causes greater feelings of betrayal than sexual abuse by stepfathers and is therefore more traumatic. However, data will be presented in chapter 16 to show that we found important differences between incestuous abuse by biological fathers and stepfathers in our study that might help explain why stepfather abuse was reported as equally traumatic.

Table 10–6 indicates a great variation in the percentages of incest experiences with different perpetrators that were described as considerably or extremely traumatic, ranging from 38 percent for the incidents with female perpetrators to 82 percent for those with stepfathers. The biggest gap, however, is between the experiences with fathers, both biological and

TABLE 10–6

Type of Abusive Relative and Degree of Trauma Reported

Type of Relative	Extreme or Considerable Trauma		Some or No Trauma	
	%	N	%	N
Step-, adoptive, foster father	82	14	18	3
Biological father	81	21	19	5
Brother	60	15	40	10
Uncle	50	24	50	24
Grandfather	50	5	50	5
Other male relative	45	10	55	12
First cousin	40	10	60	15
Female relative	38	3	63	5
Total		102		79

Missing observations: 6.
Significant at < 0.05 level.

step-, and those with other relatives. After sexual abuse by fathers, sexual abuse by brothers was the next most traumatic form: 60 percent of incidents of brother-sister incestuous abuse were reported to be considerably or extremely traumatic compared to 50 percent of the incidents with uncles and grandfathers, 45 percent of the incidents with other male relatives, and 40 percent of the incidents with male first cousins (statistically significant at < 0.05 level).*

Finkelhor (1979) also found that sexual abuse by fathers was significantly more traumatic than sexual abuse by other relatives. However, the research is not in agreement even on this issue.†

Victim Economically Dependent on Perpetrator and Degree of Trauma

In 80 percent of the cases where the victim of incestuous abuse was economically dependent on the perpetrator because he was her provider, she reported considerable or extreme trauma, compared with 51 percent of

*It should be remembered that the unit of analysis here is the *experience* of sexual abuse rather than the *victim* of sexual abuse. There are very minor differences in some of these figures when the victim is the unit of analysis (see table A-3 in the appendix).

†For example, a study conducted by Tufts New England Medical Center found that children who were sexually abused by their biological fathers were not more disturbed than other sexually abused children, in contrast to those who were abused by stepfathers (Browne and Finkelhor 1985, p. 25).

the cases where the perpetrator was not her provider. (This relationship is statistically significant at < 0.01 level.)

Interpreting this finding is difficult, since clearly the role of provider is highly related to being a father. Hence we do not know whether this relationship would still hold if it were possible to control for the type of relative involved in the incestuous abuse. Yet it also seems likely that economic dependence would play a role in trapping the victim into silence and keeping her accessible to the perpetrator, thus resulting in a more traumatic experience.

Blood Relationship and Degree of Trauma

Both the law and popular wisdom consider violation by blood relatives to be more serious than violation by those unrelated by blood. However, no significant relationship was found in our survey between consanguinity and the degree of trauma reported (see table 10–7). Indeed, the trend was for incestuous abuse by those who were not consanguineally related to be reported as more traumatic. It may be that perpetrators who are not related by blood are less restrained in their abusive behavior. This appears to be the case for stepfather perpetrators (see chapter 16).

TABLE 10–7

Consanguinity of Relationship Between Victim and Perpetrator and Degree of Trauma Reported

Consanguinity	Extreme or Considerable Trauma		Some or No Trauma	
	%	N	%	N
Consanguineally related	56	48	44	38
Partially consanguineally related	50	25	50	25
Nonconsanguineally related	67	30	33	15
Total		103		78

Missing observations: 6.
Significant at <0.05 level.

Age of Onset of Incestuous Abuse and
Degree of Trauma

There is considerable disagreement among clinicians and researchers about the relationship between the age of onset of sexual abuse and trauma. Some experts have argued that younger children are more traumatized because of their lack of readiness to deal with sex in any form and because of their great impressionability. Others believe that adolescent victims are likely to be more traumatized because they are grappling with sexual and relationship issues at that age (Browne and Finkelhor 1985, p. 28).

As Browne and Finkelhor (1985) point out, the available studies do not resolve this disagreement (p. 29). Unfortunately, our study is also undefinitive on this issue. Table 10–8 reveals a trend between the age the sexual abuse began and trauma, but the relationship does not reach significance at < 0.05 level. Two-thirds (66 percent) of the girls who were incestuously abused at some time during the first nine years of their lives reported considerable or extreme trauma, compared with 58 percent of the girls who were first so abused between ten and thirteen years and 45 percent of the girls who were first incestuously abused between fourteen and seventeen years.

The mean age at which incestuous abuse began for women who reported extreme trauma was 10.62 years, compared with 10.71 years for those reporting considerable trauma, 11.33 years for those reporting some trauma, and 12.03 years for those reporting no trauma. Although a trend is apparent here, the differences between these means are not statistically significant.

TABLE 10–8

Age of Onset of Incestuous Abuse and Degree of Trauma Reported

Age of Incestuous Abuse	Extreme or Considerable Trauma		Some or No Trauma	
	%	N	%	N
2–9 years	66	37	34	19
10–13 years	58	43	42	31
14–17 years	45	23	55	28
Total		103		78

Missing observations: 6.
Not significant at < 0.05 level.

Perpetrator's Age at Onset of Incestuous Abuse
and Degree of Trauma

When extremely traumatic incestuous abuse is separated from less traumatic abuse, an interesting curvilinear relationship emerged between the
perpetrator's age and trauma. As table 10–9 shows, only 17 percent of the
incestuous abuse perpetrated by relatives under fifteen years of age was
reported to be extremely traumatic. As the perpetrators become older, the
percentages of victims reporting extreme trauma also increases. A plateau
is reached for perpetrators between the ages of twenty-six and fifty years,
with from 44 to 47 percent of the incestuous abuse being evaluated as
extremely traumatic. For perpetrators over fifty years old, however, the
percentage of victims reporting extreme trauma declined to 27 percent.
(This association is significant at < 0.05 level.)

Our finding that incestuous abuse by younger perpetrators (twenty-five
years and less) was less traumatic than incestuous abuse by middle-aged
perpetrators is consistent with those reported in the studies of Finkelhor
and Fromuth (Browne and Finkelhor 1985, p. 30). But so far other studies
have not found the same curvilinear relationship that we did, with less
trauma being reported for abuse by the older perpetrators.

The age of incest perpetrators is a complicated variable since it is highly
associated with the type of relative and with other factors such as force
or violence.

TABLE 10–9

Age of Incest Perpetrator and Degree of Trauma Reported

Incest Perpetrator's Age	Extreme Trauma		Considerable, Some, or No Trauma	
	%	N	%	N
Under 15 years	17	5	83	25
16–20 years	26	7	74	20
21–25 years	27	3	73	8
26–30 years	47	8	53	9
31–40 years	46	22	54	26
41–50 years	44	8	56	10
51+ years	27	8	73	22
Total		61		120

Missing observations: 6.
Significant at < 0.05 level.

Age Disparity Between Incest Perpetrators and Victims and Degree of Trauma

Although the age of the perpetrator and the age disparity between the victim and the perpetrator are highly related variables, they are not identical. Nevertheless, the similarity in our findings on the age of the perpetrator and trauma and age disparity and trauma will come as no surprise. There was no significant relationship between trauma and the age differences between incest perpetrators and their victims when the trauma variable was dichotomized into extreme or considerable and some or no trauma. However, when extreme trauma was separated from the other three categories, the relationship was statistically significant at <0.05 level. Once again, the relationship was curvilinear. When the age difference between incest perpetrator and victim was four years or less, only 11 percent of the victims reported extreme trauma. As can be seen in table 10–10, the percentage of victims reporting extreme trauma increased as the age difference increased, although there is little difference for perpetrators who were ten to nineteen years older than the victim and those who were twenty to thirty-nine years older. However, there was a significant drop in the percentage of victims reporting extreme trauma once the age disparity reached forty years or more.

The finding that the smaller age disparities are associated with less

TABLE 10–10

Age Disparity Between Incest Perpetrators and Victims Under 18 Years and Degree of Trauma Reported

Age Disparity	Extreme Trauma		None, Some, or Considerable Trauma	
	%	N	%	N
Perpetrator less than 4 years older than victim	11	3	89	25
Perpetrator 5 to 9 years older than victim	28	8	72	21
Perpetrator 10 to 19 years older than victim	42	10	58	14
Perpetrator 20 to 39 years older than victim	44	39	56	61
Perpetrator 40 or more years older than victim	28	8	72	21
Total		60		121

Missing observations: 6.
Significant at <0.05 level.

extreme trauma suggests that when there is less of an authority relationship, incest is less traumatic. On the other hand, elderly men such as
grandfathers—though they may have authority—may be experienced as
less threatening than middle-aged men. In addition, incest perpetrators
who were older than fifty years more frequently sexually abused their
victims at the least severe level. ,

Multiple Victimization and Degree of Trauma

Twenty-four women in our sample were victimized by more than one
incest perpetrator. Seventy percent of the experiences reported by these
multiply abused victims were regarded as considerably or extremely traumatic compared to 50 percent of the experiences reported by women who
were sexually abused by only one relative (statistically significant at
<0.05 level).

This relationship between multiple incest victimization and trauma may
be due to the fact that multiple victimization was also found to be significantly associated with the frequency and duration of the sexual abuse as
well as the degree of physical force or violence employed.

The fact that girls who were subjected to multiple incest victimization
were significantly more likely to be sexually abused more than once by
each perpetrator suggests that they were, for some reason, less able to stop
the sexual abuse than girls who were sexually abused by only one relative.
It may be that the former girls were more vulnerable prior to any incestuous abuse and were therefore less able to protect themselves from multiple
perpetrators. Future research is needed to examine this issue.

Multiple Regression Analysis

A method of analysis known as multiple regression makes it possible to
ascertain which of the factors that we were able to quantify had the
greatest weight in explaining the degree of trauma reported (using our
constructed measure). This equation enables us to see how closely associated two variables are, independent of the effect of other variables. For
purposes of this regression analysis, the unit of analysis will be shifted
from the incident to the victim. For the twenty-four victims of more than

one incest perpetrator, the experience reported to be the most traumatic was selected for inclusion in this analysis.

The nine factors that were entered into the multiple regression equation were the frequency and duration of the incestuous abuse; the severity of abuse in terms of the sex act involved; the use of force; the age of the victim, the perpetrator, and the age disparity between them; whether the perpetrator was a father or some other relative; and whether the victim was incestuously abused by one perpetrator or by more than one.

This regression analysis reveals that in our study, the severity of the sexual abuse in terms of the sex acts involved was even more highly related to trauma than whether or not the perpetrator was a father. In fact severity emerged as the most significant of all nine variables, followed by whether or not the perpetrator was a father or some other relative, the use of physical force, the age disparity between the victim and the perpetrator, and the duration of the incestuous abuse (see table 10–11). Together these factors account for 31 percent of the variance.

Finkelhor (1979) used six of these same variables in a similar regression analysis for trauma in his college student survey. The only two factors that turned out to be important in his study were the use of force and the age of the perpetrator. The severity of the abuse, the duration, and the age of the victim did not even approach significance at < 0.05 level. Also, in sharp contrast to our findings, "a more closely related relative actually decreased the negativity a tiny bit" (p. 107).

These differences could be due to the differences among victims in our two surveys (women students versus women of all ages over eighteen in all social classes and ethnic groups), the different methodologies used (total sample versus probability sample), or a number of other factors.

In contrast to our study's use of a subjective trauma measure, Canadian researchers Christopher Bagley and Richard Ramsay (1985) applied five indices of mental health: evidence of psychoneurosis, depression, suicidal inclinations, psychiatric consultation in the previous year, and self-

TABLE 10–11

Multiple-Regression Analysis for Trauma of Incestuous Abuse

Characteristics	Beta	Significance Level
Severity of sexual acts	−.301	< 0.001
Abused by father vs. other relative	−.208	< 0.01
Use of physical force	.195	< 0.02
Age disparity between victim and perpetrator	−.184	< 0.03
Duration of incestuous abuse	.164	< 0.03
Multiple R squared	.310	

concept. A multiple-regression analysis revealed that the best predictors of the victim's mental health outcome was the severity of the sexual abuse, followed by duration and sexual abuse by more than one perpetrator (p. 11). Use of force and sexual abuse by a father or stepfather bordered on significance. These factors accounted for 30 percent of the variance (p. 12).

Despite the facts that Bagley and Ramsay's study was not confined to incestuous abuse and that their measures of trauma were so much more elaborate than ours, the results of our regression analyses are remarkably similar. This enhances the significance of our findings.

11

Incestuous Abuse as a Contributing Cause of Revictimization

Given the state of our knowledge at this time, it is impossible to assess what the long-term effects of child sexual abuse will be on the basis of the short-term impact. Children may not appear upset or hurt at the time of sexual abuse; the effects may only reveal themselves years or even decades later. Hence short-term effects should never be seen as a satisfactory measure of the total picture.

The sexual abuse of children differs in this respect from the rape of adult women. An adult woman is more likely to have experienced trust in intimate relationships, to have a sense of who she is and what sex is before the traumatic attack. In contrast, children's capacity to trust can be shattered. Their sense of who they are and what sex is about is often totally or substantially shaped by the sexually abusive experience.

Chapter 10 showed that the victims' own subjective assessment of the trauma they experienced as a result of incestuous abuse was significantly related to a whole range of variables that both popular and clinical wisdom would expect: the frequency of the abuse, the duration over which it occurred, its severity in terms of the sex acts involved, the degree of force or violence employed, how closely related the victim was to the perpetrator, and the age disparity involved. This serves as a kind of validation of the usefulness of the two subjective questions on the degree of upset and the long-term effects that were used in our study to measure the degree of trauma.

However, a limitation of relying on subjective assessments of trauma is that people are often unaware of certain kinds of effects. No one mentioned that she had attempted suicide, or become a drug addict or a prostitute, or given up her childhood religious beliefs as a result of incestuous abuse. Not one woman mentioned any connection between her incest experience and later sexual victimization.

Although we didn't ask our respondents whether they had ever attempted suicide or become drug addicts or prostitutes, we did ask a great number of questions about all kinds of experiences of sexual victimization. In doing so we found an extraordinarily strong connection between childhood incest and later experiences of sexual assault. While other researchers have reported a correlation between child sexual abuse and later sexual victimization (e.g., Herman 1981; Frieze 1983; Browne and Finkelhor 1986), this was not a hypothesis I had in mind when designing this study in 1977. However, since it is such a striking and important finding, most of this chapter will be devoted to its documentation as well as to an explanation for it.

We defined rape as forced penile-vaginal intercourse, penile-vaginal intercourse obtained by threat of force, or penile-vaginal intercourse when the woman was unable to consent because she was unconscious, severely drugged, or in some other way totally physically helpless. Unsuccessful attempts at such acts were also counted as rape, as is customary in the statistics reported annually by the Federal Bureau of Investigation in the *Uniform Crime Reports* and those gathered by the Census Bureau for the *National Crime Surveys.*

Table 11–1 shows that when all cases of rape or attempted rape by relatives are excluded from the analysis, 68 percent of incest victims were the victims of rape or attempted rape by a nonrelative at some time in their lives compared with 38 percent of the women in our sample who were never incestuously abused. When all experiences of rape or attempted rape that occurred before the age of fourteen are excluded, 65 percent of the incest victims reported such an attack compared with 36 percent of the women who had never been victims of incest. Hence we see that most of the rapes did not occur concurrently with the incestuous abuse in the victim's childhood years, but took place later.

The table also reveals that 82 percent of the incest victims were victimized by some kind of serious sexual assault—including rape and attempted rape, but excluding incestuous abuse—compared with 48 percent of the women who had never been incestuously abused.*

---

*As mentioned previously, separate sexual assault questionnaires were completed for all the more serious incidents of sexual abuse. Only with incestuous abuse were separate sexual assault questionnaires obtained for the less serious cases of exploitive sexual contact. In cases of extrafamilial child sexual abuse, sexual abuse by females and by authority figures, the abuse had to be at the level of breast or genital contact or attempted contact in order to warrant a separate sexual assault questionnaire. In all other cases rape or attempted rape had to have occurred in order to warrant the completion of a separate sexual assault questionnaire. To avoid contaminating our findings, all cases of incestuous abuse (not just incestuous rape and attempted rape) are excluded from these calculations.

TABLE 11-1

Incest Victimization Before 18 Years, Rape, and Other Sexual Abuse

	Incest Victimization*		No Incest Victimization		Significance Level
	%	N	%	N	
Respondent was victim of serious nonincestuous sexual assault at some time in her life	82	123	48	373	< 0.001
Respondent was victim of rape or attempted rape excluding incestuous rape at some time in her life	68	102	38	298	< 0.001
Respondent was victim of rape or attempted rape excluding incestuous rape after 14 years of age	65	98	36	282	< 0.001
Mean number of serious sexual assault experiences with different perpetrators		3.6		1.2	< 0.001

*Missing observation: 1.

This finding raises the question of whether extrafamilial child sexual abuse is also associated with high rates of rape and other sexual abuse, or is this phenomenon—which we will call revictimization—unique to victims of incest?

For purposes of this comparison we shall focus on women who were victimized by incest before they were fourteen, not eighteen, because this was the age criterion for obtaining data on extrafamilial child sexual abuse that is most comparable to our data on incestuous abuse. In addition, all cases of least severe sexual abuse will be excluded from this comparison for both forms of child sexual abuse since our definition of incestuous abuse was more inclusive than the one used for extrafamilial child sexual abuse. Finally, in order to avoid the problem of double counting, those who were victimized by both incestuous and extrafamilial child sexual abuse were included in the incest group only, since it was the smaller group.

This comparison reveals that 65 percent of the women who were victimized by incest at the very severe or severe levels before they turned fourteen were victimized again by rape or attempted rape by a nonrelative after the age of fourteen, compared with 61 percent of the women who were victimized by extrafamilial child sexual abuse, and only 35 percent of the women who were never sexually abused before the age of fourteen.

This 4 percent difference between the victims of incest and extrafamilial child sexual abuse is very small, indicating that all child sexual abuse, not just incestuous abuse, is associated with rape and attempted rape later in life. These percentages are also nearly double the rate for all the other respondents in our sample who had no history of sexual abuse before the age of fourteen.

While the high rates of revictimization of child sexual abuse victims are shocking, the fact that as much as 35 percent of the other 930 women in our sample were victimized by rape or attempted rape after the age of fourteen is also very disturbing. The methodology that was so effective in encouraging women to disclose their experiences of incestuous abuse appears to have been equally effective in enabling them to talk about their experiences of rape.*

Incest Victimization and Other Sexual and/or Violent Abuse

Table 11–2 reveals a statistically significant relationship between incest victimization and wife rape. Close to three times as many incest victims (19 percent) as women who were never victims of incest (7 percent) reported having been raped in marriage. In addition, over twice as many incest victims (27 percent) as women who were never victims of incest (12 percent) reported that a husband had been physically violent toward them at least once, and often many times, during their marriage.†

Over twice as many incest victims as women who were never victims of incest reported at least one unwanted sexual advance by an unrelated authority figure such as a doctor, teacher, employer, minister, therapist, policeman, or much older person: 53 percent compared with 26 percent.

This table also reveals significant associations between incest victimization and a whole host of milder experiences, such as being upset by exhibitionism, a peeping Tom, and men's sexual advances on the street.

INCEST VICTIMIZATION AND PORNOGRAPHY

Table 11–3 reveals that incest victims were over twice as likely as non-incest victims to be asked to pose for pornography, as well as to have been

*I have analyzed the data on rape and attempted rape more thoroughly in two other books: *Rape in Marriage* (1982) and *Sexual Exploitation* (1984*b*).

†Based on only those respondents who were ever married, 27 percent of incest victims versus 11 percent of nonincest victims were raped by a husband; similarly, 38 percent were victims of physical violence by a husband compared to only 18 percent of women with no history of incest.

TABLE 11–2

Incest Victimization Before 18 Years and Other Sexual and/or Violent Abuse

Sexual/Violent Abuse[a]	Incest Victimization		No Incest Victimization		Significance Level
	%	N	%	N	
Respondent was a victim of wife rape	19	29	7	58	< 0.001
Respondent was a victim of physical violence by her husband	27	41	12	97	< 0.001
Respondent had unwanted sexual advances by an authority figure[b]	53	80	26	206	< 0.001
Respondent received an obscene phone call	69	104	58	453	< 0.05
Respondent upset on street by men's comments	67	101	55	431	< 0.05
Respondent upset by someone looking while undressing, nude, or making love	23	34	12	90	< 0.001
Respondent pinched or rubbed against in a public place	85	129	64	499	< 0.001
Respondent upset by someone exposing genitals before 14	44	67	24	186	< 0.001
Respondent upset by someone exposing genitals after 14	46	69	35	273	< 0.05

[a]Kinds of sexual abuse that may overlap with incestuous abuse—for example, unwanted experiences with females, childhood intercourse, or fondling—are not included here.
[b]Relatives were not counted as authority figures.
Missing observation: 1.

upset by being requested to enact behavior seen in pornographic pictures, movies, or books (significant at < 0.001 level). In contrast, there was no significant relationship between incest victimization and respondents' being upset by seeing pornography.

Table 11–4 shows that the victims of father-daughter incest were about four times more likely than nonincest victims to report being asked to pose for pornography as well as being asked to enact it. And victims of more than one incest perpetrator were three or four times more likely to report such experiences (these associations are statistically significant at < 0.0001 level).

TABLE 11–3

Incest Victimization Before 18 Years and Experiences with Pornography

Experiences with Pornography	Incest Victimization N = 151		No Incest Victimization N = 778	
	%	N	%	N
Upset by requests to enact pornography[a]	18	27	8	62
Asked to pose for pornography[a]	27	40	11	88
Upset by seeing pornography[b]	43	33	44	137

[a]Significant at < 0.001 level.
[b]Based only on women who had *seen* pornography. Not significant at < 0.05 level.

TABLE 11–4

Father-Daughter Incest and Victimization by More Than One Relative Before 18 Years and Experiences with Pornography

Experiences with Pornography	Victim of Father-Daughter Incest N = 42		Victim of More Than One Relative N = 23[b]		No Incest Victimization N = 778	
	%	N	%	N	%	N
Upset by requests to enact pornography[a]	31	13	35	8	8	62
Asked to pose for pornography[a]	43	18	30	7	11	88

[a]Significant at < .001 level.
[b]Missing observations: 1.

Incest Victimization and Fears of Sexual Assault

In addition to reporting a variety of additional experiences of sexual abuse, incest victims described significantly greater *fears* of sexual abuse than did women who had no history of incest victimization. Specifically, they were more fearful of sexual assault during their childhood years and more fearful of being sexually assaulted when in a violent situation.

Incest victims were also significantly more inclined to believe there was some likelihood that someone would try to rape or sexually assault them at some time in the future and to worry that their child or children would be the victim of sexual assault (see table 11–5).

The fact that twice as many incest victims as women who had no history of incest victimization reported fear of sexual assault in their childhood years may be due to their experience of sexual assault. This finding could

TABLE 11–5

Incest Victimization Before 18 Years and Fears of Sexual Assault

	Incest Victimization[a]		No Incest Victimization		Significance Level
	%	N	%	N	
Respondent afraid of sexual assault in childhood	42	63	21	167	< 0.001
Respondent in violent situation where she feared being sexually assaulted	15	23	7	52	< 0.001
Respondent believes someone will try to rape her in future	60	91	48	371	< 0.01
Respondent worries her child will be victim of sexual assault[b]	82	68	63	236	< 0.01

[a]Missing observation: 1.
[b]Based only on women who had a child.

be useful as a diagnostic question. When children demonstrate a fear of sexual assault, it may indicate that they have been—or are being—sexually assaulted.

Two fear variables were not significantly associated with incest victimization. Although incest victims were more inclined to think someone would try to sexually assault them at some time in the future, they did not express any more fear of sexual assault at the time of the interview than women who had never been incest victims did (approximately a third of both groups said they were "very afraid"). Nor were they significantly more likely to take precautionary measures to try to avoid being sexually assaulted. However, a sizable 81 percent of the incest victims did take such measures (compared to 76 percent of the women who had never been incest victims).

Incest Victimization and Attitudes, Knowledge, and Beliefs About Rape, Other Sexual Abuse, and Communication About Sex

Table 11–6 lists a number of attitudes about rape and incest and how these crimes are dealt with, as well as opinions about whether or not sex should be discussed and personal knowledge of rape victims. All of these factors were significantly associated with incest victimization. In addition, incest victims were significantly more likely to personally know a rape victim. They also had slightly more pessimistic views about the percentage of women in the population who have been raped.

In summary: It appears that women who have had experiences of incestuous abuse may be differentiated as a group from women who have never been incest victims as a group on a number of attitude, knowledge, and belief items—long after the abuse is over. Far more significantly, incest victimization is clearly related to much higher rates of rape, plus a whole range of other kinds of sexual abuse experiences and fears of sexual assault. How can these findings be accounted for?

TABLE 11–6

Incest Victimization and Attitudes, Knowledge, and Beliefs About Rape, Other Sexual Abuse, and Communication About Sex

	Incest Victimization		No Incest Victimization		Significance Level
	%	N^b	%	N^b	
Respondent knows rape victim personally	66	99	41	319	< 0.001
Respondent estimates 50% or more women in country have been raped	48	72	38	277	< 0.05
Respondent disagrees that most rapists end up in jail eventually	93	140	83	640	< 0.01
Respondent agrees that most rape victims are badly treated in court	87	132	80	620	< 0.05
Respondent agrees that most women experience sexual assault	77	116	54	418	< 0.001
Respondent agrees that sexual assault within families is very common	72	109	51	397	< 0.001
Respondent agrees that many/most men are capable of rape[a]	71	107	62	480	< 0.05
Respondent agrees that rape victims are not responsible for being raped	78	118	70	540	0.05
Respondent disagrees that sex is not a subject to be discussed	95	144	86	659	< 0.01

[a]Because some interviewers reported that some respondents were upset by this question, the word "many" was substituted for "most" halfway through the fieldwork period.
[b]Number of missing observations varies by variable.

Explaining Revictimization

Three arguments will be presented and evaluated for why the relationship found between incestuous abuse and later sexual victimization may be spurious.

It could be that incest victims reported higher rates of revictimization because they were more willing than women who said they had never been incestuously abused to admit such an experience to the interviewer. Some support for this explanation is provided by the following findings: (1) significantly more incest victims than nonincest victims were likely to disagree with the opinion that "sex is not a subject to be discussed" (95 percent compared with 86 percent); (2) incest victims were rated by interviewers as significantly more interested in the study than nonincest victims at the outset of the interview (47 percent were very interested compared with 34 percent); (3) interviewers said that incest victims were significantly more friendly or eager during the interview than nonincest victims (72 percent compared with 62 percent); and (4) interviewers expressed complete confidence in the honesty of incest victim respondents significantly more frequently than in the case of nonincest victims (85 percent versus 77 percent); in only 3 percent of the interviews with incest victims were the interviewers "not very confident" of the validity of the data obtained, compared with 10 percent of the interviews with nonincest victims.

Although these findings were all statistically significant at < 0.05 level, the differences between the incest and nonincest victims were all less than 14 percent. Therefore, it seems likely that while a greater willingness to disclose sexual abuse experiences may partly explain the statistical relationships between incestuous abuse and other sexual assault, it is far from being the only factor involved.

A second possible explanation for the differences in revictimization rates is that incest victims might be more sensitive to, and easily upset by, experiences such as sexual advances by authority figures, sexual comments by men on the street, propositions to pose for pornographic pictures, and so on. They might therefore also be more inclined to remember such experiences. However, it seems most unlikely that this explanation could account for the larger number of rape and other more serious experiences of sexual assault reported by incest victims.

A third possible explanation is that repressed memories of childhood sexual abuse may sometimes be triggered by an experience of sexual assault in adulthood. This process of "unrepression" is likely to be particularly common for victims of adult rape and might contribute to the correlation found in our survey between child and adult experiences of sexual abuse.*

*This hypothesis was suggested by Ann Maney. Personal communication, 1983.

These three possible explanations may contribute to the higher rates of revictimization reported by incest victims. However, some of the differences in revictimization rates were very large, and it seems likely that the relationship between incestuous abuse and later victimization is a real one. What, then, are some of the reasons why incest victims might be more vulnerable to nonincestuous sexual assaults than women with no history of incestuous abuse?

Researchers Ronnie Janoff-Bulman and Irene Frieze (1983) believe that victims of any victimizing event must deal with "the tremendous psychological toll exacted by these extreme events" (p. 3). Much of this psychological toll, they suggest, "derives from the shattering of very basic assumptions that victims have held about themselves and their world" (p. 3). These assumptions include: (1) the belief in personal invulnerability; (2) the perception of the world as meaningful and comprehensible; and (3) the viewing of ourselves in a positive light. Victimization calls into question each of these primary postulates of our assumptive world, and by doing so destroys the stability with which we are ordinarily able to function.

Although Janoff-Bulman and Frieze do not discuss whether one victimization experience makes a person more vulnerable to another, this conclusion follows easily from their analysis. For example, they suggest that "once victimized, it is relatively easy to see oneself in the role of victim once again" (1983, p. 5). For some victims, they observe, "the anxiety associated with this new perception of vulnerability may be paralyzing" (p. 5).

In addition, Janoff-Bulman and Frieze (1983) argue that "the trauma of victimization activates negative self-images. Victims see themselves as weak, helpless, needy, frightened and out of control." They are also "apt to experience a sense of deviance" (p. 6). Thus, effective coping with victimization requires not only coming to terms with a world in which bad experiences happen to oneself, but also restoring a damaged self-image.

Needless to say, many victims are not able to follow these prescriptions for coping effectively. Instead, self-blame and a sense of worthlessness often prevail. These feelings place a victim at greater risk of revictimization, which in turn makes it even more difficult to achieve effective coping strategies. So it is easy to see how a downward spiral can be set into motion.

One of the chief shortcomings of Janoff-Bulman and Frieze's analysis is that they tend to discuss victimization as if it is either a one-time experience or a rare occurrence. Our survey, in contrast, shows that even when we limit our analysis to sexual victimization, revictimization is extremely common. Some of the more detailed case histories in chapters 12, 14, and 24 emphasize this point quite dramatically.

FINKELHOR AND BROWNE'S THEORY OF LONG-TERM EFFECTS

Finkelhor and Browne (1985) have developed a theoretical model for analyzing child sexual abuse in terms of four trauma-causing factors: traumatic sexualization, stigmatization, betrayal, and powerlessness. They refer to these factors as traumagenic dynamics, and suggest that they "alter children's cognitive and emotional orientation to the world, and create trauma by distorting children's self-concept, world view, and affective capacities" (p. 531).

This model is extremely helpful in suggesting explanations for the strong association found between incestuous abuse and revictimization.

Traumatic Sexualization. "Traumatic sexualization," write Finkelhor and Browne, "refers to a process in which a child's sexuality (including both sexual feelings and sexual attitudes) is shaped in a developmentally inappropriate and interpersonally dysfunctional fashion as a result of sexual abuse" (1985, p. 531). Several of the behavioral manifestations of traumatic sexualization suggested by the authors might contribute to the sexual revictimization of incest victims.

One example of a behavioral manifestation evident in some child victims is a preoccupation with sex. Some victimized children, for example, engage in "repetitive sexual behavior such as masturbation or compulsive sex play" (1985, p. 534). They may also "display knowledge and interests that are inappropriate to their age, such as wanting to engage school age playmates in sexual intercourse or oral-genital contact" (p. 534). Such behavior may make the children very vulnerable to revictimization. Adults and older children are likely to perceive such behavior as seductive and as encouragement to act sexually toward these children.

A common pattern observed by many clinicians is that victims of child sexual abuse respond to their earlier traumatic sexualization by becoming promiscuous as adolescents or adults. Some of these women see sexuality as a commodity—something they can use to gain money, favors, or rewards of some kind. Incestuous abuse can serve as a perfect training ground for prostitutes in this way—particularly when combined with economic pressures it may alienate the victim from her sexuality and train her to expect to be bribed in one way or another in exchange for sexual submission. Some studies provide empirical confirmation that victims of child sexual abuse are at high risk for becoming prostitutes (James and Meyerding 1977; Finkelhor and Browne 1985, p. 534).

Women who cope with their incestuous abuse by becoming promiscuous are likely to be very vulnerable to rape and other sexual assault. Frequently labeled "bad women" or "whores," their right to refuse sex is often denied. Some people want to attack such women, not because they've been rejected by them sexually but to punish them for their sexual image or behavior. Some well-known serial murderers provide dramatic examples of this phenomenon; for example, most of the victims of the so-called Yorkshire Ripper in England and the Green River murderer in Seattle, Washington, were prostitutes.

Another response to traumatic sexualization is the development of an aversion to sex in adolescence or adulthood. As Finkelhor and Browne (1985) point out, "Sexual contact associated in a child's memory with revulsion, fear, anger, a sense of powerlessness, or other negative emotions can contaminate later sexual experiences" (p. 535). The aversion may include "flashbacks to the molestation experience, difficulty with arousal and orgasm, and vaginismus, as well as negative attitudes toward their sexuality and their bodies" (p. 534). In dating and intimate relationships these women may be more inclined to reject unwanted sexual advances, which sometimes leads to sexual violence. In my analysis of rape in marriage, this dynamic appeared to be operating in some cases (Russell 1982). It might also help explain why incest victims are more likely to report physical violence by their husbands.

Betrayal.   Betrayal is the second traumagenic dynamic described by Finkelhor and Browne. It refers to the dynamic in which "children discover that someone on whom they were vitally dependent has caused them harm" (1985, p. 531). This is a particularly significant factor in the occurrence of cross-generational incestuous abuse as well as sexual abuse by siblings, in contrast to sexual abuse by strangers.

One common consequence of the manipulation of a child's trust and vulnerability is an impaired ability to correctly judge the trustworthiness of others. This impaired capacity, in turn, may make victims more vulnerable to subsequent abuse, both sexual and nonsexual. Mistrusting people who are worthy of trust can have sad or even tragic consequences. But trusting people who are untrustworthy can also be highly dangerous. It is easy to see how sexual revictimization may occur as a result.

As Finkelhor and Browne (1985) point out, "the degree of betrayal is also related to a family's response to disclosure. Children who are disbelieved, blamed, or ostracized undoubtedly experience a greater sense of betrayal than those who are supported" (p. 532). The response of family members to reports of incestuous abuse is often particularly rejecting and unsupportive because in such cases the family structure itself is at stake, unlike in cases of extrafamilial child sexual abuse.

Powerlessness.   Powerlessness—"the dynamic of rendering the victim powerless"—is the third traumagenic factor suggested by Finkelhor and Browne. It refers to "the process in which the child's will, desires, and sense of efficacy are continually contravened" (1985, p. 532). These researchers hypothesize that "a basic kind of powerlessness occurs in sexual abuse when a child's territory and body space are repeatedly invaded against the child's will" (p. 532). Both the feeling and reality of powerlessness are further reinforced when a child's attempts to stop the abuse are frustrated. Repeated victimizations—which occur more frequently with incestuous abuse than with extrafamilial child sexual abuse—may play a more significant role in the trauma of incest than in the trauma of sexual abuse by nonrelatives.

Two of the psychological consequences of this powerlessness hypothesized by Finkelhor and Browne are the child's perception of herself as a victim and a lowered sense of efficacy. So, for example, "having been a victim on repeated occasions may make it difficult to act without the expectation of being revictimized" (p. 536). The connection between these effects and revictimization are obvious. The child was, after all, unable to protect her bodily and psychological boundaries from being violated. Such an experience can socialize a child into the role of victim. If a child has been unable to prevent a brother or father from sexually abusing her, she may be less able to muster the confidence and assertiveness required to reject unwanted sexual advances from others.

Once again, Finkelhor and Browne (1985) point out that "a situation in which a child tells and is not believed will also create a greater degree of powerlessness" (p. 532).

Running away from home is another behavioral manifestation of powerlessness mentioned by Finkelhor and Browne. As is made so clear by the story of the runaway girl described in chapter 14, this behavioral manifestation renders girls particularly vulnerable to sexual revictimization.

Stigmatization. Finkelhor and Browne's fourth traumagenic factor is stigmatization. This refers to "the negative connotations—e.g., badness, shame, and guilt—that are communicated to the child around the experiences and that then become incorporated into the child's self-image" (1985, p. 532). These negative connotations may be communicated by the perpetrator and/or they may be a consequence of the child's awareness of the taboo against child sexuality and the even stronger taboo against incest. They may also be reinforced by victim blaming or shocked responses upon disclosure, as well as the literal stigmatization for being a victim of sexual abuse by friends, family, and other significant adults—particularly if it involves a family member.

Nondisclosure, however, does not necessarily lessen the stigmatization. Indeed, Finkelhor and Browne (1985) suggest that "keeping the secret of having been a victim of sexual abuse may increase the sense of stigma, since it reinforces the sense of being different" (p. 533).

In general, girls in this culture, whether or not they disclose the experience, are likely to internalize the notion that they have lost their "purity"
and have become "damaged goods." The psychological impact of this
internalization, according to Finkelhor and Browne, are feelings of guilt,
shame, lowered self-esteem, and a sense of being different from others.
Because of the isolation and sense of differentness experienced by many
victims of child sexual abuse, they "may gravitate to various stigmatized
levels of society. Thus they may get involved in drug or alcohol abuse, in
criminal activity, or in prostitution" (p. 535). These activities in turn place
victims at high risk of being sexually revictimized.

We see then that all four of Finkelhor and Browne's traumagenic factors
may be useful in explaining why incest victims—as well as victims of
extrafamilial child sexual abuse—are so often revictimized by other perpetrators in both their childhood and adult years. Three of the factors—
betrayal, powerlessness, and stigmatization—are all likely to be more serious problems for incest victims than for victims of extrafamilial child
sexual abuse; this may help to explain why incestuous abuse is often more
traumatic than sexual abuse by nonrelatives.

Finkelhor and Browne's theoretical model for analyzing child sexual
abuse in terms of the four traumagenic factors has proven exceedingly
helpful in shedding light on the possible causes of revictimization. But
there is one major problem with our application of it: It tends to explain
revictimization in terms of the psychological impact of incest victimization
on the victim. A complete explanation of revictimization requires a more
central place for the perpetrator.

THE ROLE OF THE PERPETRATOR IN REVICTIMIZATION

In order for child sexual abuse to occur, someone has to want to behave
sexually toward a child. In addition, he or she must override any internal
inhibitions he or she may have against acting out this desire as well as any
social inhibitions that may exist, such as fear of being caught (Finkelhor
1984).

In his discussion of pedophiles psychologist Kevin Howells maintains
that "there is good reason to think that such persons form a minority in
the total population of people who become sexually involved with children" (1981, p. 62). Howells proceeds to cite Kurt Freund's research
findings that suggest that "normal males show sufficient penile response
to children to allow the possibility that children might become 'surrogate'
partners when an adult partner is not available (as in the situational
offender)" (p. 80). In addition, this research showed that "the female child
elicits stronger reactions than the male child in normals and might be
regarded as a more likely surrogate" (p. 80). These findings suggests that

there is a vast number of males in the population with a potential interest in sexually abusing children.

Sexual offenders or potential offenders' knowledge about prior incest victimization may disinhibit their abusive tendencies toward these victims. This phenomenon can operate in various ways (see examples in Russell 1975; Frieze 1983). Some people apparently find the information that a child has participated in a taboo sexual relationship exciting and provocative, regardless of the involuntary nature of the child's victimization. Incest victims, for example, appear to be particularly at risk of revictimization by male therapists and psychiatrists.

Potential perpetrators' titillation at knowing about incest victimization may be stimulated or further increased by victims who react to their abuse by becoming sexually informed and precocious beyond their developmentally appropriate age. This excitement and titillation can in turn undermine potential perpetrators' internal inhibitions against acting out their desires. The common view that sexually experienced females are "damaged goods" who, once violated, cannot be violated again, also may disinhibit such acting out.

As Janoff-Bulman and Frieze (1983) further point out, "people tend to see victims as responsible for their fate, and are thereby able to maintain their own beliefs in personal invulnerability" (p. 11). This victim blaming can also serve as an ideological disinhibitor. "She must have been asking for it" can easily turn into "she's asking for it now too."

Clinical accounts indicate that sexual offenders who do not know about a child's previous victimization may be experts at picking up cues of vulnerability, such as a low self-image or a strong but unsatisfied need for affection, approval, and attention.

Along with picking up cues of psychological vulnerability in children or adults, would-be perpetrators are also good at detecting social vulnerability. The girl who is frequently alone, appears to have few friends, and has a poor relationship with her mother and other family members, for example, may be more attractive as a victim to a would-be perpetrator because he may surmise that she's less likely to report him.

Some states have introduced sexual abuse prevention programs in which children are taught to distinguish "good" touch from "bad" touch, to defend themselves, and to tell a trusted and helpful adult about any sexual abuse. A major function of such programs is to encourage would-be perpetrators to restrain their impulses. If victims could count on getting support from those they told, and if they told right away, the problem of child sexual abuse would be greatly ameliorated. Social inhibitions would thereby become a more important factor in the prevention of sexual victimization as well as revictimization.

Conclusion

Given the many different experiences of sexual assault in the lives of incest victims, it is hardly surprising that they are more fearful. Indeed, their fears may have as much and sometimes more to do with other abusive experiences as with the incestuous abuse. It is also not particularly surprising that incest victims are more inclined than nonincest victims to believe that sexual assault within families is common, that many men are capable of rape, that most women experience sexual assault, and so on.

In the past, accounts of revictimization were often interpreted as proving that victims are responsible for their own victimization. Victims of repeated rapes and sexual abuse have been blamed for consciously or unconsciously placing themselves in vulnerable situations out of a masochistic desire to be sexually assaulted. Such interpretations are not only cruel and wrong, they also reveal a failure to understand some of the destructive effects of child sexual assault suggested in this chapter. An example of this failure of understanding is evident in the 1974 edition of psychiatrist Myre Sim's *Guide to Psychiatry.* After mentioning the "fact" that "a 9-year-old girl may be capable of seduction" in his chapter on child psychiatry, Sim describes one of his own patients "who was referred for importuning lorry drivers" (p. 777). Instead of seeing this behavior as probably resulting from her victimization by her father, Sim implies that her propositioning truck drivers suggests she probably importuned her father as well, or at least enjoyed the sexual relationship.

Sim then quotes the "finding" of two researchers—Gibbens and Prince —that two-thirds of the child victims of sexual assault in their study were "sufficiently willing participants to cooperate in assaults more than once or by more than one assailant" (1974, p. 777–78). He concludes his discussion of girls who are victimized by adult men as follows: "The surprising thing is, how little promiscuous children are affected by their experiences, and how most settle down to become demure housewives. It is of interest that Henriques lists two categories—the unaffected and the guilty—and that seems to put the matter in a nutshell" (p. 778).

Blaming the victims of child sexual abuse for their revictimization as well as their initial victimization helps to keep the widespread prevalence of both a hidden problem. Many victims of revictimization in particular are smart enough not to disclose such experiences because they know they will be held responsible for them.

Yet our survey data and analysis lead us to conclude that the incest experience itself could have stripped away some of the victims' potential ability to protect themselves. For example, our study reveals that the girls and women who are being asked to pose for pornography and/or to enact other sexual behavior seen in pornography are significantly more often those who have already been sexually abused by a relative. Men appear to be selecting previously victimized females for further pornography-related victimization. They are females who may have particular difficulty in handling such experiences. In a society that raises males to behave in a predatory fashion toward females, undermining a young girl's defenses is likely to be exceedingly perilous for her.

12

Ravaged Lives:
Three Women's Stories

The lives of each of the three women included in this chapter—one Afro-American, one Latina, and one white—were devastated by repeated experiences of sexual assault. Each of them had multiple experiences of incestuous abuse as well as extrafamilial child sexual abuse. Although there is no way to separate the possible long-term effects of the incestuous abuse from those of the extrafamilial child sexual abuse, these three cases illustrate many of the points made in chapter 11 on revictimization.

Victims of one experience of sexual abuse have frequently been blamed for their victimization; but women and girls who have been sexually abused several times are far more likely to be blamed. The amount of sexual abuse to which each of these women was subjected may strike readers as incredible. It is therefore important to remember that these cases were obtained from a probability sample of women who, furthermore, were living in the community outside of institutions such as mental hospitals, prisons, halfway houses, brothels, and drug abuse treatment centers. Clearly, if our sample had included such institutions, we would have interviewed many more extreme casualties of sexual assault than we did. Nor should we forget that other victims were not alive to be interviewed because they had succeeded in ending their traumatized lives by killing themselves, or were murdered in addition to being sexually victimized. Since each woman is so different, we hope that introducing the reader to their battered lives will serve to challenge stereotypes about multiple victims.

Dorothy Tomkins

At the time of the interview, Dorothy Tomkins was a forty-two-year-old Afro-American woman who was living alone. She had raised three children and was separated from her first husband.

Dorothy had attended but did not graduate from college, and was working full time as a warehouse checker at the time of the interview.

Her earliest experience of sexual assault occurred when she was eleven years old. Two male acquaintances in their late teens attempted to rape her.

Two boys I knew followed me from a movie. They forced me into the old Catholic Church and tried to rape me. I screamed. They got my clothes off and one of them tried to insert his penis while the other one was holding me. A man heard me screaming and came into the church, so they ran away. (Did they make verbal threats?) Yes, they had knives and they said they would cut me. I got a whipping from my aunt for that. That's why I was scared to tell later.

(Upset?) Extremely upset. (Effect on your life?) A great effect. I started being afraid of boys then, and I was more careful about being out by myself. And because my aunt whipped me, I was afraid to tell when it happened again.

One year later when Dorothy was twelve, she was sexually abused by a forty-eight-year-old deacon at her church. She was living with her parents at the time that this incident occurred.

I sang in a church choir. One time a member of the church, a deacon, offered me a ride home. We were on the way home when he tried to pull me to him. He was feeling on my breasts and trying to rub them. I kept pushing his hand away and I told him I would tell if he didn't stop. (Did he use verbal threats?) Yes, he threatened to tell the church that I had tried to tempt him. He used to try to get me by myself, but I wouldn't cooperate after what happened.

(Upset?) Extremely upset. (Effect on your life?) A great effect. I had a nervous breakdown. I had bad dreams after that; some man would be standing at my bed and I would wake up screaming. I was under the doctor's care for a while. I had seizures and everything. I was afraid to be with men. It seemed that the way I was had something to do with men wanting to have sex with me.

When Dorothy was thirteen she had her first experience of incestuous abuse. The perpetrator was the first of three different brothers-in-law to sexually abuse her. This first brother-in-law was twenty-eight years old when he raped her. These attacks were repeated from two to five times over a period of a year.

He and my sister had gone to a party. He came back on the pretense of getting something. He got into bed with me and his baby and tried to insert himself in me.

(What did he try to insert?) His penis. I screamed so loud the baby woke up, and he stopped.

The next time he was supposed to be taking me home after I was babysitting when he tried to have intercourse with me. He thought I was not a virgin, but when he found I was bleeding, he stopped. I was screaming so loud after the second time that I began to have seizures. He cried after he found out I was a virgin. I had to go to the doctor because he had damaged the entrance to my vagina. I jumped out of the car in my nightgown and I don't know how I got home. I was afraid to tell my mother, but I told my brother and he told my mother. I was afraid my mother was going to whip me. I had something like a nervous breakdown.

(What ended it?) After my brother told my mother, she told my father. He threatened to kill my brother-in-law. I don't see my sister now. She and he broke up after that. (Did he have a sexual relationship with other relatives?) Yes, with my niece. She was thirteen at the time. She was sent to a foster home and now she is wacky. She tried to hurt herself several times. [Dorothy's niece was presumably her brother-in-law's daughter.]

(Upset?) Extremely upset. (Effect on your life?) A great effect. I'm sure I drove my husband to drinking because my view of sex is that it's obscene. I can't stand to see people kissing. After having my baby, it got worse. I couldn't have sex at all. If the experiences hadn't been so close to home, it wouldn't have been so bad. Men only have one thing in mind and that's to mutilate the body. I've been to several psychiatrists but it doesn't seem to go away.

Dorothy was sixteen years old the one time another twenty-six-year-old brother-in-law molested her.

My brother-in-law was supposed to take me to the store. On the way home he stopped and tried to force me to have intercourse. After what happened with my other brother-in-law, my father told me to let them get on top of me and then cut them. I had a razor on me, and after he kept pushing me down and I saw he wasn't going to stop, I let him get on me, then I cut him in the back. Then I jumped out of the car. I was scared to tell anyone because my sister would think that it was my fault. (Did he make verbal threats?) He said: "If you don't do it, I'll tell your sister you did it anyway."

(Upset?) Extremely upset. (Effect on your life?) A great effect. It was a terrible experience. I was afraid to tell anyone because they would say it was my fault. Sometimes now when I wake up, I think some man is standing at my bed. If a strange man says something to me when I go out, I'm liable to turn around and cut or stab him. It's so deep-seated, even now at forty-two I'm still affected. I can't seem to get over it. I'm paranoid.

Dorothy was eighteen when she was attacked by a twenty-four-year-old policeman and his colleague. Both were white. She was married at the time.

I was standing at the bus stop at about six in the morning. A policeman stopped and asked me for identification, then told me to get in the car. He asked me how much money I'd made. I told him I worked at a hospital and had not been paid. The other policeman in the front told him that I probably was a nurse. I had on a white uniform and white shoes and stockings. The first policeman started to take my clothes off and feel all over me. He pushed me down on the seat and inserted his finger in my vagina. I was screaming and the policeman in the front of the car got nervous. A black man pulled up alongside the police car and saw me struggling. He got out of his car and came over to see what was going on. They told him that I was being searched. He said I should be taken down to the police station and searched by a woman. After that they took me to the hospital with the man following behind. He was an important black man.

(Upset?) Extremely upset, though upset is not the best word. (Effect on your life?) A great effect. "Why me?" I wondered. I found out that I was pregnant at the time it happened. I started to have grand mal seizures. I was terrified. It took a long time to get back to some sense of having a normal life. I was under a doctor's care for quite a while. When my husband tried to touch me after that I would jump out of the bed and start screaming.

I will never get over it. It's like a hammer over my head that might fall at any time. I still see my psychiatrist sometimes when I get depressed and keep thinking about it. When I see police now I try to get as far away from them as I can.

When Dorothy was twenty-four, the husband of a good friend tried to rape her. He was twenty-three at the time.

A very good friend's husband saw me on the street and offered to give me a ride. I had just had a baby about three weeks prior to that. Instead of giving me a ride he took me to the park and started to try to pull my clothes off. I resisted, but I knew he was stronger than me. He tried to penetrate me, but I had a knife, so when he tried to get on top of me I stabbed him in the neck and back, then I jumped out and ran. I did like my father told me, and let him think he was going to go through with it, then let him have it. But I was beaten and bloody by the end. The police found him lying on the seat of his car with his pants down, unconscious. (What happened as a result of the police investigation?) I don't know.

(Upset?) Extremely upset. (Effect on your life?) A great effect. I stopped having sex with my husband. I just couldn't get ready. I think that's why my husband started to drink more and more. I didn't want anything to do with men. I cared about my husband but I couldn't go to bed with him. He would come home and get in bed and I would hop out.

One year later, when Dorothy was twenty-five, she was attacked by an acquaintance in his late twenties who also tried to rape her.

I was up in an apartment with two women and a man. I thought the two women were my friends. The man asked me to go to the store with him. Before we left he went into a room to get some money and called me in. When I went in, he threw me on the floor and tore off my clothes and tried to rape me. The two women stood in the door laughing. Then my husband came up to the apartment; the women vanished and the man stopped. The man was very frightened because my husband threatened to kill him.

(Upset?) Extremely upset. (Effect on your life?) A great effect. It just kept piling up. It seems like it was never going to stop. I kept thinking it must be something about me to cause all these things to happen.

Dorothy was twenty-seven years old when her first cousin, who was also twenty-seven, tried to rape her with the help of another man and woman.

My cousin was a pimp, though I didn't know this at the time. He took me up to his place and he started to beat me across the face. He wanted to swap me and another woman with another guy. They said everyone was doing it—changing partners and everything. The idea was that he would start with me. They took off my underpants, but I really struggled and I bit him on his penis. The girl pulled my hair and I bit her too. They were passing pills and tried to get me to use the needle. After they beat me up pretty bad, he [her cousin] stopped.

(Did he use verbal threats?) Yes, he said, "I'll shoot you." He had a gun. (Upset?) Extremely upset. (Effect on your life?) A great effect.

When Dorothy was forty years old, a third brother-in-law attempted to rape her. He was thirty-eight at the time.

My husband was at work and I was in the bed with my two small children. I slept with my window open and he came in through it. I heard the noise but thought it was my husband because he went to the bathroom. Then he got in bed with me without any clothes on. He put his arms around me and tried to get on top of me. We fought and I hit him with a lamp. After it was all over he said that he was sorry. (Upset?) Extremely upset. (Effect on your life?) A great effect.

Dorothy believed that her dislike of sex had driven her husband to drink and that it had also resulted in his assaulting her from eleven to twenty times over a period of thirteen years. She described her husband's attacks on her as follows:

It was just like rape. He forced himself on me. He hit me, then pinned me down and had sex with me. Sometimes he would come home after drinking and he would wake me up and force himself on me. He would hold me down and take it. One time he came home after he had been out drinking and he wanted to go to bed with me and we had a fight about it. He started hitting on me and finally I stopped fighting. He had sex with me and then went to sleep.

Of all her experiences of sexual assault, Dorothy considered the experiences with her brothers-in-law to be the most upsetting.

Dorothy said that her fear of sexual assault affected her behavior in the following ways:

I'm afraid of police; I'm afraid of men. I always try to carry a weapon. I always have a man like my brother in the house. I put a chair up to the door so that I feel more secure and people don't come in.

Dorothy Tomkins's history of relentless sexual assault both bewildered and devastated her. Some victims of multiple assault become numbed by the repeated traumas, but for Dorothy the trauma of each successive experience seemed to be cumulative. In response to the devastating experiences of sexual abuse in her childhood, Dorothy developed an abhorrence of sex. This placed her at great risk of sexual assault in her intimate relationships. She herself believed that her dislike of sex accounted for her husband's raping her. Hence her case illustrates well one of the possible causes of revictimization discussed in chapter 11.

A striking aspect of Dorothy's story is the assertiveness she developed in order to defend herself. She used a knife to cut one of her brothers-in-law as he was attempting to rape her. She also stabbed a good friend of her husband's who tried to rape her and left him unconscious. On the other hand, she appeared to behave very submissively toward the two white policemen who picked her up, one of whom sexually abused her. Perhaps as an Afro-American woman she was fearful that any kind of assertive response on her part could be highly dangerous in that situation. The fact that there were two of them and that they were policemen in uniform may have added to her sense of vulnerability.

Given Dorothy's generally assertive, even militant methods of self-defense, how can the repeated victimizations by nonintimates be accounted for? Since the interview was not conducted to address this question, we cannot be sure. But it seems possible that her ability to know when and whom to trust was severely undermined by her traumatic childhood experiences of both extrafamilial and incestuous abuse.

Rachel Goodner*

Rachel Goodner, who described her ethnic identification as Spanish, was twenty-six years old at the time of the interview. She had had some college education and worked as a nurse's aide. She was separated from her husband and living with her four-year-old child when interviewed.

Rachel's first experience of sexual abuse occurred when she was six years old. The perpetrator was her eleven-year-old cousin, who molested her from six to ten times over a period of seven years.

I was really sick. My cousin was staying with us and we had chicken pox at the same time. We all slept in bed together [Rachel's brother, sister, and she]. When my cousin came he slept with us. He tried to get me to touch his erection. I got

*A much edited version of Rachel's story was published in Russell, *Sexual Exploitation* (1984*b*).

the measles and chicken pox internally [in the vagina] because of my cousin. I almost died. Most of what I know about it I overheard.

(Did he do anything else sexual with you?) Yeah, he'd flash [show his penis] at his house. He exposed himself a lot. When he had an erection and I was alone he'd try to come in my room. I had to really try to keep my distance and let him know I wasn't willing. One time he tried to climb in bed with me. He was naked and he put his hand over my mouth. I was indignant and furious and I bit his hand. I let him know he'd have to force me. (Did he force you?) Yes, he did that time he climbed in bed with me.

(How did it end?) He had an affair with his best friend. I think that did it. He was in love with his friend and no longer sexually interested in me.

(Upset?) At first, I was extremely upset. (Overall?) Very upset. (Effect on your life?) A great effect. It probably reinforced my feeling that I was a whore and a slut. That was the main effect. I was already suspicious of men. It also gave me a warped sense of male sexuality. My bitter feelings were later cancelled by his confiding in me and his respecting me. All of these factors together affect me, but how they do is a complex matter.

Rachel's cousin continued to sexually abuse her until she was thirteen or fourteen. Four or five other people also sexually abused her during those years. The first of these perpetrators was a twenty-seven-year-old female neighbor who was a friend of Rachel's mother. This woman was married but her husband was away a great deal. She sexually abused Rachel from six to ten times over a period of six months.

I was nine or so. She was an alcoholic and she'd come over to our house drunk. I would have to stay at her house, and I slept in her bed. She needed me to be there to sleep with her. She didn't force me to do anything to her but I would wake up in the middle of the night and she'd be holding and touching me. (Where?) My breasts and genitals. I'd pretend I was sleeping and later we'd pretend that nothing had happened. (Did anything else sexual happen with her?) No. (How did it end?) She moved.

(Upset?) Extremely upset. (Effect on your life?) A great effect. You're trained to be hassled by men, but it's not expected with women. I was made to go over there and play daughter or lover, but I didn't want to. Neither she nor my mom cared what I felt. My needs were ignored. It made me uncomfortable around lesbians because I feel a threat that I'll have to do something with them if I'm affectionate. It makes me not be affectionate.

Rachel's next experience of sexual abuse occurred when she was ten years old. A fourteen-year-old babysitter molested Rachel, her brother, and her girlfriend. These incidents occurred from six to ten times over a period of a year.

He was our babysitter for a long time. When my girlfriend spent the night, he wanted us to undress and take our clothes off and do things to each other. We wouldn't do these things so he tied us up in the shower with my mom's nylons. He tied our wrists together, then tied our hands to the shower. We were there for about an hour.

He showed my brother and me pornographic pictures. After we refused to do it [have sex] he would barricade us in the bathroom and make us watch him jerk off. He also made us touch him. (Where?) On his genitals. He'd show us pictures and he'd demonstrate a hard-on for us so we'd know what it was. He made fun of my brother because he was so little.

Sometimes he would dress up in my mom's clothes. He'd take us out and do other stuff we weren't supposed to do. (Did he attempt intercourse?) No, but one time he asked me to open my mouth wide so he could put his penis in. I refused. Then he'd lock us in the bathroom. He must have known we wouldn't do it, so maybe he was into punishing us. He was only fourteen. (Did he threaten you verbally?) Yes, he said, "If you don't do this, then I'll do something to you." If we said no, then he'd lock us up in the bathroom with him or he'd tie us up.

(How did it end?) After the time my girlfriend and I were tied up, we went to her house and she told her mother, and her mother told mine. We got a new babysitter after that. (Was the experience reported?) I think so, but I don't know for sure. I think there was some confrontation my mom had with his mom. Then he moved and we also moved.

(Upset?) Extremely upset. (Effect on your life?) Some effect. It totally upset my life. My mom was so angry at finding the stockings. My girlfriend's mother was sympathetic but my mom was angry at having to quit her job. And she was mad at me; she thought I'd provoked it.

That was my first real exposure to sex in a way that I couldn't ignore—sex as an impersonal act where not all the people are consenting. A sick feeling and a memory of the pornographic pictures stayed with me for a long time. (Other effects?) Because of being tied up, I don't like to wear bracelets. Also I guess his having that power and control over me might have made me more passive around men after that, because I was afraid of saying no and then being tied up—bonded. I get angry now at porn pictures of women being tied up and enjoying it.

(Has pornography had any effect on your ideas or feelings about sex?) Yes. This was my first exposure to them. The babysitter showed me eight-by-ten glossy photos of people fucking. I felt repulsed and that it was ugly and wrong. I didn't want to grow up and have to do it. I thought about becoming a nun and I became more religious. I didn't feel good about my body. It took me a long time to feel comfortable with sex and certain sexual positions.

The interviewer noted that Rachel felt that her mother would not believe her because the perpetrator was the babysitter, and that's why she didn't tell her sooner. Although her mother did believe her, she apparently blamed Rachel for provoking the experience. So Rachel's lack of trust in her mother appears to have been sadly appropriate.

At the same time that Rachel was being molested by the babysitter, she was sexually abused when she was ten by a thirteen-year-old neighborhood boy. The incident occurred once.

He was a friend. We were playing hide and seek and I was hiding under the bed. He found me there and tried to get me to kiss him. Then he stopped trying to do that and he took my hand and put it on him when his pants were unzipped. That was it. He was always teasing me and trying to get me off in the bushes to teach me to french kiss. He made fun of my awkwardness and fear and offered himself as my education. It was a schizophrenic experience for me as I already knew a lot but I was trying to play innocent. (Upset?) Not very upset. (Effect on your life?) A little effect.

Rachel appears to have discounted her distress about this experience as well as the sexual abuse by her brother, which started when she was eleven, right after the experience with the babysitter. The incidents with her brother occurred from two to five times over a period of two months.

It wasn't exactly upsetting. It may have been more mutual than against my will. In the summer after sixth grade, I moved back home. My brother had started junior high, and he had changed a lot; we used to be really close. Because we had shared that experience with the babysitter, he knew that I knew as much about sex as he did. We were alone in the house a lot, and he would corner me and expose himself to me. A tension was always there when we were alone, like he'd say, "You know about it, so why don't we do it!" He made it impossible to forget the experiences [with the babysitter].

The most traumatic part was that any physical affection was taken by him as sexual. One time I was in shorts and a halter top. He started talking to me about sex, and then he lay on top of me and dry-humped me, saying "It doesn't feel bad. It doesn't hurt." He tried to convince me to take off my clothes, but I wouldn't; I found it morally wrong. Then my sister walked in.

My brother was contemptuous of me as a sexually permissive person. He must have believed my mother's attitude toward me—that I had brought it all on myself.

One time when my cousin was spending the night I went into their room in the morning to wake him and my brother up and they told me to shut the door. They both had erections and they wanted me to touch them. I left the room, but it was scary because he was in on it too. Their attitudes were "Don't play innocent. You've seen this before." But I didn't want to do it.

(Did anything else sexual ever happen with your brother?) I touched him on his genitals. (Did he touch you?) Yeah. (Where?) My genitals. (Else?) No. (How happen?) We were alone in the house a lot. (How did it end?) When my sister caught us.

(Upset?) Not very upset. (Effect on your life?) Some effect. It affected my relationship with my brother a lot. We never talk about it. I know he still has those attitudes toward me, because his relationship with our sister is different. I still feel his disrespect for me. It reinforced what Mom said, that I brought on the sexual things that happened to me. She called me a slut and I believed it. If my own brother wanted to have sex with me, she must be right. It made me uncomfortable with my first sexual feelings.

Not even being a fellow victim with her brother saved Rachel from her brother's double-standard judgment. Having been abused by the babysitter, she had lost her purity in her brother's eyes; therefore she had also lost her right to be respected and even her right to say no. The fact that a fellow victim who was also a member of her immediate family responded by sexually abusing her himself demonstrates how stigmatization can result in revictimization.

When Rachel was thirteen, her stepfather started touching her. This occurred from two to five times over a period of one year.

After I started my period, which was really traumatic because I didn't know what was going on, my mom made me read this book. It introduced me to a whole lot of taboos. I felt unclean. I was laying in bed and my dad came in. I told him I didn't want to grow up and become a woman. He started touching me and saying "You're going to grow breasts here, and pubic hair here," while touching me on my breasts and genitals. He told me not to be afraid, and he said I had to accept it. I felt comforted by him, but furious that I couldn't change things.

I slept with him when I had nightmares, and sometimes he'd hold me. It was cuddling up, not sexual. He and my mom wanted to be open about their bodies. He'd walk around naked in front of me, which embarrassed me. I knew not to be that way around him.

(How did it end?) My mom accused me of sleeping with him. (Upset?) Not very upset. (Effect on your life?) Some effect. I think it affected my relationship with him. And I guess it reinforced my feelings of my being a sexually promiscuous person. It seemed that accepting my sexuality meant accepting that someone would always be taking advantage of it. I really loved him, and I probably would have slept with him if it would have gotten me some approval.

Six years later, when Rachel was eighteen, she had a very narrow escape from a rape experience when she was hitchhiking.

I was hitchhiking in the evening and these guys offered me a ride. I said no, but I realized that if I didn't get in the car, they would come back for me, and I was scared to go off into the woods. They took me up a back road that did not go to the next town. They harassed me and said the car was broken. The guy that got out of the car took out a flashlight and a gun. I cried when I saw the gun. Then they became paternal toward me and took me to a friend's house. They pushed her [their friend] around and left for a case of beer. They left me on her couch, and one of them tried to kiss me on his way out. I felt scared and threatened. Their friend said that if they came back she couldn't protect me, so she drove me thirty miles away from her place and left me bus money. (Was there any further physical contact?) Aside from one of them trying to kiss me, it was all overtones and threats.

(Upset?) Not very upset. (Effect on your life?) A great effect. The friend's caring really meant a lot to me, and I felt I was a good person compared to them.

Even though Rachel came so close to being raped, she said that she was not very upset by the incident, and she described all the effects in positive terms. However, it is understandable that someone who has been abused so often can be touched and grateful when someone is unexpectedly kind toward them.

Rachel described another narrow escape.

It was a similar situation. I was walking with a friend and a car pulled over. A man and a woman offered us a ride. The man was driving but while the car was moving, they switched places. They were talking about having fun, and the man picked up a gun and aimed it at me. They were drunk and out of it, so we were able to assert ourselves and they let us out of the car.

On being asked whether she had ever been upset by anyone trying to get her to do what they'd seen in pornographic pictures, movies, or books, Rachel mentioned her husband. She also said that her husband had raped her more than twenty times over a period of two years. She was twenty-one years old when he first raped her.

It was real hard for me to enjoy oral sex. I didn't want to do it with him but he made me. I would ask him, "Why are you making me do something I feel uncomfortable with?"

There were certain positions I didn't want to do. I'd tell him so and he'd get defensive. He would fuck me real fast and get it over with. I didn't like oral sex at all. I thought it was degrading and that he should respect my feelings but he'd force me to do it. He'd push my head down on top of him and hold it there. He made me do it because I was his wife. "It's your duty," he said.

He'd be drunk and not affectionate. When I didn't want to have sex, he'd do it anyway. Once he wanted to have anal intercourse. I didn't want to so he held me down and did it. He didn't care that it hurt. When I was in pain—when sex was painful—he didn't care. (How did it end?) I left him.

(Upset?) Extremely upset. (Effect on your life?) A great effect. I don't ever want to get married again. I was very untrusting of men for a long time, and very afraid of physical violence. For a long time I didn't want to have any sex with anyone. I went through a long period of celibacy after I left him. I feel like I want to be in control of my sexual experiences. I've become real self-centered about my sexuality, real protective of my sexual space, refusing to let myself be somebody else's sexual object.

(Other physical violence?) Yes, right before I left him. We had just come from seeing a marriage counselor whom I'd been seeing alone. He'd been making excuses for not going, but he finally went with me. I was bewildered at his anger, as *I* was the one who was angry. When we got home, he grabbed me and pushed me out of the car. We were on the sidewalk and he was sitting on my chest, punching me and beating my head on the sidewalk with my hair. I was screaming. Then he left and ran off.

We had many steps to the house and he finally came back to help me up them. He was sorry and gentle by then.

Rachel said her husband's physical violence toward her occurred from two to five times over a two-and-one-half-year period. Aside from her experience with the babysitter when she was ten years old, Rachel reported three other unwanted sexual experiences with authority figures. She said that the first one occurred with a "higher-up in the church."

> I was at an interview and I needed him to recommend me. He asked a lot of sexual questions which humiliated me.
>
> One of my employers kept making me interview over and over. He implied that if I was looser with him he would hire me, but I never gave in. I talked to other waitresses and learned that he did the same thing to them. (Was there any physical contact?) No, it was just innuendos.
>
> Another time a bartender-employer gave me a hard time. He said if I would be friendlier he'd make it easier for me. (Was there any physical contact?) Nothing more than that.

Finally, Rachel reported two additional experiences of rape, once by a stranger and once by her boyfriend.

Even though Rachel described herself as "not very upset" by her stepfather's touching her, the effects she described were in fact considerable. Her feelings of being a whore and her belief that being sexual meant being taken advantage of were reinforced and likely contributed to the damage already done by her earlier experiences. Rachel was able to acknowledge that because she loved her stepfather and wanted his approval, she probably would have had intercourse with him if he had initiated it. This statement provides an important insight into a common consequence of child sexual victimization, particularly multiple sexual victimizations: The child (and/or the woman she becomes) often finds it difficult to say no when she doesn't want sex. She becomes accustomed to seeing sex as a commodity that, on the one hand, is her most valued asset to males but, on the other hand, is the cause of her being devalued.

Although both Rachel and Dorothy were blamed for being sexually victimized as children—Dorothy's aunt beat her and Rachel's mother treated her like a slut—their ways of coping with their many traumatic experiences were very different. Dorothy totally rejected sex and became frigid. Rachel internalized her mother's and brother's view that she was a slut. Her case illustrates the trauma of blame as much as it shows the trauma of sexual abuse itself. Rejected by her mother and emotionally needy, Rachel would have slept with her stepfather if it could have gotten her his approval. And, in general, she became "passive around men" and "afraid of saying no."

We also see how Rachel's brother used his knowledge of her prior victimization to sexually abuse her himself. Rachel herself became unclear about what she did and didn't want. Of her obviously traumatic revictimization by her brother, she said: "It wasn't exactly upsetting. It may have been more mutual than against my will."

Holly Jones

At the time of the interview, Holly Jones was a thirty-year-old white woman and mother of three children who was separated from her husband. She had been to high school but did not graduate. When interviewed, she was working part time as a cashier. The interviewer reported that Holly became progressively more withdrawn and pained as she recounted her many experiences of sexual abuse. Her first experience occurred when she was four years old and her fifty-year-old stepgrandfather started fondling her. He repeated this abuse from two to five times over a five-year period.

He took me out in the barn and tried to get me to play with him. Also, a few years later when I was asleep, he came in and started playing with my female organs. I woke up and started yelling. (Did anything else sexual occur with him?) Not that I can remember. (What ended it?) I started getting older and he realized he couldn't get away with it. I told my mother and she confronted him.

(Upset?) Not very upset at the time. (Effect on your life?) A great effect. It didn't go far, but it scared me. I think he could have been doing that with other little girls. I stay away from dirty old men. I guess if I ever have any female children I'll try to keep them away from older men.

Holly's assertiveness in yelling at her stepgrandfather and telling her mother is striking. The fact that her mother confronted him is also a positive aspect of her experience, but it didn't prevent a series of later revictimizations. When Holly was thirteen she was attacked by a stepuncle whom she described as her mother's foster sister's husband. She was living with him and her aunt at the time, and economically dependent on them. He was forty-seven or forty-eight then.

We lived in the country. I was in high school then. One night he picked me up after a school dance, and all of a sudden he pulled off the road and started kissing and grabbing me. I slapped him real hard and he stopped. He never tried it again. (Did he touch your breasts?) Yes, and he was trying to fondle my body, grabbing me all over. (Did he touch your genitals?) No. After I said I'd tell my aunt, he stopped. (Did he attempt intercourse?) No, but I think that's what he had in mind.

(Upset?) Very upset, because I was just starting to understand what sex was about. I was also upset because he was a relative. (Effect on your life?) No effect. I haven't thought about it in years.

Holly's next experience of sexual assault occurred when she was seventeen. She was raped by two men in their twenties who were strangers to her.

I had run away from home and I was out walking when two guys stopped and asked if I'd like to go for a ride. After I got in the car they turned off the road, and one grabbed me and held me down while the other one did it. When he'd finished the first one held me down while the other one did it. Then they drove me back to town. (So they raped you?) Uh-huh. [Holly nodded.] (Upset?) Very upset. (Effect on your life?) A little effect. It was upsetting, but I got over it. I didn't resist; I knew they'd kill me if I did. It didn't affect me till the next time. It's getting so it's like an everyday thing.

After this experience of rape, there appears to have been six years of freedom from sexual assault for Holly, or at least freedom from sexual assault severe enough to warrant a separate questionnaire. When she was twenty-three years old she had a sexual experience with her twenty-seven-year-old brother.*

Eight years ago I went to visit him in another city. He took me out drinking and we got drunk. Later he had me up on a table and he took my clothes off. I was drunk and laughing. I don't think we did anything. I don't remember if I stopped him or he stopped himself. (What was his intention?) I think in his drunken stupor he thought I was some tramp off the street, and yes, he was trying to have sex with me. (Did anything else sexual happen with him?) No, except when we were children. I was ten when my brother had this thing of putting ice cream on his penis and telling us to lick it off, which we wouldn't do. It was kind of funny. I don't know how many times he did it.

(Upset?) Very upset. It still bothers me because I don't actually know if he did anything or not. (Effect on your life?) A little effect, though in my own mind it bothers me a lot.

Three years later, when Holly was twenty-six, she was gang-raped by six or seven strangers in their thirties. She said that she was separated at the time and was living on welfare.

All I know is that I was walking across this field and when I came to, I was in the backseat of a car with a guy on top of me. He hit me again, and when I came to I was at these people's house where I was staying. (You were raped?) Yes. I found out later that there was a group of six or seven of them. It could have been any or all of these guys who did it. (Did they use verbal threats?) I don't know. I was knocked out. They clubbed me with a heavy blunt object. I also found out later who they were.

(Was this reported to the police?) Yes, the nurse who took care of me where I went to get my head wound treated called the police. (What happened as a result of the report?) I saw one of the guys later, but no arrests were made.

(Upset?) Extremely upset, especially with the police. (Effect on your life?) Some effect. It taught me not to go to the police with a problem. If I saw somebody being murdered right here I wouldn't call the police because they'd say I had something to do with it.

*Since Holly was an adult when this incident occurred, it is not included in our quantitative analyses of incestuous abuse.

Holly, who had been married four times, was raped by her third husband. Although she was generally unwilling to talk about this experience, the interviewer recorded the following information:

Holly explained that she had married her third husband without knowing him well. He had kept her locked in the apartment for five weeks, raping her repeatedly. She also referred to being tied up by him and to the use of whips. It had obviously been extremely painful to her and when we got to this part of the interview all she would say was: "It happened day and night for five weeks. I don't want to talk about it any more."

Holly also referred to her experience with this husband in answer to the question on pornography about being asked to do something seen in pornography. "Yes," she replied, "my third husband tied me up against my will."

Holly described being beaten by another husband more than fifty times over a period of eight months.

He used to beat me up and push me down the stairs. He busted every rib on my left side when I was four months pregnant. That was before I married him. He threatened to kill me if I didn't marry him. I used to hide from him; I'd sleep in the attic or cellar, or under the stairs. I'd also run away. Then he'd be nice for a while.

Holly said that she was not subjected to rape or other physical abuse in her other two marriages.

When she was thirty, a few months prior to the interview Holly was raped again. The rapist was a stranger in his teens.

It happened right around the corner from where I live. Some black guy pulled a knife on me and put it to my throat. He raped me for three and a half hours. He also tied me up. (Did he use verbal threats?) Yes. Before, after, and during the rape. He had his knife to my throat. I finally convinced him to put the knife down. At leaving he said something like if I ever did anything about it, be sure to do it right. I took it to mean that if I reported him, or tried to have him killed and failed, he'd kill me. I see him on the street every day. He came up to me a couple of months ago and asked me if I was a working girl. I said no.

(Upset?) Extremely upset. I was even more upset when I realized that he lives in my neighborhood. (Effect on your life?) A great effect. It scares me to death because I see him almost every day that I go out. I saw him only today. So I haven't been going out much. But it wouldn't do much good to report him. He'd just get out on bail or something and come after me. He's a psycho. He's really going to hurt somebody.

Holly was raped again by another stranger just weeks before the interview. He was in his forties.

I was hitchhiking and he was driving. He pulled a gun on me. I was found by the side of the road and taken to the hospital. He beat me so bad that I lost my baby. That's what they said at the hospital. He hit me with the gun. (Did he use verbal threats?) Yes, he said he was going to kill me if I didn't do what he wanted. (Was this reported to the police?) Yes. (What happened as a result of the report?) Nothing. I don't know if they even wrote down the report. I was semiconscious at the time.

(Upset?) Extremely upset. It killed my baby. (Effect on your life?) I can't say; it only happened a few weeks ago. I don't hitchhike anymore.

In answer to the question about unwanted sexual advances by authority figures, Holly reported an experience with a policeman.

I had heard a lot about this cop who would come on to girls and if you didn't stop him right away he'd go all the way. So, when he came on to me, I turned him off right away. (Did he come on verbally or physically?) Just verbally, to me.

When asked which of all her experiences of sexual assault was the most upsetting, she replied: "The most recent one."

The interviewer commented that Holly "looks as though she has had a very hard life. There's a lot of bitterness and pain in her voice and eyes. By the time we got to the questions about her husband, she was quiet and tense and staring off into space."

In answer to a question about the ways in which sexual assault affects her behavior, Holly replied: "I don't go out at night. I often don't go out in the day. I don't go out alone, and I take a cab rather than a bus. I call a friend with a car when I have to go three or four blocks." Holly also described herself as "very worried" about her children being the victims of sexual assault.

At the end of the interview, the interviewer noted that what Holly had told her was "hard to believe, not because I distrust her, but because it's too much to take in. But," the interviewer added, "I do think her reporting is accurate."

Unlike Dorothy, whose devastation by her multiple experiences of sexual abuse appeared to be cumulative, Holly seemed to become numb and to discount some of the less traumatic experiences. For example, about her rape by two strangers when she was seventeen, she said it only had "a little effect" on her, even though she believed they'd kill her if she resisted. "It didn't affect me till the next time," she said. "It's getting so it's like an everyday thing." Similarly, she described a gang-rape involving six or seven strangers when she was twenty-six as having only "some effect."

Holly finally gave up hitchhiking after being raped by a stranger a few months prior to the interview. This means that she was still hitchhiking in early 1978—when most women had long since accepted that it is an extremely dangerous method of transportation. Perhaps Holly's willingness to place herself in such a risky situation despite numerous previous rapes reflects the low self-regard so common among victims of repeated sexual abuse. Women who place or find themselves in risky situations in the predatory world in which we live are quite likely to be raped. This does not, of course, mean they *want* to be raped, or that they don't mind it. It means that their self-esteem may be so damaged that they don't feel they deserve their own loving self-protection. This, in turn, can result in repeated victimizations, each one of which can undermine a woman's self-esteem still further.

Some victims of repeated sexual abuse do not live to tell their stories. Others rarely have the opportunity to tell them. Those who do tell often get little sympathy. The extent to which some women's lives can be ravaged by repeated sexual assaults is difficult for many people to take in. The typical response is that the victim must be doing something to invite all this abuse. Even those people who have learned not to blame the one-time victim are often less understanding of the victim of multiple attacks. It is hoped that this chapter, by revealing both the prevalence of multiple victimization and some of the dynamics involved, will contribute to ending all forms of blaming victims of sexual assault.

13

Some Long-term Effects of Incestuous Abuse

Since most knowledge about incestuous abuse prior to our community survey has been based on cases that have come to the attention of therapists or other authorities, we will begin by evaluating how similar or different incest victims look from these two perspectives. To this end a comparison was made between Judith Herman's sample of 53 women outpatients who participated in short-term therapy groups for incest victims at a clinic in the Boston area and the 152 incest victims identified in our survey (Herman, Russell, and Trocki 1985).*

As can be seen in table 13–1, the abuse histories of the patient group differed markedly from those in our survey. The types of experiences generally described as least traumatic by our respondents were rarely found in Herman's patient group, while the types of histories judged to be most traumatic in our survey group were common. For example, a much higher proportion of the patient group reported incestuous involvement with a father or stepfather, violent abuse, and abuse of long duration. Women in the patient group were also more likely to report abuse by more than one incest perpetrator. In addition, the mean age of onset of incestuous abuse in the patient group was considerably lower than in our survey.

Although the differences between the groups are apparent by inspection, no formal analysis of the significance of these differences was attempted because the differences in methods of selection and demographic composition of the two populations do not permit statistical comparison.

It may be remembered that incest victims identified in our survey were significantly more likely than women who had never been incestuously abused to be divorced or separated at the time of the interview, to be

---

*Sections of this chapter were written for a coauthored paper by Judith Herman, Karen Trocki, and I (1985).

TABLE 13–1

Abuse Histories of Incest Victims: Patient Versus Survey Group *

	Patient Group (%) (N = 53)	Survey Group (%) (N = 152)
Perpetrator		
Father	75	28
Brother	26	13
Uncle	11	30
First cousin	2	20
More than one relative	23	16
Age of Onset		
5 or younger	30	11
6–9	30	19
10–13	21	41
14 or older	11	29
Unknown	8	0
Average age in years	8.2	11.2
Duration		
Less than 6 months	8	63
6 months–2 years	19	18
Over 2 years	51	19
Unknown	22	0
Degree of Force or Violence		
None	37	65
Force	40	31
Violence	23	3

*The percentages for these two groups do not equal one hundred because many victims were abused by more than one kind of relative.

younger at first childbearing, and to have defected from the religion with which they were raised. What other differences emerge—if any—when we differentiate between incest experiences according to the degree of trauma reported?

Since it is the most traumatized incest victims in our community sample that are most comparable with the kinds of incest victims seen by clinicians, it will be interesting to see if our respondents who reported extreme trauma as a result of incest victimization suffered from more negative long-term effects than those who reported less trauma. Our analysis in this section will focus on the 152 incest victims rather than the 187 experiences with different relatives.

Before analyzing possible effects, however, we will see whether or not any relationship exists between the degree of trauma reported and the race or ethnic identity of the victims. Once again, for simplicity, we shall report the dichotomized form of the trauma variable unless this conceals findings of interest.

Incest Victim's Race or Ethnicity
and Degree of Trauma

It turns out that there is a statistically significant relationship between the race or ethnicity of incest victims and the degree of trauma reported. Eighty-three percent of Latina incest victims reported extreme or considerable trauma compared with 79 percent of Afro-American victims, 50 percent of Asian victims, 49 percent of white victims, and 71 percent of incest victims from other race or ethnic groups (significant at 0.05 level). What might explain these findings?

Other data from our survey indicate that white women report more experiences of incestuous abuse than Afro-American women that qualify as least severe, suggesting that white women may have been more willing to report milder experiences of abuse to our interviewers than Afro-American women were. However, differential reporting thresholds appear to be only a partial explanation, at best. It may also be that incest carries a greater social stigma in certain racial or ethnic groups, which could add to the trauma of the experience. Or it could be that women who were living in more stressed circumstances at the time of the interview recalled their past experiences as more traumatic.*

Psychologist Gail Wyatt was the first researcher to design a large-scale community study to explore similarities and differences in the prevalence and responses to child sexual abuse of Afro-American and white women. Her findings are based on a nonclinical probability sample of 248 women aged eighteen to thirty-six years. While her data are not limited to experiences of incestuous abuse, they do include these experiences.

Wyatt (1984) reported that there were no statistically significant differences in the short-term effects of child sexual abuse for white and Afro-American women (p. 14). However, she found that "a greater percentage of white women than Afro-American women reported no lasting effects," and "a greater percentage of Afro-American women than white women reported being less trustful and more cautious" as a result of child sexual abuse (p. 17). In general, Wyatt came to the following conclusion about the particular impact of child sexual abuse on Afro-American women:

Afro-American women tended to seek more internal reasons, such as their physical development, as the cause for their victimization. . . . This finding, along with Afro-American women's highly negative reaction to abuse, their tendency not to disclose incidents as often to nuclear family members or to police and to disclose

*This hypothesis was suggested by Judith Herman. Personal communication, 1985.

abuse to extended family members, some of whom have been found to abuse them, place Afro-American women at risk for more severe consequences of abuse. (Pp. 21–22)

Research data on Latina and Asian women that might help shed light on this issue—as well as many others—are unfortunately not yet available.

Incest Victim's Marital Status and Degree of Trauma

Those who consider a woman's decision to marry to be a sign of psychological health will be particularly challenged by our findings that the incest victims who reported the most severe trauma were more likely to marry. Specifically, 78 percent of the victims who reported extreme or considerable trauma had married compared to 62 percent of those who reported only some or no trauma. This relationship was statistically significant at < 0.05 level. However, when finer distinctions are made between the degrees of trauma reported, incest victims who reported only some trauma were the most likely of all four groups never to marry. Almost half of them (47 percent) remained single (see table 13–2).

Table 13–2 also reveals a significant and perfectly linear relationship between the outcome of marriage and the degree of trauma reported. Thirty-seven percent of victims who reported extreme trauma were divorced or separated at the time of the interview, compared with 31 percent of those who reported considerable trauma, 22 percent of those who reported some trauma, and only 7 percent of those who reported no trauma.

Maternal Status and Degree of Trauma

Interestingly, the victims who reported extreme or considerable trauma as a result of the incest were much more likely to have raised one or more children than those who reported some or no trauma. Sixty-six percent of those reporting more trauma were mothers compared with 43 percent of those reporting less trauma (this relationship is significant at < 0.01 level).*

*Stated another way, the victims who were most traumatized by their incest experience had raised a significantly higher mean number of children (0.86) than those who were less traumatized (0.59). (This difference in means is statistically significant at < 0.05 level.)

TABLE 13–2

Incest Victims' Marital Status and Degree of Trauma Reported

Marital Status	Extreme Trauma		Considerable Trauma		Some Trauma		No Trauma	
	%	N	%	N	%	N	%	N
Married	35	19	39	10	25	9	56	15
Widowed	7	4	4	1	6	2	11	3
Divorced or separated	37	20	31	8	22	8	7	2
Never married	20	11	27	7	47	17	26	7
Total	99	54	101	26	100	36	100	27

Missing observations: 9.
Statistically significant at < 0.05 level.

However, there was no relationship between the degree of trauma and the age at which a woman first bore a child.

The fact that the more severely traumatized incest victims were more likely to marry at some time in their lives might explain why they were also more likely to have raised one or more children. But it may also be that the more traumatic experiences of incest increase the likelihood that the victim will accept the traditional female role of both marriage and motherhood. Indeed, there was a statistically significant relationship between the degree of trauma and traditionality (at < 0.05) (see chapter 9 for a description of the traditionality measure). The victims who reported extreme trauma were more traditional than those who reported considerable trauma or some trauma (with mean scores of 2.8, 3.3, and 3.5, respectively). However, the relationship was a curvilinear one; victims who reported no trauma were also more traditional than those reporting some or considerable trauma (with a mean score of 2.6).

Social Class of Victims Later in Life and Degree of Trauma

It may be remembered that we found no relationship between incest victimization and the victim's social class later in life. (See chapter 9 for a thorough discussion of this finding.) But does a relationship emerge between social class and incest victimization when we differentiate experiences that were rated more or less traumatic? Data on the following measures of social class will be presented: the education and occupational status of the victim; the education and occupational status of the victim's husband if she was married at the time of the interview; and the victim's total household income one year prior to the interview.

INCEST VICTIM'S EDUCATION AND DEGREE OF TRAUMA

While there was no statistically significant relationship between the education of incest victims and the degree of trauma reported, an interesting and quite linear trend is evident. Those reporting the least trauma were more likely to have attended college (but not necessarily to have graduated from college). Specifically, 74 percent of those reporting no trauma went to college, while 69 percent of those reporting some trauma, 65 percent of those reporting considerable trauma, and 63 percent of those reporting extreme trauma went to college.

Similarly, 15 percent of the incest victims who reported extreme trauma never graduated from high school compared with 7 percent of the incest victims who reported no trauma and 8 percent of those reporting some or considerable trauma.

INCEST VICTIM'S OCCUPATIONAL STATUS AND DEGREE OF TRAUMA

When the occupational status of incest victims at the time of the interview is used as the measure of social class, the relationship between social class and trauma is statistically significant. As can be seen in table 13–3, just over one-third (34 percent) of the victims who reported extreme trauma had lower-class occupations, compared with only 4 percent of those reporting considerable trauma, 6 percent of those reporting some trauma, and 24 percent of those reporting no trauma. Similarly, only 21 percent of those reporting extreme trauma had upper-middle-class occupations, a lower percentage than those reporting the three lesser degrees of trauma.

However, the relationship between these two variables is a curvilinear one. Those reporting no trauma are more similar to those reporting extreme trauma in that fewer have upper-middle-class occupations and more have lower-class occupations than women reporting the intermediate categories of trauma. The reason for this curvilinear relationship is unclear. Whatever the explanation, this analysis reveals that extreme trauma may have a depressing effect on social class later in life.

HUSBAND'S OCCUPATIONAL STATUS, EDUCATION, AND DEGREE OF TRAUMA

Although the relationship between the degree of reported trauma and the education and occupational status of the incest victims' husbands is not statistically significant, a clear trend is evident in a direction identical with

TABLE 13–3

Incest Victims' Occupational Status and Degree of Trauma Reported

Occupational Status	Extreme Trauma		Consider- able Trauma		Some Trauma		No Trauma	
	%	N	%	N	%	N	%	N
Upper middle class	21	11	32	8	42	15	28	7
Middle class	45	24	64	16	53	19	48	12
Lower class	34	18	4	1	6	2	24	6
Total	100	53	100	25	101	36	100	25

Missing observations: 13.
Significant at <0.01 level.

that just described for the respondent's own occupational status, including the curvilinear relationship. Of the victims who reported extreme trauma, 39 percent had husbands with lower-class occupations compared to 0 percent for those reporting considerable trauma, 11 percent for those reporting some trauma, and 23 percent for those reporting no trauma.

Similarly, of the incest victims who reported extreme trauma, only 53 percent had husbands who had some college education, compared with 78 percent of those reporting considerable trauma and 67 percent of those reporting some or no trauma. And while 16 percent of the victims who reported extreme trauma had husbands who had not graduated from high school, none of the victims who reported lower levels of trauma were married to husbands with so little formal education.

The numbers for our analysis of the education and occupational status of the victim's husbands are small because many were not married at the time of the interview; this may be a factor in their lack of statistical significance. When the incest victims who reported extreme trauma are compared with victims who reported a lesser degree of trauma, the difference in the educational status of their husbands becomes statistically significant at <0.001 level.

These findings on the education and occupational status of husbands are consistent with the findings based on those of the victim. Taken together, these four variables suggest that whether or not a woman is currently married, a very traumatic experience of incest in childhood may have an impact on her social class status such that she ends up in a lower social class than those women who reported less traumatic incest experiences.

INCEST VICTIM'S HOUSEHOLD INCOME IN 1977 AND DEGREE OF TRAUMA

Although the figures are not statistically significant, table 13–4 reveals once again that the most traumatized group of incest victims had the lowest household income in the year prior to the study. Only 22 percent had a household income of $15,000 or more compared with 44 percent, 38 percent, and 46 percent for the other three less traumatized groups. Similarly, 41 percent of the women reporting extreme trauma had a household income of less than $7,500 a year prior to the interview, close to twice the percentage of women reporting no trauma (23 percent).

This difference in economic well-being at the time of the interview becomes statistically significant at < 0.05 level when the three lesser degrees of trauma are combined and compared with extreme trauma.

RELIGIOUS DEFECTION AND DEGREE OF TRAUMA

Although incest victims were significantly more likely than women who had never been incestuously abused to defect from their religion of upbringing if they were Protestants or Catholics, there was no significant relationship between the defection rate and degree of trauma. The only trend evident was for Catholics: 65 percent of those who were extremely traumatized by incest had rejected Catholicism at the time of the interview compared with 50 percent of Catholics who reported one of the three lesser degrees of trauma.

SUMMARY AND DISCUSSION

Of the five different indicators used to evaluate social class status at the time of the interview, three were significantly related to the degree of trauma: the victim's occupational status, her husband's educational status, and her total household income at the time of the interview. In addition, the other two measures of social class revealed trends consistent with the three that reached statistical significance. More specifically, our data show that incest victims who reported extreme trauma held significantly lower-status occupations in their adult lives than the victims who reported lesser

TABLE 13-4

Total Household Income in 1977 and Degree of Trauma Reported

Household Income	Extreme Trauma		Considerable Trauma		Some Trauma		No Trauma	
	%	N	%	N	%	N	%	N
$7,499 or less	41	21	24	6	38	13	23	6
$7,500–$14,999	37	19	32	8	24	8	31	8
$15,000 or more	22	11	44	11	38	13	46	12
Total	100	51	100	25	100	34	100	26

Missing observations: 16.
Not statistically significant at < 0.05 level.

degrees of trauma. They were also less likely to have attended college, were more likely to be married to husbands with less education and lower occupational status than less traumatized women, and reported a lower household income for the year prior to the interview.

Although positive correlation does not prove causation, it seems reasonable to hypothesize on the basis of these findings that extremely traumatic incest experiences have a depressing effect on the socioeconomic status of a disproportionate number of their victims.

Our survey shows that the most traumatized group of incest victims were more inclined to marry at some time in their lives, but they were also more likely to be divorced or separated at the time of the interview. Indeed, victims who reported extreme trauma were over five times more likely than incest victims who reported no trauma to be divorced or separated when interviewed in 1978.

The more traumatized incest victims were also more likely to raise one or more children. In general, they were significantly more traditional than incest victims who reported considerable or some trauma, but they were not more traditional than those who reported no trauma.

It is important to emphasize that although we will repeatedly consider the possible effect of various kinds of incestuous abuse experiences on marital stability, we do not consider that it is better to be married than divorced or single. One's evaluation of which is the better state is a personal value judgment, both for the evaluator and for the victim. Although victims were not asked how they felt about their marital status, a few volunteered that they were distressed about not being able to find a satisfactory marriage partner. A few others mentioned that they felt they had spent a richer life of work and travel than they would have been able to enjoy had they married. In a couple of these cases, the woman was quite aware of a connection between her singleness and the incest experience.

Similarly, we do not consider religious disaffection to be negative, though we are fully aware that some people do.

Finally, some research suggests that a relationship exists between child sexual abuse and homosexuality. Since we did not ask our respondents what their sexual preference was and only a very few volunteered that they were lesbian or bisexual, our survey data cannot answer this question. However, it may be that some or many of the incest victims who never married (as well as some of those who later divorced or even stayed married) are lesbians. Some data outside of our survey, as well as clinical evidence, suggest that one response to the trauma of incest is to turn away from heterosexuality and to embrace a lesbian orientation and life style. If such a relationship between incest and lesbianism exists, given the prevalence of homophobia in this society, this would indeed be evidence of the trauma of incest. Whether or not this outcome is viewed positively or negatively, however, is entirely a matter of opinion.

Objective Measures of Long-term Effects

Our analysis of the trauma of incest in this chapter has focused so far on the victims' subjective evaluation of the consequences of the abuse. Here we will start by determining whether or not a number of negative life experiences were related to incestuous abuse. These are referred to as objective measures because the victims did not necessarily perceive any connection between them and their incest experience.

A nine-factor negative life experience scale was developed (see method of scoring at the bottom of table 13–5). It included three measures of repeated victimization, three measures of instability in marital and reproductive life, two measures of downward social mobility, and one measure of poverty at the time of the interview. These nine factors were chosen because they were the only life experiences about which we had information that most people would agree represent negative experiences.

The first question to be addressed is whether or not there is a relationship between incest victimization and scores on the scale regardless of trauma. As already mentioned, when asked to specify how their experiences of incestuous abuse had affected their lives, many victims spontane-

TABLE 13–5

Negative Life Experience Scale

---

1. Serious sexual assault (at least one experience other than incestuous abuse)
2. Marital rape
3. Wife beating
4. Early childbearing (at the age of 19 or younger)
5. Motherhood without marriage (the woman had never married but had raised one or more children)
6. Separation or divorce
7. Poverty (a total household income below $7,500 at the time of the interview in 1978)
8. Downward social mobility (the woman had a lower occupational status than her mother)
9. Downward social mobility (the woman had a lower educational status than her mother)

Mean scores were obtained for each woman by making a simple count of one for each of the nine items on the scale, then dividing the total by the number of items for which pertinent information was available. Missing data or inapplicable items (such as, for example, marital rape or divorce for women who had never married) did not lower a woman's score.

The lowest score possible was 0, the highest 1.0. Women with scores at or above 0.39 were rated as having the worst outcomes, those with scores in the range of 0.23 to 0.38 as intermediate, and those with scores of 0.22 or below as having the best outcomes.

ously mentioned negative feelings about men, sex, or themselves. But few women made a direct connection between their childhood victimization and later life experiences such as adolescent pregnancy, marital separation or divorce, or repeated sexual victimization. Such experiences, however, were far more common among women who had been incestuously abused than among those who had not.

As can be seen in table 13–6, only 33 percent of the incest victims had scores on the negative life experience scale that fell into the best outcome range, compared to 59 percent of the women with no incest history. And whereas 30 percent of the incest victims had scores that placed them in the worst outcome category, only 13 percent of the women who had never been incestuously abused had a sufficient number of negative life experiences to place them in this group (significant at < 0.001 level).

Similarly, the mean score on the negative life experience scale was 0.31 for the incest victims in our survey compared with a mean score of 0.20 for women who had not been incestuously abused (significant at < 0.001).

Having established this highly significant relationship between incest victimization and scores on the negative life experience scale, it seems reasonable to hypothesize a causal connection between them. However, it must be remembered that the scale does not represent a complete inventory of negative experiences that might be related to a childhood history of incest. Psychological distress symptoms (e.g., nightmares, flashbacks, depression, or sexual dysfunction) were not included in the scale, nor were aspects of a psychiatric history such as suicide attempts, hospitalization, or drug or alcohol abuse. Moreover, the scale is clearly an artificial construct, since it gives equal weight to experiences that may have very different meaning and importance to each woman. However, the scale has the virtue of being entirely independent of either the respondent's or the interviewer's assessment of the respondent's psychological state, since it depends only on information about actual life events.

The second question to be addressed is whether or not there is a signifi-

TABLE 13–6

Outcomes on the Negative Life Experience Scale: Incest Victims Versus Nonincest Victims

Outcome	Incest Victims (N = 152) %	Nonincest Victims (N = 778) %
Best	33	59
Intermediate	37	28
Worst	30	13

Significant at < 0.001 level.

cant relationship between the subjective measures of trauma reported by the incest victims and their scores on the negative life experience scale. As can be seen in table 13–7, a highly significant relationship was evident. Fifty-two percent of the incest victims who suffered the worst outcomes reported extreme trauma as a result of their experiences compared to 23 percent of the incest victims who enjoyed the best outcomes (significant at < 0.01 level).

This positive correlation is important because it shows that subjective measures can be useful—even years later—as indicators of long-term negative life experiences.

When the trauma measure is differentiated into degree of upset and extent of long-term effects, a multiple regression analysis revealed that the best predictor of overall negative life experiences was the subjective long-term effects question. When differentiating the revictimization experiences from marriage and reproductive history and economic and downward mobility, the subjective measure of long-term effects was also the best predictor of revictimization, and upset was the best predictor of marriage and reproductive history; downward mobility and poverty were not predicted by either of these subjective measures.

At the end of chapter 10 the results were reported of a multiple regression analysis undertaken to determine which of nine characteristics of victims' incestuous experiences had the greatest weight in explaining the degree of subjective trauma reported. The five characteristics that were statistically significant, in order of importance, were the severity of the abuse in terms of the sex acts involved, whether the perpetrator was a father or some other relative, whether or not force was used, the age disparity between the victim and her relative, and the duration of the incestuous abuse. Are these same five characteristics also significantly related to scores on the negative life experience scale?

When the negative life experiences were broken down into three differ-

TABLE 13–7

Degree of Trauma Reported and Outcome of Incestuous Abuse

Degree of Trauma	Worst Outcome		Best Outcome	
	%	N	%	N
Extreme	52	27	23	13
Considerable	25	13	19	11
Some	15	8	28	16
None	8	4	30	17
Total	100	52	100	57

Significant at < 0.01 level.

ent factors—repeated victimization, marital and reproductive history, and downward mobility plus poverty—three significant relationships emerged. First, the five characteristics together were significantly associated with the three marital and reproductive factors (at < 0.05 level), although the severity of the incestuous abuse was the only one that was individually significant (at < 0.05 level). Second, the duration of the incest victimization was significantly related to revictimization (at < 0.03 level). And third the severity of the incestuous abuse was significantly related to the poverty and downward mobility factors (at < 0.05 level).

These regression analyses show that particular aspects of the incest experience, most notably the severity of the sexual violation, were related to long-term negative life outcomes. Additional victimization, however, was best predicted by the duration of the incestuous abuse. Given the enormous number of factors that shape people's adult lives, it is remarkable that any of the characteristics of the incestuous abuse were significantly related to these marital, economic, and revictimization experiences in the victims' adult years.

14

Incest Runaway:
A Case Study

Everything that's happened to me since in my life has been a
result somehow of that experience.—Jacqueline Bell, speaking
about her stepfather's sexual abuse of her

Jacqueline Bell's story, like the three described in chapter 12, is another
example of a life ravaged by sexual assault. She is one of two respondents
in our survey who was sexually abused by both her stepfather and her
biological father.

It is becoming increasingly well known that many girls and young
women who run away from home are incest victims. The repeated experiences of sexual abuse to which Jacqueline was subjected fit what is coming
to be recognized as the plight of many who become runaways. Her life
illustrates some of the dynamics offered in chapter 11 to explain revictimization. But most of all it illustrates the tragic dilemma of underage girls
whose healthy desire to leave an abusive home places them at great risk
of what appears to be an endless series of other abusive experiences. The
fact that they so often prefer to take their chances on the street rather than
return home is a testament to the extremity of their suffering in the families from which they flee.

At the time of the interview, Jacqueline was a twenty-year-old woman
who had never been married. She described her ethnicity as half white and
half Native American.

Jacqueline was uncomfortable and evasive when asked what her current
employment was, if any, and replied simply, "I don't do anything." She
had had some college education but had not graduated. She said that she
had worked less than half the time in the job market since she left school.

Her most consistent job had been as a gardener, and she reported an income of only $3,000 to $5,000 in the year prior to the survey.

In answer to a question regarding the ways in which her fear or her family's fear of sexual assault had affected her behavior before she turned fourteen, Jacqueline described a sexually repressive atmosphere in her family of origin.

My mother pounded into my brain that being a female made me vulnerable. She told me not to talk to strangers. (Did you?) Yes, but not as much as I would have otherwise. And it gave me a fear of sex in general. It was all hush hush [about sex] in my family. I was very sheltered until I was fourteen.

Jacqueline's previously sheltered childhood ended abruptly when her stepfather sexually abused her at age fourteen. He insisted on having intercourse with her more than twenty times over a period of six months. Since this was one of only four cases of incestuous abuse reported to the police, it was included in chapter 6.

Jacqueline selected the experience with her stepfather as the most upsetting of all her experiences of sexual abuse. After running away from home, she was attacked again while she was still only fourteen years old.

I was hitchhiking with my girlfriend. We were on the run. Two men picked us up and decided they weren't going to let us out of the car. They were going to have a little fun. They kept us in the car and tried to convince us we couldn't leave until we each took one of them. Then they started getting a little forceful, grabbing at us, trying to feel us, laying their hands on us. We were protesting. We said, "Let us out of here. We're not going to do anything with you." They didn't get too far because I had a knife under my pants leg, and I pulled it out and said, "Look, I'm tired! Will you let us out?" They bought it. They let us out. But it was very close.
(Were they attempting intercourse?) Yes, they said: "We want to fuck you." There's a certain look they get. They were talking between themselves, like "Which one you gonna take?" and saying what they wanted to do to us. Oral sex is what they wanted; you can't "get down" in a Volkswagen. (Did they use force?) They grabbed at us. That was about it. (Did they make threats?) They said they wouldn't let us out of the car until they got what they wanted. (Upset?) Not very upset. (Effect on your life?) A little effect.

Jacqueline's next experience of sexual assault during her fourteenth year occurred twice in the space of twenty-four hours. She described this perpetrator as a junkie. When asked which of the two experiences with this man she had found most upsetting, she replied:

The time in the shower. The whole time I'd been on the run I hadn't washed myself or my clothes. I was washing my body and my clothes in the shower but I couldn't do it in peace. He came in with no clothes on. He cornered me in the shower, pressed against me with his body, and tried to have sex with me. He got his penis between my legs, but I wouldn't let him in me. I don't know how I got out of it, but I did. (Did he use force?) Yes, he mauled me. He was holding me in place, pinning me, forcing me in different positions, holding me in a corner.

The other time he tried to force me to have intercourse on a bed. He was really stoned, really ripped. He made my girlfriend sleep on the floor, then tried to make love to me. He tried to force me to kiss him a lot. (How try to force?) He had his face all over me. (Did he attempt intercourse?) Yes, that's what he was doing. I got out of it by compromising. I told him I'd do it manually, but he was too stoned and he lost it anyway.

(How did it end?) I left his house. (Upset?) Somewhat upset. (Effect on your life?) A little effect.

Jacqueline soon found herself at the mercy of a "protector" who raped her from two to five times in the space of two weeks. She was still only fourteen years old.

It was somebody I was tripping around with. I was dependent on him. He was an ex-Hell's Angel and was very heavy. He said, "If you want to live in my house, you have to do what I say." (Could you describe the most upsetting time?) One time he came into my room at 5 A.M., woke me, and demanded sex. He jumped on top of me for half an hour. He was so heavy I couldn't breathe. He was all over me like Glad Wrap on a sandwich. I had no birth control so I was worried. Also, he was in poor health, and I'd seen him keel over several times, so I was scared that would happen. But what could I do? He physically forced me to give him a blow job. He pushed my head down on him. I couldn't hack that, oh, no! But I couldn't do anything about it. I was a runaway and I was dependent on his protection. I had to have *some* place to be!

(Did he use any verbal threats?) Yes, he said, "I'm gonna kick you out!" (Did he have a weapon?) He didn't need one. All he had to do was sit on me; he weighed that much! (How did it end?) I finally left. I asked him to drive me to my father's house and I turned myself in. I couldn't stand it. To leave my stepfather and walk right into that!

(Upset?) Very upset. (Effect on your life?) Some effect. It closed me up socially. It closed me up more and more to relating to men.

After moving in with her biological father, Jacqueline was raped by him when she was fifteen years old. The rapes occurred eleven to twenty times over a period of two or three months. Jacqueline answered the question about the most upsetting time as follows:

I was so numb that all the times were equally upsetting. The first time he woke me up at 5 A.M. and said, "Come on." He's a real cold person who never shows affection. He said, "It's about time your dad showed you some affection. Come over here and sit on my lap." I was fifteen years old and I knew what was coming. So I went into the bedroom with him and we did it. We had sex. (Intercourse?) Yes. He was constantly comparing me with my mother in sexual ways. He'd compare my genitals with my mother's. (Did he use physical force?) No, other than pulling me around and stuff. He was a really violent man with a bad temper. I was afraid of him. He is an alcoholic, as was my stepdad. My father doesn't take no for an answer. (Did he use physical force?) Yes, I didn't want to do it but he forced me to. (How did it end?) I don't know. I think I just avoided him and got distant. Maybe he started feeling guilty because he backed off too at the same time.

(Upset?) Somewhat upset. (Effect on your life?) Some effect. It constantly makes me feel I was taken advantage of *again,* but there was nothing I could do about it. It was one against one. He never really hurt me but it was unwanted. It doesn't really bother me that much now. I've always felt that I should feel worse about it than I do. Maybe I'm repressing a lot of deep and intense feelings about it but after all that's happened to me in my life, when I think about this experience, it really doesn't make me feel that bad.

The next person who sexually abused Jacqueline was also a relative. She was still fifteen years old at the time. She described this perpetrator as a foster uncle. She later explained that her foster grandmother, who lived across the street from her father, had adopted her. The thirty-year-old son of this woman was the person who sexually abused her.* Jacqueline explained, "Besides being related, I also babysat his children." This man sexually assaulted Jacqueline seven times over a period of one and a half years.

The first time he sweet-talked me a lot. And he threatened to tell my father some things I had done if I didn't cooperate with him, because I did a lot of shoplifting at that time. He took me into the bedroom and did his thing. (What do you mean?) He made love to me. (Was it vaginal intercourse?) Yeah. It wasn't really that bad. It was more of a mental thing. (Did he use any physical force?) No. He used that threat. It was blackmail. It happened seven times.

(How did it end?) My foster uncle lived across the street from my father, so I ran away. I put myself in a children's shelter. (Upset?) Not very upset. (Effect on your life?) Some effect. Well, it had a weird effect. At first it upset me because I was blackmailed into it. But after a year and a half it ended up being a pleasurable experience. I felt taken advantage of at first, but in the end I felt better about myself. He made me feel wanted, and not in a really used way. Out of all the lovers I've had, he was one of the best. [Jacqueline showed the interviewer a large framed photo of him.] He's not bad looking either, and he knew how to use his experience. He made me feel real good.

As happens so often with women who have been repeatedly abused from a young age, Jacqueline appears to have become so accustomed to severe abuse that she hardened herself to the less severe experiences. For example, she frequently described what appeared to be a frightening and degrading experience as having no or only a little effect on her life. And

*Whether this man should be considered a foster uncle or a much older brother by adoption is difficult to determine, so we placed him in the "Other" category.

finally, with her foster uncle, she evolved into seeing it as a positive, nonabusive experience.

Jacqueline's next experience of sexual abuse was by an acquaintance in his early thirties. This incident also occurred when she was fifteen years old. It happened once. She described this perpetrator as a movie director.

I was in his apartment one day, and he sort of physically fast-talked me. It's hard to describe what happened. He wanted to know how I'd be in this movie he was making. He wanted to see what I was like. (Did he use physical force?) Well, I felt physically threatened because he had a real bad temper and he displayed it a lot. He got mad at me for the slightest thing. (Did he use physical force?) It was more of a threatening type of situation. He threatened to hit me. He said he was a black belt in something, and I really felt physically threatened. He showed me some martial arts stuff. I never was sure whether he wanted to teach me or whether he was getting off on showing me his power, but I felt real threatened by him. (What did he do?) Oral sex. (Did he have a weapon?) He showed me a knife. And since he had a black belt in martial arts his hands and feet were weapons. (Upset?) Somewhat upset. (Effect on your life?) A little effect.

It appears from Jacqueline's description that this rapist may have been making a pornographic movie.

At the age of sixteen, Jacqueline reported an experience of attempted rape by her seventeen-year-old lover.

He was my boyfriend. I went over to his house, and we were listening to records, and he just didn't know how to ask or how to take no for an answer. I told him no when he asked. (Asked what?) "Do you want to fool around?" I said, "What kind of fool around?" He said, "Fuck fool around." I said, "No." Then he locked his door, turned the music up, and went through the typical rape scene. He took off his clothes and tore off my blouse. I was sitting on the bed trying to convince him to let me go to the bus stop. He was real drunk and I guess he didn't understand. (Then?) He pulled me down on the bed and he kept getting on top of me. He unbuttoned my pants, then ripped them open. He got my pants partway down and tried to have intercourse with me. But he couldn't do it. He couldn't get into me. I didn't let him. (How?) By holding his shoulders away from me and saying no. I ended up beating him up because he wasn't that big. (Did he fight back?) No, he was too surprised. He didn't expect that. He wouldn't understand verbal pleas, nor me pushing him away, nor anything else, so I had to lay in to him. (Upset?) Somewhat upset. (Effect on your life?) A little effect.

When Jacqueline was seventeen years old she was sexually abused by a male nurse during a stay in the hospital. She was institutionalized in a girls' group home at that time.

I was in my hospital bed and he [a male nurse] stayed in my room all the time. He checked my vital signs every half hour. Then one time he started feeling me all over. (Breasts? Genitals?) Yeah. I caught on what he was doing when he started to try to masturbate me. (Were you conscious?) I was semiconscious. I was heavily drugged. But I caught on and I kept moving and making noises to make him stop. Finally I flipped over in one big movement, yelling at the same time. He tried one more time to lay his hand on me; I moved a little more and he stopped. Then he pulled my nightgown back down.

(Did you report him to the police?) No, but I reported him to the hospital authorities. (What happened?) Nothing. They finally caught him doing it to someone else at another hospital and fired him.

(Upset?) Somewhat upset. (Effect on your life?) A great effect. It made me think about people in official positions—about what they can get away with, and that I was not believed. It made me feel really crazy to go to a hospital where you're supposed to get taken care of and to get sexually assaulted!

Since Jacqueline downplayed so many of her abusive experiences, it is interesting that she described this incident with the male nurse as having a great effect on her. Most of her other abusive experiences occurred within the context of intimate relationships. Perhaps she saw them as relatively untraumatic since none of them was as disturbing as the first one with her stepfather. In contrast, her experience with the male nurse was the first time she had been abused by an authority figure who was a stranger.

Another of Jacqueline's experiences was disqualified because, although it was unwanted, the man was not related to her and it was not forced. Nevertheless, it reveals that Jacqueline sometimes had difficulty refusing sex even when she didn't want it. This appears to be quite a common consequence of sexual abuse.

Jacqueline said the unwanted sexual experiences with a twenty-eight-year-old friend of her father's occurred twice over a period of a couple of months.

I was fifteen. It was the first day at my father's house after being on the run. I was sleeping on the floor, and he happened to be sleeping right next to me. He woke me up by feeling all over me though his wife was right next to me in bed. Then he tried to say that I had lured him into it. (Was it against your wishes?) Well, I knew it was wrong. I didn't want to do it because he was married. I liked him a lot and I wanted to please him, but I didn't want to have sex with him. (Did he actually force you to have intercourse?) Yeah. I mean, he knew what he wanted and he really wanted me to do it.

The second time he took me out to a shed. I made a compromise with him. I said I'd take care of him manually instead of having intercourse or oral sex. (Did you do that?) Yeah, I got him off manually, but I didn't want to. (Why did you do it if you didn't want to?) I don't know. It's real hard to say. I knew it wasn't right, but he mentally forced me by saying what good friends we were. (What did he actually do?) He had his hands all over me. (Did he use physical force?) No, not real force except he made me kiss him. That was the only real physical force that he used.

(How did it end?) I don't know. He just disappeared. He moved or his wife had

a baby or something. We just didn't see him again. (Were there verbal threats?)
No, not really. There was a hint of, well, why-are-you-so-seductive? type trip, and
calling on our friendship. (Upset?) Not very upset. (Effect on your life?) No effect.

Most readers will be struck by the number of experiences of sexual
abuse Jacqueline reported. Although this is not an uncommon history for
a runaway, the question remains: Why does this happen?

Many different factors combine to make female runaways extraordinarily vulnerable. First, they often have nowhere to go but the street,
where they easily become dependent on anyone who offers them food and
protection—even if unwanted sex is part of the bargain that they knowingly or unknowingly make. Second, it may be difficult for them to become
outraged at someone taking sexual advantage of their helplessness since
that is precisely what happened in their own homes. Third, they have few,
if any, choices. The fact that many runaway girls do not return home
despite the abuse they are often subjected to on the streets is a measure
of how much they hate what was happening to them at home. Fourth, their
socialization has often not prepared them to take care of themselves or to
successfully confront or avoid the predatory sexual behavior that many
males exhibit, whether they are peers or elders.

The first of these reasons—having nowhere else to go—applies equally
well to boys who run away from home because of abuse. The second and
third reasons—the difficulty of being outraged and having few alternatives
—also apply to boys who have been sexually abused, though current data
suggest that many more girls are sexually abused within the family than
are boys (e.g., Finkelhor 1979; Herman 1981). However, the fourth reason
—faulty socialization—definitely places females at a much greater disadvantage than males. Young boys do not have to worry about older women
hovering around bus stations with sexually exploitive or violent intentions
toward them; like girls, they *do* have to worry about older males, but even
here, they have often had more opportunity than girls to develop at least
some street wisdom and self-sufficiency. Indeed, as long as male sexuality
continues to be as exploitive as it is today, girls will continue to be more
vulnerable than boys.

Jacqueline, however, appeared to have a certain amount of street wisdom and a capacity and willingness to defend herself. For example, she
successfully intimidated the two men who threatened to rape her and her
girlfriend by pulling a knife on them; she was also successful in preventing
two would-be rapists from penetrating her and effectively defended herself physically against a man whom she described as a lover.

Although Jacqueline was more able to take care of herself than some
runaway girls are, her ability was far from sufficient to protect her from

the predatory world in which a young girl on the streets usually lives. And her relatives were no less predatory than the strangers and acquaintances and boyfriends she encountered. Repeated experiences of sexual abuse seem to undermine a girl's or a woman's capacity to avoid further victimization. We saw, for example, that Jacqueline was willing to forgive her foster uncle for blackmailing her into having intercourse with him and subsequently enjoyed their sexual relationship. This experience must be understood in the context of her many previous abusive experiences.

Although Jacqueline did not admit to being a prostitute, the interviewer reported that she became uncomfortable and evasive when asked about her current employment, and maintained that she didn't do anything. Yet she was not living on welfare and reported an income of $3,000 to $5,000 in 1977. The interviewer's assessment was that Jacqueline was working as a prostitute. Certainly her history is a common one for girls and women who become prostitutes.

The extreme vulnerability of runaways to sexual and other abuse must be recognized and addressed. Life histories like Jacqueline's represent a compelling challenge to society to develop alternatives for runaways, as well as better methods of preventing the sexual abuse from which they so frequently are attempting to escape. Children and adolescents must not be subject to arrest for running away from abusive home situations, and well-advertised shelters that are safe, attractive, and accessible to runaways must be set up throughout the country.

PART FOUR

THE PERPETRATORS

15

Who Are the Perpetrators?

One of the major purposes of this book is to extend our understanding of incestuous abuse to include perpetrators who are brothers, uncles, grandfathers, cousins, and female relatives—as well as fathers. Part 4 is dedicated to this end. Our analysis in these chapters will draw heavily on the victims' own descriptions of their experiences (except for this introductory chapter) and on the quantitative data. We will begin by looking at the frequencies of incestuous abuse by different relatives.

Some authors believe that father-daughter incest is the most frequent type of incestuous abuse. Others consider brother-sister abuse to be the most common, despite the fact that it rarely comes to the attention of clinicians and law enforcement agencies. Given the absence of any sound basis for knowing the answer to this question, this disagreement is hardly surprising.

In our probability sample survey, neither fathers nor brothers were the most common perpetrators; *uncles* were. But only just. As can be seen in table 15–1, the forty-eight uncles constitute 25 percent of the total number of incest perpetrators—just 1 percent more than the fathers.*

Thirty-eight percent of these incest perpetrators were members of the nuclear family, that is, they were parents or siblings (including stepparents and half siblings).

In order to ascertain the prevalence rates for incestuous abuse by different relatives, we need to shift our focus from the number of perpetra-

---

*A few of these figures vary slightly from those previously published. For example, three experiences of incestuous abuse involving pair or group attacks had been counted as if they had only involved one perpetrator, instead of two or three. Stepgrandfathers were categorized as "other male relatives," whereas for most purposes they will now be combined with biological grandfathers. Two female perpetrators have been added to the eight mentioned in prior publications. One case had been classified as an acquaintance, since a male acquaintance was the primary perpetrator together with a female second cousin. The second was a borderline case that had been disqualified; consultation led to its being reclassified.

TABLE 15–1

Incest Perpetrators of Female Relatives

Relative	N	%	
Father (biological)	27	14	
Father (adoptive)	1	1	24
Stepfather	15	8	
Foster father	1	1	
Mother (biological)	1	1	
Brother (biological)	23	12	13
Half brother	2	1	
Sister (biological)	3	2	
Grandfather (biological)	8	4	6
Stepgrandfather	3	2	
Uncle	48	25	
First cousin, male	30	16	
First cousin, female	3	2	
Brother-in-law	7	4	
Other male relative	15	8	
Other female relative	3	2	
Total perpetrators	190[a]	103[b]	
Total incidents	187[a]		

[a]Since one incident involved two first cousins together and another involved three, there were three more perpetrators than there were incidents of incestuous abuse. In the rest of this chapter, however, these two pair or group incidents will be counted as if they involved only two perpetrators.

[b]The percentage column adds to 103 because of rounding to the nearest whole number.

tors to the number of women in our sample who had been victimized by each type of relative. In cases where a woman had been sexually abused by, say, both an uncle and a cousin, each experience was counted. However, when a woman was victimized by two or more of the same type of relative—several brothers, for example—the experiences were only counted once.

As can be seen in table 15–2, 4.5 percent of our probability sample of 930 women were incestuously abused by a father before the age of eighteen—including stepfathers, one foster, and one adoptive father as well as biological fathers. If we were to extrapolate from this figure to the population at large, it means that in any gathering of one hundred women, between four and five of them have been sexually abused by their fathers.

Sexual abuse by uncles was only very slightly more prevalent than father-daughter incest, with 4.9 percent of the women in the sample reporting at least one experience of abuse by an uncle before the age of eighteen.

Given that brother-sister incest has often been assumed to be the most

TABLE 15–2

Number and Percent of Women Under 18 Years Reporting Incestuous Abuse by Type of Perpetrator

Incest Perpetrator	Number of Women with One or More Experience*	% Women in Sample (N = 930)
Father (biological, step-, foster, or adoptive)	42	4.5
Mother (biological, step-, foster, or adoptive)	1	0.1
Grandfather (biological or step-)	11	1.2
Brother (biological or half)	19	2.0
Sister (biological or half)	3	0.3
Uncle	46	4.9
Brother-in-law	7	0.8
First cousin (male or female)	30	3.2
Other relative (male or female)	17	1.8

*If a woman was sexually abused by more than one category of relative, she is included in each. If she was sexually abused by more than one relative within a particular category, she is included in this category once only.

common form of intrafamily sexual abuse, it may surprise some people that only 2 percent of our respondents reported being victimized by a brother. Nevertheless, extrapolating from this small figure means that for every million women, at least 20,000 may have been sexually abused by a brother.

The prevalence rates for incestuous abuse by any kind of female relative were strikingly low: only 0.1 percent of the sample had been incestuously abused by a mother, 0.3 percent by a sister, and 0.3 percent by some other female relative.

In all, there were only ten female perpetrators of incestuous abuse in our probability sample survey, that is, 5 percent of all incest perpetrators. Had males as well as females been interviewed, the percentage of female perpetrators may well have been higher. Why the overwhelming majority of incest perpetrators are male will be discussed at some length in chapter 19.

Comparison with Other Studies

Judith Herman (1981) presents data on the frequencies of different types of incest perpetrators reported in five studies undertaken since 1955. Parent-child incest was by far the most prevalent type of incest reported in all these studies (varying from 69 percent to 95 percent of the cases) (p.

19). None of them, however, were based on random samples, let alone probability household samples.*

As was mentioned in chapter 4, David Finkelhor's findings (1979) on perpetrators who abuse their female relatives is most comparable with ours because it was also based on survey data—albeit a population of students who were not randomly selected. Some striking similarities as well as differences are apparent in our findings on incest perpetrators (or partners, in the case of Finkelhor's data). Fathers and stepfathers constitute 24 percent of the incest perpetrators in our survey compared with only 4 percent in Finkelhor's survey. Uncles constitute just over one-quarter (26 percent) of the incest perpetrators in our survey, but only 9 percent in Finkelhor's. Brothers were by far the most common incest perpetrators in his survey—39 percent of all relatives—three times higher than our 13 percent figure (p. 87).

In general, as these differences suggest, far more cross-generational incestuous abuse was reported in our survey than in Finkelhor's. If we exclude the categories of "other" male and female relatives (since generation is not self-evident for them), 60 percent of incestuous abuse in our survey was cross-generational compared with only 14 percent in Finkelhor's study.†

Another difference between our findings and Finkelhor's is that 62 percent of incestuous abuse in our survey occurred outside the nuclear family, in contrast to only 47 percent in his survey.

One noteworthy similarity is that no aunts or grandmothers were reported as sexually abusive in either study, and only one mother was cited in both studies. In general, in each study a minority of the perpetrators were female. However, in our survey only 5 percent of all incest perpetrators were female; Finkelhor reported 19 percent.

What might account for some of these differences in the prevalence of sexual abuse by different incest perpetrators? Two factors may combine to explain some of the disparities. First, as has already been pointed out, Finkelhor's definition of what constitutes a sexual experience was much broader than ours. Second, he did not differentiate between abusive and nonabusive experiences. Many more cases of harmless sexual experimentation and flirtation between relatives who are in the same generation are likely to be volunteered in response to a definition that includes verbal propositions and exhibitionism and that does not disqualify nonabusive experiences.

*In order to be able to generalize to the population at large, a probability household sample is considerably more valuable than a random sample of students, of patients attending an outpatient clinic, or of any other already highly selected group.

†This is a very approximate method of measuring cross-generational abuse since siblings, in-laws, and cousins, for example, may not always be in the same generation.

Some of the differences may also result from the different methods used to obtain information from respondents. Women may be less likely to disclose the more taboo experiences of father-daughter and other cross-generational incest on a self-administered questionnaire completed in a classroom situation (as was required by Finkelhor's methodology) than in a face-to-face interview with well-trained interviewers who have developed good rapport with them.*

The Perpetrators of Incestuous and Extrafamilial Child Sexual Abuse

The old myth used to be that most perpetrators of child sexual abuse are strangers. It is now common for people to say instead that most child sexual abuse is perpetrated by members of the child's own family. Our survey reveals, however, that when all cases of incestuous and extrafamilial child sexual abuse are combined, *the majority of the perpetrators were not relatives.* Specifically, 11 percent were total strangers, 29 percent were relatives, and 60 percent were known but unrelated to the victims. We must be careful that we do not simply replace the old myth that perpetrators are usually strangers with a new one that they are usually relatives.

We will now examine who the incest perpetrators in our survey were in terms of their ages, social class, and race or ethnicity.

Age of Incest Perpetrators

The stereotype of the child molester as a "dirty old man" who accosts children who are strangers to him in the schoolyard is a hard one to break, despite increasing proof to the contrary. The current stereotype of the incest perpetrator is that he's a middle-aged father. What light does our sample shed on the perpetrator's age?

Just over a quarter (26 percent) of the perpetrators who sexually abused

*Another difference between our surveys is that Finkelhor used no age limit for the "victims" of incestuous experiences. However, when we included in our analysis the forty cases of incestuous abuse that started when the respondent was already an adult (i.e., over eighteen), there was little impact on this analysis of the differences between the studies with regard to the frequencies of different kinds of perpetrators.

their female relatives before they turned eighteen years were themselves under eighteen years of age. This means that more than one in every four incest perpetrators was a juvenile offender.

The average age of our survey's incest perpetrators was thirty-three years. Only 20 percent of these men and women were older than forty-six years. As can be seen in the total column in table 15–3, the thirty-six-to-forty-five-year age group was the next largest for incest perpetrators after the under-eighteen age group.

Thus the stereotype of the old man who preys on children is equally inappropriate for incest perpetrators as it is for extrafamilial child sexual abuse. On the other hand, from the child's perspective a thirty-three-year-old man would likely be seen as a "dirty old man." Indeed, a twenty-five-year-old man might be seen as such. So the stereotype may not be as inaccurate in children's eyes.

As with table 15–3, the tables that follow will also include a separate breakdown of quantitative information for all the incest perpetrators. These tables will serve as reference tables for the analyses in the chapters on incest perpetrators to follow.

It is important to bear in mind that the total numbers for some incest perpetrators are very small, particularly the ten female relatives and eleven grandfathers. Findings based on such small numbers must be regarded as tentative only. Because it would add unnecessarily to the complexity of discussing our findings to routinely report numbers as well as percentages, it is hoped that this cautionary statement to the reader will suffice.

Since chapter 16 provides a comparison of incestuous abuse by biological fathers and stepfathers, all the fathers will be combined into one category for the analysis in this chapter.

Social Class of Incest Perpetrators

Our examination of the social class background of incest victims in chapter 8 has already revealed how false is the stereotype of incestuous abuse as a predominantly lower-class phenomenon. Given that relatives within the nuclear family can be assumed to have the same social class and that those outside the nuclear family are *usually* in the same social class, it would be surprising if our focus here on the occupations and education of the perpetrators were to yield a different conclusion. And indeed it doesn't.

Of those incest perpetrators whose occupations were known to the victim—or where the occupations of the providers of the perpetrators were known—approximately a third (32 percent) had upper-middle-class occupations, a third (34 percent) had middle-class occupations, and a third (34 percent) had lower-class occupations.* It is truly remarkable to find the incest perpetrators so evenly distributed by social class.

As can be seen in table 15–4, when looked at separately, most of the incest perpetrators were also pretty evenly divided among social classes.

The high number of missing observations on the education of incest perpetrators makes these data unreliable, so they will not be reported.

Race and Ethnicity of Incest Perpetrators

Table 15–5 presents the data on the race and ethnicity of the different types of incest perpetrators. The percentage of our survey respondents who belonged to each race or ethnic group included in the rightmost column of the table provides some indication of the amount of incest victimization that might be expected if race and ethnicity were to be totally unrelated to incest by different types of perpetrators.

As with social class, the table reveals that there was no significant relationship between the race or ethnicity of the incest perpetrator and incest victimization in general. In addition, when looked at separately, most of the incest perpetrators were distributed roughly in proportion to the percentages of our survey respondents in each racial or ethnic group —except where the numbers were very small, (e.g., for grandfathers and female perpetrators).†

Characteristics of Incestuous Abuse by Different Perpetrators

FREQUENCY OF SEXUAL ABUSE BY DIFFERENT INCEST PERPETRATORS

There was a statistically significant relationship between the frequency of incestuous abuse and the type of relative involved.

*Because a large number of the incest perpetrators were young, there are many missing observations on their occupations and education. For example, 17 percent of the incest perpetrators were under fifteen years old and had therefore not completed their education and did not yet have an occupation. Because it was assumed that perpetrators under twenty-five years of age might still be in the process of obtaining their education, information on this item was only requested for those twenty-five years or older. Information on occupation was only requested if the perpetrator was largely self-supporting. Where this was not the case, the occupation of the primary breadwinner in the perpetrator's family was requested.

†The high percentage of incestuous Asian brothers is largely a consequence of one Asian woman being sexually abused by several different brothers.

TABLE 15-3

Age of Perpetrators by Type of Incest Perpetrator

Age in Years	Fathers (N = 44) (%)	Brothers (N = 25) (%)	Grandfathers (N = 10) (%)	Uncles (N = 48) (%)	First Cousins (N = 25) (%)	Other Males (N = 22) (%)	All Females (N = 9) (%)	Total %	Total N
Less than 18	0	72	0	8	68	14	56	26	47
18–25 years	2	16	0	2	20	32	33	11	21
26–35 years	27	4	0	19	12	36	0	18	33
36–45 years	57	4	0	33	0	9	11	25	45
46–55 years	9	4	20	17	0	5	0	9	16
55+ years	5	0	80	21	0	5	0	11	21
Total	100	100	100	100	100	101	100	100	183
Mean age	39.9	17.9	60.9	41.7	17.4	27.5	19.1	32.9	

Missing observations: 4.
Significant at <0.05 level.

TABLE 15-4

Occupational Status of Incest Perpetrators or Their Providers by Type of Perpetrator

Occupational Status	Fathers (N = 43) (%)	Brothers (N = 19) (%)	Grandfathers (N = 9) (%)	Uncles (N = 44) (%)	First Cousins (N = 19) (%)	Other Males (N = 19) (%)	All Females (N = 8) (%)	Total (N = 161) (%)
Upper middle class	35	42	33	25	53	11	38	32
Middle class	37	42	33	32	16	37	38	34
Lower class	28	16	33	43	32	53	25	34
Total	100	100	99	100	101	101	101	100

Missing observations: 26.
Not significant at <0.05 level.

As can be seen in table 15–6, fathers were the most likely to sexually abuse their daughters eleven times or more, followed by grandfathers. No female perpetrator sexually abused a relative eleven times or more. Only a very few male first cousins and brothers did so.

Grandfathers were the least likely to sexually abuse their victims once only, and female relatives were the most likely to sexually abuse their victims on one occasion only.

DURATION OF INCESTUOUS ABUSE BY DIFFERENT INCEST PERPETRATORS

The duration of the incestuous abuse and the type of incest perpetrator were also significantly associated.

Sexual abuse by grandfathers was the most likely to continue for more than a year, followed by sexual abuse by uncles and fathers. It appears, then, that incestuous abuse is more likely to occur over an extended period of time when it is cross-generational (see table 15–7). A likely explanation is that these are the relationships in which power and authority play a more significant role than is usually the case for brothers and sisters, cousins, and brothers-in-law.

VIOLENCE AND PHYSICAL FORCE BY DIFFERENT INCEST PERPETRATORS

A gun was used in the course of the incestuous abuse by one relative who was classified as "other male relative." Other weapons were used by two fathers and two first cousins. This was the extent of weapon use in our 187 cases of incest.

Verbal threats accompanied the incestuous abuse in only a small fraction of the cases (9 percent). No grandfather used a verbal threat, and only 2 percent of the uncles did so.

Physical force was *not* used in two-thirds of the cases of incestuous abuse (see table 15–8). Brothers, first cousins, and other male relatives were the most likely to use physical force, though most of them used the least serious level of pushing or pinning their victims. Perhaps these relatives, lacking the power and authority of fathers, grandfathers, and uncles, found it more necessary to resort to force.

SEVERITY OF INCESTUOUS ABUSE BY DIFFERENT INCEST PERPETRATORS

Table 15–9 reveals that there was a statistically significant relationship between the severity of the sexual abuse in terms of the sex acts involved and the kind of relative who abused the child (at < 0.001 level). Fathers were the most likely of the incest perpetrators to sexually abuse their victims at the very severe level. In contrast, no female relative or grandfather sexually abused their victims at that level.

The table also shows that when incestuous abuse occurred within the

TABLE 15–5

Perpetrators' Race and Ethnicity by Type of Incest Perpetrator

Race/Ethnicity	Fathers (N = 44) (%)	Brothers (N = 25) (%)	Grandfathers (N = 10) (%)	Uncles (N = 48) (%)	First Cousins (N = 25) (%)	Other Males (N = 22) (%)	All Females (N = 9) (%)	Total (N = 183) (%)	Survey Respondents (%)	Survey Respondents (N)
White	77	72	90	69	76	73	78	74	67	627
Afro-American	9	8	0	15	4	14	0	9	10	90
Latino	9	0	10	10	12	5	0	8	7	66
Asian	0	16	0	4	4	9	22	6	8	70
Other	5	4	0	2	4	0	0	3	8	77
Total	100	100	100	100	100	101	100	100	100	930

Missing observations: 4.
Not significant at <0.05 level.

TABLE 15–6

Frequency of Incestuous Abuse by Type of Perpetrator

Frequency	Fathers (N = 42) (%)	Brothers (N = 25) (%)	Grandfathers (N = 11) (%)	Uncles (N = 48) (%)	First Cousins (N = 27) (%)	Other Males (N = 22) (%)	All Females (N = 10) (%)	Total (N = 185) (%)
1 time only	36	36	18	42	59	46	70	43
2–10 times	26	56	55	38	37	50	30	40
11 or more times	38	8	27	21	4	5	0	18
Total	100	100	100	101	100	101	100	101

Missing observations: 2.
Significant at <0.02 level.

TABLE 15-7

Duration of Incestuous Abuse by Type of Perpetrator

Duration	Fathers (N = 42) (%)	Brothers (N = 25) (%)	Grandfathers (N = 10) (%)	Uncles (N = 47) (%)	First Cousins (N = 27) (%)	Other Males (N = 21) (%)	All Females (N = 10) (%)	Total (N = 182) (%)
1 time only	36	36	20*	43*	59	48*	70	43
1 week– < 1 year	29	48	10	17	19	33	20	26
1 year– < 5 years	21	16	60	32	15	14	10	23
5 years or more	14	0	10	9	7	5	0	8
Total	100	100	100	101	100	100	100	100

*These percentages differ slightly from those in table 15–6 because there were 3 more cases of missing information on the duration of incestuous abuse than on its frequency.
Missing observations: 5.
Significant at <0.05 level.

TABLE 15-8

Use of Physical Force by Type of Incest Perpetrator

Use of Physical Force	Fathers (N = 44) (%)	Brothers (N = 25) (%)	Grandfathers (N = 11) (%)	Uncles (N = 48) (%)	First Cousins (N = 27) (%)	Other Males (N = 22) (%)	All Females (N = 10) (%)	Total (N = 187) (%)
Physical force used	34	44	18	21	44	50	10	33
No physical force used	66	56	82	79	56	50	90	67
Total	100	100	100	100	100	100	100	100

Significant at <0.05 level.

TABLE 15-9

Severity of Incestuous Abuse Before 18 Years of Age by Relationship with Perpetrator

	Fathers		Brothers		Grand-fathers		Uncles		First Cousins[a]		Other Male Relatives		All Female Relatives		Total	
	%	N	%	N	%	N	%	N	%	N	%	N	%	N	(%)	(N)
1. Very severe sexual abuse: Completed and attempted vaginal, oral, anal intercourse, cunnilingus, forced and unforced[b]	34	15	24	6	0	0	17	8	26	7	32	7	0	0	22	42
2. Severe sexual abuse: Completed and attempted genital fondling, simulated intercourse, digital penetration, forced and unforced[b]	32	14	64	16	27	3	29	14	56	15	27	6	80	8	41	76
3. Least severe sexual abuse: Completed and attempted acts of intentional sexual touching of buttocks, thigh, leg or other body part, clothed breasts or genitals, kissing, forced and unforced[b]	34	15	12	3	73	8	54	26	19	5	41	9	20	2	37	69
Total	100	44	100	25	100	11	100	48	101	27	100	22	100	10	100	187

Significant at <0.001 level.
[a]The two incidents in which the victim was sexually abused by more than one of her first cousins are counted here as if they involved two perpetrators.
[b]The term "force" includes physical force, threat of physical force, or inability to consent because of being unconscious, drugged, asleep, or in some other way totally physically helpless.

same generation, fewer of the least severe incidents were reported. Only 12 percent of the incidents with brothers and 19 percent with first cousins involved abuse at this level, compared with 73 percent of the incidents with grandfathers and 54 percent with uncles. It may be that even relatively mild experiences are remembered because they are more disturbing when they are cross-generational than when they are not. Or it could be that because the incest taboo is weaker for brothers and cousins, they are less inhibited from engaging in more seriously abusive behavior.

AGE OF INCEST VICTIM BY TYPE OF INCEST PERPETRATOR

As can be seen in table 15–10, the mean ages of the victims of incestuous abuse by different relatives ranged from 9.8 years for grandfathers to 12.1 years for female perpetrators and those classified as "other male relatives." However, the relationship between the age of incest victimization and the type of incest perpetrator is not statistically significant at <0.05 level.

Aside from the age of incest victims when first victimized, there was a statistically significant relationship between the type of incest perpetrator and the mean age of the victim at the time of the interview. The average age of the victims of female relatives was by far the oldest: 47.2 years. At 31.8 years old, the victims of first cousins were over fifteen years younger than the victims of female relatives.

One possible explanation of these findings is that incestuous abuse by female relatives, uncles, and grandfathers has declined in recent years, while incestuous abuse by first cousins and brothers has increased. Unfortunately, the numbers of incest perpetrators in each group are insufficient to evaluate the trends over time for each of them separately.

INCEST PERPETRATORS KNOWN TO SEXUALLY ABUSE OTHER RELATIVES

Given the tremendous secrecy that usually surrounds incestuous abuse, it was surprising to discover that in almost a third (31 percent) of the cases of incestuous abuse, the victim said that the perpetrator had also sexually abused some other relative. In 54 percent of the cases, the victim reported that the perpetrator did not sexually abuse another relative, and in 15 percent of the cases, she said she didn't know if this had occurred (see table 15–11).

Grandfathers were most likely to be known to have sexually abused another relative: 44 percent compared to only 5 percent of brothers.

TABLE 15–10

Age of Victims Sexually Abused by Type of Incest Perpetrator

Age of Victims (In Years)	Fathers (N = 44) (%)	Brothers (N = 25) (%)	Grandfathers (N = 11) (%)	Uncles (N = 48) (%)	First Cousins (N = 27) (%)	Other Males (N = 22) (%)	All Females (N = 10) (%)	Total (N = 187) (%)
Less than 9	27	32	55	31	41	18	30	32
10–13	36	52	18	44	30	50	40	40
14–17	36	16	27	25	30	32	30	28
Total	99	100	100	100	101	100	100	100
Mean age at victimization[a]	11.7	10.7	9.8	10.5	11.1	12.1	12.1	11.1
Mean age at time of interview[b]	36.4	33.8	37.4	41.0	31.8	38.9	47.2	38.1

[a]Not significant at <0.05 level.
[b]Significant at <0.05 level.

TABLE 15–11

Sexual Abuse of Other Relatives by Type of Incest Perpetrator

Sexual Abuse of Other Relative	Fathers (N = 39) (%)	Brothers (N = 19) (%)	Grandfathers (N = 9) (%)	Uncles (N = 46) (%)	First Cousins (N = 19) (%)	Other Males (N = 20) (%)	All Females (N = 8) (%)	Total (N = 160) (%)
Known to have abused another relative	39	5	44	41	16	30	25	31
Known not to have abused another relative	54	79	56	44	42	65	50	54
Don't know either way	8	16	0	15	42	5	25	15
Total	101	100	100	100	100	100	100	100

Missing observations: 27.
Significant at <0.01 level.

Primary Strategy Used by Incest Perpetrator

Incest victims were not specifically asked about the strategies of their perpetrators, but two members of the research staff read through each account to try to ascertain what primary strategy had been employed. The perpetrators' primary strategies in order of frequency were force or threat of force (27 percent); taking the victim by surprise so that refusal was impossible (17 percent); taking advantage of the victim when she was asleep, unconscious, drugged, ill, or physically helpless in some other way (9 percent); deception—for example, by telling the victim that he or she wanted to show her something, or that her mother had said she needed a ride (3 percent); use of a threat other than force (2 percent); bribery—for example, offering sweets, money, other treats, or privileges (1 percent); and using a manipulative argument such as telling the victim that sexual taboos are silly, touching each other sexually is proof of love, or the victim needs to be educated sexually by doing it with the perpetrator (1 percent).

However, the "other" category was by far the largest—40 percent—because it included cases in which the perpetrator used a combination of strategies from which it was impossible to isolate the primary one as well as cases where there was no information on the perpetrator's strategy. Some examples of combinations of strategies follow.

Six-year-old Sonia was sick in bed when an eleven-year-old relative (she refused to divulge the precise relationship) asked her to play doctor. Then he forcibly stuck his fingers in her anus and vagina, pinning her down while she cried and kicked. The strategies included force, use of a manipulative suggestion, and taking advantage of the victim when she was sick.

Aside from force and threats, nine-year-old Babette's stepfather used the manipulative argument that "you're old enough to know about these things." Some of his behavior was impossible to resist; for example, he would masturbate in a room that faced the kitchen window so his daughter couldn't avoid seeing him while she washed the dishes.

Nine-year-old Ingrid's brother would grab her and rub his penis against her stomach until he ejaculated. His strategies included taking her by surprise, physical force, and threatening "to tell on me, like I was doing something wrong."

When she was twelve, Nan's biological father would go to her bedroom and grab her pajama top so that she had to move toward him. Then he would grab her breast. He did this as though in fun. These strategies included force, deception, and being taken by surprise.

Jacqueline's stepfather used the manipulative argument: "I've been your father since you were three. I've been a good father, so you owe it to me."

He also threatened his fifteen-year-old daughter with loss of privileges: "He said if I didn't do it, I couldn't go skating."

The first time Pauline's uncle used deception: He had her sit on his lap to let her steer the car, then he touched her genitals. The second time he touched her breasts when she was asleep.

Shirley's biological father used force as well as manipulation: "That was the way he taught me about sex," she said.

One time fourteen-year-old Faith's stepfather took her by surprise when he touched her buttocks. Other times he offered her money if she would have sex with him (she refused).

Here are some examples of the verbal threats used by incest perpetrators: Zelda's cousin's brother-in-law said "he'd beat the hell out of me. He said if I didn't let him, he would tell everyone I did it anyway." Ten-year-old Abby's stepfather told her if she said anything, "he would smother me to death." Dorothy's brother-in-law told her, "If you don't, I'll tell your sister you did it anyway."

These quotations make it clear that many incest perpetrators used multiple strategies, and that the primary ones were often difficult or impossible to determine. However, a primary strategy was ascertained in 60 percent of the cases. Force or threat of force was the most common primary strategy for fathers (23 percent), brothers (44 percent), first cousins (33 percent), and "other" male relatives (46 percent). Taking the victim by surprise was the most common primary strategy used by uncles (29 percent).

Conclusion

Although fathers were the second largest group of incest perpetrators after uncles, most incestuous abuse is perpetrated by relatives other than fathers. While 4.5 percent of our respondents were victims of father-daughter incestuous abuse, 12 percent were victims of other relatives. Since these statistics on incestuous abuse were published in 1983, many people cite the overall 16 percent figure for the prevalence of incestuous abuse, then proceed to talk exclusively about father-daughter incest as if this figure applied to this one form of incestuous abuse. This focus on father-daughter incest is understandable, but our statistics suggest that it is time to pay attention to the other types of incestuous abuse as well.

Although father-daughter incest is the subject of the next two chapters, the five chapters to follow will provide the first systematic examination of sexual abuse by brothers, grandfathers, uncles, first cousins, and female relatives.

16

Father-Daughter Incest: The Supreme Betrayal

Both clinical and popular opinion believe father-daughter incest to be the most traumatic form of incestuous abuse. This opinion is strongly confirmed by our probability sample. Over half (54 percent) of the victims of fathers reported being extremely upset by the sexual abuse compared with a quarter (25 percent) of the victims of all the other incest perpetrators combined (significant at <0.01 level). And over twice as many of the abused daughters reported great long-term effects as a result of the incest —44 percent compared with 19 percent of the other victims (significant at <0.001 level).* (See tables A–1 and A–2 in the appendix.)

Some of the factors that may have contributed to the greater trauma reported by the daughters—aside from the special significance of the father-daughter relationship—include the following:

1. Fathers were more likely to have imposed vaginal intercourse on their daughters than the other incest perpetrators—18 percent versus 6 percent (significant at <0.05 level).
2. Fathers sexually abused their daughters more frequently than other incestu-

---

*The tabular sources of information for this chapter can be found in chapter 15 and in the appendix. These tables compare all the major types of incest perpetrators investigated by our survey. The significance levels reported for these tables refer to the entire tables; they don't necessarily inform us about which of the within-table differences are statistically significant. However, when comparisons are made between incestuous abuse by fathers and incestuous abuse by all other incest perpetrators combined, additional computer runs were conducted using this simplified dichotomization of the incest perpetrator variable. This made it possible to explore the ways in which sexual abuse by fathers was significantly different from sexual abuse by all other abusive relatives combined.

The reader may observe that the figures in the total columns for all incest perpetrators in chapter 15 and the appendix sometimes differ from those reported in this and the following chapters for "all other incest perpetrators." This is because the latter figures do not include the perpetrators—for example, fathers—with which all other perpetrators are being compared.

When *all* perpetrators are included—as in the tables in chapter 15 and the appendix—the totals are often referred to as revealing "the norm" for all incest perpetrators for the variable under discussion. Careful reading is necessary to be clear on exactly which comparison is being used.

ous relatives (significant at <0.01 level): 38 percent of the fathers sexually abused their daughters eleven times or more compared to 12 percent of the other incest perpetrators.

3. Although the overall numbers of incest perpetrators who used force or violence in the perpetration of the sexual abuse were extremely low, fathers were more likely than other relatives to use physical force (significant at <0.05 level).

4. In contrast to the other incest perpetrators, the vast majority of fathers were also the victim's provider: 86 percent compared to 2 percent (significant at <0.001 level).

5. Most of the fathers were also at least twenty years older than their victims: 89 percent compared to 45 percent of the other incest perpetrators (significant at <0.001 level). The average age of incestuous fathers was approximately forty compared to an average of thirty-one for the other incest perpetrators (significant at <0.001).

All these factors have been shown to be related to the trauma reported by incest victims. The question we will address next is whether biological fathers and stepfathers are equally responsible for the greater trauma of father-daughter incest. And aside from trauma, how does biological father–daughter incest differ from stepfather-daughter incest?

Biological Fathers and Stepfathers: A Comparison

Incest has long been legally defined as "the crime of marrying, and/or having coitus with a person or persons who are biologically closely related (consanguineous)" (Beserra, Jewel, and Matthews 1973, p. 145). Because this definition is limited to what are popularly known as blood ties, it has been common to consider stepfather-daughter incest as being much less serious than biological father–daughter incest.*

In an effort to counteract the discounting of sexual abuse by stepfathers or other surrogate parents, many contemporary experts on child sexual abuse have pointed out that the violation of the parent-child relationship is just as serious when the relationship is nonconsanguineal as when it is consanguineal. For example, Judith Herman (1981) maintains that "from the psychological point of view, it does not matter if the father and child are blood relatives. What matters is the relationship that exists by virtue of the adult's parental power and the child's dependency" (p. 70). Consequently cases of sexual abuse by biological and

---

*For example, in a recent anthology of personal descriptions of child sexual abuse, the accounts of victims of biological father–daughter incest were separated from all other relatives including stepfathers "because of the unique character of this type of abuse in terms of betrayal and devastation . . ." (Bass and Thornton 1983, p. 21).

stepparents have often been combined, thereby obscuring any differences between them. While recognizing the sound reasoning behind this practice, it seems important to explore what can be learned by separating incest perpetrators who are biological parents from those who are step-, adoptive, or foster parents.

The first question is: Which form of father-daughter incest is the more prevalent?

Prevalence of Incestuous Abuse by Biological Versus Stepfathers

We noted in chapter 15 that there were twenty-seven cases of incestuous abuse by biological fathers, fifteen by stepfathers, one by an adoptive father, and one by a foster father. Although these figures show there were almost twice as many incestuous biological fathers as stepfathers, it must be recognized that only a minority of girls have stepfathers.

The best way to evaluate the extent to which stepfathers in our sample are overrepresented as incest perpetrators would be to calculate what percentage of our respondents who had ever lived with a stepfather were sexually abused by him. This percentage could then be compared with the corresponding calculation for biological fathers.

Unfortunately, we only asked our respondents whether or not a stepfather was one of the major figures with whom they lived in the first fourteen years of their lives—*not* whether they had ever lived with a stepfather, even for a brief period.* Hence we must calculate instead what percentage of women in our sample who were actually *raised* by a stepfather (i.e., he was mentioned as a primary person with whom they lived in their first fourteen years) were sexually abused by him.

Since our questions focused on the first fourteen years, we will consider here only those cases of incestuous abuse that occurred before the victim turned fourteen. The one adoptive father will be combined with the twenty-seven biological fathers,† and the one foster father will be combined with the fifteen stepfathers.

Ten of the sixteen stepfathers sexually abused their stepdaughters before they turned fourteen. But only five of these ten stepfathers were

*The specific questions asked were: "Were you living with both parents most of the time, up until you turned fourteen?" If the respondent replied affirmatively, she was asked: "Was that with your natural parents, or with step- or foster parents?" If she replied negatively, she was asked: "Who *were* you living with most of the time?"

†The reason the one adoptive father was included with the biological fathers for this analysis of prevalence is that they were combined in the precoded answers to the question on whom respondents were living with up until they turned fourteen.

mentioned as primary parent figures. This means that the other five stepfathers were all more transitory figures in their stepdaughters' childhood
years.

Of the twenty-nine women who mentioned a stepfather as one of the
primary people with whom they resided during their first fourteen years,
17 percent were sexually abused by one of these stepfathers. This means
that *one out of approximately every six women who had a stepfather as a principal figure
in her childhood years was sexually abused by him before she reached the age of fourteen.*

Of the 749 women who mentioned a biological father as one of the
primary people with whom they resided during their first fourteen years,
only 2.3 percent were sexually abused by one of these biological fathers.
Thus only *one out of every forty-three women who had a biological father as a principal
figure in her childhood years was sexually abused by him before the age of fourteen.* *

This analysis reveals that *women who were raised by a stepfather were over seven
times more likely to be sexually abused by him than women who were raised by a biological
father.* Some of the implications of this startling finding will be discussed
in the next chapter.

Since most of our analysis focuses on incestuous abuse before the age
of eighteen, not fourteen, it should be noted that 2.9 percent of the women
in our sample, or one out of every thirty-four, who had a biological or
adoptive father as a principal figure in her childhood years was sexually
abused by him *before eighteen years of age.* (From this point on, the one adoptive father who sexually abused his daughter will be combined with the
fifteen stepfathers and one foster father, since they all share the characteristic of nonconsanguineality.)

Frequency of Father-Daughter Incestuous Abuse

Not only was incestuous abuse by stepfathers disproportionately more
prevalent in our survey than such abuse by biological fathers, but incestuous stepfathers were found to sexually abuse their victims significantly
more frequently than incestuous biological fathers. As can be seen in table
16–1, 41 percent of the incidents with stepfathers occurred more than
twenty times, compared with 12 percent of the experiences with biological
fathers. And while almost half of the victims of biological father–daughter
incest reported that the sexual abuse occurred only once, this was the case

*Only one out of the eighteen biological fathers who sexually abused their daughters was
not a primary parent figure with whom the victim had resided in her childhood years.

for only 18 percent of the victims of stepfather-daughter incest (significant at < 0.05 level).

We noted earlier that some clinicians believe that father-daughter incest never occurs only once and that a woman who reports one incident is likely repressing others. One of our respondents, Maria, agrees—at least in her case. Although she could remember her biological father sexually abusing her only once when she was fifteen, she believed that the abuse had probably occurred more often. Her words follow.

I only remember one incident, but it seems like he was probably sexually aggressive other times in my life and I don't remember them. This is really difficult to talk about. It's almost as difficult as therapy, but I keep thinking that talking about it will help somebody else.

Once when I was fifteen everyone had gone to bed except my father and myself. He called me over to his chair and he seemed to regress to childlike behavior. He put his arm around my waist and his hand up my dress and up my panties, and started rubbing my genitals. Then he asked me to go lie down on the couch. For a second I was very afraid of my father, but then I told him I had to go study. He seemed to accept that and told me not to let any of the boys at school do that to me. Then I went upstairs and that was the end of it.

(Upset?) Extremely upset. (Effect on your life?) A great effect. It's caused me not to be able to have friends. (How so?) Well, I guess I went completely inside myself. I'm only now beginning to come out after five years of intensive therapy. My education and intelligence were hindered because of my father. I could write a book about what it has meant and done to my life. There probably isn't one area it hasn't touched because without a solid family foundation you don't have anything. I think I completely missed adolescence.

Whether or not Maria was sexually abused by her biological father once or many times, it is clear that she was extremely traumatized by the experience.

TABLE 16–1

Frequency of Incest Victimization by Biological Fathers and Stepfathers Before 18 Years

Frequency	Biological Fathers		Stepfathers	
	%	N	%	N
One time only	48	12	18	3
2 to 10 times	20	5	35	6
11 to 20 times	20	5	6	1
Over 20 times	12	3	41	7
Total		25		17

Missing observations: 2.
Significant at < 0.05 level.

Duration of Father-Daughter Incest

Given that sexual abuse by stepfathers was reported to occur more frequently than such abuse by biological fathers, it is not surprising to learn that the period of time over which it occurred was also longer. In almost half the cases (47 percent) of stepfather-daughter incest the abuse occurred for a year or longer, compared with 28 percent of the cases of biological father–daughter incest. In nearly a quarter (24 percent) of the cases of incestuous abuse by stepfathers, the abuse continued for more than five years—compared with 8 percent of the abuse by biological fathers. Although these associations did not reach statistical significance at < 0.05 level, the trend evident is consistent with the findings on the greater frequency of sexual abuse by stepfathers.

Physical Force and Violence Accompanying Father-Daughter Incest

Not one of the twenty-seven victims of biological father–daughter incest said that their fathers threatened them verbally in connection with the sexual abuse. In contrast, 35 percent of the seventeen stepfathers verbally threatened their stepdaughters (significant at < 0.01 level). Perhaps the additional authority wielded by biological fathers makes them more readily able to get what they want from their daughters. Or it may be that the biological bond makes them less willing to use this form of coercion.

With regard to actual behavior, there was only a small and statistically insignificant trend toward stepfathers using more physical force than biological fathers (41 percent versus 30 percent). And only one biological father and one stepfather used weapons to coerce their daughters into a sexual relationship.

Camille's experience provides an illustrative example from our survey of a stepfather's use of force. She was nine years old when he first raped her. Camille said that her stepfather had sexually assaulted her more than twenty times over a period of six years. When asked to describe the most upsetting time, she replied:

> Every time was upsetting. He forced me to have [vaginal] intercourse and oral intercourse with him. (What kind of force?) Physical force with his hands. He'd hold me down. That was enough. (How did it end?) I threatened to tell my mother. In fact, I didn't just threaten; I was *going* to tell her.
> (Upset?) Extremely upset. (Effect on your life?) A great effect. Initially it created

in me a real terrible feeling about men that I had to overcome. Sexually I was very messed up for a long time. I feel that I could have ended up in a mental hospital from the experiences. I'm lucky I didn't, but it will affect me forever.

Florence's experience provides an example of a biological father's use of force as well as psychological manipulation. His daughter was seventeen years old at that time.

It was after I left home. I had gone back to visit my grandparents after I had run away. They told me to call my father even though they knew we didn't get along.

We [Florence and her father] kissed when we met, and I was suspicious of the kind of kiss he gave me. We went to dinner and afterward we went to my apartment. All of a sudden he said that from an academic standpoint, he thought incest would be interesting. Then he pushed me down on the couch and tried to kiss me again. I screamed bloody murder. I was furious. He was caught off guard, and my roommate came in soon after. (Did he touch you anywhere when he tried to kiss you?) He had his hands on my shoulders to push me down on the couch. (Did he use force?) I suppose he was using force, though he could have been more forceful. When I screamed, he stopped immediately.

I didn't see him for a long time afterward. It really threw me for a loop. It took me a long time to get over hating him. When I did see him a long time later, there was always someone there and we never spoke of it. But I loved the academic question about incest. (Florence laughed sardonically.)

(Upset?) Extremely upset. (Effect on your life?) Some effect. It didn't affect my relationships with other people. But it affected my relationship with my father, and it kept me from having a stronger relationship with my father's family. I didn't see him for nine years after that, and consequently I also didn't see my half brother and sister, whom I missed. My father is old now and probably doesn't remember any of this.

When asked which of her experiences of sexual abuse was the most upsetting, Florence replied that it was the one with her father. Her other experiences included rape by an acquaintance when she was nineteen and sexual abuse by a professor who was a friend of her father's when she was fifteen.

The Severity of Father-Daughter Incest

When stepfathers sexually abused their daughters, they were more likely than any other relative to abuse them at the most severe level in terms of the sex acts involved. Although the difference between stepfathers and biological fathers in the severity of the abuse did not reach statistical significance, there was a marked trend toward stepfathers being more abusive. Specifically, in almost half the cases of sexual abuse by stepfathers

(47 percent), the abuse reported was very severe, compared with 26 percent of the sexual abuse by biological fathers. Only 24 percent of the experiences of sexual abuse by stepfathers were at the least severe level, compared with 41 percent of the sexual abuse by biological fathers.

In order to provide a clearer sense of the distinctions being made between the different levels of severity for incestuous abuse, as well as to give the reader a better idea of the kinds of sexual abuse perpetrated by the incestuous fathers, four examples will be cited. They illustrate cases at both the most and least severe levels of incestuous abuse for both biological fathers and stepfathers.

Kate's experience is an example of sexual abuse by a biological father at the least severe level. She was fourteen years old when he first fondled her breasts. When asked which incident with him was the most upsetting, Kate replied as follows:

The last time. That was the time I let him know that I knew what he was doing. He approached me in a friendly manner, calling me his baby and things, and he put his hands on my breast. He didn't try to go any further; he got his thrills out of touching my breast. I let him know I didn't appreciate what he was doing. (Did anything else sexual occur with him?) No.

(Upset?) Extremely upset. (Effect on your life?) A great effect. It affects how I feel about him up till today. I feel guilty now because he's old and needs lots of attention, but I don't feel anything for him so I can't give it to him. (Other ways?) Men can't be trusted. I told my daughters so that they would be able to tell me if it happened with them. It did happen, and my daughters told me about it.

Shirley provides an example of a daughter who was sexually abused by her biological father at the very severe level. Her father started to fondle her sexually from the age of two or three. These experiences occurred more than twenty times over a period of fifteen years. Shirley was upset and crying when asked to describe these experiences.

This will have to be vague. I can't handle talking about it too much. I've only talked about it once or twice before. I told my first husband and it made our relationship with my parents very difficult. I haven't told my second husband. My father will die soon so it doesn't matter. (It was your father?) Yes. That is the way he taught me about sex. That was his standpoint. I thought it was wrong from the first time. We were in bed and the doorbell rang and he said, "Quick, go upstairs." (Did you have intercourse?) Not until he knew that I'd had sex with a boyfriend when I was seventeen. He performed cunnilingus on me. I think he—Jesus, it is so hard to remember! I remember as a small child objecting to him coming into the bathroom to wash me. (Did he force you to do anything to him?) Yes, he forced me. (Did he force you to masturbate him?) Yes. (Did he use verbal threats?) I don't know. I guess it was more or less pleading. (How did it end?) When I left home.

(Upset?) Extremely upset. (Effect on your life?) A great effect. I was very emotionally upset as a teenager and a young adult. I was angry. I don't know what else to say. I was an unstable person. I flunked out of three colleges. [Shirley became very upset and started crying again.] (Which experience was the most upsetting?) The one with my father. Had I had someone to talk to at the time, I wouldn't have spent half my life trying to work it out, and maybe I would even have gotten help for my father.

Shirley said that although her father had denied it, she knew that one other sister was definitely also a victim of father-daughter incest. She suspected that another younger sister had also been victimized by him, but they had never talked about it.

Faith was fourteen years old the first time her stepfather propositioned her. Her experience is an example of sexual abuse at the least severe level. Faith said that her stepfather had made sexual advances toward her from six to ten times over a period of two years.

He'd asked me to go to bed with him, and offer me money. My mother had a job and he used to wake me up in the morning as soon as she left for work. He'd come into my room and invite me into his bed. I'd wake up my sister. (Did he try to force you?) No, he never forced me, he just offered me money. One time I was walking by him and he touched my ass. I slapped him, and he never tried that again. He'd say things like "I wish I had you in bed." (Did he want sexual intercourse with you?) Yes, he told me that he did.

(How did it end?) I got pregnant intentionally so that I could get married and get out of the house. (Upset?) Extremely upset. (Effect on your life?) No effect. I really don't think about it. It makes me leery of guys. I've got to get to know a guy before I sleep with him. I've got to know what kind of guy he is.

Faith said that her younger sister was also sexually abused by her stepfather. "That was when my mother left him," she added.

Despite Faith's claim that the abuse had no long-term effects, she nevertheless said that she became pregnant at the young age of sixteen in order to escape her stepfather's sexual advances.

One of many examples of sexual abuse by a stepfather at the very severe level is provided by Abby. She was ten years old when her stepfather raped her. This was the first of two incidents that occurred over a period of six months.

My mother worked at night. One night when she was at work my stepfather came into my bedroom when I was asleep. He got me out of my bed and put me in his bed with him. He said if I hollered he would smother me with his pillow. He was kissing me and I started to fight him off, but he was a big strong man. He started feeling all over me, my breasts and my genitals. He took his fingers and forced them into my vagina. Then he started to force his penis into me. He got part of the way in when I remembered that my mother kept a hammer under the bed. I reached down, got it, and hit him on the head with it.

(Verbal threats?) He said if I said anything he would smother me to death. When he tried it again, I wasn't asleep and I stopped him. I told him that if he bothered me any more, I'd tell my mother and the police. My mother left him soon after that.

(Upset?) Extremely upset. (Effect on your life?) Some effect. When I first met my husband it was hard for me to make love to him, although he tried to reassure me.

Abby's courage and assertiveness are quite remarkable. At ten years old she defended herself physically and verbally against an adult man who threatened her with death in his attempt to have intercourse with her. Although her stepfather partially penetrated her, she was successful in interrupting the rape; and despite his threat to kill her if she spoke about it, she told him she would tell her mother and the police if he ever bothered her again.

While Abby's handling of her stepfather was extraordinary, we must remember that she was also lucky; her mother left her stepfather shortly after the second attack. There is no way to know if she would have continued to be as successful had she been forced to live with him for many years like so many other victimized daughters. And, despite her resourceful and determined efforts to protect herself, she was unable to keep from being raped by her stepfather.

Age of Daughters

The average age of the victims at the time of the interview was significantly different: thirty-eight years for the victims of biological fathers and thirty-two years for the victims of stepfathers. This difference in ages may reflect the increasing number of stepfamilies in recent years.

Although the victims of biological fathers were close to a year younger than the victims of stepfathers—11.4 years compared to 12.1 years—this difference is not statistically significant.*

Some researchers believe that very young children may be less traumatized than older children by sexual abuse because their developmental level makes the experience less confusing to them. Rena was only five when her biological father started touching her sexually. Even though the sexual abuse was at the least severe level, she described it as quite traumatic. The abusive incidents occurred from eleven to twenty times over a period of five years.

*Biological fathers were very slightly more likely to sexually abuse their daughters when they were less than nine years of age than were stepfathers (24 percent and 30 percent, respectively). A third of the victims of biological fathers were ten to thirteen years old, and 37 percent were fourteen to seventeen, compared with 41 percent and 35 percent, respectively, of the victims of stepfathers.

He had a habit of tickling us girls between our legs. It was not like foreplay; it would just be in the course of playing. We mostly had our clothes on, at least I did. It wasn't overly sexual, but it was *where* he chose to tickle us that was strange. It was right between our legs. (Did he touch your genitals?) Yeah. (Were you ever undressed when he did this?) Yeah. (Did he penetrate you with his fingers?) No, he wasn't that bad. (Did he use force?) Well, in playing he would hold us down. That's not really force, but he could tickle us that way. (How did it end?) I suppose he sensed I didn't like it and felt guilty because I was getting older, so he didn't do it any more.

(Upset?) Somewhat upset. (Effect on your life?) Some effect. It inhibited my own sexual growth, like in having sex with men and being comfortable with my own body. Enjoying sex with men wasn't easy. (What advice would you give to someone in the same situation?) At that age, there wasn't much you can do. Maybe to speak to someone who can do something about it. My mother was in the same boat as us, but maybe some other relative could have helped.

Rena said that her father had touched the genitals of all four of his daughters in this manner.

Valerie's sexual abuse by her stepfather illustrates the same point. She was only five years old when her stepfather started molesting her, but she felt very traumatized by these experiences. Her stepfather continued to abuse her for the next six years.

He said he'd take me out to get root beer and buy presents or toys for me. He got me root beer, but that was all. Then he'd feel me. (Where?) My crotch and breasts. (Did he actually touch your genitals?) Yes. It was upsetting because he did it under the pretext of being nice. He also put my hand on his genitals. And he'd lay on top of me a lot while I'd be watching TV or reading a book. He'd squirm and rub his groin on me. I could feel his hard-on. He'd never take it out; he'd just rub it against me. (Did he use physical force?) Yes. He'd lay down on top of me so I couldn't move. (How did it end?) He left the house.

(Upset?) Extremely upset. (Effect on your life?) A great effect. I can't have normal relationships with men. I can't trust men at all. I don't go near them much, I'm very shy. I'm totally turned off to men and I'm scared of them. It's disturbed my whole sexuality.

When asked which of her experiences she found the most upsetting, Valerie mentioned the one with her stepfather. She was more upset by this than an attack by a cousin and three of his friends who used force to try to have intercourse with her when she was nine.

Age of Fathers

The average ages of the biological fathers and stepfathers when they started sexually abusing their daughters was very close indeed: 39.6 years and 40.4 years, respectively.*

No incestuous fathers were less than twenty years old when they began to abuse their daughters. While all the biological fathers were twenty or more years older than their daughters, four stepfathers (24 percent) were less than twenty years older than the stepdaughters they sexually abused.

Fathers Who Sexually Abuse More Than One Relative

All victims of incest were asked if they knew whether or not their perpetrator ever had any kind of sexual relationship with any other relative. In exactly half the cases of incestuous abuse by stepfathers, the victim reported that she was aware of at least one other relative who was also sexually abused by him. This compares with approximately a third (32 percent) of the cases of incestuous abuse by biological fathers. However, this difference does not quite reach significance at <0.05 level.

Given the intense secrecy that so often surrounds cases of incest, and given how common it is for victims to assume that they are the only ones to have been victimized, these two figures should probably be regarded as underassessments. Even as underestimates, these percentages are very high. This finding has important implications for what we will call the family dynamic theory of father-daughter incest. According to this theory, all members of the family contribute to the making of an "incest family." One version stresses the role of the wife who withholds sex from her husband and rejects the housewife role. The validity of this theory is jeopardized by cases in which fathers also sexually abuse a niece or some other relative outside the nuclear family. The same is true if he sexually abuses a neighbor's child or some other nonrelative, but unfortunately we did not ask our respondents whether they knew about occurrences of extrafamilial child sexual abuse perpetrated by their abuser.

*Seven percent of the biological fathers were twenty-one to thirty compared to 18 percent of the stepfathers; 59 percent of the biological fathers were thirty-one to forty compared to 47 percent of the stepfathers. And 33 percent of the biological fathers were over forty years old compared to 35 percent of the stepfathers. These differences are not statistically significant.

Lenore's case provides an example of a biological father who was believed to have sexually abused a cousin as well as his daughter. Lenore described only one incident that involved bodily contact with her father. It occurred when she was fourteen.

One of the most striking insights offered by this case is the considerable degree of trauma that resulted from what many people would regard as a quite marginal experience of sexual abuse.

My mother and father used to argue a great deal, and my father, when angry, would walk around nude. This upset me and my sister. We weren't nudists. We'd close our eyes and hide under our pillows. He did it to show her [their mother], and he'd also do it when drinking. (Did he touch you?) No, but once he tried to. He hugged me, and I connected it with those other things. My sister and I wanted to be away from him; we had the feeling something was wrong.

(What happened when he tried to touch you?) Once I was getting money to go to the movies. He was in the bedroom, and he said, "Come and get it." He was stark naked and he wanted to hug me. He said, "That's all right," and tried to hug me. I backed off. "What the hell's the matter with you?" he asked in broken English. I tore down the hallway, very upset. (Did he hug you?) Not quite. When he gave me the money he reached out; it wasn't a close body-hug, though he did have his arm around me. Then I backed off and left the house. From that time on we were at odds with one another.

Later when we had a big argument I reminded him about that incident, but he denied it had ever happened. He said, "You're lying! It never happened." That was the only incident like that. I told my mother he was walking around in the nude, and he denied that too. My mother told him, "Put your robe on when you go to the bathroom."

(Did he have any kind of sexual relationship with any other relative that you know of?) Yes, from hearsay, he had made advances toward a young cousin. I really don't know more about it but I think he did have sexual problems.

(How upset?) Extremely upset. Looking back on it, I was disillusioned, confused, and hurt. (Effect on your life?) A great effect. My number-one feeling was that I had to get out of the house. I was living with the fear that it would happen again, and that it might be worse the next time. (Other ways?) I was defiant and I ran off and got married. But I wasn't prepared for marriage. I went from one bad situation to another. My life has gone on, but if this hadn't happened a different future would have been in store, I feel. (Other effects?) Not anymore. But I think my bad sex life with my first husband was largely because of my father. The decision I made to escape into marriage was wrong.

(Who was most helpful in dealing with this experience?) My sister. (What advice would you give to someone in the same situation?) That's difficult. I should have discussed it with my mother immediately, but she was having such problems with him. Still, I believe you should discuss it with someone in the family. The person doing it definitely has problems, and the problem has to be taken care of because it could get worse. It scars a kid to abuse the sacred trust. It is difficult to forgive and to understand. (Which of your experiences was the most upsetting?) The first one when I was fourteen years old with my father.

Reported Trauma of Father-Daughter Incest

Most people would probably surmise that victims of biological fathers would be more traumatized by the experience than victims of stepfathers because of a greater sense of betrayal. Hannah—one of our respondents—specifically admonished her stepfather that he shouldn't make advances toward her because she considered him to be "like my own father," not just a stepfather.

Hannah was fifteen years old the one time her stepfather approached her sexually. Because no physical contact was attempted, this incident did not meet our definition of sexual abuse.

> I was taking a shower and he came in. I didn't know he was watching me. I heard a noise and said, "Who's there?" Then I saw a shadow. I said, "Dad, what are you doing in here?" He said, "Do you want me to get you soap?" I said, "No, I have some right here." He said, "Turn around and I'll put soap on you." I was very reluctant. In Filipino families, authority plays a great part; you never question your elders. As he opened the curtain, I was standing there naked. I knew that he wanted to touch me, and he also had a bulge in his pants. Whatever was in his mind, I talked him out of it. I had to think quickly. I said, "I respect and love you like my own father." He sat down on the toilet seat and started crying. He admitted that a desire to touch me had crossed his mind. (Upset?) Not very upset. (Effect on your life?) A great effect.

Our survey cannot confirm or disconfirm the belief that other things being equal, sexual abuse by a biological father is more traumatic than sexual abuse by a stepfather—because other things were *not* equal. And since in our study stepfathers more often than biological fathers sexually abused their stepdaughters in ways that are related to trauma—for example, frequency of abuse, use of force, severity, and so on—it is not surprising that stepdaughters also reported significantly more upset than biological daughters. More specifically, 82 percent of the victims of stepfathers reported being very or extremely upset by the sexual abuse compared with 62 percent of the victims of biological fathers. (This relationship is statistically significant at < 0.05 level.)

The victims of stepfathers also more frequently reported great long-term effects as a result of the sexual abuse than the victims of biological fathers —53 percent versus 39 percent, respectively—but this relationship did not reach statistical significance.

In order to provide a better sense of the different levels of trauma that were reported as a result of father-daughter incest, three examples of varying responses will be cited next.

Elaine reported no real trauma as a result of her biological father's one-time sexual advance toward her. She was seventeen years old at the time.

He didn't speak very well. He spoke in broken English and German. It was hard to understand him sometimes. I had my back to him and he came up behind me and put his arm around me and squeezed me. (Where?) Around my waist, I think. He said, "Your mother's not much to make love to." I pulled away and told him to get lost. (Did anything else sexual ever happen with him?) No, I told my mother if he touched me again he was going to be in big trouble. He said [to Elaine], "You don't have any sympathy." (Upset?) Somewhat upset. (Effect on your life?) A little effect.

Elaine is one of the few victims of father-daughter sexual abuse to report that it only had a little effect on her. In contrast, Peggy reported considerable trauma resulting from the one time her biological father started touching her sexually. She was thirteen years old at the time.

My father was an alcoholic, and he was at home one evening when I returned from school. I didn't live with him; my parents were divorced ever since my mom was pregnant with my younger sister. I was over visiting him and he opened a bottle of wine and asked me if I wanted some sips. I said fine. We were sitting in front of the TV, and he asked if I wanted a backrub. My dad then pulled up my shirt and started rubbing my back. Then all of a sudden he started rubbing my hips. I was freaked out. I didn't know how to react. I was real young, and it was a crucial time for me. I turned over to ask what he was doing, and he bent over to kiss me on my lips. I started crying and he sat up and said, "What's the matter?" I kept crying and wouldn't answer. He got up and said it was okay and went into the other room.

(Upset?) Very upset. (Effect on your life?) Some effect. My father had a strong effect on my life in general. He was never there, and when he was, he was never there in a fatherly way. I was deprived of that as a child. I think having only a mother image and not a father image makes you too dependent on one person, especially other women. Although my mother found someone else to provide a father image, it wasn't the same. It has affected my relationship with other men. For a long time I was searching for someone who could be a father to me, who would take care of me. (Which of your experiences was the most upsetting?) What happened with my father.

The other experiences of sexual abuse reported by Peggy included an attempted rape when she was less than fourteen years old (about which she refused to divulge any further information because she said it was a "sore spot"; she also mentioned that she had discussed this experience with different people including psychiatrists), being forced to touch the penis of her mother's lover when she was twelve, an attempted rape by a friend when she was twenty-one, and an experience of forced breast contact by her boyfriend's father when she was seventeen. The fact that Peggy considered her father's rubbing her hips and kissing her more upsetting than all these experiences reveals once again how traumatic even a relatively mild sexual experience can be when the perpetrator is one's father.

Wanda provides one of many possible examples of considerable trauma as a result of sexual abuse by a stepfather. Wanda was eleven the one time her stepfather approached her sexually.

He got drunk. I shared a bedroom with my two brothers and a sister. He came in when we were all asleep and he got in bed with me. (Were you the oldest?) Yes. I said, "I'll go sleep with Mom." It scared the shit out of me. This happened when I was eleven. It took years of work with a psychiatrist to even get me to think about it. (What did he do?) He was just in bed with me. That was enough! (Was it sexually threatening?) Yes, it took me eighteen years to get over it. I remember the threat but not him doing anything in particular. (What was his threat?) When he was leaving the room, he said, "I'll kill you if you ever tell your mother."

(Upset?) Extremely upset. It was threatening sexually. I was afraid to be home alone with my stepfather. (Effect on your life?) A great effect. I would never trust a stepparent with children, especially a daughter. (Other effect?) Not consciously, but I know it's had a deep psychological impact. That's why I can't remember the details.

As already mentioned, repression often blots out memories of incestuous experiences because they are so upsetting. Sometimes the repression is selective, and the victim's feelings about the experience may be inaccessible to her although the actual incident can be remembered. Sometimes the opposite is true. Wanda specifically mentioned that it took her years of work with a psychiatrist to even think about what had happened with her stepfather. Even with professional help, she realized that she was still not fully aware of the impact of the experience on her life. At the time of the interview—eighteen years after the incident with her stepfather— Wanda believed that she had finally recovered from it. One wonders what she might have to say about this ten years hence. Charlotte Vale Allen, author of *Daddy's Girl* (1980)—an autobiographical book on father-daughter incest—described many different stages in her life during which she thought she was no longer affected by the experience, only to learn later that this was not the case.

Edith—a victim of stepfather-daughter incest—was particularly eloquent about the traumatic effects of this experience on her life. She was eight years old the first time her stepfather tried to get her to touch his penis. He sexually abused her more than twenty times over a period of eight years until she left home at sixteen.

The most upsetting experience was when I was fourteen. My parents were alcoholics and would stay up till 4 or 5 A.M. drinking and fighting. When my mother would pass out, my father would get my sister and me out of bed for "family discussions." He thought my mother was sexually inhibited and he said he was going to help my sister and me through it so we wouldn't be inhibited too. One night I got up to go to the bathroom and my father was still up. He picked me up bodily, sat me on the table and kissed me. Because he was so drunk and couldn't stop me, I got off the table and after fifteen minutes of argument, I managed to leave and go to bed.

(What about other times?) Right after they were married, when I was about eight and my mother was out, I asked if I could go to bed with him. Being young and without a father, I wanted to be close to him. He said yeah, but when in bed, he asked me if I knew the difference between boys and girls. He said, "Give me your hand." He was going to put it on his penis. I said, "I'd better go to my bed."

(Did you have other sexual experiences with him?) Yes. He'd do little things like say "Give me a kiss," then he'd turn his face so I'd have to kiss him on the mouth. I was careful around him at all times, and tried to avoid physical contact with him. My sister and I never wore just robes or underwear around him.

(What ended it?) I left home at sixteen. (Upset?) Extremely upset. (Effect on your life?) A great effect. It had a much greater effect than being raped by a stranger—someone you'll never see again. I never told my mother. It would have broken her heart and I don't know if she would have believed me. It's so awful on Christmas, birthdays, and especially Father's Day. I have to send the bastard a card for her sake, and I spend hours in card shops looking for a card that's not mushy—that doesn't say "what a wonderful father you are."

I wanted a father—someone to be close to—not someone I had to be afraid of every moment I was with him. It's very, very sad. My own father left us, so my father image is bad. Because of my father and my stepfather, I felt all men were rotten. It became really hard to relate to men and to trust them. However, I've discovered they have feelings and they're not all bad.

It inhibited me sexually for a long time. There has to be a certain kind of trust for me to have sex with a male. Every time anyone makes a sexual comment or yells at me on the street, I ask myself, "What kind of image am I projecting? Is it the way I walk, or dress, or look? There must be something about me—an aura—that brings that out in people that pass by. Or is it just chance?" The thing that's kept me going is I've been a strong person. I left home early and put myself through school. I'm a fighter. I can't spend the rest of my life brooding about this. I can't jump off bridges, so I just move on.

I've thought of another effect and this is a biggy! My mother is a very sexually inhibited person. She became an alcoholic and thereby avoided it [sex]. After marrying my stepfather, my mother gained an incredible amount of weight and became unattractive to my stepfather. I realize that I did the same thing; I gained about fifty pounds and still can't get rid of the extra weight. I ate constantly also to make myself unattractive to men and to not have to deal with them.

(What did you find most helpful in dealing with the experiences with your stepfather?) Myself. Getting away from the household. And I took psychology courses in college to get more understanding of what had happened.

Edith's strategies included cautiousness, avoidance of physical contact, arguing, physically fleeing the situation, and finally leaving home when she was sixteen. This was not submissive behavior, yet still she was unable to avoid considerable abuse—abuse that appeared to have an enormous impact on her life.

At the end of the interview, interviewers evaluated how upset the respondent had appeared to be during the interview. The answers to this question serve as a kind of validation of the long-term trauma of incestuous abuse. According to our interviewers' reports, victims of father-daughter incest (both biological and stepfathers combined) were significantly more upset during the interview than victims of the other incest perpetrators—43 percent versus 21 percent, respectively (significant at < 0.02 level). This finding confirms the respondents' own subjective evaluations: that generally speaking, father-daughter incest is the most traumatic of those we investigated.

We will now examine the extent to which the background factors included in our survey differentiate biological father- and stepfather-daughter incest. Any differences that emerge will help to suggest risk factors for incestuous abuse by these two kinds of perpetrators.

Background Factors

Jean Giles-Sims and David Finkelhor (1984) endeavored to examine the evidence for the widespread presumption that children are at increased risk of abuse by stepfathers. They conceded that the evidence from reported cases suggests an overrepresentation of stepparents among perpetrators, but argued that the evidence is inconclusive because stepparents are known to be overrepresented among lower socioeconomic groups, from which the majority of child abuse reports come (p. 409).

Giles-Sims and Finkelhor's analysis raises the question: Are some of the differences in the characteristics of sexual abuse by biological fathers and stepfathers found in our survey due to social class or race or ethnic differences rather than to consanguineality or lack thereof?

VICTIMS' RACE AND ETHNICITY

Although the numbers of victims of father-daughter incest for all minority race and ethnic groups is small, and should therefore be read with caution, table 16–2 reveals a few suggestive findings about the percentages of women from different groups who were victimized by their fathers. Since 2.9 percent of the sample of 930 women were sexually abused by a biological father before the age of eighteen, any percentage above that figure for a particular race or ethnic group is higher than the average. Any percentage above 1.8 percent for stepfather abuse is higher than the average for that form of incest.

The findings that more than one-quarter (27.3 percent) of the Native

TABLE 16–2

Rates for Victimization by Biological Fathers and Stepfathers for Different Racial and Ethnic Groups

| Race/ Ethnicity of Victims | Women Victimized (N) | | Survey Partici- pants (N) | Victimization Rate/100 | | |
	by Bio- logical Fathers	by Step- fathers		by Bio- logical Fathers[a]	by Step- fathers[a]	by Bio- logical and Step- fathers[b]
White (non-Jewish)	20	10	563	3.6	1.8	5.3
Jewish	0	0	64	0	0	0
Afro-American	1	3	90	1.1	3.3	4.4
Latina	3	2	66	4.5	3.0	7.6
Asian	0	0	70	0	0	0
Filipina	0	0	41	0	0	0
Native American	3	1	11	27.3	9.1	36.4
Other	0	1	25	0	4.0	4.0
Total	27	17	930			

[a]The differences between these rates of incestuous abuse for different racial and ethnic groups are not significant at <0.05 level.
[b]The differences between these rates of incestuous abuse for different racial and ethnic groups are significant at <0.01 level.

American women in the sample were sexually abused by a biological father, and 9.1 percent were sexually abused by a stepfather, are provocative but unreliable because there were only eleven Native American women in our sample of 930 women.

Only 1.1 percent of the Afro-American women in our sample were incestuously abused by their biological fathers compared with 3.3 percent who were sexually abused by their stepfathers. This slight underrepresentation of Afro-American women as victims of biological fathers and their slight overrepresentation as victims of stepfathers presumably reflects the fact that stepfamilies are more prevalent among Afro-Americans than among whites.

Latina women were slightly overrepresented as victims of both biological fathers and stepfathers. White non-Jewish women were slightly overrepresented as victims of biological fathers, but not as victims of stepfathers.

No Asian, Filipina, or Jewish women were sexually abused by either a biological father or a stepfather.

VICTIMS' SOCIAL CLASS

When using the victim's father's education and occupation as the measures of social class, the victims of stepfathers were not significantly more lower class than the victims of biological fathers. There was a noticeable

trend, however, for the victims of stepfathers to be less well represented
in the upper middle class than the victims of biological fathers. The explanation may be that stepfamilies are less common in the upper middle class.
Or it may be that stepfathers are more common in Afro-American families
who are in turn underrepresented in the upper middle class.

Because of the small numbers of victims of biological fathers and stepfathers in the different racial and ethnic groups, it is impossible to further
analyze whether factors that may be related to race or ethnicity contribute
to the differences found in our survey between biological and stepfather
incestuous abuse. Hopefully, future research will shed more light on this
question.

RELIGIOUS UPBRINGING

When comparing women who were raised Protestant, Catholic, Jewish,
or with some other religion, as well as those who were raised with no
religion, there was no statistically significant relationship between religious upbringing and father-daughter incest. However, when the fifty-
nine women who were raised as Jews are compared with all those who
were raised as non-Jews, the fact that there was no case of father-daughter
incest reported by a Jew is statistically significant at < 0.05 level.*

Before endeavoring to explain these findings, it would be helpful if other
research would be conducted to evaluate their validity.

MOTHER'S EMPLOYMENT OUTSIDE HOME†

Several of our respondents who were victimized by their fathers said
that the abuse occurred when their mothers were away at work. Is there
a relationship between the mothers' employment histories and father-
daughter incest?

Respondents were asked what percentage of time their mothers worked
outside the home during the first fourteen years of their lives. As can be
seen in table 16–3, only 11 percent of the cases of biological father–daughter incest occurred in homes where the mother was working most of the
time in her daughter's childhood years compared with 56 percent of the
cases of stepfather-daughter incest and 19 percent of the women who were
not victimized by their fathers. This suggests that when their mothers
worked most of the time outside the home, daughters with stepfathers
were much more vulnerable to sexual abuse by them than was the case for
daughters with biological fathers. Indeed, while well over half the cases of
sexual abuse by stepfathers occurred when the mothers worked in the

*The number of Jewish women who were raised in the Jewish religion is five less than the
number identified as Jewish in table 8–3 because some women who identified as Jewish at
the time of the interview had not been raised in that religion.

†I am indebted to Nancy Howell and Karen Trocki for their assistance with the data
analysis on this topic.

labor force most of the time during their daughter's childhood, nearly half the cases (48 percent) of biological father–daughter incest occurred when the mother did *not* work during these years.

We need to determine, however, whether these findings could all be an artifact of the different work patterns for mothers in stepfamilies and mothers in biological families. This is done in table 16–4. However, because we don't know how many respondents had ever had a step-father—only how many had been *raised* by one—this table is necessarily limited to fathers who raised their daughters (recall the discussion on page 234). Table 16–4 shows that the mothers' work practices were indeed highly related to whether or not they were in stepfamilies; 31 percent of the mothers in stepfamilies worked most of the time compared to only 15 percent of the mothers in biological families; and only 21 percent of the mothers in stepfamilies never worked compared to 60 percent of the mothers in biological families (significant at <0.001 level).

In order to try to ascertain whether or not the findings reported in table 16–3 are confounded by the fact that women in stepfamilies are more apt to work, we have to separate out the three variables in question: mothers' work practices, being raised by a biological father or a stepfather, and being victimized by a biological father or a stepfather (see table 16–5, to which the same caveat, above, applies).

Interestingly, table 16–5 suggests that mothers' work status has little effect on the likelihood a stepdaughter will be sexually abused by her stepfather. While 21 to 22 percent of the girls raised in families where the mother worked outside the home were abused by their stepfathers, the figure for girls whose mothers never worked was (an insignificantly differ-

TABLE 16–3

Amount of Time Respondents' Mothers Worked During Childhood Years and Incestuous Abuse by Biological Fathers Versus Stepfathers Before 18 Years

Work Status	Women Victimized by Biological Father		Women Victimized by Stepfather		Women not Victimized by Father	
	%	N	%	N	%	N
Mother worked most of time	11	3	56	9	19	169
Mother worked some of time	41	11	31	5	25	214
Mother never worked	48	13	13	2	56	488
Total	100	27	100	16	100	871

Missing observations: 1 on victims of stepfathers, 15 on women not victimized by fathers.
Significant at <0.001 level.

TABLE 16–4

Relationship Between Respondent's Family of Origin and Mothers Working
Outside the Home During Daughters' Childhood Years

Mother's Work Status	Women Raised by Biological Father and Mother		Women Raised by Stepfather and Mother	
	%	N	%	N
Mother worked most of time	15	109	31	9
Mother worked some of time	26	193	48	14
Mother never worked	60	446	21	6
Total	101	748	100	29

Missing observations: 161 women raised by other parent figures.
Significant at < 0.001 level.

ent) 17 percent.* Similarly, there was little variation in incestuous abuse
rates by mothers' work status in biological father families (2 to 4 percent).
Although these findings are tentative (since they are based on a limited
sample of fathers), they do provide some evidence that the greater propen-
sity of stepfathers to abuse their daughters is not attributable to the mothers' higher rates of labor-force participation.

Possible Social Effects of Father-Daughter Incest

The victims of stepfathers were, on average, almost three years younger
when they first bore a child than the victims of biological fathers: 19.8
years compared to 22.6 years, respectively. Indeed, the victims of stepfathers were younger than the victims of all the other types of incest perpetrators when they had their first child. Although these differences did not
reach statistical significance at < 0.05 level, future research should investigate this finding. If replicated, researchers should address to what extent
this finding may be due to some of the differences that emerged between
biological and stepfather incest, and to what extent it may be due to other
factors such as the overrepresentation of stepfathers in Afro-American
families. (The average age of first childbearing is younger for Afro-American women than for white women.)

Similarly, the statistically significant finding that 41 percent of the vic-

*This analysis focuses on victimization before eighteen years; hence the figures are slightly
different from those reported on page 235, which apply to sexual abuse before fourteen.

TABLE 16–5

Mother's Work Status, Family of Origin, and Victimization by a Father Before 18 Years

1. Mother Worked Most of Time

	Raised by Biological Father		Raised by Stepfather	
	%	N	%	N
Respondent victimized by father who raised her	3	3	22	2
Respondent not victimized by father who raised her	97	106	78	7
Total	100	109	100	9

Significant at < 0.001 level.

2. Mother Worked Some of Time

	Raised by Biological Father		Raised by Stepfather	
	%	N	%	N
Respondent victimized by father who raised her	4	8	21	3
Respondent not victimized by father who raised her	96	185	79	11
Total	100	193	100	14

Significant at < 0.001 level.

3. Mother Never Worked

	Raised by Biological Father		Raised by Stepfather	
	%	N	%	N
Respondent victimized by father who raised her	2	11	17	1
Respondent not victimized by father who raised her	98	435	83	5
Total	100	446	100	6

Significant at < 0.001 level.

tims of biological fathers were college graduates compared with only 12 percent of the victims of stepfathers may be due to the same cultural factor just noted.

Aside from these two variables, none of the other possible social effects were significantly different for the victims of biological fathers and stepfathers.

Comparison of the Victims of Incestuous Fathers and Other Incest Perpetrators

When the victims of father-daughter incest were combined and compared with the victims of all the other incest perpetrators, the following significant findings emerged:

- Only 17 percent of the victims of father-daughter incest were married at the time of the interview compared with 43 percent of the victims of other incest perpetrators (significant at < 0.05 level).
- Forty-three percent of the victims of father-daughter incest reported having been asked to pose for pornography compared with 21 percent of the victims of other incest perpetrators (significant at < 0.02 level).
- Thirty-one percent of the victims of father-daughter incest reported being upset by someone asking them to enact what they had seen in pornographic pictures, movies, or books compared with 13 percent of the victims of other incest perpetrators (significant at < 0.02 level).

Our finding that fewer than one in five victims of father-daughter incest was married at the time of the interview suggests that this form of incestuous abuse may have a particularly destructive effect on marital relationships. This will come as little surprise to most people.

More unexpected, perhaps, is our finding that the victims of father-daughter incest were not more likely than the victims of other relatives to be raped by a nonrelative, beaten by a husband, or subjected to more of the other forms of sexual abuse investigated, except for the two pornography items just cited.

Conclusion

The victims of stepfathers were not significantly more lower class than the victims of biological fathers, but there was a trend for stepdaughter victims to be less well represented in the upper middle class. However, this may reflect the fact that stepfamilies are less common in the upper middle class, rather than indicating any significant risk factor associated with social class background (Giles-Sims and Finkelhor 1984).

Our survey found statistically significant differences in the rates of victimization by fathers (biological and stepfathers combined) for different racial and ethnic groups. Although the number was unreliably small, 36 percent of the Native American women in our sample had been sexually abused by a father, compared to 7.5 percent of Latina women, 5.4 percent of white non-Jewish women, and 4.4 percent of Afro-American women. There were no cases of incestuous abuse by biological or stepfathers for Asian, Jewish, and Filipina women.

Despite appearances (for example, the findings presented in table 16–3 and some of the case material), careful analysis of our survey data suggests that girls with mothers who worked outside the home most or part of the time in their daughters' childhood years were not more at risk of sexual abuse by a biological father *or* a stepfather than girls with mothers who never worked outside the home. This finding has extremely important implications for women who work in the labor force.

Our survey found that biological father–daughter incest occurred more frequently than stepfather-daughter incest. However, when taking account of the fact that many more daughters are reared in families with biological fathers, it emerged that at least 17 percent of the women in our sample who were reared by a stepfather were sexually abused by him before the age of fourteen, compared to 2 percent of those reared by biological fathers.

In addition, stepfathers were more likely than biological fathers to sexually abuse their daughters more than once as well as more than twenty times, to sexually abuse them over a longer duration, to use force, and to abuse them at a more severe level of violation in terms of the sex acts involved.

Although the victims of stepfathers were, on average, significantly younger than the victims of biological fathers at the time of the interview, there was no significant difference in the fathers' ages at the time they started sexually abusing their daughters, nor in the ages of the daughters at the onset of the abuse.

This analysis suggests that there are many significant differences between sexual abuse by biological fathers and stepfathers that are hidden when researchers combine them into a single group.

In the next chapter we will consider various explanations for some of the differences found in our survey.

17

Explaining the Differences Between Biological Father and Stepfather Incest

In order to explain why child sexual abuse occurs, David Finkelhor (1984) suggests that the following four questions have to be answered. First, what predisposes a person to want to sexually abuse a child? Second, what undermines his or her internal inhibitions against acting out this desire? Third, what undermines the social inhibitions against sexually abusing a child? And fourth, what undermines the child's ability to avoid or resist such sexual abuse? Since this fourth question suggests that the child *can* avoid or resist the sexual abuse if his or her capacity is not undermined, it will be rephrased as follows: What increases the child's vulnerability to sexual abuse?

This four-factor theoretical model provides an excellent framework for discussing some of the differences found in our survey between incestuous abuse by biological fathers and stepfathers.

Researchers are often prone to search for a single theory to account for phenomena, and to see theories as competing with, rather than complementing, each other. One of the advantages of Finkelhor's model is that it discourages such a singular search and highlights the fact that different theories address different levels of explanation.

The discussion to follow will focus on theories that might explain the differences between incestuous abuse by biological and stepfathers, not those that address any father's reasons for abusing his daughter.

Different Predispositions to Child Sexual Abuse

The first question to be addressed is: Are stepfathers more predisposed than biological fathers to sexually abuse their daughters?

The answer is they may be, for several reasons.

MEN WITH AN ACTIVE SEXUAL INTEREST IN CHILDREN MAY BE OVERREPRESENTED AMONG STEPFATHERS

Since the classic pedophile does not have sexual or marital relationships with adults, men who marry are rarely placed into that diagnostic category. But, clinical terminology notwithstanding, men with an active sexual interest in children may in fact seek out women to marry who already have children whose age, sex, appearance, and vulnerability meets their needs.

Many experts believe that incest perpetrators have very little in common with perpetrators of extrafamilial child sexual abuse; the term "pedophile" is therefore usually reserved not only for men who don't marry but for those who molest children outside of their families. Stepfathers are an interesting anomaly in this theoretical dichotomy, since in some cases the children they may be attracted to start out by being "extrafamilial" but then become "intrafamilial." A case from our survey in which a stepfather appears to have been interested in the children prior to marrying their mother bears this point out.

Zelda was twelve years old the first time her stepfather molested her. She said these incidents occurred from two to five times over a period of three to four months.

I thought he loved my mother, but I later realized he married her only to be near kids. I used to have nightmares. Because of this my mother brought me in to sleep in my parents' bed one night. He started feeling around on me. (Where?) My breasts and genitals. I was terrified but I couldn't get up. It would have woken my mother and she would have wanted to know why I left. (Did he penetrate you?) No. This was three or four years after my experience with my uncle, and I was too hip to let him get too far.

One time my family went on a trip together. He told my mother to sleep with their son and he would sleep with me. He tried to make me feel his genitals, but I got out of the bed. (How did he try?) He grabbed my hand and tried to stick it down his underwear. I left home soon after that. I was really upset.

(Did your stepfather ever have any kind of sexual relationship with any other relative that you know of?) Yes. He raped his brother's older daughter, and he tried to rape the younger one, but she had been warned by her older sister.

(Upset?) Extremely upset. (Effect on your life?) A great effect. If I had a daughter I wouldn't get married again. Even with my little boy, I would never be able to trust any man not to molest him.

In addition to Zelda's own conviction that her stepfather married her mother in order to be near her children, the fact that he also raped or tried to rape two of his nieces suggests that he had quite an active sexual interest in young girls.

Zelda mentioned that because of her previous experiences with her uncle she was "too hip" to let her stepfather go any further. Her uncle had sexually abused her more than twenty times over a period of three to four years. When asked how it ended she replied: "By my becoming aware that it was sexual." Zelda's story suggests that if children know what kinds of sexual abuse they might have to contend with, they may be better able to prevent it or stop it from becoming more serious.

Researcher Kathleen Coulborn Faller reports that in about half of the cases of stepfather-daughter incestuous abuse and sexual abuse by the mother's live-in boyfriend in her study of over 150 cases of child sexual abuse in Michigan, the sexual abuse began quite soon after the relationship with the mother was established. "In such cases," Faller observes, "one often finds the perpetrators simultaneously courting mother and daughter" (1984, p. 15). Nevertheless, she stated that the perpetrators could be diagnosed as pedophiles in only about 5 percent of her case sample (p. 55). But then, as Kevin Howells has pointed out, the majority of sexual offenders against children would not be diagnosed as pedophiles (1981, p. 62).

The stepfather of Karen—one of our respondents—started touching her sexually when she was fifteen years old, shortly after he married her mother.

He tried to put his hands on me. I woke up, saw him in my bed, and screamed. He got out fast. (Did he ever use force?) No. Then, after we buried my mother, the next morning he was in bed with me. [This incident was twenty-five years later.] But he didn't get very far. (Exactly what did he do?) He slapped my behind. (Did he try to touch your genitals?) No. I imagine if he had gotten by with touching my breasts he would have.

(Did he have sexual relationships with other relatives?) Yes, he tried with my older sister, but not with the younger one. My older sister confronted him about it. I also discussed it with her once.

(Upset?) Extremely upset. When it's a relative who does this sort of thing, it's worse than a stranger. (Effect on your life?) A great effect. I don't like to think about him now. It was repulsive to me. I've never liked to think about or talk about it with my sister. I wish I never had that experience.

At the end of the interview Karen said that she had married young and had always disliked sex. She also mentioned that she had never revealed this experience to anyone before except her older sister. The interviewer noted that after the question about sexual contact with relatives, Karen had needed to be reassured about confidentiality before revealing the experience with her stepfather. At the age of seventy-nine, when her stepfather must have long been dead, she was still determined to protect his reputation—or, perhaps, her own.

Some clinicians have observed that some adults with a sexual preference for children are so fixated on children of particular ages that as soon as a child exceeds the ceiling age, they lose interest in that child. This may be true in some cases, but it appears not to apply to Karen's stepfather.

Obviously, our data are inadequate for arriving at diagnoses of the incest perpetrators in our sample. But it seems reasonable to assume that the more children the perpetrator was known to have sexually abused, the more active his sexual interest in children probably was. The following case provides an example of a biological father who did not confine his sexual abuse to family members.

Nan reported that her father's sexual abuse of her began when she was twelve and occurred from two to five times over a period of a year.

My sister and I slept in bunk beds. My mother had gone shopping and my dad tucked us in. He would reach his arm over and lift my pajama top. I'd roll over so my back was to him, but he'd hold on to my pajama top so I had to roll back. Then he would grab my breast. He did it as though it was in fun. (Did he touch you anywhere else?) No. (Did he also do this to your sister?) No. (Were you older?) Yes, I was five years older. She told me later that he was doing it to other fourteen-year-old girls in the neighborhood.

(How did it end?) After I got chased home by a man. When I was about twelve, I walked my girlfriend halfway home at about 10:30 one night. Someone hid behind a building, then ran after me. He almost caught my shoulder, but I outran him. I was screaming and he got scared off. It shocked him [her father] into stopping it.

(Upset?) Extremely upset. (Effect on your life?) Some effect. I learned to dress myself down, rather than dress up. I guess I felt responsible for what happened. I clammed up with him. Previously I had tried to make myself cute for him but I stopped after that. And I have a hard time relaxing in sexual relationships. (Relaxing?) It's hard to enjoy it because he made me afraid of physical contact.

Despite this case, it seems possible that men with an active sexual interest in children may be overrepresented among stepfathers as compared with biological fathers. The findings that stepfathers were so overrepresented among incestuous fathers and the trend for more stepfathers than biological fathers to be known to sexually abuse other relatives besides the respondent provide some support for this hypothesis.

OTHER CHARACTEROLOGICAL DIFFERENCES BETWEEN STEPFATHERS AND BIOLOGICAL FATHERS

Men who have difficulty maintaining long-term relationships with adult women may also be more prevalent among stepfathers than biological fathers. Finkelhor (1984) hypothesizes that four components contribute to the making of a child molester: emotional congruence, sexual arousal, blockage, and disinhibition. "The first three factors," he writes, "explain how a person develops a sexual interest in a child or children in general. The last factor explains how this interest is translated into actual behavior" (p. 37).

The finding that many child molesters appear to feel more emotionally comfortable with children than with adults is cited by Finkelhor as evidence for the emotional congruence component of child molesters. According to Finkelhor (1984), "they experience themselves as children," and have childish emotional needs, and thus prefer relating to children (p. 38).

With regard to the sexual arousal component, Finkelhor (1984) argues that "there is very good experimental data, using physiological measurements, that child molesters, including incest offenders, do show unusual levels of sexual arousal to children" (p. 39).

The third component of child molesters—blockage—refers to the fact that these people appear to be "blocked in their ability to get their sexual and emotional needs met in adult heterosexual relationships" (1984, p. 43).

Future research is needed to explore whether any one of these three factors is found more commonly in stepfathers than in biological fathers. (Why conventional inhibitions against having sex with children may be overcome more readily by stepfathers than by biological fathers—the disinhibition component of Finkelhor's four factor theory—will be considered in the next section.) These are but some of the possible ways in which differences between stepfathers and biological fathers may disproportionally predispose stepfathers to have more sexual interest in children.

Differences in Internal Inhibitions

The second question to be addressed is: What are some of the factors that might undermine the internal inhibitions of stepfathers more than biological fathers against acting out their sexual impulses toward their daughters?

STEPFATHER–STEPDAUGHTER INCEST TABOO MAY BE WEAKER OR ALTOGETHER ABSENT

Stepfathers, because they are not consanguineally related to their daughters, may feel less bound by the normative disapproval of incest. Many stepfathers who feel desire for their stepdaughters and do not act on their feelings may recognize that to do so would violate their step-daughter's trust, betray their wives, breach the norms and laws against relating sexually to a child, and so on. Biological fathers have all these factors to consider *plus* the incest taboo.

Louise Armstrong (1978) has argued that incest is not taboo, but talking about it is. Since she articulated this hypothesis, it has become widely accepted by those concerned about the problem of incestuous abuse. Although the prevalence of incestuous abuse may seem to support this conclusion, our comparison of biological fathers and stepfathers who sexually abuse their daughters suggests that it may be somewhat misleading, if not seriously erroneous. Weak as the incest taboo may appear to be, it nevertheless may help to explain why relatively few biological fathers compared with stepfathers sexually abuse their daughters.*

Although foster fathers are not relatives, their parental role has much in common with that of biological fathers and stepfathers. Presumably the incest taboo is either absent or weaker for foster fathers than for biological fathers (this is why the one foster father who sexually abused his foster daughter in our survey was combined with stepfathers for the analysis). There is no evidence in Sarah's case, for instance, that her foster father had any familial feelings toward her.

Sarah was sixteen years old when her foster father insisted on having intercourse with her. He assaulted her in this way more than twenty times over a period of three to four months.

Since my "uncle" [foster father] was footing the bill, he wanted something from me. He put me in a compromising position. He didn't force me, but I didn't have anywhere else to go, so I complied with his demands. (Was it unwanted?) Yes. It was the democratic system; I was the only "nay" vote. (Did you have intercourse?) Yes.

He was the father of my friend. My friend's mother didn't like the way I was raised, so she took me in. It was a mental rape more than a physical one. I knew that if I said no, I'd have to leave the house. (This was how you earned your keep in the house?) Right. The family accepted it. (Verbal threats?) There were no threats during the act of assault, but there were threats like: "If you're letting other men screw you, then you let me, because I'm supporting you." I was promiscuous as a teenager. (Was there any physical force?) There was in the sex act itself, because he was a rough man.

*Both Finkelhor (1979, p. 88) and Phelan (1981, pp. 211–16) discuss the weaker incest taboo as one possible explanation for differences between incest by biological fathers and stepfathers.

(How did it end?) I decided that I wasn't a whore and that I wasn't going to do this because he was supporting me, so I moved to another state. (Upset?) Extremely upset. (Effect on your life?) A little effect.

Although Sarah described the experience with her foster father as having only "a little effect," she considered the experience with him the most upsetting of all her experiences of sexual abuse. Her other experiences included rape by a friend when she was fifteen (described as very upsetting but as having "no effect"); a gang-rape involving six assailants when she was fifteen and a half that was interrupted by the police (described as extremely upsetting but as having "no effect"); rape at knifepoint by her mother's lover when she was sixteen (described as extremely upsetting but as having "no effect"); and rape by an acquaintance when she was sixteen (described as not very upsetting and as having "no effect").

Sarah appears most reluctant to consider that even extremely upsetting experiences have had any impact on her life. The interviewer mentioned that twenty-eight-year-old Sarah was involved in an abusive relationship at the time of the interview. Sarah told the interviewer that her boyfriend threatened to beat her up when she didn't look good.

Vulnerable as are all children to their parents, Sarah's experience highlights the even greater vulnerability of some foster children. Most daughters are not afraid that they will be cast out on the street or lose their homes if they refuse to comply with their fathers' advances. This cruel threat, apparently sanctioned by Sarah's foster family, resulted in her submission. It is not known how frequent such abuse by foster fathers is. My guess is that it is quite common.

STEPFATHER-DAUGHTER BONDING MAY BE WEAKER

Another possible explanation for the much greater prevalence and severity of sexual abuse by stepfathers is that the usual bonding between biological fathers and their daughters may not exist with stepfathers who are absent during their daughters' early years. Judith Herman (1981, p. 206) argues that if fathers shared the work and pleasures of nurturing their children with their wives, they would be much less likely to sexually abuse their daughters. Indeed, she considers this the key explanation for the enormous discrepancy in the frequency with which mothers and fathers sexually abuse their children. Although Herman does not discuss stepfathers in this context, it follows from her theory that stepfathers who enter the lives of their daughters when they are already past babyhood may be more likely to sexually abuse them.

Although these two explanations—a weaker incest taboo and weaker bonding—are quite different, they are not mutually exclusive. Both might contribute to some of the differences between sexual abuse by biological fathers and stepfathers found in our survey. An evaluation of the relative merits of these two theories would be facilitated if we knew how old the daughters in our survey were when these men became stepfathers. It would also help to know about the quality of the relationships both biological and stepfathers had with their daughters in their early childhood years, including whether or not the fathers had any long absences from the home. Unfortunately, this information is not available from our survey.

SMALLER AGE DISPARITY BETWEEN STEPFATHERS AND THEIR DAUGHTERS

One stepfather was only between five and nine years older than his stepdaughter, and three were between ten and nineteen years older. Thus 24 percent of the total of seventeen stepfathers were less than twenty years older than their daughters. In contrast, all of the incestuous biological fathers were twenty years or more older than their daughters.

Aside from the incest taboo, there is also a taboo against sexual relations between people of very disparate ages. Our data show that the breach of the age taboo was not as significant for stepfather-daughter incest as it was for biological father–daughter incest. The smaller age disparity could serve to undermine the internal inhibitions of some stepfathers against acting out their desires toward their stepdaughters. Faller (1984) mentioned that generational boundaries tend to be more blurred in stepfather-daughter cases than with biological fathers. "Our experience is that frequently the perpetrator is younger than the mother," she writes. "This age incongruity adds to the role confusion which also arises from the perpetrator having to take on the new status of parent in the household and from his concurrent courting of mother and daughter" (p. 16).

Differences in Social Inhibition

The third question to be addressed is: What are some of the factors that might undermine the social inhibitions of stepfathers more than biological fathers against acting out their sexual impulses toward their daughters?

STEPFATHERS MAY HAVE MORE OPPORTUNITIES THAN BIOLOGICAL FATHERS TO SEXUALLY ABUSE THEIR DAUGHTERS

It seems reasonable to assume that the more time mothers spend in the work force, the more opportunity fathers will have to sexually abuse their daughters. Since mothers in stepfamilies are more apt to work in the labor force (see table 16–4), stepfathers may sexually abuse their stepdaughters because they have more opportunities to do so.

Despite first appearances, our survey data do not support this hypothesis. As was discussed at some length in chapter 16, our analysis suggests that the mother's employment history in her daughter's childhood years had little impact on the likelihood that she would be sexually abused by a biological father or a stepfather who raised her. Whether or not the more transitory stepfathers were more likely to sexually abuse their stepdaughters could not be determined from our data, however, because we lacked information on this group of fathers.

MOTHERS MAY HAVE LESS POWER IN STEPFAMILIES THAN IN BIOLOGICAL FAMILIES

Judith Herman (1981) has pointed out that fathers who sexually abuse their daughters often have a great deal of power in their families. They are patriarchs who believe themselves to be king of their castles and their wives and daughters to be their sexual property. Although we have no information on how patriarchal the incest perpetrators in our survey were, it seems possible that very tyrannical and abusive husbands may be over-represented among stepfathers. It is known, for example, that most husbands who are left by wives they batter remarry.

On the other hand, it is generally believed that women who work in the labor force have more power in their marriages than women who do not, since their increased economic power is presumed to carry over into other spheres. In support of this theory, some studies have shown that wives who do not work in the labor force are significantly more likely to remain in abusive marriages (Russell 1982; Pagelow 1984).

From this line of argument it follows that mothers who worked most of the time during their daughters' childhoods have more power than those who were not working. If we then apply the theory that the daughters of women who are particularly powerless in relation to their husbands are most at risk of sexual abuse by them, we would expect less sexual abuse by fathers in homes where the mother was working most of the time during the most vulnerable childhood years.

Our data show that mothers in stepfamilies were more likely to work outside the home most of the time than mothers in biological families (see table 16–4), yet their daughters were much more likely to be victimized by their fathers. Hence, this theory is not supported by our survey. However, since mothers' employment is being used as both a measure of women's power as well as a measure of the father's opportunity to abuse, better measures than these need to be developed for testing these competing hypotheses.

For example, another way of measuring the mother's power is to compare the educational levels and occupational status (for those who had jobs) of the biological father perpetrators, the stepfather perpetrators, the fathers who were not incest perpetrators, and their wives. Such comparisons reveal no significant differences in the percentages of fathers with higher occupational or educational status than mothers for women victimized by biological fathers, stepfathers, and those who were never victimized by incest.

By these measures, then, mothers in our survey did not appear to have significantly less power than their husbands in families where father-daughter incest occurred, and mothers in stepfamilies did not have less power than mothers in biological families. However, because of the small numbers involved, this conclusion is very tentative.* In addition, it does not mean that significant power differences do not exist by other criteria.

Differences in Daughters' Vulnerability

The fourth and final question to be addressed is: Are there factors that increase the vulnerability of stepdaughters more than biological daughters to sexual abuse by their fathers?

INCEST TABOO WEAK OR ABSENT FOR STEPDAUGHTERS

Just as it appears that the incest taboo may be weak or sometimes absent for stepfathers, so it may also be for stepdaughters. Of course there are many other factors that make stepfather-daughter incest a taboo activity: for example, it involves a sexual relationship between an adult and a child who are in a parent-child role relationship. In addition, the stepfather is the husband of the girl's mother, and therefore a very powerful infidelity is inherent in such breaches of the taboo. Nevertheless, when a stepfather makes a sexual advance toward his daughter, she may not feel quite the same sense of abhorrence or betrayal as the daughter who is approached by her biological father feels.

STEPDAUGHTERS MAY BE MORE VULNERABLE BECAUSE OF PRIOR VICTIMIZATION

Faller (1984) hypothesized that one of the reasons a sexual relationship between a stepfather and his daughter might evolve so quickly after he

---

*Information on the educational discrepancy between stepfather perpetrators and their wives was missing in eight out of the seventeen cases. And since many mothers never worked in the labor force, the numbers involved in the comparison of occupational status were also unreliably small for fathers who were incest perpetrators and their wives.

enters the new family is that "the child may have been victimized by her own father or other men with whom the mother has had relationships" (p. 16). Our survey data does not support this hypothesis. As already mentioned, there were only two cases in which a girl was sexually abused by both her biological father and her stepfather. In both cases the sexual abuse by the stepfather preceded the sexual abuse by the biological father. And more generally, the victims had been previously sexually abused by someone else—either a relative or a nonrelative—in 35 percent of the cases of stepfather-daughter incest and in 30 percent of the cases of biological father–daughter incest. This difference doesn't approach statistical significance.

STEPDAUGHTERS MAY BE MORE VULNERABLE BECAUSE OF GREATER NEEDINESS

A common clinical assumption is that children who are deprived of attention, affection, or love are particularly vulnerable to child sexual abuse. While stepchildren are not necessarily deprived in these ways, the distress and insecurity that children of divorced and remarried parents commonly feel, at least for a period of time, may make them extra needy and less able to avoid or reject their stepfathers' advances. For example, Rachel, whose many experiences of sexual abuse were described in chapter 12, said of her stepfather: "I really loved him, and I probably would have slept with him if it would have gotten me some approval."

FAMILY DYNAMICS MAY MAKE STEPDAUGHTERS MORE VULNERABLE

Finkelhor (1979) suggests that "something in the Oedipal triangle may make the child more vulnerable. The daughter may feel betrayed by her mother, who has now married, or she may feel that her mother is paying less attention to her. She may be competing with her mother for the attention of the stepfather" (p. 124).

The danger of the fourth precondition of Finkelhor's four-factor theoretical model is that it can so easily be used to introduce victim-blaming hypotheses. For example, a translator of a synopsis of a previously published article of mine apparently could not resist going beyond his or her role to interject the following explanation of my finding that stepfathers are so much more inclined to sexually abuse their daughters than biological fathers: "a young woman of seventeen or eighteen might have a seductive attitude toward her stepfather, which she would be constrained from having toward her own father" (Russell 1984a). Identifying a seductive attitude on the daughter's part may not necessarily mean that the incestuous relationship is therefore considered to be her responsibility. But given the long and relentless history of blaming allegedly seductive daughters for their father's incestuous abuse of them, it is very difficult to contemplate this hypothesis without hearing it as victim blaming.

While four different theories have been offered here to explain why stepdaughters might be less able than biological daughters to resist or avoid their fathers' sexually abusive behavior, other theories support the opposite conclusion. For example, stepfathers may have less authority over their stepdaughters, particularly if they enter the family when the children are already teenagers. This factor could make it easier for stepdaughters to resist their stepfather's propositions and active sexual advances. This hypothesis emerged from reading the descriptions of father-daughter incest in our survey. Some of the stepdaughters seemed much more assertive and determined in their resistance than were the biological daughters. However, since the stepfathers also acted with more force and violence toward their stepdaughters, it is impossible to disentangle the direction of causation here.

Faller (1984) offers another theory that might enable stepdaughters to more effectively avoid, or be better able to end, sexual abuse than biological daughters. She found in her study of 150 cases of child sexual abuse that "mothers in stepfather/boyfriend cases can usually be differentiated from mothers in the classical incest family by their ability to extricate themselves from relationships with problematic men. They do this by separation and divorce, throwing them out, or having them arrested" (p. 16). The mothers have, after all, been through at least one marriage already. They have broken the divorce taboo once and, according to Faller, are more willing to do so again.

Furthermore, our data show that mothers from stepfamilies were almost twice as likely as mothers from biological families to have worked outside the home most of the time or some of the time (see table 16–4). This might be another explanation for Faller's observation that these women were more willing to leave their second or third husbands. Since it is their economic and psychological dependence on their husbands that often makes it difficult or impossible for wives to side with their daughters when their husbands are the perpetrators, the greater independence of the remarried women might make it easier for stepdaughters to resist their stepfathers' sexual approaches.

Future research will have to test and evaluate these and other theories to explain the differences that emerged in our survey between incestuous abuse by biological fathers and stepfathers.

Some Implications

The finding that stepfather-daughter incest is far more prevalent and severe than biological father–daughter incest has considerable implications. The most obvious ones are not only that the daughters of women who remarry are at much greater risk of being sexually abused by their stepfathers, but that it is a substantial risk. For those stepfathers who become a primary parent in their stepdaughters' lives, our data suggest a one-in-six risk factor; for those stepfathers who are around for shorter lengths of time, the risk may be considerably higher.

In addition, if the disproportionate prevalence of stepfather-daughter incest over biological father–daughter incest is due to the weaker incest taboo felt by stepfathers, one might expect a prevalence rate for foster father–daughter incest even higher than the 17 percent found for stepfathers in our study.

Another implication of these findings is that women with daughters might be more cautious about marrying again if they were to recognize the consequent risk to their daughters. We interviewed many women whose trust in men had been so undermined by their experiences of sexual abuse that they chose not to remarry or to entrust any man with the care of their children, even on the most temporary basis. However, facing this risk of remarriage may in turn discourage some women from divorcing abusive first husbands. They may reason that because remarriage is risky and because they don't want to live alone for the rest of their lives, they should stay in their first marriages, no matter how detrimental to them.

An alternative and more constructive response to the findings reported here would be for women to be more careful in their evaluation of prospective male friends, lovers, or marriage partners. They need to seriously evaluate the interest of these men in their daughters, observe the way they relate to them, avoid placing their daughters in vulnerable situations with them, warn their daughters about the danger of incestuous abuse, and work even harder than they otherwise might to establish a relationship of trust between themselves and their daughters. Then, if the daughters feel any discomfort about the way their stepfathers relate to them, they are more likely to confide in their mothers about it.

One case was cited in which a victim of stepfather-daughter incest believed that her stepfather had married her mother especially to gain access to the children. This appears to be a definite strategy employed by some men with a sexual preference for children. The more women know about it, the less effective a strategy it will become.

Herman has emphasized that a strong mother-daughter bond is the best strategy for the prevention of father-daughter incest as well as the best remedy in those cases where it has occurred. Working to make this bond a strong one is likely to be a much more effective means of protecting daughters than remaining in abusive marriages with the concomitantly destructive role models they provide for the children.

18

Brother-Sister Incest: Breaking the Myth of Mutuality

Much has been made of the fact that in a few societies, marriage between siblings was permitted or even required, as among the royal families of the ancient Egyptians and the Incas (e.g., Ford and Beach 1951, p. 112). Even in these cultures, however, brother-sister incest was not tolerated outside of the royal families.

Journalist Philip Nobile blithely maintains that "brother-sister relations are attended by fewer complications [than father-daughter cases], since domination is not a factor" (1977, p. 157). Author Warren Farrell—whose still unpublished research involved advertising for accounts of incest experiences, especially positive ones—reported that "the overwhelming majority" of the two hundred cases he analyzed were positive. More specifically, he claimed that "cousin-cousin (including uncle-niece and aunt-nephew) and *brother-sister* (including sibling homosexuality) *relations,* accounting for about half of the total incidence, *are perceived as beneficial in 95% of the cases*" (Nobile 1977, p. 126; emphasis added). It turned out, in fact, that it was frequently the *perpetrator* who perceived the experience as beneficial (Herman 1981).

Social anthropologist Robin Fox, one of the few researchers to give attention to brother-sister incest and to develop a theory to try to explain it, appears to assume that all sex between prepubescent children is harmless mutual sex play (1980). He also implies that incest occurring after puberty is equally mutual, though he does not say whether or not he regards it as innocuous.

Even David Finkelhor, one of the finest researchers on child sexual abuse, contributes to this sibling-incest-is-positive point of view. For example, he writes:

Women who had sibling sexual experiences have markedly higher sexual self-esteem than women who had other kinds of childhood sexual experiences. Nor does it make any difference if a distinction is made between positive and negative childhood experiences. . . . Positive sibling childhood experiences had an impact that other positive childhood experiences did not. Something about the fact of having a positive experience with a sibling rather than some other partner seemed to be important for affecting adult self-esteem. (1980, p. 187)

These are but a few examples of how brother-sister incest has been discounted as a serious form of sexual abuse. The fact that it almost always occurs within the context of a power relationship is usually ignored, because the power relationship is almost always so much less serious than it is in father-daughter incest. This way of viewing brother-sister incest—as perpetually in the shadow of father-daughter incest—is one of the greatest obstacles to seeing it in a more realistic light.

While brother-sister incest shares this problem with all nonparent-child forms of incestuous abuse, it suffers more than any of the others from the stereotype of mutuality. For example, authors Joann DeLora and Carol Warren (1977) maintain that: "Incestuous sisters are more likely to be willing participants or even aggressors than are incestuous daughters" (p. 244). While, strictly speaking, this is likely correct, it leaves an impression that sisters may often be willing or aggressive incest partners. The one case of sibling incest they cite without comment reinforces this impression, and conveys further that incest between siblings is often a highly positive experience for both parties (p. 246). As researcher Mary de Young (1985) points out, the failure to recognize the difference between exploitive and nonexploitive brother-sister incest "has created scientific support for a general social apathy about sibling incest. The topic evokes little ire so that the taboo against the behavior is quite relaxed" (p. 81).

In this chapter we shall explore to what extent the stereotype of mutuality is justified. But first, a few basic facts about brother-sister incest will be presented.

Prevalence of Brother-Sister Incestuous Abuse

Nineteen women—or 2 percent of our sample of 930—reported at least one sexually abusive experience with a brother before the age of eighteen.* One of these women was sexually abused by three of her brothers and

*Previous publications report twenty, not nineteen, women as the victims of brother-sister incest. One case was later disqualified because it was nonabusive when it started, at age ten, and only became abusive after the woman became an adult.

another by five. Hence there were twenty-five cases of brother-sister incestuous abuse, two involving half brothers. (The reader should note that
the analysis will sometimes focus on the nineteen victims and sometimes
on the twenty-five experiences.) None of the incestuous brothers molested
his sister with a companion, and each of the sisters was alone at the time
of the abuse.

But our 2-percent prevalence figure for brother-sister incestuous abuse
underestimates the problem because many girls have no brothers and
therefore are not at risk for this form of abuse. Just as our prevalence rate
for wife rape was based only on women who had ever been married, our
brother-sister incestuous abuse rate should ideally be calculated on the
basis of women who had at least one brother.

It could even be argued that because sibling incestuous abuse almost
always involves an abuse of power in which an older brother sexually
abuses a younger sister, an even more accurate prevalence rate should be
based only on women with at least one older brother. Unfortunately, we
did not determine whether our respondents had siblings, let alone what
their ordinal positions and genders were.

The only case of brother-sister incestuous abuse in which the girl's
brother was actually younger than her will be cited next.

Jean was sixteen years old when her thirteen-year-old brother started to
molest her while she was asleep.

As kids we'd had a lot of sexual experiences together and with other kids. My
three brothers, myself, and my mother were on vacation together. L. and I slept
in the same bed in the hotel. I woke up in the middle of the night to find that his
hands were on my breasts. I was surprised, and I lay there wondering what he was
up to. I decided to wait to see what would happen. He kept touching me and then
I rolled over. That finished it right there. There were no other advances. He didn't
know that I'd even woken up. I thought about confronting him but I decided to
just let it lay. I didn't want to embarrass him. I thought it might hurt our relationship.

In trying to explain why brother-sister incest occurs, Fox (1980)
hypothesizes that "the intensity of heterosexual attraction between coso-
cialized* children after puberty is inversely proportionate to the intensity
of heterosexual activity between them before puberty" (p. 50). In other
words, the more intensely brothers and sisters play with each other sexually before puberty, the less likely they are to have sexual relations after
puberty.

While one exception doesn't prove or disprove a theory, Jean's experience is inconsistent with Fox's hypothesis about sibling incest.

*Children socialized together in the same environment.

Frequency and Duration

Brother-sister incestuous abuse was significantly less likely than such abuse by all other perpetrators to occur over a period of more than a year: 16 percent and 33 percent, respectively (significant at < 0.05 level).

One explanation for the finding that brother-sister incestuous abuse rarely continued for more than a year may be that sisters are better able than other incest victims to stop the abuse at some point—perhaps because the power relationship is less severe than in most other incestuous relationships. Or it could be that brothers become less motivated to continue the abuse—perhaps moving on to another phase of their lives in which they look outside the family for satisfaction of their sexual or aggressive needs.

Is Mutuality a Myth?

In chapter 3 we addressed the fact that some cases of incest are nonabusive. When sex between brothers and sisters or cousins is mutually desired and enjoyable—or at least neutral—and when it occurs between peers, it is not abusive. The fact that there can be nonabusive brother-sister incest sets it apart in yet another way from father-daughter incest, which, by our definition, can never be nonabusive, no matter what the age of the parties or the feelings of the daughters.

Clearly, there will always be some cases that are borderline in terms of abusiveness, particularly since we have insisted on the importance of recognizing that sexual abuse also occurs between peers. Ten of the twenty-five brothers who sexually abused their sisters in our survey—or 40 percent—are considered peers because they were less than five years older than their sisters. These cases would not qualify as sexual abuse for most researchers. Let us see what kinds of experiences most researchers are discounting.

Pamela was twelve when her sixteen-year-old brother first suggested they have intercourse. She said she could remember her age "because I got my period soon after this began." When asked how many times something sexual happened with him, Pamela chose the category of from two to five times over a period of two years.

> He was physically mature and older than me. I remember once when the family was out he said, "Let's try it." He completely undressed, and I ran into my room

and locked the door. I think the most upsetting part was that he said that Mother said it couldn't come to any harm because I wasn't menstruating yet. I'll never know if she gave her blessing or whether he made it up, but it made me upset at my mother for a long time. (Describe what he did.) He felt my breasts and said they were getting to be a good size, and he tried to take my clothes off. (Did he intend intercourse if you hadn't locked yourself in your room?) He definitely did. (Other unwanted sexual experiences with him?) Yes, he would touch me whenever he could get the chance. He made me feel I had to hide from him, and that he'd try to get me when we were home alone. My mother made me feel she encouraged it.

(Upset?) Very upset. (Effect on your life?) Some effect. Because it was with such a close relative, it made the experience more disagreeable. I've always been an idealist and it shook my feelings toward my brother. I thought he was above that.

When asked which of all her experiences of sexual abuse she found the most upsetting, Pamela chose the experience with her brother. Her other experiences of sexual abuse included having her genitals fondled by a stranger in his late twenties when she was twelve ("He almost raped me," she said), which she described as "a terrifying experience" that "had a great effect on my early teens"; an attempted rape by a stranger when she was seventeen or eighteen after which she said "I was terrified for a long time of strangers"; another attempted rape by a coworker when she was twenty or twenty-one; wife rape from eleven to twenty times over a period of ten years starting in her early thirties; and unwanted intercourse with her brother-in-law when she was thirty-four. Pamela also mentioned that she had never before told anyone about most of these experiences.

Only one case of forcible rape by a brother was disclosed by our sample of 930 women. Thelma was first raped by her nineteen-year-old brother when she was sixteen. She said his assaults occurred two to five times over a period of a month.

My parents weren't home. He just grabbed me, dragged me down the hall, knocked me on the bed and started doing it. (Doing it?) Having sex. (What kind?) He put his penis in me. (How did he knock you?) He pushed me down. He did more or less the same thing a second time. (Did he have intercourse?) Yes. (How did it end?) He left home. (Did he have any kind of a sexual relationship with any other relative?) Yes, he had intercourse by force with my sister—most likely more than once.

(Upset?) Extremely upset. (Effect on your life?) A great effect. It changed my way of thinking. I think now that all men are out there for what they can get. You can't even trust your own brother. I was afraid to tell my parents because of what might have happened; he'd have gotten beaten. Also it was embarrassing for me.

Audrey was ten years old when her thirteen-year-old brother started abusing her. He did so five or six times over a period of six months or more. Her description conveys very eloquently how wrong it would be to infer enjoyment or lack of trauma from a passive response to abuse.

I trusted my brother. He was a good friend who defended me against others. I was in bed when I was awakened by someone fondling my breasts. I was horrified, but I didn't want to get him into trouble, and it was too awkward to turn him in.

One time he made me lay down, then he fondled my breasts and touched my pubic area. I was about ten and he was about thirteen. It was so inappropriate and I felt very weird. I definitely didn't want it; it was against my wishes. I was always wondering how he ever had the nerve. I would lay there in dread, really worried about it.

I had forgotten about all this. I've been interacting with him as an adult without being conscious of what happened, but now it comes back. I would actually lay there and pretend it wasn't happening. I definitely know I didn't enjoy it. Perhaps later he tried to have intercourse, he tried to enter me, I can't quite remember. I do remember him approaching me, and I froze, but I couldn't get myself to say no. I looked up to him and admired him and I didn't have the nerve to stand up to him. I was afraid to tell my father who probably would have killed him.

(Did anything else sexual happen with him?) No. I imagine if I'd let it progress, there would have been a next step. I just had a flash of someone grabbing my hand, guiding it. He must have had me touch him. I'm not sure whether it was my brother, but it probably was. (How did it end?) I finally mustered enough courage to squirm out of situations. At first, I lay there and offered no resistance.

(Upset?) Extremely upset. (Effect on your life?) Some effect. I didn't generalize the experience to other men, but I have a certain degree of shame and disrespect for my brother. I think what he did was unclean and unright. I can't imagine approaching *him*. Though it is less and less relevant, there is always some shame between us. But it doesn't affect my present sex life.

Clearly cases like the three just cited should be regarded as abusive. Just because there is less than a five-year age difference between these siblings does not mean that consent was involved, or that they were mutually wanted or enjoyable experiences. Even though Audrey's brother was only three years older than her, she said: "I couldn't get myself to say no. I looked up to him and admired him and I didn't have the nerve to stand up to him."

Both Pamela and Thelma expressed particular disillusionment because their abuser was a brother. "You can't even trust your own brother," concluded Thelma. And for Pamela the fact that "it was with such a close relative" was evidently what made the experience with her brother so traumatic for her. It is precisely this feeling that sets incestuous abuse apart from extrafamilial child sexual abuse.

Another thing that distinguishes sexual abuse by a brother from abuse by a stranger or an acquaintance is the protective feelings some sisters have toward their brothers. For example, Thelma was afraid to tell her parents because she believed her brother would have been beaten up for raping her, and Audrey was afraid because if she told, she believed her father "probably would have killed him." Aside from the apparently unreciprocated compassion that these two young girls felt toward their brothers, these responses also reveal their recognition of the serious and taboo nature of what their brothers did to them.

Since age has been used as a major criterion for evaluating sexual abuse in childhood and the age disparity between perpetrator and victim has often been found to be related to trauma, it might be helpful at this point to provide a more thorough picture of the age factor in brother-sister incestuous abuse.

Age

The average age of brothers who sexually abused their sisters was 17.9 years compared to 35.3 years for all the other incest perpetrators combined. The average age of the sisters was 10.7 years at the time of the first abuse, quite close to the overall mean of 11.1 years for all incest victims. We see, then, that the average age disparity between abusive brothers and their sisters was slightly over seven years. This age difference represents a very considerable power difference in childhood and adolescence.

Close to three-quarters (72 percent) of the incestuous brothers were juveniles—that is, under eighteen years of age—compared to only 18 percent of all the other incest perpetrators.

We have already mentioned that in 40 percent of the cases of brother-sister incest, there was less than five years difference in age. In 40 percent of the cases, the age difference was between five and nine years, and in 20 percent of the cases, it was ten or more years.

Almost a third (32 percent) of the sisters who were sexually abused by their brothers were less than nine years old. Just over a half (52 percent) were ten to thirteen years of age, and only 16 percent were fourteen to seventeen. Fewer sisters were molested for the first time in the fourteen- to seventeen-year age group than was the case for any of the other perpetrators. It may be that sisters are better able to protect themselves as they get older.

Ambivalent Victims

When we differentiate all the experiences of sexual abuse that were completely unwanted from those that were mostly unwanted or where there was some ambivalence on the part of the victim, only 70 percent of the cases of brother-sister incestuous abuse qualified as completely unwanted compared with 88 percent of all the other cases of incestuous abuse (significant at <0.06 level). Can we consider the cases that were not completely unwanted or where there was ambivalence mutual and/or benign? Let us hear how two of these sisters described their experiences.

Rona was thirteen years old when her eighteen-year-old brother proposed having sexual intercourse with her. Rona said that there had been sexual contact with this brother three times over a period of three months.

He came into my room in the middle of the night with a towel. I asked why he had a towel. He said something about it being messy, and that's when I became aware that he was going to attempt to have intercourse. I told him to go back to his room and that I never wanted to do that. (Had he had intercourse with you before?) No, he never did, and he didn't that time either. I told him not to come back again. (What made you think he wanted intercourse?) Because that's what he said. He said, "When that happens everything gets wet and you need a towel to soak it up." (What did he mean by "that"?) Intercourse. (Did he say anything else to indicate that?) I just know that's what he meant.

Before the incident with the towel, he came into my room a couple of times. We'd lie together in bed and cuddle and talk but I didn't feel threatened and I wouldn't say that what happened was unwanted. (What happened?) He touched me on the breasts. He didn't touch my genitals, and I never touched his. But when he brought the towel, I felt threatened and frightened, and I told him never to come back. (Would you call it attempted intercourse?) Well, he wanted to do that, and I didn't. That was clearly his intent. But he didn't actually try to do anything to me. (Did he ever use force?) No, he didn't force me to do anything to him.

(Upset?) Somewhat upset. (Effect on your life?) It had a great effect on my relationship with him, but in no other way. (How affect relationship with him?) I don't like him. I don't want to be close to him though he's indicated that he wants to be close to me. We've talked about the incident, but I keep him away from me. It's had no other effect on my life.

Rona emphasizes that the experience with her brother affected only her relationship with him. But a ruined sibling relationship is a very significant thing, particularly when it was previously a close and valued one. Furthermore, it seems highly unlikely that this disappointment could have remained totally encapsulated and without any effect on any of her other feelings, attitudes, or relationships, particularly since what happened grew out of wanted sexual experiences with him.

Lorna was sexually abused by three brothers and a sister. Though two of the experiences to be described were partially wanted, Lorna felt they had a serious effect on her intimate relationships. She was six when her thirteen-year-old brother started fondling her. Though Lorna reported that two of her brothers abused her during the same period of time, there is no indication that they acted as a pair. The sexual abuse by this brother occurred from two to five times over a period of five months.

It was my older brother. He wanted to touch my breasts and genitals. He *did* touch them several times. I was caught between two systems. I would say I wasn't supposed to do this, and he'd say it's okay. (Did he ever use physical force?) No, he pleaded and I'd give in. Even when I said no, I yielded, so I can't say he forced me. (Was it wanted or unwanted?) Partially wanted. I knew I shouldn't do it. I would always say no, but I gave in. (How did it end?) I had to stop it; I refused to yield.

(Upset?) Somewhat upset. (Effect on your life?) Some effect. In intimate relationships I've had a hard time determining where my sexuality is and being free with myself. This experience and the other one and the association between them has left a deep mark on me.

Six-year-old Lorna's eight- or nine-year-old brother also touched her sexually from two to five times over a period of five months.

It was very similar to what happened with my older brother. It involved episodes of fondling. He'd touch my breasts and genitals. He never asked for it to be reciprocal. (Was it wanted or unwanted?) It was wanted at first and then it got to be unwanted. The experience with my older brother happened at the same time. After I was locked in a room and punished for it, it became unwanted. (How exactly did it happen?) I didn't feel I could say no. It was part of an everyday living kind of thing.

(Upset?) Somewhat upset. (Effect on your life?) Some effect. It made me over-cautious in intimate relationships.

Lorna also described an experience with a twenty-three-year-old brother who was married at the time of the abuse. She was thirteen when this brother started examining her genitals. She said he did this from six to ten times over a period of six months.

I wasn't really upset. I was more perplexed. This brother was married and he would examine me on an examination table. He was a doctor. I would go help him at work and he would ask me to get on the table and then he would examine me. It was more exploring for him. He lacked knowledge of sex and he was trying to get educated. It was mainly examining my genitals. (Examining?) Yes, he was looking at and touching my genitals. (Did anything else sexual happen with him?) No, nothing. (Were these experiences wanted or unwanted?) I didn't choose them. (How did it end?) He just stopped doing it. (Upset?) Not very upset. (Effect on your life?) A little effect. (Of all your experiences, which was the most upsetting?) The experiences with my two brothers where I had to stop their demands. (Which one was most upsetting?) The first one [the one with her thirteen-year-old brother].

Lorna's case demonstrates that relying on whether or not the sexual experience was wanted at the time would be a poor single criterion of sexual abuse. Her brothers' refusal to take her "no" seriously and her general sense of powerlessness to stop them touching her genitals comes out clearly, despite the positive feelings she also experienced: "I didn't feel I could say no. It was part of an everyday living kind of thing."

To what extent the ineffectiveness of Lorna's saying no to her first two brothers resulted in her passivity toward her eldest brother, we do not know. But Lorna was quite definite about there being harmful effects as a result of the sexual abuse by her two younger brothers.

At one point in the interview Lorna referred to having been mentally ill, but she made no connection between this and her experiences of child sexual abuse. Lorna's experience of sexual abuse by her sister will be cited in chapter 19.

Rona's brother's attempt to have intercourse with her was preceded by two episodes in which he touched her breasts when they were talking and cuddling together in bed. She said these experiences were not unwanted —rather than that they were actually wanted. But Rona was clearly appalled by her brother's desire to have intercourse and his apparent presumption that she would cooperate. It would be ridiculous to assume that because the earlier two experiences had been neutral or positive the third one was any less traumatic. Indeed, in some cases it could be just the opposite. There may be more self-blame or sense of betrayal when a mutually enjoyable intimacy is taken as permission to engage in a much more intimate act without even being consulted on the matter than if no positive experiences preceded the abuse.

So, although Rona and Lorna described their sexual experiences with their brothers as being partially wanted at some point or at least quite neutral, the experiences could hardly be described as mutual.

After reviewing the meager literature on brother-sister incest, Mary de Young (1982) concluded that "quite a few of the sibling incest participants report that the sexual experience is pleasurable. This assessment reflects the mutuality of most of these types of sexual encounters" (pp. 87–88). The danger of not differentiating between abusive and nonabusive sibling incest has already been noted. The point we wish to emphasize here is that experiencing sexual pleasure in no way mitigates the abusive nature of the interaction in nonpeer relationships. And in peer relationships, the sex may start out to be consensual and mutual but become abusive. Just as a husband can rape his usually consenting wife and lovers and dates can rape their usually cooperative companions, so can a nonabusive sibling relationship become sexually abusive. Because the age difference in most cases of brother-sister incestuous abuse is smaller than in most cases of cross-generational incest, the sexual encounter itself may often be less stressful. Indeed, it may sometimes be positive or pleasurable. But when such pleasure occurs in an abusive context, the fact of having experienced pleasure may actually intensify the trauma because of the added guilt, shame, and self-blame it may induce. This, indeed, may be an additional aspect of the trauma of some cases of brother-sister incestuous abuse.

The tone of this discussion is so tentative because it was, in fact, so rare for the victims of brother-sister incestuous abuse in our survey to describe positive or pleasurable feelings about the sexual aspect of their experiences with their brothers.

Stepbrothers and Half Brothers

Only one of the twenty-five incestuous brothers in our sample was a stepbrother and only one a half brother. In Yvette's case, the fact that he wasn't a biological brother seems to have been very salient to her. Yvette was thirteen years old when her half brother, who was in his forties, started fondling her. She said the incidents occurred from two to five times over a period of three months.

He was a half brother. He was in prison for seven years, so he was not really like a brother. He was my mother's son. His wife had a baby and I went there and tried to help. He started kissing me and touching me on my genitals. He didn't go any further. I did not accept or reject what he did. I loved him. He was handsome. I thought maybe he liked me more than his wife. I was both going along and not going along with it. I knew it wasn't good, but I wondered what was happening. (Force?) No, he did those things and I just stood there. (Other times?) He kissed me and touched my genitals again a couple more times when he was in my home. I didn't think he wanted more than that. I was young and he had a fantasy [about young girls]. I didn't do anything; I didn't know what to do. (Did you want it?) I don't know. I didn't know what was happening and wondered what to do.

(How did it end?) He got the message that I didn't like it. I made him nervous because I'd get away from him when he came over, and I would try not to be close to him. (Upset?) I knew it wasn't right. I was not at all upset but it was wrong. I guess I was very unhappy. (Upset?) Very. (Effect on your life?) Some effect. It made me nervous and suspicious about people.

Yvette's feeling that her abuser was "not really like a brother" seems to have contributed to her considerable ambivalence about his fondling of her. This case illustrates again how problematic it is to use whether the experience was unwanted as the criterion for determining whether it qualifies as abuse. Yvette didn't seem to know whether she wanted the experience; she was equally confused on the question of how upset she was by it.

Celia was fourteen the one time her fifteen-year-old stepbrother attacked her. Her experience is unlike those described by the victims of biological brothers in our survey.

We were at a party, dancing; most people were drinking. My stepbrother asked me to dance. It was a slow dance and he started rubbing against me. I told him to stop. I went to the bathroom, and he came in the bathroom behind me. He grabbed me and started trying to pull my pants down. We struggled for a few minutes. Then I told him I would tell Daddy, so he looked at me then walked out of the bathroom. (Did anything else sexual occur with him?) No, nothing else. (What were his intentions?) He wanted to have intercourse.

(Upset?) Somewhat upset. (Effect on your life?) No effect. (Which of your experiences would you now say was most upsetting?) The incident with my stepbrother.

The other serious experience of sexual assault described by Celia was an attempted rape by an acquaintance. A lack of consistency is evident in that she said that the attempted rape experience made her "very upset" and had "some effect" on her life, while she described herself as only "somewhat upset" by the experience with her stepbrother and said that it had no effect.

The fact that Celia's stepbrother started his advances toward her in a public situation makes this case unlike the other brother-sister cases in our survey. It appears that he may not have felt inhibited by the incest taboo that biological brothers face, ineffective as it sometimes is as a restraint.

Trauma

Almost half (48 percent) of the sisters reported being very or extremely upset by their brother's sexually abusing them, and 24 percent reported being somewhat upset. The former figure is close to the norm for all incest cases (53 percent), and identical with the degree of upset reported for incestuous abuse by male first cousins and uncles.

Four percent of the sisters said they were "not at all upset" and 24 percent that they were "not very upset."

While only 12 percent of sisters reported suffering from great long-term effects as a result of their brothers' sexual abuse, 44 percent reported some long-term effects. This means that well over half (56 percent) of the victims reported some or great long-term effects. This percentage is very close to the norm of 52 percent for such effects reported by all incest victims.

On the other hand, 28 percent of the victims of brother-sister incestuous abuse reported no long-term effects at all. While this is close to the norm of 22 percent for all incest victims, it is significantly higher than the 5 percent of father-daughter incest victims who reported no long-term effects (significant at the < 0.05 level). But this finding will surprise no one.

There is a strikingly wide range in the degree of trauma reported by victims of all kinds of incest. Ellen is an example of a woman who reported considerable trauma as a result of her brother's one-time attack. She was fifteen years old when her thirty-year-old brother came to her bed while she was asleep.

I was lying down and asleep. I woke up when he was about to touch my genitals. It scared me and I jumped up. I thought someone had broken into the house. He's retarded and I thought he maybe didn't know any better. I told my father and he spoke to my brother about it. My brother said he was sorry and that he had been half asleep.

It really hurt me. About a year ago I dreamt about it and I woke up crying. Afterward I was afraid for a man to touch me. I think it affected me a great deal. It affected me when I started having intercourse. I think about what happened and I get a cold standoffish feeling. It turned me off. I'm barely getting over it now. (Where else did he touch you?) My pelvic parts. I think about what happened and I freeze up. (Upset?) Extremely upset. (Effect on your life?) Some effect. I didn't want any man to touch me, and I had dreams about it.

Ellen's answer to the direct question on the effect of the experience did not yield nearly as rich information as the questions about the incident itself. When asked which of all her experiences was the most upsetting, she said, "The one with my brother because I was so young then." The significance of her answer is clearer when one learns that her other experiences include an attempted rape by a friend when she was sixteen or seventeen, a completed rape by a violent lover when she was seventeen, and a completed rape by a friend of her family when she was twenty. All three of these experiences were described in traumatic terms, yet she considered the abuse by her brother to be the most upsetting.

However, there were a few cases of brother-sister incest that—while they met our definition of incestuous abuse—appeared to result in very little or no trauma. Let us consider two such cases.

Olive was eleven or twelve when her brother, who was five years older, first started lying on top of her. She said this happened from two to five times during a one-year period. When asked about the most upsetting time, she replied as follows:

There was not one most upsetting time. It probably happened three times. Jim is a very physical person and when we were kids he used to beat up on me a lot. On other occasions we'd start fighting and wrestling good-naturedly and then he'd straddle me, holding me down as if we were fighting, and then he would lie on me. We'd end up watching TV on the couch with him laying on top of me. He'd have an erection and he'd press his weight against me. That was it.

(Did he ever use verbal threats?) No, not in connection with sex. He would often threaten me at other times; he'd say he was going to kill me, but that was like a brother. (Did he use physical force?) Only in the sense that we'd start out fighting. (How did it end?) Just growing up. He was in a transitional stage with his interest in girls then. He was five years older than me, and he came to channel his interest toward his peers. My parents were probably home more often too. (Upset?) Not very upset. (Effect on your life?) No effect.

Penny was ten years old the one time her sixteen-year-old brother sexually abused her. Though she reported very little distress about this experience, it is considered abusive not only because it was unwanted but because she was only ten at the time and her brother was six years older.

A girlfriend who was a neighbor and I were trying on clothes at my house. I don't know if my brother was already in the house or came in later, but somehow he tried to get on top of me when I didn't have any clothes on. He had his clothes on and I think he must have unzipped his fly because he was in direct contact— his penis on my stomach. I was sitting on the edge of the bed. I thought he was going to tie me to the bed or do something like brothers usually do. (What did he actually do?) He rubbed his penis on my stomach. (For how long?) About two minutes. Then he got up. I think my girlfriend was in the other room and he went to her. (Upset?) Not very upset. (Effect on your life?) No effect.

It is interesting to note how both Olive and Penny discount their brother's violence. Olive said, for example, that her brother "would say he was going to kill me, but that was like a brother," and Penny mentioned that she "thought he was going to tie me to the bed or something like brothers usually do." One wonders if they discounted the consequences of the sexual abuse in a similar fashion.

Effective Strategies and Trauma

In the two cases of brother-sister incestuous abuse to be cited next, the brothers were only one year older than their sisters. Both experiences only occurred once, and the sisters were able to employ effective strategies for stopping the sexual abuse.

Daisy was thirteen when her fourteen-year-old brother tried to get her to touch his penis. Her knowledge about sex seemed helpful in her ability to assertively avoid it.

My brother was maturing, and he wanted me to get him excited. He was in the barn and I walked in unexpectedly. He was playing around with young calves and he had exposed himself. He was trying to get excited with a calf, and I became a substitute. He said, "Come here!" He was playing with his penis, and he tried to get me to touch it. I knew what he wanted because I had been around animals and knew enough about sex. I think I said something nasty to him and left. (Physical force?) No. (Anything else sexual with him?) No, nothing.

(Upset?) Not very upset. (Effect on your life?) No effect.

It may be that, other things being equal, the smaller the age difference between brother and sister, the easier it is for the sisters to defy their brothers' suggestions and approaches. However, in contrast to Finkelhor's student survey finding (1980), we found no statistically significant relationship between the age disparity between the victimized sisters and their brothers and the degree of trauma reported.

Although there was only a one-year age difference between twelve-year-old Bonnie and her thirteen-year-old brother, she had a harder time ending the abuse than Daisy had, since he approached her when she was asleep.

Bonnie's brother molested her from two to five times over a period of a month.

I would be asleep and my brother would sneak under my bed, and his hand would reach up and feel my breasts. It happened several times. (Did he touch your genitals?) No, nothing else. This experience scared me, and I would freeze. I was afraid to tell my mother. (How did it end?) When I finally told my mother.

(Upset?) Very upset. (Effect on your life?) Some effect. I have no feelings in my breasts, which could possibly be due to that experience.

In summary: Although it was more common for victims of brother-sister incestuous abuse than other incest victims to report an ambivalent or positive response to the sexual encounter at some stage of the relationship, these feelings were almost always overwhelmed by more substantial negative reactions. This is hardly consistent with the notion of mutuality that pervades most accounts of brother-sister incestuous abuse. Indeed, some aspects of this type of abuse—to be presented next—particularly contradict the assumption of benign reciprocity. In addition, it is important to remember that even if we take the absence of reported trauma at face value and assume that denial or repression did not occur, this would not make their brothers' behavior toward these victims nonabusive.

Violence and Physical Force

Only three brothers (12 percent) physically threatened their sisters in connection with the sexual abuse. None used a weapon. None were physically violent at the two most serious levels: hitting or slapping and beating or slugging. However, 44 percent used force at the less serious level of pushing or pinning. This percentage was not significantly higher than the norm for the use of physical force for all incest cases (33 percent).

However, the trend for brothers to use more physical force reaches statistical significance when we focus on the *primary strategy* used by incest perpetrators. Although respondents were not specifically asked what primary strategy the perpetrator employed, in most instances coders were able to ascertain this from the descriptive accounts. In 44 percent of the cases of brother-sister incest, the primary strategy was physical force compared with 25 percent of all other cases of incestuous abuse (significant at < 0.05 level). The following case provides an example of a brother's use of force on his sister.

Vicki said she was accosted by her nineteen-year-old brother on one occasion when she was twelve years old.

My brother came into my room late at night and asked me to come into his room. He was ready for bed and he had his shorts on. When I came in he asked me to touch him. He exposed himself and placed my hand on his genitals. It frightened me and I tried to leave. I got up but he forced me to sit back down. He held me by the arm and he kept asking me to touch him. (Did he force you to touch his genitals?) Yes, he forced me to touch it, then finally he let me go. (Did he ever try to do anything else sexual to you?) No, nothing.

(Upset?) Extremely upset. (Effect on your life?) Some effect. For a long time I thought there was something very wrong with my family for this to happen. I think this was the first time I was threatened about sex. It made me a little afraid of boys after that.

Another relevant finding is that in 28 percent of the cases of brother-sister incestuous abuse, coders were able to ascertain from the accounts that a good relationship existed prior to the sexual abuse. This compares with only 10 percent of all the other cases of incestuous abuse (significant at < 0.05 level).

It appears, then, that incestuous brothers may either try to trade on their good relationships with their sisters or, failing this, use force more readily than most other incest perpetrators. Even though brothers often have considerable authority over their younger sisters, clearly fathers, uncles, and grandfathers usually have still more.

Severity of Sexual Abuse

Another factor that undercuts the stereotype of brother-sister incest as benign and mutual is the fact that only 12 percent of such incestuous abuse occurred at the least severe level compared with 40 percent of all the other types of incestuous abuse combined (significant at < 0.01 level). (What might account for this finding was discussed in chapter 15.)

Although the percentage of brother-sister incestuous abuse at the very severe level was very close to the norm for all incest perpetrators (24 percent and 23 percent, respectively), the fact that so few mild cases were reported contradicts the notion that the experiences of these girls are often benign.

Possible Effects

If we compare victims of brother-sister incest with the victims of other types of incest and, more important, with women who were never sexually abused by a relative as children, then we can get another version of the likely effects of the victimization besides the victim's own account. The term "likely" is used because positive correlations never prove causation; it could be that some other factor is the mutual cause of both incest and a particular outcome. The reader should bear this cautionary statement in mind. While it seems a plausible hypothesis that the incest may have played a causative role, this connection remains hypothetical only.

One of the most startling findings about brother-sister incestuous abuse is that almost half (47 percent) of the victims never married. This is the highest nonmarriage rate reported by any of the victims of different incest perpetrators and compares with 27 percent for all the other incest victims combined. However, it does not quite reach statistical significance at the < 0.05 level.

Only one of the victims of brother-sister incest out of the ten who married ever remarried (10 percent). Only the victims of first cousins had a lower rate of remarriage (one out of twenty, or 5 percent). The remarriage norm for all incest victims was 28 percent, and for women who were never victimized by incest, it was 25 percent. Despite the fact that this association also does not reach statistical significance at the < 0.05 level, these findings suggest that brother-sister incest may have a considerable effect on a victim's marital history. Further research based on a larger sample of incestuous brothers is needed to evaluate the validity of these trends.

Revictimization

Since we found such a strong association between incestuous abuse and all kinds of revictimization (see chapter 11), it is interesting to see which kinds of revictimization might differentiate victims of brother-sister incest from women who have never been victims of incestuous abuse.

Victims of brother-sister incest reported the following victimization experiences significantly more frequently than did women who had never been victimized by incest (all at < 0.05 or < 0.01 levels): Having a husband or ex-husband be physically violent toward them: 50 percent versus 18 percent; having an unwanted sexual experience with an authority figure: 58 percent versus 27 percent; having an unwanted sexual experience with a girl or woman: 26 percent versus 6 percent; being upset on the street by men's sexual comments or advances: 90 percent versus 56 percent; being asked to pose for pornographic pictures: 32 percent versus 11 percent; being upset by a peeping Tom: 32 percent versus 12 percent; being upset by an exhibitionist before they turned fourteen: 58 percent versus 24 percent.*

As already mentioned, separate sexual assault questionnaires were completed for all the more serious experiences of sexual assault reported by our sample of 930 women. The victims of brother-sister incest completed significantly more of these questionnaires than did women who had never been incestuously abused—a mean of 4.16 compared with 1.2.

Fears of Sexual Victimization

The victims of brother-sister incest reported being more fearful of sexual assault as children than women who had never been incestuously abused (63 percent versus 21 percent; significant at < 0.001 level). Indeed, a higher percentage of them reported fear than the victims of all the other incest perpetrators combined: 38 percent (significant only at < 0.07 level).

Seventy-nine percent of the victims of brother-sister incest believed there was some likelihood that they would be sexually assaulted at some time in the future, compared with 48 percent of the women who had never been victims of incest (significant at < 0.02 level).

We see, then, that women who reported having been sexually abused

---

*Of all these victimization experiences, the only one that was also significantly different from those reported by the victims of the other incest perpetrators was being upset about men's sexual comments and advances on the street (90 percent, compared to a norm for all incest victims of 66 percent).

by a brother were more likely than women who had never been sexually abused by a relative to also report a whole range of victimization experiences and fears of victimization. Presumably, the explanations for revictimization offered in chapter 11 are applicable to the victims of incestuous brothers too.

Why the victims of brother-sister incest might be more afraid of sexual assault in childhood than the victims of all other incest perpetrators is unclear. It makes sense that it might be more frightening to be sexually abused by someone with whom one lives. But this situation applies to the victims of incestuous fathers as well. Again, further research is needed to replicate and clarify this unexpected finding.

Religious Preference and Defection

We have seen that defection from the religion of upbringing is associated with incest victimization in general. Does this also apply to victims of brother-sister incest?

Over half (53 percent) of the victims of brother-sister incest didn't subscribe to any religion at the time of the interview. Only 5 percent were Catholic; 37 percent preferred a Protestant religion; 5 percent, some other religion; and none chose Judaism.

Almost two-thirds (65 percent) of these victims had defected from their religion of upbringing at the time of the interview. This is significantly higher than the 35-percent defection rate for women who had never been incestuously abused (at < 0.01 level).

Although the numbers are too small to warrant applying a statistical test of significance, it is interesting to note that the defection from Catholicism by victims of brother-sister incest was substantially greater than the defection from Protestant religions: 86 percent versus 50 percent. It will be interesting to see if this tentative finding is replicated in future research.

Summary

We see then that experiences of brother-sister incestuous abuse in childhood were associated with a number of possible effects.

Victims of brother-sister incest may be less likely to marry than victims of other incest perpetrators. Almost half of the nineteen victims in our sample never married. Although this association did not quite reach statistical significance, the trend was strong. This finding is very provocative and deserving of further research, particularly in light of the very low 10-percent remarriage rate for victims of brother-sister incestuous abuse (an association that also did not reach statistical significance). It could be that a marriage relationship—which conventionally involves women who are a few years younger than men—is perceived as too reminiscent of older brother–younger sister incestuous relationships and therefore to be avoided.

Victims who did marry were more likely to be subjected to physical violence in their marriages than women who were never incestuously abused. And regardless of marital status, victimized sisters were more likely to report unwanted sexual advances by an authority figure, and a host of other experiences of sexual harassment or abuse, than were women with no incest history.

Victims of brother-sister incest were significantly more likely to defect from their religion of upbringing than women who had never been victimized by incest.

Such victims were more fearful about the likelihood of sexual assault at some time in the future than women who had never been incest victims. They had also been more fearful of sexual assault as children than other incest victims or women who were never victimized by incest.

There may also be many long-term effects of brother-sister incestuous abuse that were not investigated by our survey—particularly psychological ones. Some clinicians, for example, have observed that victims of brother-sister incest are more inclined to have problems in maintaining long-term relationships, in or out of marriage (Thompson 1983*).

Whether or not this is the case, our survey data show that the notion that brother-sister incest is usually a harmless, mutual interaction is seriously wrong. Although there are cases that are nonabusive and although a few cases in our survey resulted in little trauma, many others were seriously abusive and some were extremely traumatic. We must stop allowing the fact that some cases may be harmless to continue to blind us to the realization that most cases are not.

One of the consequences of the myth of mutuality may be that when brother-sister incestuous abuse is discovered or reported, there may be even less support for the victim than in other cases of abuse. This hypothesis is supported by one of our survey findings. Although we didn't specifically ask the victims about people's responses to their victimization, in 57

---

*Workshop on sibling incest conducted in San Francisco, October 1983.

percent of the cases of brother-sister incest where a response was ascertainable it was *unsupportive*. This compares with 17 percent of the responses to all the other cases of incestuous abuse. This difference is significant at < 0.05 level.

So far this chapter has mainly focused on information that has some relevance to the issue of mutuality. However, there are other important findings about brother-sister incestuous abuse that don't relate to this question.

Family Background

Some clinicians and researchers have suggested that one kind of family structure associated with brother-sister incest involves large families and absentee parents. For example, Karin Meiselman (1978) writes that the incestuous brother "is often the oldest brother in a large family with weak or absent parents and thus has the intrafamilial power to effect incestuous relationships with his sisters" (p. 293).

David Finkelhor (1979) also found that girls who were sexually abused by their brothers were more likely to come from large families. Although we didn't ask about family size directly, we did ask about the number of people who were dependent on the total household income at the time the sexual abuse started. Over three-quarters (77 percent) of the victims of brother-sister incest came from families where six or more people depended on the family income compared to only 32 percent of the victims of other incest perpetrators (significant at < 0.001 level). This serendipitous finding makes sense. As already pointed out, girls with one or more older brothers are more at risk of this form of incestuous abuse than girls with younger brothers, and girls with no brothers are not at risk at all.

One of our respondents who was a victim of brother-sister incestuous abuse specifically mentioned that she came from a large family. Wilma was ten when her eighteen-year-old brother first sexually abused her. She said he fondled her half a dozen times over a period of a year.

I'm the youngest of twelve children. One of my oldest brothers would come into my room after I was asleep. He wanted to see my breasts. I was ten and I didn't know what to do so I'd pretend to be asleep. He would lift up my nightgown or pull down my pajamas and proceed to rub against me. This happened more than once, but he never attempted intercourse. It was very upsetting, but I was afraid to say anything so I pretended I was asleep. (How did it end?) He just stopped coming into my room. I think he finally grew up. (Upset?) It's hard for me to remember how I felt as a kid, but I'd say very upset. (Effect on your life?) No effect.

Pretending to be asleep is a common strategy of incest victims. It is one that easily allows the perpetrator to imagine that his behavior is harmless. Indeed, if he is perceptive enough to realize that his victim is pretending, he can even tell himself that she must be enjoying it since she doesn't try to stop him and shows no signs of distress.

Another very suggestive finding that did not quite reach statistical significance is that the father had a higher education than the mother in only 13 percent of the cases of brother-sister incest. In contrast, 36 percent of all the incest victims had fathers with a higher education than their mothers. The victims of brothers and the victims of female perpetrators were very different from all the other types of incest victims in this regard.

It is the norm in this culture for men to have a higher education than their wives. The fact that this was the case in only 13 percent of the families in which brother-sister incest occurred suggests that fathers may play a less dominant role in these families, perhaps permitting an older son to play a more dominant and sometimes abusive role unchecked. This interpretation is consistent with Meiselman's theory and deserves further research attention.

Only in one case (5 percent) was a victim aware that her brother was sexually abusing another relative compared to 35 percent of the victims of other types of incest perpetrators combined (significant at < 0.05 level). This finding is particularly noteworthy since sisters may be more likely to know about the abuse records of their brothers than the records of other, more distant relatives. Or could it be that there is less secrecy about more distant relatives? Contradicting this possibility is the fact that incestuous fathers are among the perpetrators known to have abused their other relatives most frequently.

Another possible explanation is that since sexual abuse is more often perpetrated by males who are older than their female victims, the older generations of men have more potential victims to molest. Some brothers may have no more than one younger sister to abuse.

Conclusion

An unwanted sexual experience with a brother requires the victim to deal not only with the trauma of unwanted sex but also with the trauma that results from the breach of the brother-sister incest taboo. A very significant relationship in a woman's life is affected by this form of incestuous abuse, sometimes devastatingly so. Despite this Meiselman (1978) points out that "there seem to be no theories about family conspiracies, role reversals, or unconscious motives for the occurrence of incest, probably because sexual contact between brother and sister is seen as an understandable, completely natural consequence of a lack of parental guidance" (p. 269). Breach of the taboo by siblings is seen as mutual sexual acting out rather than the sexual abuse it so often is.

The fact that some sexual contact between siblings who are peers is nonabusive has been used to deny the large number of abusive cases. Because mutuality is most frequently presumed to occur with siblings, brother-sister incestuous abuse is the most discounted of all the forms of sexual abuse by relatives. So strong is the myth of mutuality that many victims themselves internalize the discounting of their experiences, particularly if their brothers did not use force, if they themselves did not forcefully resist the abuse at the time, if they still continued to care about their brothers, or if they did not consider it abuse when it occurred. And sisters are even more likely than daughters to be seen as responsible for their own abuse. For example, Meiselman (1978) offered the following explanation for the finding in her psychotherapy sample that victims of brother-sister incest had more often been rape victims than victims of father-daughter incest: "Since some of the sisters later appeared to be sexually masochistic, it is possible that they unconsciously wanted to be raped and actively invited it" (p. 283).

Meiselman (1978) also maintains that "the usual absence of a dependency relationship between brother and sister and the less intense taboo against their sexual contact have led to fewer predictions of severe disturbance as a result of sibling incest" (p. 263). What is overlooked here is that intense dependency relationships and power relationships *do* exist among siblings. Even a one-year age difference between siblings has enormous power implications for both parties. Our survey data show that the average age disparity between incestuous brothers and their sisters is seven years. In some cases the brothers even play a surrogate father role. Such cases are likely to share some of the same dynamics as father-daughter incest.

Though he minimizes the exploitation involved in all forms of incestuous abuse,* psychiatrist Narcyz Lukianowicz is particularly blind to the myth of mutuality in brother-sister cases. His study was based on interviews with patients attending a psychiatric outpatient clinic, a child guidance clinic, and a hospital in Northern Ireland. Among these seven hundred male and female patients, fifteen had been involved in brother-sister incest. Lukianowicz concluded that, with the possible exception of one mother-son and one uncle-niece case, "there were no real cases of rape in our group" (p. 309). Yet in his discussion of the psychodynamics of broth-

*For example, he writes that with the possible exception of two of the incest victims he studied, "all other children, male and female, were far from being innocent victims; on the contrary, they were willing partners and often provocative seductresses" (1972, p. 309).

er-sister incest, he mentions one case that lasted for fourteen years. Although he acknowledges that "in some stages it was continued by the aggressive and violent psychopathic brother against the sister's wishes," this apparently does not meet his definition of rape (p. 310). Given Lukianowicz's apparent lack of understanding that violence often does not occur in cases of child sexual abuse, his other conclusions must be read with considerable skepticism. He maintains that:

All remaining cases followed the pattern of sexual exploration, play, and later real heterosexual intercourse as found among siblings in different remote societies . . . and also in overcrowded households of working class families in our own Western society. The parents usually turn a blind eye to such behavior in their children (as long as the girls have not begun to menstruate); hence there is no scolding, no threats, no punishment, and so these children do not develop feelings of guilt and later find it easy to substitute for their siblings new sexual partners from outside the family. As a result of this permissive attitude of their parents, and of their subculture, these youngsters usually do not come to any psychological harm. . . . It seems to be almost a "normal" usually a short-lasting phase in the sexual development of children from some social groups. (Pp. 310–11)

Later, in discussing the twenty-nine cases of nonpaternal incest, Lukianowicz reiterates that the incestuous activities "did not result in any bad effects" (1972, p. 312). One wonders then why these people required psychiatric care! It is highly doubtful that seeking psychiatric help is either fashionable or affordable to the majority of the population in Northern Ireland. On the contrary, particularly given the subculture so prejudicially described, it would likely be only quite unhappy or disturbed people who would seek, or be forced to seek, such services.

In contrast to Meiselman, Lukianowicz, Fox, and Farrell, psychologists Stephen Bank and Michael Kahn (1982) consider brother-sister incest as serious as incestuous abuse by other family members. In general, they believe that the significance of sibling relationships in the development of personality as well as in the psychic lives of adults has been greatly underestimated. "It is clear to us," they write,

that the breaking of the incest taboo by siblings is special, and that its greater frequency does not mean that its ramifications are any less significant than are those of the least frequent type, that between mother and son. . . . We believe that sibling incest has profound implications for personality development because it is a basic attack on social custom and taboo and often involves such contradictory feelings as guilt, love, shame, empathy, and anger as well as the processes of identification. (P. 169)

In spite of their strongly stated views about the detrimental effects of sibling incest (which Bank and Kahn define very restrictively as heterosexual activity involving at least one experience of vaginal intercourse or oral-genital contact), these authors often appear unable to distinguish between abuse and mutuality. While they make a distinction between what they refer to as power-oriented, phallic, aggressive incest and nurturing, erotic, loving incest, their examples of the latter are difficult to comprehend. They describe the case of Patty, for example, in which they claim that "although one sibling initiated sexual contact, it became acceptable to both and developed a momentum that neither child chose to slow down" (1982, pp. 171–72). Because Bank and Kahn are unique in apparently taking incestuous abuse by brothers so seriously, the fact that they too are unable to recognize the coerciveness in the sibling relationships they themselves describe will be demonstrated in some detail.

Patty, who was only six years old when her eleven-year-old brother asked her to touch his penis, told her therapist that she had always been frightened of her brother because: "He used to beat me up. He had an uncontrollable temper. He knocked me out twice when I was little by pushing my head into a wall" (1982, p. 172). The therapist asked her: "What do you think about these memories as we bring them up now?" Patty replied: "I just feel scared, very scared. I'm almost reliving it. I'm *panicking, frightened,* because now I remember I was afraid if I didn't go along with what he wanted, that he would beat me up" (p. 173; authors' emphasis). Later Patty added that: "I've lied to myself so much that I believed it never happened. I was so sickened by it" (p. 174). After hearing about Patty's fear and the repression of her feelings, why, one wonders, do Bank and Kahn consider the sexual behavior as becoming acceptable to both parties?

The authors describe Patty as idealizing her brother Shawn as well as being dependent on him because of parental absence and neglect ("Shawn was the only one entrusted with Patty's well-being" [1982, p. 173]). The fact that the sexual relationship (which involved oral, genital, and masturbatory sex) occurred over many years is not in itself evidence that Patty wanted or enjoyed it. But Bank and Kahn offer no other evidence for their conclusion. It seems clear from their description that Patty was very attached to her brother and that there were positive aspects to the relationship, but this does not make the sexual part of it mutual or nonabusive. Along with physical intimidation, the positive elements may help to explain why Patty tolerated the abuse. Yet Bank and Kahn conclude their discussion of this case as follows: "Sibling incest such as Shawn and Patty's must be understood in its family context. In this larger sense, no one is a total victim and no one is a total victimizer. Shawn needed Patty, and she needed him; in a family in which there was depression and despair, *everyone* was a victim" (p. 176).

No. Patty was the victim. Shawn was the perpetrator. And the parents failed to protect their daughter. In some of the other cases they describe, Bank and Kahn also show a similar blindness to the coerciveness and nonreciprocity in the sexual relationships between brothers and sisters.

For sibling incest, the myth of mutuality is tenacious indeed. The cases presented in this chapter indicate that incestuous abuse by brothers is not usually as traumatic for the victim as father-daughter incest. But they also reveal that such experiences are often upsetting, sometimes exceedingly so. And the effects are often long-lasting. Because father-daughter incest is usually (though by no means always) a more serious offense is no justification for continuing to neglect the problem of incestuous abuse by brothers.

19

Female Incest Perpetrators: How Do They Differ from Males, and Why Are There So Few?

Just as it was assumed until recently that boys are rarely victims of sexual abuse, it has also been commonly believed that very few women sexually abuse children. Past studies on the gender of perpetrators confirmed this assumption. Recently, however, some researchers have begun to question this well-established finding.

Some particularly shocking cases of child sexual abuse involving female perpetrators have recently received wide publicity. The most sensational example involves a multiplicity of molestation charges against a grand-mother, several other women, and only one man at the Virginia McMartin Preschool in Manhattan Beach, California. Other cases have occurred at several day care centers throughout the country. These cases have increased public skepticism about the rarity of female perpetration of child sexual abuse.

Nicholas Groth, a prison psychologist, is one of the experts who believes that there has been a serious underreporting of female perpetrators. Although he encountered only 3 women out of 253 adult offenders against children (1 percent) in his professional work prior to 1979, he concluded his discussion of the female offender by arguing that sexual victimization of children by women "may not be as infrequent an event as might be supposed from the small number of identified cases" (1979, p. 192).

Groth (1979) offered the following explanation of his view. First, he said, women may "mask sexually inappropriate contact with a child through the guise of bathing or dressing the victim" (p. 192). Second, the sexual offenses of females are "more incestuous in nature, and the children are more reluctant to report such contact when the offender is a parent (i.e., their mother) and someone they are dependent upon" (p. 192). Third, boys may more frequently be the targets of female offenders than girls are, but it may be difficult to confirm this hypothesis because "boys are less likely to report or disclose sexual victimization than girls" (p. 192).

Kenneth Plummer, a sociologist of sexual behavior, argues that the notion that pedophiles are all men is an inaccurate "stereotype" (1981, p. 27). He maintains that there is a "considerable degree of adult female–child sexuality" (p. 228). Like Groth, Plummer suggests that such "activity" (he appears to deliberately avoid using the word "abuse") is hidden "because of the expectations of the female role which simultaneously expect a degree of bodily contact between woman and child and deny the existence of sexuality in women" (p. 228). Plummer goes so far as to argue that the physical affection that is socially prescribed for women may result in prison sentences for men.

Psychologists Blair Justice and Rita Justice suggest that so few cases of mother-son incest are reported in the literature because this form of incest is the least likely to come to light. "In our experience," they write, "mothers engage more frequently in sexual activity that does not get reported: fondling, sleeping with a son, caressing in a sexual way, exposing her body to him, and keeping him tied to her emotionally with implied promises of a sexual payoff" (1979, p. 179).

Frequently when the issue of female perpetrators is discussed, the definition of sexual abuse becomes much broader. Notice how Justice and Justice, for example, extend their notion of sexual abuse by women to include keeping a son emotionally dependent by being covertly sexually suggestive.

Since we interviewed only women, our survey data provide only a partial basis for evaluating these hypotheses. Nevertheless, we shall see what light our data shed on this issue.

Our probability sample of 930 women reported a total of only ten cases of incestuous abuse by females. These perpetrators include a biological mother, three sisters, three first cousins, and three more distant relatives. These ten relatives constitute only 5 percent of all incest perpetrators reported in our survey and affected only 1 percent of the 930 women interviewed. The percentage of female perpetrators of extrafamilial child sexual abuse in our survey was virtually the same—4 percent.

These low prevalence figures provide strong evidence to contradict the view that there are many more female perpetrators of child sexual abuse —against females, at least—than was previously believed. It is strong evidence because these figures are based on a probability household sample specifically designed to evaluate prevalence issues. Clearly, however, it provides no data on the frequency with which females sexually abuse males. This issue will be discussed later in this chapter.

Despite our small number of female incest perpetrators, some interesting and statistically significant findings emerged from the quantitative analysis, suggesting that when females sexually abuse their relatives, they do so in different ways from males. Not only was incestuous abuse by female perpetrators very rare, it also appears to have been less serious and traumatic than incestuous abuse by male perpetrators. This conclusion is supported by the victims' descriptions of their experiences. Although some of these accounts may seem unworthy of quotation, it is this, ironically, that makes them of such interest. Several appear to have been quite borderline in terms of abusiveness. This is precisely what our nonclinical sample suggests may differentiate sexual abuse by females from sexual abuse by males. Citing these cases, then, provides valuable qualitative confirmation of our major finding about incestuous female relatives.

Finkelhor (1979) also noted that victims of females reported less trauma than victims of males. The comparisons to follow suggest a possible reason. But first, three examples of borderline cases will be cited.

Rare as mother-son incest is, mother-daughter incest is reported even more rarely. In a thorough annotated bibliography on incest published recently, there were only four citations for mother-daughter incest, and the total number of cases discussed in these publications was five (de Young 1985). The only case in our survey is so borderline that the interviewer did not believe it met our definition of sexual abuse. In addition, the respondent mentioned the experience only after the interview had been concluded, not in response to the question on sexual contact with relatives. Hence the interviewer did not complete the separate sexual assault questionnaire required for all qualifying incidents. Consequently we do not know how old the respondent was when the following incident occurred with her mother, except that she was under fourteen years of age.

At the end of the interview, "completely out of nowhere," Marlene told the interviewer that when she was young she had chafed her genitals. Her mother had her lie with her legs apart on a bed while she put lotion on them. Marlene said that her mother stopped and examined her for the longest time without any expression, and without saying a word, almost as if she'd never seen female genitals before. Marlene reported that, "It made me feel very weird. I remember it and still wonder what she saw and thought then. I was very uncomfortable."

A strong argument could be made against considering this incident a case of sexual abuse. First, Marlene did not mention it in answer to the question about whether a relative had ever had sexual contact with her at any time in her life. Second, she described it as making her feel "weird," rather than saying that she felt it was sexual in some way. Third, our definition of sexual abuse is limited to experiences involving sexual contact or attempted sexual contact, but it was her mother's looking at her genitals rather than her putting lotion on them that made her uncomfortable. Out of our desire to err in the direction of inclusion rather than exclusion of female perpetrators, Marlene's experience was counted as a case of incestuous abuse.

Beatrice was five years old when she had the following experience with a fifteen-year-old second cousin.

My grandfather died, so we went to their house. She had me get on top of her. (What happened?) Nothing. I just laid on top of her. (Was it unwanted?) I didn't know what it was all about, so I don't know if it was unwanted. (Was force used?) No. (Was she caressing you anywhere?) I really don't remember. (Did she ever try anything else sexual with you?) No.*

Beatrice recounted this incident after being asked whether she had ever experienced sexual contact with a relative. This indicates that she perceived the contact to be sexual in some way. In addition, there was a ten-year age difference between Beatrice and her second cousin. Therefore this incident was counted as a case of sexual abuse.

Sharon refused to say exactly how the person who abused her was related to her, but she said the perpetrator was a woman. Regarding the relationship, Sharon would only say that it was "a close relation." When the interviewer asked her to be more specific, Sharon said she had blocked out the experience and couldn't really talk about it. The interviewer noted that Sharon was quite upset and uncomfortable at this point. To add to the confusion, Sharon started out describing the perpetrator as a male, and for several reasons the interviewer continued to think that it was a man.†

---

*The interviewer decided that Beatrice's experience would not qualify as sexual abuse so did not complete the questions routinely asked about incidents that qualify, including how upset the respondent was and what the long-term effects of the abuse were.

†For example, when information about the perpetrator's occupation was requested, the interviewer described Sharon as "at a loss, and she seems stressed." Her first answer was that she didn't know, but she then said, "some kind of clerical, secretarial work," followed by the statement: "I was too young." The interviewer noted that Sharon seemed defensive and also that her father was a clerk. The interviewer also commented, "I think she may have been

However, since Sharon insisted the perpetrator was a woman, we have classified the experience as such.

Sharon was thirteen at the time the sexual abuse started. It occurred six to ten times over a period of six months. The perpetrator was about forty years of age at the time it started.

We had to share the same bed because of crowded conditions and he would fondle me at night when I was asleep. (Where did he touch you?) In the genitals. It was a woman by the way. She would fondle me and that would be it. She would stroke my genitals. (Was it something you wanted?) No, I didn't know what to do about it. (Did you ever express that you didn't want it?) No, she was older. (Did anything else sexual occur?) No.

(Upset?) Extremely upset. (Effect on your life?) A great effect. Trust was lost. I learned you just can't trust anyone no matter how close, and that you should always leave room for doubt. The person could be taking advantage of that trust.

If I had a little girl I would be a lot more careful about who I let her stay with, and question her more about what went on. I'd probably not let her stay with an adult alone.

We will focus now on some of our basic findings about female incest perpetrators and how they compare with male perpetrators. When no information about the significance level is reported in the following comparisons, it should be understood that the findings do not reach the < 0.05 level of significance. Most of the findings for female relatives will be reported in percentages despite the small numbers involved, because this makes it easier to comprehend the comparisons with male incest perpetrators.

Characteristics of Incestuous Abuse by Females

Seventy percent of the incestuous abuse by female relatives occurred one time only compared to 41 percent for male perpetrators. Of the eight different kinds of incest perpetrators compared in our study, females were the least likely to sexually abuse their victims more than once. Only one female relative continued to sexually abuse her victim over a period of a year or more.

The only case of a female relative using a verbal threat in connection

---

troubled because the occupation might have been a clue to the identity of the person, for example, her father or mother." The interviewer also noted that Sharon had answered negatively when asked a question at an earlier point in the interview about whether or not she had ever had any unwanted experiences with a girl or woman.

with the sexual abuse was an attack led by a male acquaintance of the victim. This was also the only one of the ten cases of sexual abuse by a female relative in which the abuse involved any physical force. Except for this one incident—which was dominated by a male—no female relatives used force, a weapon, or a verbal threat.

This is how Yvonne—the victim in the one exceptional case—described the experience. She was thirteen when attacked by her female first cousin and a male neighbor who was a friend of her family. Yvonne's cousin was fifteen and her neighbor was sixteen at the time.

He tried to "pants" me: to get me down on the ground and pull off my underwear and run off with it. It was traumatic. He and my cousin took me on a snipe hunt. They grabbed me and threw me on the ground. My cousin held me while he tried to take my panties off and open my shirt and get off my new bra. (Did he touch your breasts or genitals?) My breasts. Then I started screaming so loud that they let me go. I had to walk home alone on a dark country road. (Did they use verbal threats?) Yes, but I can't remember what they were.

(Did your cousin ever have any kind of sexual relationship with other relatives?) Yes, with my uncle. I saw it from a tree. He came and grabbed her. (Upset?) Very upset. (Effect on your life?) A little effect.

Note Yvonne's response to the question—asked of all incest victims—on whether the incest perpetrator was known to have had a sexual relationship with any other relative. This question never yielded a similar disclosure of incest victimization experiences for male incest perpetrators. Could it be that when females become perpetrators of incestuous abuse, they usually have a history of being sexually victimized themselves?

Yvonne's case is consistent with a common finding: When females participate in pair or group sexual victimization with one or more males, they often play an adjunctive rather than a primary, initiating role (see, e.g., Finkelhor and Hotaling's analysis of the National Incidence Study [1984]). Also, they often do not participate directly in the sexual acts.

Only one of the other female incest perpetrators was reported to have had a sexual relationship with another relative besides the respondent. This stepcousin perpetrator participated with two young boys in a Tarzan and Jane game. Rita's experiences occurred over a period of two years, starting when she was ten and her female stepcousin was twelve.

We were into "Tarzan and Jane" games and she staged it so we'd take off our clothes and romp around like Tarzan. This sometimes also included her younger five- and six-year-old brothers. She tried to role play love scenes with me always as the boy. It involved kissing, hugging, and basically being aggressive. She wanted us to pretend we were making love. She wanted me to touch her. What made it confusing was she didn't touch me enough. (Was what she did against your wishes?) Yes, I didn't want to do these things. (What did her two younger brothers have to do?) Take off their clothes. (What did she do to them?) She was not sexual with them; she would help them get dressed. (What ended it?) We moved.

(Upset?) Not very upset. (Effect on your life?) Some effect. Sometimes I wonder about my sexual identity. (Explain.) Because she made me like her, and I was sometimes confused about the boy's role, and wondered what girls are like.

As she described it, Rita's experience was quite ambiguous; she seemed distressed that her stepcousin didn't touch her enough, but she also said that she "didn't want to do these things," and she was upset by the confusion that resulted. Another factor that makes Rita's experience a borderline case of sexual abuse is that her stepcousin was only two years older than her. This falls within our definition of a peer relationship.

With regard to the issue of multiple victimization, the two young boys were made to undress, but according to the sexually abused respondent, "she was not sexual with them." So neither of the cases in which female perpetrators were known to have a sexual relationship with another relative are straightforward instances of multiple perpetration of incestuous abuse. This is yet another way in which the male and female incest perpetrators in our sample were different.

Severity of Incestuous Abuse

Not a single case of incestuous abuse by a female relative occurred at the very severe level of sexual violation (significant at < 0.01 level). Two cases involving female first cousins will be cited next: one at the severe level of abuse (genital fondling) and the other at the least severe level.

Phyllis was nine years old when her ten-year-old female first cousin initiated genital fondling with her.

I was on vacation with a female cousin. The experience was mostly her feeling my genitals. She knew so much more than me, and she was able to get me to feel her genitals too. We were behind locked doors and my mother wanted to know what was going on. We were both severely punished. (Did anything else sexual occur with her?) No, but I felt very guilty.

(Upset?) Very upset. (Effect on your life?) Some effect. It probably had some effect in making me sexually repressed for a long time. My mother was very religious and I knew what I had done was wrong. I never heard anything about sex when growing up, so I didn't know anything about it. My husband had to be very patient with me the first year we were married. I am determined not to do the same thing with my child. (Same thing?) Be closed about sex with her. I want her prepared. I think she will be happier. You have to be open about sex in order to enjoy it as well as for protection.

(Which experience was most upsetting?) The one with my cousin, because of the punishment and guilt involved.

Phyllis considered this experience with her first cousin to have been more upsetting than an attempted rape by a friend when she was nineteen years old. However, the trauma she reported seems largely associated with her mother's punitive response to the incident. It is unfortunate that the interviewer did not probe more carefully for Phyllis's reaction to the sexual experience itself.

Nina was fifteen the one time her eighteen- or nineteen-year-old female first cousin cuddled with her in a way she found sexual and unpleasant.

My cousin was visiting and we slept in the same bed. I was aware that there was more to her cuddling than the need for warmth. (Do you remember her touching you specifically?) No, she just kept getting closer to me. She was pressed very close against me, and I remember how warm she was. She tried to hold me tight and I remember turning my back to her and moving away. I remember thinking something was wrong but I didn't know then that there was such a thing as a lesbian. (What else did she do?) Nothing else. She left me alone after that. (Did she touch you on your breasts or genitals?) No, but she might have wanted to if I had responded. (Upset?) Not very upset. (Effect on your life?) No effect.

Significantly, in all three cases of incest involving female first cousins, the parties were peers (i.e., within five years of age of each other). In addition, all three cases occurred on one occasion only.

Age

Female incest perpetrators were significantly younger than male incest perpetrators when they sexually abused their victims. For example, 44 percent of the female perpetrators were under fifteen years of age, compared to 17 percent of the males. And only two female perpetrators (22 percent) were older than twenty, compared to 71 percent of the males. (These differences were significant at < 0.05 level.) However, the ages of the *victims* of female relatives were very similar to those for male perpetrators.

The age disparity between female incest perpetrators and their victims was also much smaller than was the case for male incest perpetrators. More specifically, 56 percent of the female perpetrators were less than five years older than their victims, compared to only 13 percent of the male perpetrators (significant at < 0.01 level).

Another interesting finding is that the average age of the victims of female perpetrators was forty-seven years at the time of the interview—significantly older than any of the victims of male incest perpetrators, the mean for whom was thirty-seven—a whole decade younger (significant at < 0.05 level). Why the female incest perpetrators were so much older than the males is unknown. Although the small number involved makes conjecture about this finding particularly precarious, one possibility is that there was more sexual abuse by female relatives some time ago than in recent years. This suggestion runs counter to the recent speculations of many experts that sexual abuse by females is increasing. On the other hand, our data are not totally current; the interviews were undertaken in 1978, and the respondents' childhood years often occurred many years or even decades prior to that date. So it could be that sexual abuse by females declined prior to our data collection, but has increased more recently.

Trauma

Browne and Finkelhor (1985) point out that very few studies to date have examined the impact of sexual abuse according to the gender of the perpetrator (p. 29). In their review, they cited only Finkelhor's 1979 study and ours. In his survey he found that "adults rated experiences with *male* perpetrators as being much more traumatic than those with females perpetrators" (1985, p. 29).

Thirty-eight percent of the victims of female incest perpetrators in our survey reported being very or extremely upset by the sexual abuse, the second lowest percentage after victims of grandfathers. In contrast, 53 percent of the victims of male relatives reported being very or extremely upset.

Thirty-eight percent of the victims of female relatives also reported great long-term effects, compared with 52 percent of the victims of male relatives. Although these associations did not reach statistical significance at < 0.05 level, by both these measures of trauma incestuous abuse by female perpetrators appears to be less distressing to the victims.*

---

*There are a number of reasons why these comparisons probably did not reach statistical significance. In two of the ten cases of female perpetrators the interviewer erroneously did not qualify the experience as sexual abuse because it was so mild or questionable as a sexual incident. Therefore, the data on upset and long-term effects were missing. In a third case, the sexual abuse occurred with a female cousin and a male acquaintance who orchestrated the

Incestuous abuse by female relatives may be less traumatic because many of the factors associated with trauma were absent or less pronounced with female incest perpetrators. For example, there was less force or violence associated with sexual abuse by female relatives than male relatives. The sexual abuse was more likely to occur once only and less likely to occur over a long duration. The age difference between the victim and perpetrator was smaller with female relatives than with male relatives. And the sexual abuse never occurred at the most severe level of violation for female relatives, whereas 24 percent of incestuous abuse was at the most severe level for male relatives.

As already mentioned, the case material on incestuous abuse by females also suggests lower levels of trauma than is the case for male incest perpetrators. For example, the three accounts of sister-sister incestuous abuse to follow—only one of which involved peers—appear to be milder than most of the brother-sister cases cited in chapter 18. Although Brigitte reported low trauma, hers was the most distressing of the three experiences of sister-sister incestuous abuse disclosed in our survey.

Brigitte was fifteen years old on the one occasion her sixteen-year-old sister climbed on top of her and proceeded to satisfy herself.

> We slept in the same bed. We were going to bed and she tried to have an orgasm. She didn't wait for me to agree, she just started in. She got on top of me and worked herself up to an orgasm. After that I didn't want to sleep in the same bed with her. (Were you clothed?) We both were. She had a pillow between us, and she got an orgasm on the pillow. (The pillow was on top of you?) Yes. She said, "I'll be the man." (Did she have body contact with you?) No, I'm sure she didn't. But it frightened me. She had a bad temper and we never got along. I was a little afraid of her. She got in trouble when she was eighteen. She later had eight children. (Did you change beds?) Yes, after that. (Upset?) Somewhat upset. (Effect on your life?) No effect.

Yvette was also fifteen years old the one time her sister, who was twenty-four or twenty-five, sexually abused her.

> We were sleeping together in bed, and she started kissing me. She touched me all over with her fingers. She touched my breasts. (Genitals?) Yes. She did the whole act. She got on top of me and rubbed against me and finished. (She had an orgasm?) Yes, she climaxed. (Did anything else happen?) No. She never tried it again. (Did you want it?) I didn't know what she would do. It happened normally.

---

attack. The trauma measure of course reflects the whole experience, not just the female relative's role in it. In a fourth case discussed previously—the only one with a female perpetrator reported to be extremely upsetting and to have great long-term effects—the interviewer was unclear whether the perpetrator was really a female because the respondent referred to the person as "he" (among other reasons).

She started with kissing. It felt funny. I never felt anything against her. (Was it wanted or unwanted?) It seemed normal to me at the time. I guess I was going along with it because I loved her very much. It was funny to me. It didn't upset me too much at the time, but since then I've been thinking about it. (How do you feel now?) I figure she and everyone else gets excited sexually.

(Upset?) Not at all upset. It was just funny. (Effect on your life?) No effect.

Lorna was thirteen years old when her twenty-year-old sister first approached her. The sexual incidents occurred from two to five times over a period of six months. This case is complicated because Lorna reported that the experience had a great *positive* effect on her feelings about her sexuality. It appears to have been unwanted at the time, though even on this issue she fluctuated between saying it was unwanted and that she felt indifferent about what happened. Nevertheless, because of the age difference involved, these experiences constitute a clear-cut case of sexual abuse.

The most upsetting time was initially. It was a new experience. It was with a sister. She has large breasts and she wanted me to fondle them. She was kind of loose for her time. I did fondle her breasts and I feel it was strictly for her gratification. (Did anything else sexual happen with her?) No, that's it. It was the same thing every time. (Was it wanted or unwanted?) It was not wanted. I was indifferent. Sex didn't make that much difference to me at that time. (How did it happen?) We were sleeping in the same room and she kept requesting it. (What ended it?) She moved away.

(Upset?) Somewhat upset. (Effect on your life?) A great effect. I feel that I accepted my own sexuality a lot better because this was an intimate thing with a woman. Sex was not an above-the-table subject in my family, so I feel I learned to accept my sexuality a little better.

Lorna was also sexually abused by three brothers, two of whom abused her when she was six and the third when she was thirteen (see chapter 18). In contrast to her experience with her sister, Lorna reported a fair amount of trauma as a result of two of her experiences with her brothers.

Chapter 3 emphasized the importance of distinguishing between abusive and nonabusive sexual contact between relatives who are peers. It is assumed that mutual, voluntary sex play between siblings and other children who are peers is healthy—or, at least, harmless. As already noted, only 22 percent of the experiences of brother-sister incest reported by our sample of 930 women qualified as nonabusive compared to 50 percent of the cases of sister-sister incest.

Not only are girls much less likely to be sexually abused by a sister than a brother, but it appears that when sister-sister incestuous abuse occurs, it may be less upsetting and may have a less negative impact on the victims' lives.

Possible Effects

Because of the small number of female perpetrators, our analysis here will be limited to one observation of interest.

Some people believe that a childhood sexual experience with someone of the same sex—even an abusive experience—may result in the victim becoming homosexual later in life. Although marriage is not proof of heterosexuality, it is nevertheless suggestive that all ten of the women who had been victimized by a female relative married. This sets them apart from all the other victims of incest perpetrators. Only 68 percent of the victims of male relatives married. This 100-percent marriage rate also sets the victims of female perpetrators apart from the women who had never been victimized by incest, only 69 percent of whom had married.

In addition, exactly half of the victims of female incest perpetrators were still married at the time of the interview—the second highest percentage for the victims of different incest perpetrators. And the victims of female incest perpetrators had raised the highest average number of children (one each) of any of the victims or of the women who had never been victimized.

Presumably the relatively high childbearing rate of our female incest perpetrators is related to their high marriage rate. What might explain their high marriage rate is unknown. It is important to note, however, that three out of the ten victims of female incest perpetrators were also victimized by male relatives. Given the small number of female perpetrators, it becomes impossible to further analyze the possible effects of female perpetrators independently of males.

In conclusion, because there appear to be significant differences in the dynamics and possibly the consequences of sexual abuse of females by other females than for sexual abuse of females by males, it seems advisable for future researchers to do separate analyses by the gender of the perpetrator whenever possible.

The Gender Gap Among Perpetrators of Child Sexual Abuse: Fact or Fiction?

The increasing tendency among many experts on child sexual abuse to view the extent of sexual abuse by females as having been seriously underestimated was discussed at the beginning of this chapter. Because of the popularity of this view, sociologist David Finkelhor and I undertook to thoroughly review the literature on this topic and evaluate the arguments. The results of our review are published at length in our most recent books (Russell 1984*b*; Finkelhor 1984).* The data collated from the studies we reviewed on both extrafamilial and incestuous child sexual abuse confirmed that most sexual offenses against children are perpetrated by males. We concluded that *only about 5 percent of all sexual abuse of girls and about 20 percent of all sexual abuse of boys is perpetrated by older females.*

Since sexual abuse of female children occurs at least twice or three times as frequently as does sexual abuse of male children, the theory that perpetrators of sexual abuse are primarily men seems clearly supported (Finkelhor 1979, 1984). However, various objections have been raised against using the available data to resolve the issue of male preponderance, and these objections need to be addressed.

(1) *Is sexual abuse by adult female perpetrators less often perceived as abusive than abuse by men?* Some observers speculate that much contact between children and older or adult women goes unnoticed in surveys, because the children do not feel abused or victimized or even upset. Some children, in fact, may consider it pleasurable.

By avoiding judgmental terms like "sexual abuse" or "victimization," several studies contradict these speculations. Bell and Weinberg (1981), for example, asked only about sexual contacts that respondents had had before puberty, and then asked for the age of the "partner" (as distinct from "perpetrator"). Their figures are based on contacts with "partners" older than age sixteen, regardless of whether they were positive or negative experiences.

Similarly, students in Finkelhor's (1979) student sample were asked simply to note experiences that they had had before the age of twelve with a person over sixteen and experiences they had had before age twelve with any other persons. Experiences were included in the tally based on meeting certain age-difference criteria, not because they were considered either positive or negative, upsetting or pleasurable. Thus the figures in both these studies were not limited to experiences perceived as abusive by the respondents. Positive experiences with older females would have been included in these figures.

The question of what difference it makes whether the experiences examined are considered abusive by the respondent can be looked at with some of the data from Finkelhor's (1984) Boston survey too. In that survey, adult respondents were asked to list any experiences they had had before the age of sixteen with a person five years older than themselves (irrespective of whether it was considered abusive). The males listed twenty-four such

*The following discussion is an edited excerpt from a chapter I coauthored with David Finkelhor that is published in both of our books.

experiences, five of which (or 21 percent) were with older females. Later the respondents were asked whether they considered the experience to be abusive. Thirteen of the experiences were considered abusive, including two (or 15 percent) of the experiences with females.

So, asking only about abusive experiences *was* found to make some difference (though it was insignificant statistically). But it is not accurate to say that a much larger percentage of experiences with older women is disclosed when respondents are asked about both positive and negative experiences.

(2) *Can women mask sexually inappropriate behavior more easily than men?* Both Groth (1979) and Plummer (1981) believe that since women have more socially prescribed and acceptable physical intimacy with children, their sexual contacts with children might go unnoticed. A woman could, for instance, have a three- or four-year-old child suck on her breasts as a way of gaining sexual gratification, without having this behavior identified as abuse.

There are indeed some caretaking activities that could mask abuse by a woman. Breast-feeding and bathing young children are two of these. It seems unlikely, however, that women could mask the activities that comprise the vast majority of abuse engaged in by men: having the child fondle the adult's genitals, putting the penis on or in the vagina, performing oral sex. A woman engaging in comparable activities would have a hard time disguising them as normal mothering. And even if the mother-child relationship is hidden from the scrutiny of other adults, the mother is still left with the difficult task of masking the sexual activity from the children themselves.

Professionals who work with children believe that most of them are very good at distinguishing touch that is affectionate from touch that is sexual and intended for the adult's gratification. It is especially hard to imagine that preadolescent boys, who are particularly inclined by their peer culture to see sexual content in behavior, could fail to notice an older woman being sexual with them.

Like men, women may try to disguise the sexual nature of their activities with children by telling them that they're just playing a game or expressing affection. Children may believe such deceptions for a short time, but most eventually realize their true nature. It is possible that, at the time of sexual contact, women can deceive children more easily than men can. But any consistent sexual activity would surely show up in reports of older children who, when looking back on their younger years, realize that women were being sexual with them. In fact, few such reports occur.

Therefore, what this discussion actually reveals is that despite the ample opportunities for sexual abuse that mothers have, remarkably few seem to take advantage of them. Breast-sucking, for example, has the dual characteristics of being both a typical act of sexual lovemaking and a basic nurturant interaction between mother and child. As such, it seems fraught with possibilities for abuse. Yet reports from clinical populations or general surveys reveal extremely few cases of inappropriate breast-sucking of mothers by their children.

In contrast, suppose that it was a basic part of the early nurturing process for children to fondle their father's penis. Given the nature of male sexuality common in this culture, we might expect that many fathers would be reluctant to give up this activity and would try to get a child to repeat this act long after the child had outgrown it. The contrast shows well the apparent restraint that is the norm in relations between women and children. Although some sexual activity may be masked, the amount would seem to be small.

(3) *Do women commit special kinds of sexual abuse that go unnoticed and unmeasured?* In discussions of sexual abuse by women, certain activities are mentioned that are not considered in discussions of sexual abuse by men. Justice and Justice (1979), for example, referred to "sleeping with a son . . . exposing her body to him, and keeping him tied to her emotionally with implied promises of a sexual payoff" as forms of sexual abuse by women that go unrecorded (p. 179). The giving of frequent enemas by mothers is also sometimes mentioned.

Studies of sexual abuse of children by adults have not usually asked about such behaviors, which are generally judged to be in a different category. In their extreme forms, these activities constitute psychological rather than sexual abuse (which is characterized by children being used for the direct physical gratification of an adult's sexual needs). It is not at all clear that women engage in more of this psychological abuse than men do. Judith Herman (1981) points out that a large number of fathers have "seductive" relationships with daughters that border on overt sexual abuse but never quite cross the line. There are also forms of psychological abusiveness often used by men: making sexual references to their daughter's breasts or body or exposing children to pornography. Women seem to engage in such behavior far less frequently.

The point about male preponderance is not that women never do harmful things to children's sexuality. It is that women do not seem to use children as often or in such serious ways as men do for their own direct physical sexual gratification. If the question of sexual abuse is to be broadened to include a wider range of psychological sexual abuses, then the behavior of both women *and* men must be submitted to this kind of more inclusive scrutiny.

(4) *Are sexual offenses by females less likely to be reported because they are primarily incestuous?* There is some speculation that the quantity of abuse by females is obscured because it so often occurs within the family. The assumption

here is that incestuous child abuse is less subject to public reporting than is extrafamilial child sexual abuse.

However, no evidence substantiates the first of these ideas. In our study as well as in Finkelhor's student survey, the ratio of female perpetrators involved in incestuous abuse was not significantly different from those involved in extrafamilial child sexual abuse. Moreover, this speculation does not explain why sexual abuse by females is so rarely evident in these self-report studies.

(5) *Is sexual abuse by females obscured because they more often abuse boys, who are more reluctant to report the abuse than girls?* While prior research does indicate that boys are less likely to report abuse either to parents or to public agencies (Finkelhor 1979), it is not necessarily true that most abuse by females occurs to boys. In studies done on both reported cases and self-reports, a greater *absolute* number of cases involved females abusing girls, not boys. For example, in Finkelhor's (1979) student survey, 67 percent of the female perpetrators sexually abused girls, and only 33 percent abused boys (p. 79); and in a study conducted by the American Humane Association (1981), while the percentage of female offenders against boys was higher than the percentage of female offenders against girls (14 percent vs. 6 percent), there were also a great many more girl victims than boy victims. Six percent of 5,052 girls is substantially higher than 14 percent of 803 boys (303 vs. 112). Thus the stereotype that women are most likely to abuse boys than girls is not supported by the available research.

Moreover, this explanation would only apply to underreporting of sexual abuse in public records, not self-report studies. In fact, since sexual contacts between young boys and older women would seem to be among the least stigmatized of the cross-generational contacts, candor about such experiences in self-report studies would be expected to be even higher (Finkelhor and Redfield 1984).

Conclusion

This review supports the conclusion that the extent of sexual abuse by adult female perpetrators is small and that child sexual abuse is primarily perpetrated by males. Furthermore, our survey data indicate that male perpetrators may be responsible for more serious and traumatic levels of sexual abuse than are female perpetrators. So why are so many experts in the field currently arguing that the number of female perpetrators has been seriously underestimated?

At least two factors account for this wave of speculation about hidden sexual abuse by females. On the one hand, clinicians are seeing (and also noticing) more cases of sexual abuse by females than ever before. The number of such cases may have jumped dramatically, but the fact is that the number of cases of sexual abuse *of all types* coming to light has increased dramatically. The types of cases coming to attention are therefore more varied. Because very few or no cases of female perpetrators came to light in the past, as they now emerge in proportion to their actual prevalence they may give the illusion of representing a dramatic new development. This increase (or sudden appearance) has led to questioning of the traditional beliefs about female perpetrators.

Some people assumed in the past that sexual abuse by females *never* occurred. This assumption was wrong and requires correction. Sexual abuse by women *does* occur in some fraction of cases: current evidence suggests about 5 percent of abused girls and 20 percent of abused boys are abused by females. But to take the appearance of some cases of sexual abuse by women to mean that sexual abuse is not primarily committed by men is also wrong and is not supported by the data.

There is another important reason for the current questioning of the long-held presumption of a preponderance of male sexual abusers of children—the fact that some mental health professionals and researchers are ideologically uncomfortable with the idea. Due to their discomfort, they may be overly eager to accept the possibility that it might not be true.

In a cultural climate where feminists have called upon men to relinquish certain traditional modes of behavior, the fact that it is primarily men who commit sexual abuse bolsters feminists' arguments and may thus create defensiveness in those who oppose feminist thinking. Some people find the problem of sexual abuse an easier cause to promote when it is not entangled in "gender politics." Political support for issues of general "human" concern is easier to mobilize than support for issues that appear to benefit one social group more than others—particularly when that group, women, is a stigmatized one of lower status.

But reality must not be twisted to suit ideological or political needs. The widespread and destructive problem of child sexual abuse can be solved only if we face the truth about it. This truth is well documented by the evidence and consistent with our current understanding of sex roles and male and female sexuality.

20

Grandfather-Granddaughter Incest

In our survey, sexual abuse by grandfathers was reported less frequently than any other category of male relatives except brothers-in-law. Uncles, for example, constitute 26 percent of the total number of incest perpetrators compared to only 6 percent for grandfathers. On the other hand, one more case of sexual abuse by grandfathers was reported than sexual abuse by all female incest perpetrators combined (eleven versus ten cases). These eleven cases represent a prevalence rate of 1.2 percent for grandfather-granddaughter incest.

With an average age of sixty-one years at the time they started to abuse their granddaughters, three of these grandfathers were step- and eight were biological grandfathers. We have no data on what percentage of our sample had stepgrandfathers. However, this three-to-eight ratio suggests that stepgrandfathers, like stepfathers, may be more prone to sexually abuse their granddaughters than biological grandfathers.

Even less is known about grandfather-granddaughter incest than about brother-sister incest. Psychologist Karin Meiselman (1978) is one of the few scholars who has made at least some attempt to shed light on the subject. She had access to only five cases of grandfather-granddaughter incest obtained from a sample of women who were undergoing psychotherapy. Meiselman was interested in evaluating to what extent incestuous grandfathers fit the cultural stereotype of the "dirty old man." She concluded that they did not.

None was reported to have been senile, psychotic, mentally defective, or drunk. All of the grandfathers were gentle in their sexual approaches, and none of them attempted to have intercourse with a prepubertal granddaughter. They did not threaten or intimidate their incest partners, and because of their quality of gentleness the granddaughter was cooperative during the incest affair itself, although she later developed very serious misgivings about it. These women tended to blame themselves, rather than their grandfather, for the affair. As adults, they often enjoyed sexual intercourse but still manifested a number of conflicts in heterosexual relationships that they themselves attributed to incest. (P. 291)

The terms "partner" and "affair" serve to obscure the abusive and coercive aspect of grandfather-granddaughter incest, implying joint responsibility and even that the victims, like their grandfathers, had their sexual needs met in these relationships. This suggests a severely distorted perpetrator-oriented perspective in an otherwise useful book.

While Meiselman concluded that the five incestuous grandfathers in her sample didn't fit the stereotype of "dirty old men," several in our sample do. As was the case in Meiselman's tiny sample, the grandfathers in our survey did not appear to be psychotic, senile, or mentally defective, though one was reported as drunk. However, some of them do appear to be predatory old men who were attracted to young teenage or prepubescent girls, and took advantage of their naïveté and helplessness. And 44 percent of grandfathers were known to have sexually abused at least one other relative. Here are three examples of behavior that seems to fit the common stereotype:

Heather was fifteen years old when her grandfather, who was in his late sixties, started sexualizing contact with her. These incidents occurred from eleven to twenty times over a period of two years.

One had to be on one's guard at times when one kissed him hello or good-bye. You had to do it quickly or your breasts were definitely "accidentally" touched and fondled. This went on for a couple of years. You had to warn your girlfriends not to get too close to him. It was more embarrassing than frightening, especially when he did it to my girlfriends. The same thing happened with my aunts. He'd get them when they passed by him too. My mother held his hand when she kissed him hello and good-bye [presumably to stop him from touching her elsewhere]. (What ended it?) He outgrew it. (Upset?) Not at all upset. (Effect on your life?) No effect.

Gloria was fifteen years old when her grandfather started touching her sexually. This occurred from eleven to twenty times over a period of eight years.

It started when I was fifteen and my father died, and it went on until I was twenty-three. He repeatedly kissed me, fondled me, and caressed me. (Where did he touch you?) He would hug and fondle me, but when I was growing up he didn't touch my breasts or genitals. I knew he liked teenage girls. I put up with it because he was the sole financial support of my family, and I didn't want to make him mad. He made me conscious of the fact that he supported us.

When I was older we would travel together because I worked for his business. One time he came into the motel room and told me about his unhappy marriage. He said that his wife was frigid, then he lay down on the bed with me and began to kiss me and caress my breasts. I said I loved him but I could understand why his wife was frigid. That hurt his feelings and he left. I was twenty-three at that time and married. (What ended it?) I hurt his feelings.

(Upset?) Not at all upset. (Effect on your life?) Some effect. I like old men. (Any other effect?) No, he was a nice guy.

Despite the fact that Gloria felt she had to tolerate her grandfather's behavior for financial reasons, she reported no negative effects.

Erna was sixteen years old when her seventy-year-old grandfather started behaving sexually toward her.

My mother had encouraged me to visit my grandfather because she couldn't stand to visit him herself. I went to visit and talked for a while and when I got ready to leave, he gave me this big bear hug all over my body above my waist. He didn't go for my crotch or anything, but it was far more affectionate than a grandfather should be. It was a matter of touching my breast and, as much as he could, my front and sides. He would hug me and feel me up and down, and do as much as he could possibly get away with. I felt he was pressing intimacy. He would have done more if I'd let him. I didn't visit him alone after that. (Upset?) Not very upset. (Effect on your life?) No effect.

Heather, Gloria, and Erna all reported very little distress as a result of these experiences. Gloria seemed less able than the other two girls to stop her grandfather's sexual behavior toward her. She was quite clear about the reason: his role as the financial supporter of her family. This placed him in a position more comparable with many fathers. It seems unlikely that this experience was as untraumatic as Gloria claimed.

In any case, one of our survey's findings about grandfather-granddaughter incest is that the sexually abused granddaughters reported the lowest degree of upset of the victims of all the other types of incest perpetrators, either separately or together. For example, 50 percent of the granddaughters described the sexual abuse as not at all or not very upsetting compared to 19 percent of the victims of all the other incest perpetrators combined. (This relationship is significant at < 0.05 level.)

Granddaughters were also among the lowest reporters of great long-term effects, but this finding did not reach statistical significance.*

These findings raise two questions: Why was grandfather-granddaughter incest less upsetting than other forms of incestuous abuse? And why did this difference not also manifest itself in long-term effects? The latter question will be addressed first.

Victims of grandfather-granddaughter incest were significantly more likely to be victims of more than one incestuous relative than was the case for other incest victims (significant at < 0.01 level). More than half of them

*When the upset and long-term effects variables were combined for our trauma measure, victims of female relatives, male first cousins and "other" male relatives all reported slightly less trauma than victims of grandfathers (see table 10–6).

(55 percent) were so victimized compared to 13 percent of the other victims of incest. Although the question about long-term effects was asked of each perpetrator separately, it may be difficult for victims of multiple perpetrators to clearly distinguish the effects of each experience. Furthermore, there may be a cumulative effect.

Explaining Low Upset for Grandfather-Granddaughter Incest

Incestuous grandfathers were significantly more likely than other incest perpetrators to sexually abuse their victims at the least severe level. Almost three-quarters (73 percent) of them did so compared with about a third (34 percent) of the other abusive relatives (significant at < 0.05 level). And not a single grandfather engaged in sexual abuse at the very severe level. This finding is consistent with Meiselman's; no grandfather in her sample attempted intercourse with a prepubertal granddaughter either.

However, the grandfathers in our sample were not significantly less forceful than other perpetrators, as was the case in Meiselman's study. Furthermore, grandfathers in our survey sexually abused their granddaughters significantly more frequently than other incest perpetrators abused their victims: 82 percent of the grandfathers sexually abused their victims more than once compared with 56 percent of the other incest perpetrators (significant at < 0.06 level). In addition, the duration of grandfather-granddaughter incest was longer than it was for other incest perpetrators. Seventy percent of them sexually abused their victims for longer than a year compared with 29 percent of the other incestuous relatives (significant at < 0.05 level).

Since both frequency and duration of incestuous abuse are correlated with trauma, one might have supposed that the greater frequency and duration of incestuous abuse by grandfathers would have offset the milder severity of their sexual abuse. Future research is needed to evaluate our finding that grandfather-granddaughter incest was less upsetting than incestuous abuse by other incest perpetrators combined, and—if this is confirmed—to try to explain it.

Two examples of granddaughters who reported relatively low degrees of trauma as a result of sexual abuse by their grandfathers will be cited next. Edith was seven years old when her stepgrandfather, in his fifties at the time, started sexually abusing her. This abuse occurred from eleven to twenty times over a period of two years.

It was a constant thing any time we went to Grandpa and Grandma's. When my mother and grandmother would go out, my stepgrandfather would babysit me and my sister. He'd suggest we get in our nightgowns. I remember lying on a couch next to him. He was drunk and passed out, but he fondled my breasts in his sleep! (Was he really asleep?) Yes. Finally I just got up. I was able to cope with him much better than I was able to cope with my stepfather. I was cold and didn't care when he died. (Did he abuse your sister too?) No, she was five years younger than me and little more than a baby.

(What ended it?) I got older and we could babysit ourselves. (Upset?) Somewhat upset. (Effect on your life?) Some effect. That experience along with what happened with my stepfather didn't help me. But this is not something I really think of at all.

One year later when Edith was eight, her stepfather started abusing her. The much greater trauma she reported as a result of that experience may have overshadowed her experience with her stepgrandfather.

Carrie was one of the youngest victims in our survey to be able to remember an experience of sexual abuse. She was three and one-half when the incidents with her grandfather started. They continued over a period of two years. He was in his sixties at the time.

My memory is fairly general. There's not one instance that is outstanding. I would say it occurred maybe a dozen times. It was a treat for me to sleep in the guest room. When he visited me we would sleep together. He would kiss me with his tongue in my mouth and rub against me. I don't remember him fondling me though I think maybe one time he put his hand in my pants, but nothing more.

(What ended it?) I stopped sleeping with him. When I got older, I decided to sleep in my own bed. (Upset?) Somewhat upset. (Effect on your life?) No effect.

Although Carrie describes being only "somewhat upset" by her experiences with her grandfather and said they had no effect, the interviewer observed that at the end of the interview Carrie "got a bit subdued when talking about her grandfather." In addition, she selected her experiences with him as the most upsetting she had ever had, more upsetting even than an attempted rape by a stranger when she was twenty-three. This evaluation is confusing since Carrie reported that she had been "very upset" by the attempted rape and that it had had "some" long-term effects on her life.

Despite the fact that several victims of grandfathers reported low levels of upset in response to the sexual abuse, it would be a serious mistake to assume that grandfather-granddaughter incest is never very upsetting or traumatic. Not only are we dealing with a tiny sample of eleven cases, but some of these experiences were reported to have been very distressing. Two examples follow.

Winifred was twelve years old when her grandfather, who was in his

sixties, approached her sexually. This behavior occurred from two to five times over a period of one week.

My younger sister and I were staying with our grandparents for three weeks. In the middle of the second week our grandmother would leave the house, and our grandfather would come into our room. One time I was sitting in a chair and he moved his hand up my leg to my crotch. He told me how Grandma wouldn't let him share her room anymore. The second time he came into our room he patted my shoulder as close as he could get to my breast, until I moved away. The third time he came in with five dollars in his hand. He told my sister, who was very busty, that if she would take off her nightgown, he'd give her the five dollars. I was in bed listening. She yelled, "Papa, get out of here!" He threw the five dollars on the bed and said, "This is for you," and left. We were scared and decided never to leave each other alone. We put a chair in front of the door so he couldn't come in.
   The next day I took a tray of iced tea outside, and he came up to me and said, "Oh, you're taking that outside? How nice," and he patted me with his hand on my crotch. This time my sister and I decided to tell my aunt. She believed us and sent her husband over to talk to him. (Did anything else sexual occur with him?) No, that's it. I found out that he tried all of those things with my older sister, but she never told us. (What ended it?) Telling my aunt and her husband talking to him.
   (Upset?) Extremely upset. (Effect on your life?) Some effect. That was the first time I realized how people's first reaction was not to believe you about being abused, and how they covered it up if it was one's relatives. My first distrust of males started creeping in then. I realized that things are not as they seem.

Winifred's disillusionment regarding people's response to being told about sexual abuse is difficult to understand since her aunt and uncle intervened to stop the abuse. Unfortunately, the interviewer failed to delve into this inconsistency.
   Winifred and her sister were harassed by their grandfather in each other's presence; thus they did not experience the terrible isolation that is so common in cases of child sexual abuse, which their older sister may have experienced. Their mutual supportiveness is a touching aspect of Winifred's account. In general, they appear to have handled their predicament in an impressively assertive and resourceful way.
   Vivian was seven years old when her grandfather, who was in his fifties, sexually abused her. He did so from two to five times within a period of one month. Vivian was very reluctant to reveal that her perpetrator was her grandfather.

(Which time was the most upsetting?) The first time. I was so young—about seven. It was a relative and he pulled off my pants, put his finger in me, and then took my hand and put it on his crotch. (In you?) In my vagina. I don't think it happened more than twice. The second time was just an attempt. Through my growing up years I hated his guts. I didn't show any family-type affection for him.

I discussed it with a cousin and my younger sister years later, and the same thing happened to them at about the same age.

(What ended it?) My avoiding any situation where it could happen again. I stopped being alone with him or sitting on his lap. (What was the relationship between you and this person?) [Vivian did not wish to disclose her relationship with this man. She said that he was dead, but that his family wasn't. The importance of knowing the relationship was explained and she was assured of confidentiality.] He was my grandfather.

(Upset?) Extremely upset. (Effect on your life?) Some effect. I certainly avoided any contact with him. I worried about my younger sisters. I developed great animosity toward him and I was relieved when he died. It might have affected my show of affection, I don't know. It created a big split with me and my mother because I told her about it when my sister was about that age and she refused to believe me. It caused difficulties between us for a number of years. (Which experience of sexual abuse was most upsetting?) The experience with my grandfather had the most lasting effect.

The other experiences that Vivian recounted included one that she described as "exactly the same as with my grandfather except he was a friend of the family. I was the same age and it was the same event. I was sitting on his lap and it was like they'd gotten together! I might have gotten the two people confused because they were so much the same. I'm sure I repressed it for years."

Vivian was also the victim of an attempted rape by a date when she was sixteen, an attempted rape by an acquaintance when she was twenty-four, and an attempted rape by another acquaintance when she was thirty-one. Given these other sexual assaults, the fact that Vivian found the experience with her grandfather to be the most upsetting is all the more significant.

Grandfather's Role in Multiple Victimization

We noted earlier in this chapter that 55 percent of the victims of grandfathers were sexually abused by more than one relative. This raises the question: Are the grandfathers the first relatives to incestuously abuse their granddaughters, or do they sexually abuse them only after they have already been incestuously abused? If the latter were the case, it might suggest that the grandfathers—along with other perpetrators—were picking up on cues of premature sexualization in their granddaughters' behavior.

In three of the five cases of granddaughters who were multiple incest victims, their grandfathers were the first relative to sexually abuse them;

in another case (Vivian's) an uncle sexually abused the girl at the same age, and it isn't known who did so first; and in the fifth case an uncle and a cousin sexually abused the victim before the grandfather did. Even though the severity of the sexual abuse grandfathers engaged in was mild and relatively untraumatic, this analysis suggests the possibility that some grandfathers may play an initiating role in what became a history of revictimization for their victims.

Because of the very small numbers, this hypothesis is extremely tentative, but worthy of further investigation.

Social Class of Victimized Granddaughters

An unexpected finding about the victims of grandfathers was that 86 percent of them came from upper-middle-class homes (as judged by the occupational status of their fathers) compared with 41 percent of the victims of other incest perpetrators (significant at < 0.06 level). However, the numbers involved are particularly small because of missing information on father's occupation for four out of the eleven victims of grandfather-granddaughter incest.

This upper-middle-class overrepresentation of the victims of incestuous grandfathers was also reflected in the occupational status of the victims themselves; 55 percent had upper-middle-class occupations compared with 27 percent of all the other incest victims and 29 percent of the women who had never been victimized by incest (significant at < 0.06 level). Similarly, these granddaughters' fathers also had significantly higher job prestige than the fathers of other incest perpetrators (significant at < 0.05 level).

In addition, all but one of the incestuous grandfathers was white.

Again, future research is needed on a larger sample of incestuous grandfathers to evaluate these findings.

Conclusion

To some extent, our study supports Meiselman's analysis of grandfather-granddaughter incestuous abuse. Incestuous grandfathers appear to be most comparable to female incest perpetrators in that most of them sexually abused their victims at the least severe level and their victims reported relatively low levels of trauma. Despite this rather mild picture, grandfathers were more inclined than other incest perpetrators to sexually abuse their victims more than once and over a longer duration.

Yet a very different picture of grandfather-granddaughter incest emerges from a study of ten cases that had been referred to the police or a protective service hotline (Goodwin, Cormier, and Owen 1983). Sexual intercourse was involved in five of these cases. Psychiatrists Jean Goodwin, Lawrence Cormier, and John Owen considered that nine of the victims were in need of treatment and only two of them were without symptoms (p. 169). They conclude that the results of their study "cast doubt on the assumption that grandparent incest is a benign form of abuse" (p. 163).

Of course, it is to be expected that it is the more serious cases of incest victimization that are reported to the authorities. Therefore it is not reasonable to assume that these cases can provide an accurate picture of incestuous grandfathers in the population at large. However, the findings of Goodwin, Cormier, and Owen serve as a valuable reminder that grandfather-granddaughter incest can be far more severe and traumatic than the cases that emerged in our probability sample. Presumably, had our sample been much larger, we would have encountered cases more comparable with those assessed in their study.

In Goodwin, Cormier, and Owen's study (1983), eight out of ten of the incestuous grandfathers had also sexually abused their own daughters. Indeed, the ten grandfathers were known to have sexually abused a total of thirty-three victims (p. 165). Also, "of the 18 grandchild victims, eight had been sexually abused by other perpetrators in addition to grandfather"; and "five of these children were re-abused by other perpetrators after the grandfather incest stopped" (pp. 167–68).

Unfortunately, we did not ask the victims of grandfather-granddaughter incest in our survey whether or not their mothers had also been victimized. However, as already noted, 55 percent of our victims of grandfathers were sexually abused by more than one relative and 44 percent of the grandfathers were known to have sexually abused another relative. In these two respects, then, our findings are similar.

Given their findings, it is not surprising that Goodwin, Cormier, and Owen (1983) conclude that "there is some justification for the fears expressed by adult incest victims about visitation between their children and the [grand] father-perpetrator" (p. 163).

Our findings about grandfather-granddaughter incest raise several questions: Why was sexual abuse by grandfathers less upsetting than such abuse by other incest perpetrators? Are most incestuous grandfathers only interested in having sexual contact at the least severe level, or do they restrain themselves from attempting more severe acts of abuse? If so, why do they restrain themselves: for fear of being caught, concern for the victim, or some other reason? Why are granddaughters more frequently the victims of more than one incest perpetrator than most victims of other relatives? And finally, to what extent do incestuous grandfathers play an initiating role in their granddaughters' history of revictimization?

The three cases of stepgrandfather-daughter incest were all reported to be quite or very traumatic. (See the case histories of Holly in chapter 12 and Ann in chapter 24.) Two of these victims responded with considerable assertiveness—behavior that also occurred more frequently with stepfathers than with biological fathers. And all three of the victims of sexual abuse by stepgrandfathers were multiple victims of incest and sometimes other sexual abuse as well.

Just as we found many significant differences between incestuous abuse by biological fathers and stepfathers, it appears that there may be similar differences between sexual abuse by biological grandfathers and stepgrandfathers. Further research is needed to explore this hypothesis as well as the many other questions raised in this chapter.

21

Uncles Who Sexually Abuse Their Nieces

Cases of uncles who sexually abuse their nieces are scattered through the incest literature. But rarely have they been separated from other types of perpetrators to compare them to incestuous fathers, brothers, or other relatives. Yet our survey shows uncles to be the most common perpetrators of incest ($N = 48$), slightly more common than fathers ($N = 44$). And the Kinsey study (1953) found over twice as many cases of uncle-niece incest as father-daughter or brother-sister incest (p. 118). It is indeed past time to take a careful look at incestuous uncles.

The fact that uncle-niece incestuous abuse occurs outside the nuclear family makes it particularly important theoretically. Some theorists have attributed the occurrence of incestuous abuse within the nuclear family to certain types of family problems, for example: a mother who is weak, sick, or unavailable; a wife who rejects all aspects of the traditional wife role, particularly sex with her husband; a daughter who plays the role of little mother (see, e.g., Herman 1981; Mrazek and Bentovim 1981; de Young 1982; Thorman 1983). Clearly such explanations are irrelevant to uncle-niece incest. This fact alone does not, of course, invalidate the possible usefulness of these theories in explaining father-daughter incest. However, it does raise *questions* about their usefulness, especially when they are considered the only causal factors. It it doubtful that incestuous fathers and uncles are altogether different kinds of men and that the dynamics of father-daughter incest and uncle-niece incest have nothing in common.

True, for most people the incest taboo is probably considerably stronger between father and daughter than uncle and niece. Hence a complete and satisfactory explanation of father-daughter incest has to account for the overcoming of greater social and presumably internal inhibitions against acting out incestuous feelings by fathers than by uncles. Nevertheless, the widespread prevalence of uncle-niece incest provides a significant challenge for those who consider family dynamics to be a complete and satisfactory theory of incestuous abuse.

Once again Karin Meiselman is one of the few researchers to discuss uncle-niece incest as a distinct type of incestuous abuse. And once again her analysis was based on only five cases, all of whom had sought psychotherapy. Since there were, in contrast, thirty-six cases of father-daughter incest in her sample, Meiselman (1978) speculated about uncle-niece incest that "there are a large number of women in the general population who were not particularly unsettled by such experiences" (p. 285).

She also surmised that the "typical" uncle-niece case probably "involves an uncle who is quite distant from the niece's nuclear family and has no important role in her upbringing" (1978, p. 288). She suggested that "uncle-niece incest has the potential for being extremely disturbing" but only "if it is violent or if its occurrence disrupts the child's relationships within the nuclear family" (p. 288). The implication of Meiselman's argument here is that adult-child sexual relationships in general are traumatic only if they are violent and disrupt the nuclear family.

Our probability sample survey provides an ideal opportunity to evaluate Meiselman's conclusions. The average age of the incestuous uncles in our survey was forty-two years. Because there is almost always a substantial age difference between uncles and nieces, all cases of sexual contact that occurred before the niece reached the age of eighteen were considered abusive. Our survey found that in only two of the forty-eight cases of incestuous abuse by uncles did nieces have any positive feelings about the sexual contact; only one was described by the niece as wholly positive. (This case was cited in chapter 3.) Overall, 96 percent of the experiences of uncle-niece incest appeared from the descriptions to have been completely unwanted compared to 83 percent of all the other cases of incestuous abuse (significant at < 0.05 level).

Dina is one of the nieces who expressed some positive feelings about the sexual contact with her uncle, but as we shall see, these were far outweighed by—and added to—the trauma. Her uncle started molesting her when she was three years old. Dina estimated that he did so from two to five times over a period of from one to three years. He was in his fifties at the time.

It occurred when I was a small child. It also happened to all the others in the family; we compared notes later. It started with caressing. Then the caressing moved to the genital area—to the outer lips of my vagina; there was no interior exploration of the vulva. He kissed me too, but not on the mouth. It occurred when I was alone in a room with him. I wasn't all that close to him, and I saw him only occasionally. I would sit on his lap, but I was not unclothed—my underpants were not removed and nor was I hurt. I did not struggle; I was very passive. It was like an awakening experience for a very small child. (Was it pleasurable?) Oh, yes. (Did he ever use physical force?) No. (What ended it?) I can't remember. In life your patterns change. You get too big. Other smaller ones come along. You don't go to the same places or do the same things.

(Upset?) Very upset. I was troubled by it; knowing you're doing something you shouldn't do but fascinated by it. It made me nervous, upset. It occupied quite a lot of my thinking time. (Effect on your life?) For a long time it made me shy and fearful of males at the same time as being fascinated. I had ambivalent feelings toward them. It took quite a while to put things into perspective. I'm fortunate in that I've never been assaulted in a hurtful way. It lost its impact for me when I found out it had happened to my three female cousins who were both older and younger than I. I was a teenager when I found that out, so I carried it around for quite a while. The upset was when I was alone with this dark, dark secret.

(Which experience was the most upsetting?) The one with my uncle probably had the most emotional impact on me. Traumatic things that happen when you're young seem to be the most upsetting.

The other experiences Dina reported included an attempted rape by a date when she was sixteen as well as sexual abuse by a chiropractor when she was nineteen and by a medical doctor when she was twenty-six.

We shall see throughout this chapter that many of the incestuous uncles sexually abused more than one relative.

Age

Eight percent of the uncles were under twenty years of age, 13 percent were twenty-one to thirty, 35 percent were thirty-one to forty, 15 percent were forty-one to fifty, 23 percent were fifty-one to sixty, and 6 percent were over sixty.

Four percent of the uncles were only five to nine years older than their nieces; 12 percent were ten to nineteen years older; 54 percent were twenty to thirty-nine years older; and 29 percent were over forty years older. The age disparities between uncles and their nieces were somewhat greater than for fathers.

Approximately a third (31 percent) of the nieces were under nine years of age when their uncles sexually abused them, 44 percent were ten to thirteen, and 25 percent were fourteen to seventeen. These percentages are very close to the norm for all incest perpetrators.

Typology of Incestuous Uncles

Four different types of incestuous uncles emerged from the descriptions reported in our survey. Some of the uncles appeared to behave in a relatively mild predatory fashion toward their nieces. They appeared to have no intention of carrying the sexual abuse further. Other uncles were definitely willing to proceed to a more severe level of sexual abuse. We will refer to these two types of uncles as mild predators and serious predators.

Another factor besides the kinds of sex acts the uncles were interested in engaging in that distinguished these incestuous uncles was whether or not they were interested in girls who were postpubertal or prepubertal. Since this typology emerged from the case material, illustrative examples of these four types of incestuous uncles may be helpful in bringing it to life.

MILD PREDATORS TOWARD POSTPUBERTAL GIRLS

The following two cases are examples of uncles who are considered to be mild predators.

Theresa was thirteen and her uncle forty when he started touching her sexually. These incidents occurred from six to ten times over a period of two years.

(Which time upset you the most?) It was all pretty upsetting. I was very young and he tried to feel me. He pinched me and touched my bosoms. He was a dirty old man. Whenever there were family dinners and he came to our house, he'd find a way to give me a little feel. Also when I visited his house. These occasions were never prearranged; it was at family gatherings.
(Did he have a sexual relationship with any other relative?) I think he tried it with my sister. We (sisters) decided once he tried to get fresh with all of us. (Upset?) Very upset. (Effect on your life?) A little effect.

Heidi was fifteen or sixteen years old when her thirty-year-old uncle started sexually harassing her. These incidents occurred more than twenty times (the maximum category) over a period of one year.

I used to wear shorts. He would put his arm around me and pinch me on the bottom. It was embarrassing at the time. He'd also say funny things like "You're going to be a good lay when you grow up." I didn't know what it meant. Older men seem to be curious about young girls. (Did he touch your breasts or genitals?) No, he was a real uncle. (How many different times did something sexual happen with him?) All the time he came to the house. (What ended it?) I told him to leave me alone. I got real embarrassed. (Upset?) Not at all upset. (Effect on your life?) No effect.

Despite her uncle's predatory behavior, Heidi seemed confident that he wouldn't touch her breasts or genitals because "he was a real uncle." The incest taboo had not really been violated in her opinion.

SERIOUS PREDATORS TOWARD POSTPUBERTAL GIRLS

Christine's uncle appeared to have been a more serious predator than Theresa's or Heidi's. She was twelve years old when her uncle, in his late twenties, attempted to have intercourse with her. These assaults occurred from two to five times over a period of one or two months.

(Which time was the most upsetting?) The times he wanted me to do it with him. One time on Christmas Eve everyone else had gone to bed. I was still up and I went downstairs. He tried to kiss me, leaned me up against the wall, then tried to do it. (What did he try to do?) He wanted to screw me. He pulled down my pants and everything and he tried. But I left, went upstairs and talked to my sister. Another time he got me and my sister out of school, bought some wine, and got drunk. When she went to the bathroom, he pulled down my pants. (What did he do next?) Nothing because my sister was coming back. (Was force involved?) Yes, he grabbed me real hard. (Did you feel physically threatened?) Yes.

(What ended it?) I told him if he didn't stop, I'd tell my boyfriend. (How upset?) Very upset. (Effect on your life?) A great effect. I think all guys are disgusting sometimes, or they can be. I don't trust them like I'd like to. I feel guilty and ashamed about it.

MILD PREDATORS TOWARD PREPUBERTAL GIRLS

Cornelia expressed repulsion for the way that several uncles embraced her, but she said that only one of these uncles touched her in a sexual way. She was seven and her uncle forty-two on the one occasion that this occurred.

My uncles would hug us and squeeze us—but not in a sexual way. I didn't care for those drunkards to touch me. They would always do this in open view. I told my mother I didn't like them. (How did they touch you?) It was mainly hugging or hanging on to me, but they were big drunken hugs. Every time they came around me, I'd run away. I was always on my guard. I hated them all for their drinking. My father would drink a lot too. I never liked any man who liked to get drunk.

(Did any of them ever try to touch you on the breasts or genitals?) Only one of them when I was really young. I was very worried about this, but I never told my parents about him because they would have been so mad at him. You are the only person I ever told about this. I was about seven. The main thing I remember is his big hand coming down like this. [Cornelia gestured to show a hand rubbing her breast back and forth several times.] It frightened me so badly. It made a lasting impression on me. I was always very afraid of all the family who were drinkers. (Did he try anything else sexual?) No, because I always stayed away from him after that. I'd always catch him looking at me and I felt this fear, and I never gave him the opportunity again. He felt my auntie on the breasts too, and that also made me afraid. I pretended to be asleep but I saw him play with her breasts.

(Upset?) Very upset. (Effect on your life?) A great effect. It scared me very much and I didn't know how to take it. I didn't want them to feel I was lying and I didn't want to get in trouble, so I always stayed away and I never set foot in my aunt's house again.

When Cornelia said she didn't want "them" to feel she was lying, she presumably meant her parents. Her response to her uncle is another example of the tremendous resourcefulness and determination shown by some young girls in avoiding and/or coping with sexually exploitive, older relatives.

SERIOUS PREDATORS TOWARD PREPUBERTAL GIRLS

The uncles of Elsa and Tamara appear to have been more serious predators. Elsa was only three or four years old the one time her uncle, who was over sixty, sexually molested her.

I was sleeping on the floor. We were over at an aunt's house and I remember I woke up and this dirty old man was messing around with me. The only memory I have is that I didn't like it and that I knew it was something wrong. So I got up and moved away and he stopped. I wasn't afraid. I just didn't like it; it wasn't the right thing to be doing. (What did he do?) He fondled me. (Fondled?) He touched my genitals. (Genitals?) My vagina. He put his hand through the leg part of my underpants. (How well did you know him?) I knew him fairly well, though he wasn't someone we visited. (Did he use verbal threats?) No, he didn't say a word. (Was this reported to the police?) No, not even to my mother and father.

(Upset?) Somewhat upset. (Effect on your life?) Some effect. It was something that stuck with me for many many years. It's a memory that I don't forget. It was distasteful. Even talking about it after all these years is very distasteful.

Why some children feel sexual advances by adults to be wrong and others do not is unknown at this time. In Elsa's case moral disapproval of her uncle's behavior seemed to provide her with additional motivation to try to avoid future encounters.

Tamara was ten years old when her uncle, who was in his forties, started to molest her. These incidents occurred from two to five times over a period of two years.

I was staying with my uncle and aunt at that time. Every day he used to give me extra money to spend. One day when my aunt was gone, he called me in and tried to get me to play with his penis. (Did he use force?) Yes, he tried to force me to jerk him off. He forced me to touch his penis, but I wouldn't jerk him off. At other times when my aunt was not at home, he used to reach out and feel my breast. I was afraid to tell my aunt because he might beat her up if I did.

(What ended it?) I left them and went to live with my mother. He tried to get me back, but I wouldn't go and my mother didn't make me. (Upset?) Very upset. (Effect on your life?) A great effect. It made me a little leery of men. I couldn't really trust them after that.

Tamara's explanation for not telling her aunt about the sexual abuse is an example of the many young girls who act against their own interests in order to protect an adult.

It is clear from some of the cases just cited that some of these uncles also behaved in a predatory and assaultive fashion toward their adult relatives. Not all the uncles can be placed into our typology. For one thing, we don't always know whether the victim was pre- or postpubertal. Nor is it always clear from the accounts whether the uncles who sexually abused their nieces at a mild level would have abused them at a more severe level if the opportunity had arisen. Nevertheless, the typology does serve to differentiate the less serious types of incestuous uncles from the more serious ones. This typology may be equally appropriate for incestuous grandfathers, and perhaps fathers as well.

Uncle-Niece Incestuous Abuse and Incestuous Abuse by Other Relatives

Only one uncle was the provider for the niece he victimized. This lack of economic dependence in most cases of uncle-niece incest constitutes a major difference between this type of incest and father-daughter incest. It is one of the factors that makes the power relationship between uncle and niece less intense than it is between father and daughter.

The two primary resistance strategies employed by victims of uncle-niece incest, where these were ascertainable, were fleeing (29 percent) and seeking assistance (23 percent). In contrast, only 18 percent of the other incest victims used fleeing as a primary strategy and only 1 percent sought assistance (significant at < 0.01 level). Presumably it is easier to flee from someone one doesn't live with. But why nieces were more ready to seek assistance is less clear. Perhaps they felt more hopeful they wouldn't be blamed. When a child tells a family member about incestuous abuse by a father or a brother, it is likely to engender a greater conflict of loyalties in the person told than when the perpetrator is an uncle or a cousin. Reporting a grandfather can also evoke loyalty conflicts since he is the father of one of the victim's parents.

This explanation is supported by the finding that where information was available on people's reactions to the incestuous abuse, it was supportive in 65 percent of the uncle-niece cases compared to only 31 percent of the father-daughter and brother-sister cases combined and 40 percent of the grandfather-granddaughter cases (significant at < 0.01 level).

The experiences of Felice and Irma provide examples of supportive responses by family members. Felice was ten years old when her uncle started hugging her in a sexual way. This behavior occurred from eleven to twenty times over a period of two years. Her uncle was in his forties at the time.

We'd be invited over for dinner and he'd be at the door. I felt his hug was an overly fond embrace. It was too friendly. I told my mother and she talked it over with her sister, my aunt. (What ended it?) My aunt finally straightened him out, and it stopped happening. (Did he have a sexual relationship with other relatives?) Yes, a girl cousin and other aunts. (Upset?) Not very upset. (Effect on your life?) No effect.

Irma was fourteen years old when her sixty-year-old uncle started sexualizing their relationship. These incidents occurred from two to five times over a period of two weeks.

It was my responsibility to babysit my younger cousins. My uncle would come and watch me and make me uncomfortable. He'd send the boys up the hill and he'd stand very close to me and breathe down my neck and say off-color things. He'd place his hands down my back and fool with my bra clasp. When I had on a swimsuit he'd undo my top, and when I'd be fumbling to get myself together, he'd give me a squeeze. He'd always want to kiss me and hug me and get me by myself. He fondled me while I had my hands behind my back trying to get my top back on. (Did he touch your breasts?) Yes, but he never did more than that. He was basically trying to touch me as if it was okay because it was all in the family. He'd say how soft and gentle and pretty I was, and how he liked to touch me.

(What ended it?) My father arrived on the scene. I had told my sister about it and she told him. I think my father punched him in the nose! He was prohibited from coming there when young women were there. (Did he ever have sexual relationships with other relatives?) I heard things to that effect, involving other girl in-laws about my age, but I don't know the specific details. (Upset?) Very upset. (Effect on your life?) A little effect. (Which experience was the most upsetting?) The one with my uncle.

Irma considered this experience with her uncle more upsetting than being forcibly raped by a friend when she was twenty-one.

Reported Trauma

We observed in chapter 20 that grandfather-granddaughter incestuous abuse was significantly less upsetting than all other forms of incestuous abuse combined. Could it be that all incestuous abuse outside the nuclear family is less upsetting than incestuous abuse within the nuclear family?

The answer is no. Although sexual abuse by uncles was less upsetting than father-daughter incest, it was quite similar to that of brother-sister incestuous abuse. Almost half (48 percent) of the nieces who were sexually abused by their uncles reported being very or extremely upset by the sexual abuse. Exactly the same percentage of sisters who were victimized by their brothers reported being very or extremely upset by the experience.

A quarter of the nieces reported great long-term effects as a result of the sexual abuse by their uncles. This is identical with the percentage reported by the victims of all the other incest perpetrators, and higher than the percentage of victims of brother-sister incestuous abuse who reported great long-term effects.*

Twenty-one percent of nieces said the sexual abuse had no long-term effects, almost the same as the norm for all incest perpetrators (22 percent) and fairly close to the percentage of victims of brother-sister incest.

We will start by citing two cases in which the victims reported no or little trauma.

Kitty was ten years old when her uncle, in his late fifties, first started touching her sexually. He did this from two to five times over a period of four to five months.

It happened a couple of times. He liked to have me sit on his lap. At the age of ten I was developing breasts and I was very aware of them. My uncle noticed them, and his hand would come up onto my breasts and he'd wiggle them, and I'd slide away and he'd do it again. He'd also pinch my arm and then slide his hand in by my breast. This usually happened when my aunts were around talking or being busy, and his excitement was in the danger of getting caught. He knew I was afraid to let on about what he was doing for fear of being blamed. I would occasionally be alone with this uncle but he never touched me when I was alone with him; he only did it in public. But I avoided being alone with him anyhow. (What ended it?) I moved. (Did he have a sexual relationship with other relatives?) Yes, he tried to with my cousin's wife. She was ten years older than I. He caressed her.

(Upset?) Not very upset. (Effect on your life?) A little effect. I became aware that just because you are related to men, they are not quite safe. I learned to avoid situations with relatives like him.

*However, when we applied our combined measure of trauma based on both upset and long-term effects, sexual abuse by brothers was slightly more traumatic (see table 10–6). But none of these differences between the trauma measures for the victims of uncles and brothers are statistically significant.

Kitty reveals that she had expected relatives not to respond to her sexually prior to her experiences with her uncle. The loss of this expectation can be a considerable disappointment for some girls, who thereafter perceive themselves as having no reliable sanctuary from sexual harassment.

Selma was ten years old the one time her forty-year-old uncle tried to molest her.

He didn't live in our town; he was there on a visit. He said, "Let's lay down and take a nap," then he started getting fresh with me. He grabbed me and started feeling around. (Your breasts and genitals?) Yes. (Did he touch them?) No, he started to but I didn't like it so I pulled away and I said I didn't want to take a nap. He said, "That's what I was afraid of," and let me go. I think he was afraid I would yell because there were other people in the house. (Upset?) Not very upset. (Effect on your life?) No effect.

Some victims whose assertive handling of the perpetrators stopped the sexual abuse from becoming more serious experience less trauma as a result.

Selma was assertive verbally; she rejected her uncle's suggestion to take a nap with him once she realized his motivation. She also physically asserted herself by pulling away. The fact that other people were around and that her uncle was afraid she would yell also helped. The case highlights the extent to which many would-be perpetrators rely on the silence of their chosen victims.

The following two girls reported far more trauma than the two cases just cited.

Rebecca was seven years old when her seventeen-year-old uncle started molesting her. These incidents occurred from two to five times over a period of a few weeks.

(Which time was most upsetting?) They were all about the same. He used to reach up under my underwear and feel around. I didn't run away because I was shocked that he would do that. (Did he touch your genitals?) Yes. (Did he do anything else?) No, that's all. I didn't know what to make of it. I think he got sexual satisfaction from doing that. I couldn't tell my parents because they wouldn't believe me—he was very religious. (What ended it?) I stayed out of his way. I wouldn't be around him alone.

(Upset?) Extremely upset. (Effect on your life?) A great effect. I tried to forget it, but when I first experienced sex, it brought it back to me. I've been afraid for my children—that it might happen to my daughter. I also worry about my son.

Rebecca's inability to forget the sexual abuse is common, particularly when the victims become sexually active. This is another case of the trauma of sexual abuse becoming apparent only long after it actually occurred.

Eileen was sexually abused by her uncle—whom she described as a bum —more than twenty times (our maximum category) over a period of fifteen years, including being raped. She was five and her uncle was in his thirties when he started molesting her.

My uncle lived with my grandmother. My mother sent me to my grandmother's to pick up something. When I got there he tried to keep me there. He pushed me into the bedroom and he was trying to go under my dress. He had his pants unzipped at the same time. He was trying to force me onto the bed when the phone started to ring. It was my mother. When he answered, she told him to send me home because she knew what he was like. When I was younger she tried to explain it to me, but I didn't understand what she was telling me till I was much older. I was five years old the first time he tried. (Did he ever force intercourse on you?) Yes. (Do you remember the first time?) No. But if my father had known he would've killed him, and I didn't want to be without my father. (You mean, if they put him in prison?) Yeah.

He had his hands on me when no one was looking every chance he got. He was always at our house, and if we were there by ourselves, he'd take the opportunity. (Did anything else sexual happen with him?) Yes. [Eileen had tears in her eyes and was very tense, so I didn't probe for further details.] (Did he use verbal threats?) Well, he used to say he'd make up things about my mother so that my father would fight her. My father used to fight her a lot. (Did he use physical force with you?) He was so much bigger than me, and I was just a child, so he didn't have to hit me. (What ended it?) His death, honestly! That's what ended it!

(Did he have sexual relationships with other relatives?) Yes, my cousin [his brother's daughter] and maybe my sister too. She mentioned something once. (Upset?) Extremely upset then; just a little now. [Eileen thought some more.] It really bothers me extremely now too. (Effect on your life?) Some effect. Well, first of all I don't trust men at all. I feel most of the time when you meet someone, they're after sex. They don't look at you as a person nor do they care how you feel.

Severity of Sexual Abuse

Although the victims of uncle-niece incest considered their abuse more upsetting than the victims of grandfather-granddaughter incest, these forms of incestuous abuse are similar in that they both involved considerable sexual abuse at the less severe level—in terms of the sex acts involved as well as in terms of the force used. Only 17 percent of the uncles sexually abused their nieces at the very severe level, 29 percent at the severe level, and over half (54 percent) at the least severe level. Uncles were second only to grandfathers (73 percent) in the frequency with which they sexually abused their nieces at the least severe level. In contrast, only 30 percent of the sexual abuse by all other incest perpetrators combined was at this level (significant at < 0.02 level).

Some typical examples of uncle-niece incestuous abuse at the least severe level will be cited next. The rituals of family affection, particularly greetings and farewells, provided one of the most common scenarios for uncles to take liberties with their nieces' bodies.

Ruth was fifteen years old when her uncle, in his fifties, started touching her sexually. These incidents occurred about once a year for four years.

(Which time was the most upsetting?) They were all basically the same. Whenever we'd greet each other, he'd grab my breasts. (Did he do this in front of others?) Yes, but covertly. I tried to pretend it didn't happen. (What ended it?) My getting married. And I don't hug him as much as I used to. It was a form of behavior modification. (Upset?) Somewhat upset. (Effect on your life?) A little effect.

Louise was fourteen years old when her forty-year-old uncle started touching her sexually. These incidents occurred from eleven to twenty times over a period of several months.

Every time he'd come to visit my house, he tried to kiss me, squeeze me, and touch my breasts. I would run away but he still succeeded in getting his hands on me. (What ended it?) He finally got the message after I screamed at him, pushed him away, and kicked him out of the house. (Upset?) Somewhat upset. (Effect on your life?) No effect.

The uncles in these two cases appear to be mild predators toward postpubertal girls. For the most part, nieces subjected to these kinds of experiences considered them unpleasant and distasteful, but they usually did not feel very traumatized by them.

Many of the least severe cases of uncle-niece incest involved situations other than those of greeting and farewells. For example, Priscilla was ten years old the one time her fifty-year-old uncle sexually abused her.

He had been drinking and I was on the floor watching TV. There were other people there when he started to tickle me. When I moved away he started to grab my breasts. I moved away again, and he stopped. (Did he use physical force?) He pushed me pretty mildly, but it was scary. (Did he have a sexual relationship with other relatives?) Yes, he did the same thing to my mother. He grabbed her breast after he was drunk. (Upset?) Somewhat upset. (Effect on your life?) Some effect.

Karla's experience provides an example of uncle-niece incestuous abuse at the very severe level. Karla was five years old when her sixteen-year-old uncle started sexually abusing her. This is one of the more severe cases of uncle-niece incest in terms of the sex acts involved. The sexual assaults occurred from eleven to twenty times over a period of two years. Karla's reluctance to talk about what happened is very evident from the segment of the interview to follow.

It was a member of the family. (Member of the family?) He was an uncle. Every time he came to the house I would cringe. He did things to me. (Things?) He made me touch his genitals and make love to him in certain ways. (Certain ways?) Oral intercourse. (Anything else?) Yes. (Did he force intercourse with you?) Yes. (Anything else?) He would touch me and make me touch him. I didn't want to do it, but I was very young. (Did he stroke your genitals?) Yes. (And how did you stroke him?) I touched his genitals—down there. (Did he use physical force?) Yes.

(What ended it?) I told my mother. (Did he have a sexual relationship with any other relative?) Yes, my twin sister. (Upset?) Extremely upset. (Effect on your life?) No effect. (You stated you were extremely upset, but that it had no effect on your life. Can you explain this?) I was very young. It all seems vague now, like a memory. I don't like to think about bad things. I was so young it didn't stay with me.

When answering the last question the interviewer commented that she felt Karla was becoming upset because she was remembering more than she wanted to.

Karla, who was twenty-two years old when interviewed, similarly claimed that an attempted rape by an acquaintance when she was nineteen was only "somewhat upsetting" and had no long-term effects. At the end of the interview the interviewer noted that when asked for details about these two experiences of sexual assault Karla "closed up, and information had to be dragged out. Although she claims the experiences had no effect on her life, I would guess that they have had an effect but are unresolved." Judging from Karla's account just cited, the interviewer's conclusion seems sound.

Violence and Physical Force

No uncle used a weapon; only one used a physical threat to accomplish the sexual abuse. Only 23 percent of the uncles used physical force. Uncles were the third least likely of the incest perpetrators to use force, following female relatives and grandfathers. Although these relationships did not reach statistical significance, when use of weapons, verbal threats, and physical force were combined according to the formula of our force and violence scale, incestuous abuse by uncles was significantly less forceful (at < 0.05 level) than incestuous abuse by all other incest perpetrators combined (77 percent and 60 percent, respectively).

Frequency and Duration

Whereas incestuous abuse by grandfathers occurred significantly more frequently and over a longer duration than sexual abuse by other incest perpetrators, this was not the case for incestuous abuse by uncles. Forty-two percent of the incestuous uncles sexually abused their nieces once only, 38 percent of them did so from two to ten times, and 21 percent did so more than eleven times. These frequencies are very close to the norm for all incest perpetrators.

Seventeen percent of the uncles who sexually abused their nieces more than once did so for less than a year. Forty-one percent of them continued the abuse for more than a year. These frequencies are also fairly close to the norm for all incest perpetrators.

Sexual Abuse of Other Relatives

Uncles were the third most likely incest perpetrator to be known to sexually abuse other relatives; they followed stepfathers (50 percent) and grandfathers (44 percent) with 41 percent. However, when uncles were compared with all other incest perpetrators combined, they were not significantly more likely to be known to have sexually abused another relative. Two examples of uncles who were believed to have sexually abused other relatives follow.

Carol's uncle was twenty-eight and she was four or five years old the first time he molested her. He abused her from two to five times over a period of five years.

Grandma sent me to the store. I had an uncle who had an auto. When I was on the way home from the store, he offered me a ride. He said, "You sit on my lap and I'll let you drive." I had these black bloomers on and he put his hand in and started feeling around and pinched me. It hurt and I said, "Don't!" and I said, "Ouch!" I hated him. He had an evil air about him. Another time I was in the bedroom with my cousin. We were both sleeping in the same bed. I woke up and he [her uncle] was feeling my breasts inside my nightgown. I said, "Uncle L., what are you doing?" He said, "Shh, you don't want to wake everyone up, do you?" He stopped what he was doing because I was awake.

(Did he have any kind of sexual relationships with any other relative?) I think he raped my mother's two younger sisters. (Upset?) Somewhat upset. I didn't trust him. (Effect on your life?) A little effect. It made me leery of men.

Theodora was ten years old the one time her thirty-five-year-old uncle molested her.

He took me to get some eggs at a ranch. Instead of going straight home afterward, we went to the river and he put me on his back to cross it. When we returned to the car I asked him if I could steer it. He said yes, so I sat on his lap. He was working the foot pedal and I was steering. I had a dress on and before I knew it, I felt this thing. He didn't button up his pants, his penis was getting hard, and I could feel it on my legs. When I saw it, I jumped off his lap, and he left and went into the bushes. When he came back I didn't say anything, and he drove home. I didn't even look at him. (Did he have a sexual relationship with other relatives?) Well, I know that he tried to bother my sister, but I don't know in what manner he touched her.
(Upset?) Very upset. (Effect on your life?) A great effect. It proved what my father told me: to stay away from relatives. It also made me curious. (Which experience did you find most upsetting?) The one with my uncle.

Theodora's other experiences included being raped by a boyfriend when she was thirteen and by an acquaintance when she was eighteen, and an attempted rape by another acquaintance when she was nineteen.

Neither Carol nor Theodora mentioned their uncles' own daughters as victims. One wonders to what extent incestuous uncles are also incestuous fathers. Or do some incest perpetrators balk at abusing their own children? If so, why? Might they adhere to a father-daughter incest taboo but not an uncle-niece incest taboo? Is the latter taboo weaker? These questions need to be addressed by future research.

In summary: Incestuous uncles were similar to incestuous grandfathers in sexually abusing their victims most often at the least severe level and without the use of force or violence. However, they sexually abused their victims less frequently and over a shorter period than did grandfathers. Nor was sexual abuse by uncles characterized by a low degree of upset, as was the case for sexual abuse by grandfathers.

Why might uncle-niece incestuous abuse be more upsetting than grandfather-granddaughter incestuous abuse? We reported earlier that there appears to be a curvilinear relationship between age and trauma, with incestuous abuse by middle-aged men being considered more traumatic than incestuous abuse by younger or older perpetrators. The difficulty in evaluating age as an explanatory factor here is that it is clearly not independent of the type of relatedness between victim and perpetrator.

Future research will hopefully continue this exploration of some of the similarities and differences found in our sample between uncle-niece and grandfather-granddaughter incest as well as the other types of incest.

Incestuous Abuse by More Than One Uncle

Twenty-four percent of the victims of uncles were sexually abused by more than one incest perpetrator. This is close to the norm of 27 percent for the victims of all incest perpetrators.

Three women reported being sexually abused by two different uncles before they were eighteen years of age. One of them, Laverne, was four when an uncle in his early twenties started touching her sexually. She said that these incidents occurred from two to five times over a period of eight years.

(Which time was most upsetting?) No particular time was more upsetting than any other. Nothing ever came of it besides his feeling my body. It was always at family gatherings and my parents were nearby. (What happened the first time?) It was at a family reunion picnic. He kept grabbing my ass, attempting to appear to be a friendly, affectionate uncle. This led to my avoiding him most of my adult life.

(Upset?) Extremely upset. (Effect on your life?) A great effect. I still don't relate to him as an adult. I avoid him.

Another uncle, who was in his forties at the time, started fondling Laverne when she was eleven years old. He touched her from two to five times over a period of two years.

It occurred in the living room of my parents' house. It was fondling, him feeling my breasts and my ass—rubbing around my butt. (What ended it?) He just stopped. Later on I talked to my aunt and sister and they had had the same kind of experiences of his fondling them and feeling their breasts and asses.

(Upset?) Very upset. (Effect on your life?) A great effect, since I never had anything to do with him again.

Carol described the first uncle who sexually abused her as an uncle-in-law. She was eight years old and he was forty the first time he molested her. These incidents occurred from two to five times over a period of four years.

The most upsetting time was when my parents had gone to church. He stayed home with me and his little daughter. I remember him getting into bed with me, taking his penis out, and fondling it against my rectum. (Did he do anything else?) No, that's all. That was enough, at that age. (Did he touch other parts of your body?) I can't remember. It turned me against him. I hated him.

The next time he tried, I ran under the house. He came under the house and pulled my panties down. His daughter came under the house too, which stopped him. I was twelve the following time. I wasn't asleep so I kept my eye on him. I heard him crawling toward me and I screamed, "Uncle Willie, where are you going?!" That stopped him. He was a rapist, gambler, and murderer. He was sent to a penitentiary for life. (Did he use verbal threats?) He would love to say "That Thing," when referring to my privates. Kids would say "pussy," and adults would call the vagina "That Thing." The way he said it was threatening. (Did he have any kind of sexual relationship with any other relative?) He tried with my youngest aunt.

(Upset?) Very upset. (Effect on your life?) A great effect. I hate him. It made me more cautious and suspicious of men. I was always looking out.

Carol's ingenuity and assertiveness in handling a middle-aged relative who was a violent criminal is quite remarkable. She was nine years old the one time another sixteen-year-old uncle tried to have intercourse with her.

My uncle was seven years older than me. He was an oversized person. I mean his penis was very, very large. It was a game to him. He pulled off my drawers. Being so little, he could just pick me up. I didn't resist. I didn't understand what he was doing. After he found out he could not enter me he stopped and went after my little brother and cousin instead. He thought it was funny—a plaything. (He tried to put his penis inside your vagina?) Yes, but he couldn't because he was too big. Later on, I found out that he didn't have good sense. I don't think he knew what he was doing. (Did he have any sexual relationship with another relative?) Yes, my younger brother and a younger cousin.

(Upset?) Not at all upset. (Effect on your life?) A great effect. In fact, it had a *terrible* effect when I realize what could have happened to me when my grandmother left me alone with those boys. It was horrifying. It didn't affect my life as much as my attitude. I'm overcautious. I watch out for signs from men. I can tell whether they're having little girls in their rooms. It wasn't in me to be a victim, but I only narrowly escaped. It makes me mad. I wouldn't think twice about hurting them. (Them?) Men in general. It had a terrible effect on my attitude to men.

Carol's report that she was not at all upset by this incident when it occurred, but that it had a great long-term effect on her life, illustrates the point made in chapter 10: Children cannot be expected to gauge at the time of the sexual abuse the trauma that the experience may cause later.

Background Factors

Forty-eight cases of uncle-niece incestuous abuse is a sufficiently large number to permit further exploration of some of the background factors associated with this kind of victimization.

While there was no significant association between social class background (when using the victim's father's occupation and education as the measures) or the race and ethnicity of the victims of uncle-niece incestuous abuse, there was a significant association between this form of incest and family background (significant at < 0.05 level). Victims of uncles were more likely to have been raised by grandparents or relatives other than

De Young hypothesizes that "the degree of relatedness, both by blood and by emotional intimacy, between the child and the perpetrator of the incest, is an important variable in determining the impact that incest will have on the victim" (1985, pp. 103–4). This seems a sound enough hypothesis. But we have seen that many other variables also affect the degree of trauma reported by incest victims, such as the severity of the abuse, the degree of force or violence used, the frequency and duration of the abuse, the age disparity between the victim and the perpetrator, and victimization by more than one relative. Implicit in any minimization of the trauma of incestuous abuse by uncles who have little relationship with the victim or her family is the assumption that sexual abuse by adult strangers, acquaintances, and unrelated authority figures is not very distressing for children. This is, of course, a very poor assumption.

Our study, the first thorough examination of uncle-niece incestuous abuse, makes it clear that this form of incest is both serious and widespread. Although there were cases in which nieces reported no trauma, particularly when the degree of violation was at the least severe level, there were many more reports of distress and some very severely traumatic consequences. Although Meiselman is quite right in her assumption that father-daughter incest is usually more traumatic than uncle-niece incest, she has nevertheless erred seriously by greatly discounting the upset and long-term effects of this type of incest. More specifically, Meiselman's suggestion that uncle-niece incest is extremely disturbing only when it is violent or disrupts the child's relationship within the nuclear family is clearly contradicted.

It seems clear from our survey data that all but one of the nieces who were victimized had no desire to be used for their uncles' sexual gratification. Indeed, it seems a tremendously self-serving theory to imagine that when adult males seek gratification by touching the genitals or having intercourse with young children, the children would enjoy these experiences were it not for the prevailing punitive attitude in our culture. This theory views children as naturally receptive and excited by sexual acts with whichever adult males happen to be interested in acting out such behavior. The literature on rape reveals this to be a common misconception about adult women. It is even more inappropriate when applied to children.

22

Brothers-in-Law, First Cousins, and Other More Distant Relatives

Sexual activity between cousins is illegal in some states in this country, while in others it is legal. In many preindustrial societies, marriage between first cousins was not only permitted but preferred. Even where sex between first cousins is illegal, it is generally considered to be by far the least serious form of incest. Consequently, there is no literature on first-cousin incestuous abuse.

Nor is there any literature on sexual abuse by brothers-in-law. Yet the victims' accounts of this form of incestuous abuse make it obvious that they were often quite traumatic.* In addition, it was clear in some cases that the relatedness contributed to the trauma experienced.

Brothers-in-Law

Out of the twenty-two incest perpetrators who were classified as "other male relatives," seven were brothers-in-law. This number is too small for meaningful quantitative analysis. However, the case material helps to convey why this form of incestuous abuse can be so distressing.

*The experiences of the one respondent, Dorothy, who was very seriously sexually abused by three different brothers-in-law, were cited in chapter 12 along with her many other experiences of sexual abuse.

Lucy was sixteen when her twenty-three-year-old brother-in-law tried to initiate sexual contact with her. She was living with her sister, who was recovering from the birth of a baby.

I was very young and he was my sister's husband and it all happened very fast. My sister was in the hospital having her baby. I was coming home from visiting her when he tried to kiss me in the car. I got out. (What was his intention?) He was a sexy guy. If I'd let him, I'm sure he'd have done anything.

(Upset?) Very upset, being so young and being that he was my sister's husband. (Effect on your life?) A great effect. He was always afraid of me after that. He was afraid I'd tell. I never have told my sister, even now after twenty-seven years when they're divorced. He didn't like me after that, and it affected my relationship with my sister.

As Lucy's experience illustrates, the relationship between brothers-in-law and sisters-in-law makes sexual abuse by these men far more complicated than abuse by strangers, acquaintances, or even friends. Among other reasons, it complicates the relationship between sisters. It can also reactivate or instigate sibling wounds and rivalries.

Although victims of incestuous abuse frequently feel guilty about the assault, victims of brothers-in-law are particularly prone to such feelings. Many also fear that their sister, if she knew, would hold them responsible. Furthermore, the closer the relationship between the sisters, the more destructive it is to keep such an experience secret and yet the more dangerous it may be to divulge.

In Dolores's case, telling her sister proved helpful in stopping the abuse from occurring again. Dolores was fifteen the one time her twenty-four-year-old brother-in-law grabbed her.

This happened when my brother-in-law was drunk one night and he grabbed me and kissed me. I pushed him away and afterward he apologized. (Did he touch your breasts or genitals?) No, he just kissed me. I think it happened because he was drunk and my sister was pregnant and he thought he'd try something. He never did anything again. My sister sensed something had happened and she asked me so I told her. He wouldn't dare try anything after that. (Upset?) Somewhat upset. (Effect on your life?) No effect.

Brenda used telling her sister as a threat to try to stop her brother-in-law's abuse. She was also fifteen when her twenty-two-year-old brother-in-law first approached her sexually. There were two such incidents over the period of a few months.

The first time my sister's husband stopped me in the hallway at my parent's home and started kissing me in a very unbrotherly fashion. I pushed away from him. He was a creep. He'd beat my sister and run around with other women. If anyone complained about his family, he'd take it out on her.

The second time was in his car. It was the same thing. He made advances toward me, kissed me, put his arms around me, and pulled me close to him. I threatened to tell my sister and told him to take me home. (What ended it?) I stayed completely away from him. If he came to the house I'd stay with my parents.

(Upset?) Extremely upset. (Effect on your life?) A great effect. I didn't want to repeat my sister's mistakes. Later I compared my husband and his acts of violence with her husband's. I asked myself whether I would go through the same thing. I decided I didn't want to live like that.

In the next case to be cited, Bernadette makes it clear that she saw sex with her brother-in-law as wrong because of their relatedness. She was thirteen when her brother-in-law—in his early twenties—first made sexual advances toward her. The sexual incidents occurred from eleven to twenty times over a period of three months.

I'd have to say, as far as I'm concerned, it was more experimentation. He touched me, I touched him. We'd be sitting on the couch watching TV. We were the only two who stayed up late. Then he'd make advances and I'd go along with him. We kissed and petted, rubbed against each other, but never had intercourse. I enjoyed it, but I knew it was wrong because he was my brother-in-law.

Yet I did feel I was being forced into it. (Forced?) It's hard to explain because I didn't say no, but I feel, looking back on it now, that I was taken advantage of. I'm resentful about it now. (Upset?) Somewhat upset. (Effect on your life?) A little effect.

It is common for victims to have a different view in retrospect from what they felt at the time. Although they often find this change in perspective confusing, there is really nothing odd about it. Children's responses to sexual abuse at the time it occurs will not necessarily reflect their feelings about it later.

In the final account of sexual abuse by a brother-in-law to be cited here, Jeanine mentioned becoming mistrustful of all in-laws as a result of her experience. She was ten years old when her thirty-five-year-old brother-in-law started molesting her. He did so from two to five times over a period of three years.

(Which time was most upsetting?) He hugged me, then touched my breasts. He hugged me very strongly and put his sexual organ against the back part of my body. That bothered me a lot. He also touched my sexual organ. All this was done with our clothes on. He'd rub against the outside. (What do you think he wanted to do?) I think he wanted to have sex with me. I started screaming and he left me alone.

I would go to the fruit trees with my nieces. They would run off to play and I would stay to cut fruit. Many times he was hidden nearby. I didn't know he was there, but then he'd start on me. Men are bad! (Did he use verbal threats?) He told me that someday he was going to make me his. (Did he use physical force?) Yes. Also, I was a little girl.

(What ended it?) I became very angry and had to tell my mother. After she

stepfathers, suggests the following hypothesis: Other things being equal, the more distant the relationship in terms of kinship and consanguinity, the greater the resistance of the victim will be. Ironically, it seems possible that the stronger the incest taboo, the more unprepared the victims may be if it is broken, and the more disarmed they may be by its very tabooness.

Relationship Between Distance of Relatedness and Victim Resistance

Our quantitative analysis of the first-cousin data offers tentative support for this hypothesis. Although victims were not specifically asked about their resistance strategies, we attempted to ascertain this from their descriptions of the sexual abuse. When comparing the primary resistance strategy employed by first cousins and all other incest perpetrators combined, 33 percent of the first-cousin victims used force compared to 19 percent of all other victims, and 39 percent used verbal strategies compared to only 10 percent of all other victims (significant at <0.02 level).

Winifred provides an example of a victim who physically resisted sexual abuse by a first cousin. She was eleven years old the one time her sixteen-year-old cousin attacked her sexually.

I was visiting my aunt's house for a family reunion. The whole family was there. At one point I was in the bedroom where all the coats were and my cousin came in. He was a few years older than me. I was eleven at the time. He jumped on me on the bed and pressed his body against me and tried to kiss me. I couldn't scream because he had me pressed down. I tried to fight him off but he was stronger than I was. He started to put his hand up my skirt and touch my crotch when his mother called him to come and do something. He jumped up and ran out. (Did anything else sexual happen with him?) No, nothing else. We both had our clothes on. I never would go anywhere alone with him, and I never would let him near me again. (Was this ever reported?) No, I never even told my mother.

(Upset?) Very upset. (Effect on your life?) Some effect. After that I was very cautious of people I thought I could trust. I didn't really know at the time that he was interested in sex, but I knew he was playing too rough and that somehow it was wrong. I was too embarrassed to tell my mother. He just leered at me whenever I saw him after that. I guess he knew I'd never tell.

Joan provides an example of a first-cousin victim who used assertive verbal resistance. She was thirteen and her cousin seventeen at the time of the sexual abuse.

He was older—seventeen. We were walking through the cornfields when he said, "Let's rest and lie down on the grass." Then he kissed me. I said, "Cut that out! Are you crazy?" But he approached me again, this time touching my breasts and then quickly touching my genitals. I jumped up and said, "I'll tell my mother if you don't stop." I was scared and ran off. That was more or less it. I had a feeling he wanted to go further, but I made myself clear to him. (Did he use physical force?) Yes, a little, by pushing me and pinning me down. (Upset?) Somewhat upset. (Effect on your life?) A little effect.

Comparison Between Brothers and First Cousins

Brothers and first cousins share the characteristic of usually belonging to the same generation as their victims. What differentiates them from each other is the closeness of their biological connection with the victim, as well as the social relationships of brothers and cousins. Just as our examination of uncle-niece incestuous abuse raised questions about a total reliance on family dynamics theory to explain father-daughter incest, sexual abuse by first cousins raises similar questions about such an explanation of brother-sister incest. If family dynamics were the only explanation, why, for example, would incestuous first cousins and brothers have almost exactly the same average ages at the time the incestuous abuse began—17.4 and 17.9 years, respectively? Why would their victims also be almost exactly the same age—on average 11.1 and 10.7 years, respectively?

In addition, brother and first-cousin perpetrators are extremely similar in terms of the degree of physical force used, the severity of the abuse in terms of the sex acts involved, and the age disparity between them and their victims. They were both also significantly less likely than other incest perpetrators to be known to sexually abuse another relative (significant at < 0.01 level).

However, there were two differences between brother and first-cousin perpetrators. First cousins were significantly more likely to sexually abuse their victims once only: 59 percent versus 36 percent (significant at < 0.02 level). But they were also more likely to sexually abuse their cousins for two years or more: 22 percent versus 8 percent. More important, however, was the fact that 56 percent of the victims of brothers reported some or great long-term effects as a result of the sexual abuse compared with 36 percent of the victims of first cousins. Although this difference is not significant at < 0.05 level, this trend was also evident in our overall assessment of the traumatic effects based on all the available information about the victim and the assault, not just the victims' answers to the one direct question on effects.

This difference in long-term effects was not reflected, however, in the degree of upset reported by the victims of brothers and cousins. This is surprising because the victims of brothers more often became upset during the interview than victims of first cousins: 32 percent versus 19 percent, respectively (although this difference also didn't reach significance at <0.05 level). In addition, the victims of brothers reported much greater fear of sexual assault in childhood than the victims of first cousins—63 percent versus 28 percent, respectively (significant at <0.05 level). Perhaps they were unaware that this fear may have been related to their brother's sexual abuse.

Given the great similarities in the kind of sexual abuse engaged in by brothers and first cousins, it seems reasonable to assume that the differences in the victims' fear of sexual assault in childhood and long-term effects are due to the fact that the brother-sister relationship is a much closer and more significant one in this culture. When it is abused, the consequences are more serious. The victims of cousins in the two cases to be cited next both reported being very upset by the sexual abuse but also that it had little long-term impact on them.

Eight-year-old Marcia described her experience with her eighteen-year-old cousin as follows:

We were playing cards. He decided whoever won got to touch the other person wherever they wanted. I was eight and I didn't know what was happening so I never stopped it. He won so he touched my genitals. Then he suggested that I touch his anyway, so I did. He was older so I did what he wanted. (Did he attempt intercourse?) No. (Upset?) Very upset. (Effect on your life?) A little effect, though after that I certainly watched what I was betting about!

Sometimes very young girls appear to be disarmed by their innocence and lack of understanding of what is being done to them. Other equally young children appear to be aware that something about the touch is wrong. For example, Kay was five or six years old when her twelve-year-old cousin sexually abused her.

We all slept together during carnival. He offered me candy, then he came next to me and tried to touch me. (Where?) My genitals. At that age there *are* no boobs. I knew the way he was touching me was different, so I got off the bed and went into the other room. I was scared of him after that, so I avoided him. I slept with my mother and I was very careful not to be alone with him again. Whenever there were family gatherings I stayed close to my mother. (Did this happen more than once?) Once with me but it happened for many years with my sister. (Upset?) Very upset. (Effect on your life?) A little effect. It made me scared of boys. I avoided older boys a lot when I was a kid.

Trauma of First Cousin Incest

Going beyond our comparison between the victims of brothers and first cousins, the degree of upset reported by the victims of cousins was only slightly below that reported by the victims of all the other perpetrators combined: 48 percent versus 53 percent. However, the 36-percent figure for some or great long-term effects reported by first cousins was substantially lower than the 54-percent figure reported by the victims of all the other types of incest perpetrators combined. Although this difference still did not reach statistical significance at <0.05 level, it does constitute a strong trend.

Still, there clearly were cases of very traumatic incestuous abuse by first cousins. Kathleen, Erika, and Sylvia provide three such examples.

Kathleen was gang-raped by three cousins when she was ten years old. They were all brothers in their late teens. They raped her twice over a period of a month.

(Which experience was most upsetting?) Both of them were, because I was very scared. They were much older than me and they used words and pocketknives to threaten me. They took me into an old shed, stripped me, then sexually molested me. All three of them had intercourse with me, as well as oral and anal copulation. (What ended it?) I don't know. I think they were afraid I'd tell.

(Upset?) Extremely upset. (Effect on your life?) A great effect. I didn't start dating until I was nineteen. I would not go out at all. I was more cautious with my other relatives, and I wouldn't go spend the night with other families.

Erika was eight when her fifteen-year-old cousin started molesting her. These incidents occurred more than twenty times over a period of five years.

We liked each other, but he was much older than me and he used to grab at me all the time. The worst time was when we were in a swimming pool, and he reached inside my bathing suit and touched my genitals. That incident really stands out. (What ended it?) I must have gotten too old. He used to spend vacations with us; maybe he quit taking them with us. There was no more contact, that's what ended it. I never told anyone about it.

(Upset?) At the time I was extremely upset. But until you asked me, I'd almost forgotten it. (Effect on your life?) A great effect. It led to a general caution toward men during my early experiences. There were times when I felt guilty about what had happened. When I finally did tell my mother years later, she was surprised but not supportive of me.

In another traumatic case the victim emphasized that her cousin had authority over her as "the man in the house." Hence it was a situation more typical of a much older brother–sister relationship than a cousin relationship. Sylvia was fifteen years old the one time her twenty-eight-year-old cousin sexually abused her.

He had authority because he was the only man in the house, and he was older than me. We were alone in the house and I was doing homework. He sat next to me on the couch, and he put his hand on my leg. I was wearing my school uniform skirt. He pulled it up and started touching me. I was scared and didn't move. He started kissing me on my mouth. (Did he touch you elsewhere?) [Sylvia nodded.] (Where?) My vagina. But he stayed on the outside. His bedroom was the next room over, and he managed to get me in there. He started kissing me while his hands were on my hips. He started to go up my skirt and he wanted to pull off my panties. He started to push them down, while still kissing me. Then my aunt came down the back stairs and he got scared when he heard her.

I told his mother and mine and everyone was aware of it. That was the only time it happened. (Would he have tried sexual intercourse if he hadn't been disturbed?) I think he would have. And being scared, I would have submitted. He had authority. He was the man of the house. (Did he use physical force?) He had a strong grip—a tight grip. (Did he take you into the bedroom forcibly?) It was only three or four steps, but he used a strong grip and made sure I got up with him. He said, "I want to show you something."

(Upset?) Extremely upset. (Effect on your life?) A great effect. I wouldn't want that to happen to my daughter. I am very careful with her. She has a lot of boy cousins and I make sure they are out in the open and stay out of bedrooms. I don't trust any boy cousins.

Age Disparity

The age disparity in 46 percent of the cases of first-cousin sexual abuse was less than five years, and in 20 percent of the cases it was ten years or more. As with brother-sister abuse, there was only one case of sexual abuse by a first cousin in which the victim was older than the perpetrator. Leila was nine and her cousin six the one time he touched her genitals against her wishes.

He was living in the same house with me then. I woke up and he was fondling my genitals. I was very surprised to find him in bed with me. I wasn't really angry but I was surprised. I told him to get out of my bed and he did. We spent a great deal of time together; there were three years when we were pretty close. This happened right at the beginning of that period. (Was it wanted or unwanted?) I had been sleeping and he awakened me. It was unwanted and unencouraged. (What were your ages?) I was nine and he was six. *I* was the authority figure! (Upset?) Somewhat upset. (Effect on your life?) No effect.

Surprisingly, there was no significant relationship between the age disparity between the first cousins and the degree of trauma reported by the victims.

More Distant Relatives

As is true of other incest perpetrators, some of the distant male relatives appear to have been sexually attracted to children in general and not just to the respondent whom they victimized. This inference is drawn from the fact that they had sexually abused other relatives besides the respondent. The experiences of Adele and Natalie exemplify this kind of perpetrator.

Adele was eleven years old when her twenty-six-year-old second cousin touched her sexually. He did so twice within one year.

The first time we were in an airplane and he was rubbing my prepuberty chest, and it felt good. I didn't think much about it. One other time we were standing in a doorway at my aunt's house and I was upset about something. He was patting my butt and all of a sudden it was in there; he touched me in the crack. He was putting his finger inside my pants in my crack. I moved away. He knew I was old enough to understand, and he left me alone after that.

(Did he ever have a sexual relationship with other relatives?) Yes, I know of three first cousins he tried this with. (Upset?) Somewhat upset. (Effect on your life?) No effect.

Natalie was seven years old the one time the thirty-year-old husband of her cousin molested her.

My cousin had a daughter my age and I was staying with them for a vacation. One night my cousin went out and left her husband babysitting. I woke from being asleep in bed to find he had my nightgown up and was touching me all over my body. (Did he touch your genitals?) Yes, the pervert! His daughter was in the same bed with me. I started crying and he told me not to wake up his daughter. I played sick the next day so that I could go home. The sad thing was that I couldn't tell my mother because I would have been accused of enticing him, even though I was asleep in bed. Later I found out that he'd done this with two other cousins as well.

(Upset?) Extremely upset. (Effect on your life?) Some effect. I'm always very scared of men. The only man I'd let hold me or whose lap I would sit on was my older brother. It made me cautious.

Conclusion

Our survey finding that only 36 percent of the first-cousin victims reported some or great long-term effects as a result of the incestuous abuse—a lower percentage than those of victims of all other types of incest perpetrators —comes as no surprise. The incest taboo is undoubtedly weaker for first cousins than for fathers, brothers, grandfathers, and uncles. The age and hence power disparity between first cousins is less than for most other relatives. Yet, unlike brother-sister incestuous abuse where the age disparity is usually also relatively small, first cousins rarely live together. Hence the dynamics of the nuclear family are less affected by this form of incestuous abuse, and it is easier for the victim to avoid the abusive relative.

All of these factors contribute to making the impact of incestuous abuse by first cousins less serious and of shorter duration. Despite this, it is noteworthy that over one-third of the victims of first cousins reported some or great long-term effects. It is not known whether the trauma reported as a result of sexual abuse by first cousins and other more distant relatives would have been the same had it been perpetrated at the same level of severity by males of the same age but who were unrelated to the victim.

Sexual abuse by cousins is significant for several reasons. First, many parents are not aware that their children may be at risk of sexual abuse by cousins. Our 2.9-percent prevalence figure and illustrative case material may help to dispel the myth that cousins and other more distant relatives are safe because they are relatives. Many parents are wary of strangers and encourage their children to be careful of them but are totally trusting of relatives unless they are known to have a sexual problem with children.

It is also quite clear that some victims subscribe to an incest taboo that extends to cousins, brothers-in-law, and other even more distant relatives. This can make sexual abuse by these relatives more disillusioning—a disillusionment that they may generalize to other relatives, thereby undermining the feeling of security from sexual abuse engendered by the incest taboo.

PART FIVE

THE FAMILIES

23

Family Members: What Role Do They Play?

Experts on child sexual abuse are unanimous in believing that the reactions of those who learn of a child's experience of such abuse are crucial to the child. Researchers such as the Kinsey team, who belittled the anguish caused by child sexual victimization, often argue that the hysterical responses of parents and other adults—and not the abuse itself—cause trauma. Others consider child sexual abuse to be a very serious and frequently devastating experience; such researchers and clinicians also believe that the responses of adults and peers can make a tremendous difference in the level of distress experienced at the time, as well as to the long-term effects on the abused child.

Every woman in our survey who reported an experience of child sexual abuse was asked whether or not she had reported the experience to the police, and if so, what the outcome was. (This information was discussed in chapter 6.) Although we did not ask who else, if anyone, was told and what his or her reaction was, ninety-five of the incest victims volunteered information about this. Of these ninety-five victims, 34 percent had told someone soon after the first incident; 19 percent had told someone later—sometimes much later; and 47 percent said that they didn't tell anyone. In these latter cases, 37 percent mentioned that someone knew about it anyway.

In the sixty-five cases of incestuous abuse for which information about people's reactions to the knowledge of the abuse was available, 45 percent were described as mostly supportive or sympathetic; 22 percent, as mostly unsupportive or unsympathetic; and 34 percent of the reactions could be placed in neither of these categories. The people mentioned as reacting in these sixty-five cases included siblings, fellow victims, friends, as well as parents and other adults.

Interestingly, there was a significant relationship between the supportiveness of those told and who the incest perpetrator was. The more distant the relationship, the more supportive the reaction (significant at < 0.01 level). Those told responded supportively in only 31 percent of the cases of incestuous abuse by fathers and brothers (combined), 40 percent of the cases involving grandfathers, 65 percent of the uncle-niece cases, and 80 percent of the cases that involved other more distant male relatives.

Of the fourteen cases where the information available indicated an unsupportive reaction by the people who were told about the incestuous abuse, 86 percent ($N = 12$) involved fathers and brothers. The two other cases of unsupportiveness involved an uncle and a first cousin. This finding makes sense since there is so much less at stake emotionally and economically for members of the nuclear family when the perpetrator is an uncle or other more distant relative.

Some people would consider Diane's experience, to be cited next, as a confirmation that the trauma of incest is caused mostly by the negative responses to it rather than by the sexual abuse per se.

Diane was two or three years old when her uncle, in his thirties, started to sexually abuse her. He did so more than twenty times over a period of twelve years.

The most upsetting time was when I finally told my parents. My uncle is retarded. I lived with him and my grandparents for a long time on and off until I was fourteen. My uncle would get me down in the basement workshop where I was sent to play with him. Little did they know! [Diane laughed.] It happened frequently. I was *very,* very young. Mainly what he did was stick his finger up my vagina, pull his pants down, then rub against me until he ejaculated all over me. That sort of thing went on for years. I never liked it, but I wasn't terrified. It was just something he did that I didn't like. Only later did I realize it was not supposed to be done. (Did anything else sexual happen with him?) He tried to make me touch him. (His genitals?) Yeah. Then he'd touch me. He'd pull my panties down and do this whole number. He'd pin me against the wall, rub against me, and I'd end up with goo all over me, which I really objected to!

The real trauma was when I finally refused to play with my uncle. My parents and grandparents finally figured out why, and my father attacked my uncle. It was really scary. (What ended it?) When I told someone. After that he caught me a couple of times, and those were the worst times because I knew it was wrong. Those times were traumatic. It stopped when I stopped being alone with him.

(Upset?) Extremely upset. (Effect on your life?) A great effect. I still have trouble with any type of sexual experience that is similar. Any type of ejaculation or gooey sort of problems are difficult for me. In later years I've been screwed up about sex, and it came from those experiences. They, and my first marriage, really fucked up my life for a long time.

(Which experience of sexual abuse was the most upsetting?) The one with S. [her husband who raped and beat her and threatened to kill her] and my uncle. They were both incredibly upsetting on different levels.

Out of the eighty-seven respondents who were raped by a husband, Diane was one of only two women to be raped by two husbands. She also had numerous other experiences of sexual assault.

According to Diane, "the real trauma" occurred when the secret was discovered after she refused to submit to her uncle any more. Not only did her father attack her uncle, but when the abuse was repeated "those were the worst times because I knew it was wrong." But even a case such as Diane's does not lead to the conclusion that the greatest trauma of incest is caused by the negative response of those to whom it is reported. This argument assumes that the child knows at the time of the abuse how much trauma has been caused by it and/or will result from it in the future. Had Diane's relatives never discovered that her uncle was sexually assaulting her, her frequent experiences of being used for her uncle's sexual gratification would likely have taken a toll on her later sexual and interpersonal development. It is not surprising that as a child she had no sense of the consequences in store for her, and would therefore report that it was after she learned that others perceived the sex acts with her uncle as being bad that those acts became much more distressing to her.

Like Diane, Zelda also saw nothing morally wrong with her uncle's sexual fondling of her from the ages of five or six to nine. However, according to Zelda's account, it was precisely her naïveté that made her so helpless. Zelda was six years old when her uncle, in his fifties, started to molest her. The sexual abuse occurred more than twenty times over a period of three or four years.

He was always trying to touch my breasts and genitals. (Did he succeed?) Yes. I would be on his lap and he would touch my breasts. He'd caress me over my shirt. (Did he touch your genitals?) Yes. I didn't know what was happening or what sex was until I was about nine and started hearing it from girls at school. Then I got upset. I couldn't tell my mother or my aunt, but when I got hip to what he was doing I would just take off. I would go into the room where they were so he never got me alone in the house anymore. We also moved soon after that. (Did he attempt intercourse?) No.

(What ended it?) My becoming aware that it was sexual. Kids can't tell their parents because they see sex as dirty. (Did he have a sexual relationship with any other relative?) Yes, two of my cousins that I know of. Also my mother; I think he was always trying to make passes at her. (Upset?) Extremely upset. (Effect on your life?) Some effect. I don't trust any old men around kids.

Again, some might argue that had Zelda not learned about sex from her peers at school, her uncle might have continued fondling her sexually without causing her distress. This argument does not acknowledge that being used by an adult for the adult's sexual gratification is exploitive, and being the victim of exploitation usually has negative consequences—not the least of which is the sense of betrayal that results from realizing that a trusted adult would take advantage of a child. By this perspective, then, children like Zelda would be best protected by being educated about the possibility of unwanted sexual touching and how to deal with it if it occurs.

This is not to imply that knowledge about sexual abuse, and training in handling it, is sufficient protection for young children. In fact, it is far from totally effective in the face of determined perpetrators. Three or four years after the sexual abuse by her uncle had ended, Zelda was molested by her stepfather (see chapter 17 for the full account). However, she maintained that her knowledge about sexual abuse gave her some protection in this situation: "I was too hip to let him get too far," she said.

When asked which experience of sexual abuse was most upsetting, Zelda replied: "It's hard to say. The rape was real upsetting, but the experience with my stepfather and uncle were more so, I guess." This reply is all the more significant after reading Zelda's account of a violent group rape when she was sixteen, which she described as extremely upsetting and having a great effect on her life.

Our study was not designed to explore the response of family members to the incestuous abuse. Hence the information obtained about it is unfortunately often not very rich. Nevertheless, because of people's interest in this subject, this chapter will examine the kinds of cases in which the reactions of relatives were mentioned.

Mothers Who Intervened

Since the literature has focused so heavily on mothers who are unsupportive of their daughters who become incest victims, let us start by citing two cases in which the mothers intervened to stop their daughters' abuse.

Wendy was fifteen years old the one time her biological father sexually abused her. She was extremely reluctant to identify her father as the perpetrator.

The person came into my room. The person had obviously been drinking and he just reached over and kissed me very passionately, which I could not understand. He held me in his arms and then he kissed me on my lips even though I didn't want him to. I had to push him away. That's about as far as it went.

(Was it someone in your immediate family?) Yes. (How was he related to you?) He was my father. It was very confusing. I talked to my mother about it, and they talked among themselves. (It was never repeated?) No. (At the time it happened, did you think that more would happen?) Not right then, but later I thought it might. (What went through your mind when this occurred?) I felt fear that my mother would find out. I wondered what she would do, and what I would do. I wondered about the consequences. My mother might get divorced, or it could develop into something further between him and myself. Family relationships would be ruined. *(How did the talk with your mother go?) She was very surprised and didn't know how to react. But she did confront my father with it. (How was she with you?) She just mostly listened. My father responded by apologizing and reassuring us that it would never happen again.* * It is an unspoken accident among us.

(Upset?) Very upset. (Effect on your life?) Some effect. I couldn't be alone with my father until a few years ago. If I was alone with him I felt very insecure. (Were there other ways?) No, I think that was the only area, because I did okay with men in general.

Wendy was twenty-five years old at the time of the interview, which means that she had felt unable to be alone with her father for about seven years. Her experience with him was the only experience of sexual abuse she reported; hence the fact that she rated it as the most upsetting has no significance. However, the interviewer specifically commented on the extreme difficulty Wendy had in talking about this experience.

Aileen was twelve years old the one time that a sexual incident occurred with her biological father.

I was twelve and we were taking a nap together in his bed and he was cuddling me face to face. He wrapped his arms around me, put my legs in between his legs, and pulled up close to me. (He pressed against you?) Yes. I didn't know what the shit was happening. (Did he touch your breasts or genitals?) No, *my mother came in and she started yelling and screaming at him.* (What do you think would have happened if your mother hadn't come in?) I don't know.

The cases of Aileen and Wendy demonstrate that confrontation of perpetrators or would-be perpetrators by mothers can work. Wendy's response also demonstrates the high level of trauma that can result from even a single occurrence of the least severe form of abuse despite a supportive and confrontive mother and an apologetic father.

*Data on the reactions of family members and the consequences of these reactions are italicized for emphasis in this chapter.

Mothers Who Were Unwittingly Protective
Because of Their Power

The daughters in the following two cases assertively rejected their fathers' advances. However, they both believed that their mothers played a crucial role in helping them avoid more severe sexual abuse, even though they didn't tell their mothers about their fathers' behavior.

Cindy was twelve years old when her biological father tried to fondle her. There were two such incidents in the space of two weeks.

The first time my father tried to molest me I was in bed with my parents. He started touching me between the legs. He didn't want to wake my mother. I kicked him away. He left me alone then. *I guess he was afraid I would wake my mother.* He was on bad terms with her most of the time. *I guess he was scared of my mother and stopped.*

The other time he exposed himself. (What did he expose?) His genitals. It was daytime and he exposed himself and I ran into the house. Again I didn't tell my mother anything.

(Upset?) Very upset. (Effect on your life?) Some effect. I have a little disrespect and distrust for all men, even fathers. It's possible that all men—including the good ones—could try to do something sexual to children.

Aside from Cindy's willingness to kick her father, his fear of her mother appears to have played a key role in her successfully avoiding more serious sexual abuse by him.

Debra was thirteen on the one occasion that her biological father sexually molested her.

My mother was in the hospital. My father was in the kitchen with his robe on but no clothes underneath. He was talking nasty. He was telling my sister that he wanted to go to bed with her. (What did he do with you?) Nothing that time. But one time he came into the bedroom with his penis hanging out. I was sleeping when I felt something on my hand. I woke up and he was rubbing his penis against my hand. I screamed at him to get out. *He left because my mother was home.* (Did anything else sexual ever happen with him?) No, nothing. (Upset?) Somewhat upset. But I was scared more than upset. (Effect on your life?) Some effect. I don't trust people.

Debra considered this incident with her father to be her most upsetting experience of sexual abuse, more upsetting than being raped by an acquaintance when she was thirteen and by a stranger when she was twenty.

Debra specifically mentioned that it was when her mother was in the hospital that her father propositioned her sister and that it was because her mother was at home that her own assertive act of screaming was effective.

As was stated earlier, Herman (1981) and Finkelhor (1979) both reported that the daughters of mothers who have power in their families are much less likely to be incestuously abused. The experiences of Cindy and Debra provide examples of fathers whose fear of their wives' responses inhibited them from further acting out their desires to abuse their daughters.

Herman has stressed the importance of both the mother's power in the family and her relationship with her daughter in the prevention or healing of father-daughter incest. A father who knows that his daughter would never tell her mother, or that his wife would never believe their daughter, has only his internal inhibitions to stop him from acting on his incestuous desires.

Incestuous Fathers Who Take Advantage of Powerless Wives

The research of David Finkelhor (1979), Judith Herman (1981), and others has shown that many mothers of incest victims are sick, absent, or in powerless or abusive situations themselves. For example, one incest victim —Beth—described her biological father's behavior as follows: "My father suspected my mother of seeing other men and began parading around the house nude demanding that she make love on the spot. She refused so he grabbed her and raped her right in front of us." The experience of Vera provides another example of such a case.

Vera was sixteen years old the first time her biological father approached her sexually. She said this occurred four times over a period of two weeks.

I was sixteen. *My mother was sick and my father was coming after me to kiss me on the mouth and touch me.* One night after he had been kissing me I was in my bed and he came into my room. I felt that he had something sexual on his mind when he came in. He came to my bed and began to put his body next to me. (Did he lie down?) Yes. I was trying to look as if I was asleep. He came nearer and nearer and I kept turning my face in the other direction. Then I told him to go, so he went away. (Did he touch you?) Oh yes, he was touching my back and my legs, and trying to kiss me. He touched the area here. [Vera pointed toward her genitals.] He also touched my breasts. (What do you think he had in his mind?) I thought he wanted to have intercourse with me.

(Upset?) Extremely upset. (Effect on your life?) Some effect. For me, a father does not have the right to act like he did. He's not supposed to come to his girl to have a sexual relationship with him. He made me feel very upset. Because my mother was sick I understood that he wanted other women, but that did not mean that he should come to me. I felt very sad and bad, but understanding. After that I was very cold with him and I never talked with him.

When asked which of her many experiences of sexual abuse were the most upsetting, Vera mentioned the one with her biological father. Her other experiences included two attempted rapes by strangers, one when she was thirteen and another when she was sixteen; unwanted sexual intercourse with a teacher who was also a prospective employer when she was seventeen; and an unwanted experience of attempted intercourse with an employer who was also a friend of her parents.

Psychologist Kathleen Coulborn Faller (1984) has found several important differences in the way mothers behave in response to father-daughter incest depending on their relationship with the father. More specifically, she compared situations where the perpetrator was (1) the biological father married to—and living with—the mother; (2) the stepfather or live-in lover; and (3) the father who was not living with the mother because of separation or divorce. She refers to fathers in the latter situation as noncustodial parents.

Faller found that mothers who were still married to the biological father were more dependent on their husbands and behaved much less protectively toward their daughters than mothers married to stepfathers. Mothers married to stepfathers were, in turn, much more dependent on their husbands and behaved much less protectively toward their daughters than mothers who were no longer living with the perpetrator.

In keeping with Faller's findings, the two cases to be cited next involved mothers witnessing the sexual abuse of their daughters but doing nothing to stop it; both were mothers living with the biological fathers.

Janet said the incidents with her biological father started when she was seven years old and occurred from eleven to twenty times over a period of four years, often in the presence of her mother.

He touched my breasts with a perfectly innocent attitude. I don't think it would ever have gone any further. I was very young; it was long before I was fourteen. It was a strange situation because we were awfully close. We would go on long walks. [Janet digressed about her good relationship with her father.] If I was around him at home, I would sit on his lap and he would always manage to touch me across the front. *My mother said that he was aware of my approaching womanhood.* It was almost as if he was keeping tabs on my development. I would always try to avoid it because I thought it was unpleasant. (Did he ever try to do anything else?) No. He was a very proper person. I didn't think of it as child molestation. But he would manage to touch me across the front—never pinching or anything—to see if I was filling out, I guess. It never happened outside the home. He didn't do it when we went for walks. (How did it end?) I got smart enough to avoid the situation.

(Upset?) Not very upset. It didn't bother me a lot. It was just something I had to avoid. (Effect on your life?) Some effect. For one thing it made me very bust conscious. And it had some effects on my relationship with my husband, though nothing I couldn't overcome. I didn't like my husband to touch my breasts. He was very understanding and I overcame it, but it did affect me in that way. (Other effect?) I get very angry when I hear about cases of child molestation today. It's made me very sensitive to the issue. And looking back, I feel anger at my mother for not having done something about it at the time.

Here we see once again that what might be considered a very mild experience of sexual abuse by some criteria, including Janet's own assessment, nevertheless had quite a substantial effect on her.

Olga said that on the one occasion that sexual contact occurred with her biological father it was witnessed by her mother.

I was in my pajamas when I went to say good night to my father. I think he had been drinking. He noticed that I was beginning to develop breasts. I'd had them long enough that they were noticeable. He said: "Look who's getting to be a big girl" and he reached inside my pajamas to feel my breasts. I protested but to no avail. You don't argue with your father. (How protested?) I pulled away. I probably said, "Don't." (Did he continue feeling you even though you pulled away?) Yes. He insisted on doing what he wanted to do. (How?) I don't think he grabbed me or anything, but I submitted in fear of being slapped.

(What happened next?) He must have followed me. The experience isn't really clear to me. *(Was your mother in the room?) Yes, she was right there and she didn't do a damned thing! They were both in the doorway of their bedroom. It all happened in the doorway. (Did your mother say something?) No. I can remember thinking: "Mother, why don't you stop him?"* But I didn't say anything. (Did he use physical force?) I don't really think so. It was mental force; my fear of not being the obedient little daughter.

(Upset?) Extremely upset. (Effect on your life?) A great effect. Whenever I'd have sexual intercourse with my husband and later with boyfriends, their touching my breasts would remind me of the experience with my father and it caused me to feel a repulsion to the sex act. This is something I consciously had to overcome. But I wasn't able to overcome this, as well as a general fear of men my own age, until two years of psychological counseling. After my divorce, even though I was over forty, I dated only men under thirty. I was repulsed by men my own age for some unknown reason, until counseling made me realize it was connected with my father and that that incident was a part of it.

I am small breasted and I have always felt that the incident stopped my breasts from growing. (Which of your experiences was the most upsetting?) The one with my father.

Olga's other experiences of sexual abuse included unwanted genital fondling by her doctor when she was eighteen, completed rape by a lover when she was forty-one, forced fellatio by another lover when she was forty-two, and completed rape by an ex-lover when she was forty-seven. The fact that Olga considered the one-time fondling of her breasts by her father to be more upsetting than all these other experiences provides further evidence of how traumatic it was for her.

Mothers Who Refused to Believe Their Daughters

The next two cases involved mothers who refused to believe their daughters' accounts of sexual abuse by their stepfathers. Faller's findings suggest that such unprotective responses are more common among mothers still married to the biological fathers of their daughters. But clearly, there are many exceptions to this generality.

Laura's case provides an example of a mother whose disbelief of her daughter amounted to collusion with her husband in his sexual abuse. Laura was seventeen years old when her stepfather started to make passes at her. He did so more than twenty times in the six months before she left home. Laura reported that her stepfather behaved in the same way toward her sister and brother when they were older.

He and Mom married six months before I graduated from high school. Frequently when I was getting dressed or undressed in the bathroom, he'd come into the room and try to feel me up. He'd say, "You sure are looking nice"—that kind of thing. (Did he touch you?) Uh-huh. (Where?) He'd try to feel my boobs. He also made passes at all my friends. (How did it end?) I left home.

(Upset?) Somewhat upset. (Effect on your life?) A little effect. *I'd tell my mom and she'd say I was lying, even though she knew it was happening. It was the same with my sister.*

The fact that Laura was already seventeen when her new stepfather approached her sexually may account for the relatively low level of trauma involved. More surprising is the fact that she did not express greater distress about her mother's response. It's possible that their relationship was already a poor one and that her mother frequently discounted what she said.

Babette was nine years old when her stepfather first molested her. She said that his sexual abuse, which included attempted intercourse, occurred more than twenty times over a period of five years.

My mother went to work and he [Babette's stepfather] pretended he was sick. I was nine at the time and she told me to take care of him. When she was gone he called me into the bedroom and said I was old enough to know about these things, and he handed me a dirty magazine to read. I didn't want to but I was so scared of him that I read it to him. He tried to put his hand down my pants, but I pushed it away. Then he took my hand and wanted me to masturbate him. I pulled my hand away and told him if he didn't stop, I would scream. We argued for a while and he finally told me I could go.

(Did anything else sexual occur with him?) He forced me to watch him masturbate. Also he would come into the bathroom and into my bedroom while I was dressing. Every time I rejected him he would have me beaten. He would hide money in my room and tell my mother I had stolen it. She would find it, and then she would beat me. (Did he attempt intercourse?) Yes, sometimes. After dinner I'd have to clean the kitchen. He placed himself in a position where I'd have to look at him; then he'd masturbate.

(Did he use verbal threats?) Yes, he said, "I'm going to tell your mother you did this. I'm going to beat you." One time he told my mother to call juvenile hall. He resented my sister and me because we rejected him and because we caused my mother a lot of problems. *She refused to face up to the fact that he was abusing us. He was sick mentally and she still won't face this fact.* (How did it end?) He tried to kill me when I was fourteen and I ran away. (Upset?) Extremely upset. (Effect on your life?) A little effect.

Babette's continuous and determined resistance to her stepfather's sexual advances is quite remarkable. She resisted him physically by pushing his hand away and pulling her hand away when he tried to make her masturbate him. She threatened to scream if he didn't stop molesting her; she argued with him; she rejected him repeatedly despite the beatings and the threat to call juvenile hall that resulted. And finally, she ran away.

Babette stated that her stepfather also sexually abused her two younger sisters. Babette's mother apparently refused to face the fact that he sexually abused all three of his stepdaughters.

Given the extreme degree of abuse Babette was subjected to by her stepfather, it is startling that she considered it to have only a little effect on her life. This is all the more confusing because she rated this as the most upsetting of several experiences of sexual abuse she had had, including an experience of forced fellatio accompanied by violence with a stranger when she was seventeen, a violent attempted rape by an acquaintance when she was eighteen, and a violent attempted fellatio by another acquaintance when she was nineteen in which she bit the man's penis as hard as she could, then jumped out of his car and ran away. Babette also discounted the effects of these experiences; she described the last one as having some effect and the other two as having no effect or a little effect. Cases like Babette's highlight the need for more objective measures of the consequences of sexual abuse.

Mothers Who Failed to be Supportive

Mabel—the only respondent in our sample to report sexual abuse by an adoptive father—was thirteen years old the one time her adoptive father raped her. The interviewer asked Mabel who had been most helpful in dealing with this experience. She replied: "I didn't find any help in dealing with it at all. *I told my mother later, but she told me not to repeat it to anybody or they'd put him in jail.*"

The interviewer described Mabel's behavior when she talked about her adoptive father as follows:

Mabel became extremely upset during these questions. At the beginning she couldn't talk. Her hands were very restless and she was squeezing them. She was crying; it was as if she were screaming silently. She shook her head and indicated that she could not go on. I tried to let her know I understood and gave her the space to feel the pain. She told me that I was the first person she had ever told aside from her mother, and that it was something she had repressed for a long time. Several times she really couldn't say anything. She was choked by tears or screams that she could not let out.

Mabel described her experiences as follows:

It was my adoptive parents that did this. My adoptive father threatened to beat me up if I didn't do what he said to do. (Exactly what did he do?) I had something in my eye. He pretended to get it out and then he. . . . [Mabel became really subdued and upset]. (Exactly what happened?) He had sex with me. I resisted, but he said, "You do what you're supposed to do because I'm the parent and you're the child." And he said that he'd beat me up if I didn't do it or if I told my mother. (Did he have intercourse with you?) Yes, that's what I've been trying to say. (Did anything else sexual occur with him?) No, I think that was enough. And once was enough. (Did he use physical force?) Yes. He was over 200 pounds; I was just a little girl. (How exactly did it happen?) He was my parent and told me what to do. Naturally you don't argue with your parents.
  (Upset?) Extremely upset. (Effect on your life?) A great effect. It affected my relationships with men. Even when I found a decent boyfriend, I'd figure that he was out to do something to me because of what had been done to me by my father. I thought badly of men in general for a long time. (Which of all your experiences was the most upsetting?) The first experience I had in my life when I was thirteen was the most upsetting. It affected my trust in people—in parents, in men. What happens to you when you're young upsets you more than at any other time.

Note that Mabel blamed both of her adoptive parents for what happened, not just her father.

Reactions to Incestuous Abuse by More Distant Relatives

Many victims of incestuous abuse outside the nuclear family were reluctant or unwilling to tell anyone about what happened to them, but as we have observed, when they did tell someone, the response tended to be more helpful than when the abuse did not involve father-daughter incest.

Jill was six years old, her younger sister was four, and her abusive first cousin was about fifteen at the time of the sexual victimization. A second sixteen-year-old cousin was also present when the incident occurred, but because he was disapproving of it, he is not considered a perpetrator.

Two of my male cousins and my sister were sitting in the backseat of a car. One cousin alternately sat my sister and myself on his lap and started to fondle us. We didn't really know what he was doing. However, the other cousin looked disapprovingly at the one who was doing this. Then I started to have feelings of discomfort and made him let me get down. (Where did he fondle you?) Here. [Jill pointed to her genitals.] (Did he insert his finger inside you?) [Jill nodded yes.] It went on for a while before I realized what was going on. Nothing was said; it was the look my other cousin gave him that made me think about getting away. (Did he attempt intercourse with you?) Not at that time. If the situation had been right, he would have. If the older people had been away for an extended period of time, the chances are probably good that he would have tried. Our folks found out. *My mother went crazy and made sure we were never around him except in a crowd.*

(Upset?) Somewhat upset. I didn't really know much about it at the time, but I was upset by my mother's reaction. (Effect on your life?) A little effect. After that I would never trust him, particularly because of my mother's reaction.

In the following two cases the incestuous abuse ended when the victims told their parents. However, one of them, Eleanor, was particularly reluctant to tell them because of their idealized view of the perpetrator.

Eleanor was thirteen years old when her fifty-eight-year-old father's cousin started grabbing at her. Note the forty-five-year age difference. These incidents occurred from six to ten times over a period of two years.

(Which time was most upsetting?) It was all upsetting. He was a very dear relative. I had loved him all my life. But when I developed female sexual characteristics, he seemed fascinated by my breasts and would grab them whenever he could, and sometimes pinch them. I didn't want to tell my parents because they believed him to be almost a saint. However, I avoided him when I could. It was most upsetting when he grabbed my breast in front of his wife. She was getting old and losing her figure. He made it clear that my figure was preferable to hers. He would also kiss me in a rather sexual way, but he never tried to carry it any further. (Did he use physical force?) Yes, he held me, not brutally, but tightly. *(What ended it?) I told my parents.* (Upset?) Somewhat upset. (Effect on your life?) A little effect.

When a perpetrator has the reputation of being a virtuous pillar of the community, his victim is frequently much less willing to tell anyone about the abuse. Often her reluctance is due to her anticipation that she will not be believed. In Eleanor's case, it isn't clear whether she was afraid of being disbelieved or of causing pain to her parents by destroying the perpetrator's image in their eyes. Not only does the person with a good reputation have a stake in that reputation, but often others do too. When reality conflicts with the reputation, some people prefer to uphold the reputation.

Patricia was twelve years old the one time her eighteen-year-old second cousin molested her. She said that telling her parents prevented the abuse from being repeated.

He said he wanted me to be with him, and he had me secluded away from everyone else. Then he exposed himself and asked me to feel his genitals. He also tried to talk me into taking off all my clothes and walking around. (Did he succeed in getting you to touch his genitals?) Yes. (Did he use force?) No, he wasn't physically forceful, but he did guide my hand. (Did he try to touch your body?) Yes. [Patricia indicated he had pulled at her clothes.] (Did he touch your breasts or genitals?) No.
(What ended it?) I told my parents. I refused to go somewhere with him and my parents wanted to know why. (Upset?) Very upset. (Effect on your life?) A little effect. (Which of your experiences was the most upsetting?) The one with my second cousin.

Patricia considered this experience to be more distressing than an attempted rape by a date when she was twenty-three.

Father's Reactions

Incest research in the past has been heavily focused on father-daughter cases. The role fathers play in preventing or colluding with the sexual abuse of their daughters by other perpetrators is a subject about which nothing has been written.

In the respondents' accounts of incestuous abuse by other relatives, the reactions of fathers were not mentioned as often as mothers were. In the first case to be cited, the father played a positive role; in the second, the role was negative.

Marjorie was thirteen the one time her uncle touched her sexually. He was in his thirties at the time.

He was my mother's brother. I remember when my breasts first started developing, I was up on a chair and he told me he would help me down. When he did so he put his arms around me and his hands right on my breasts. I don't know if he did it on purpose or not, but he didn't have to help me down. *I told my father about it and he talked to him and he never did that again.* (Upset?) Somewhat upset. (Effect on your life?) A little effect.

In contrast to Marjorie's father who stopped the sexual abuse of his daughter, Connie's father naïvely placed her in a very vulnerable situation. She was fourteen years old at the time of this incident; her uncle was in his fifties. No other sexual abuse occurred with this man.

> I went on a business trip with my father and my uncle. My father went out so I was in the hotel room alone with my uncle. I was in my bed getting ready to go to sleep. My uncle came in and sat on the edge of the bed. He started pawing me. He was touching my face and shoulders. I felt distinct sexual advances. (Advances?) The way he was stroking me and talking to me, he made it clear what it was he wanted. He was kissing me full on the mouth and trying to get me to kiss him. (Did he try to touch your breasts or genitals?) No, just my face and shoulders. I finally talked him out of it.
> (Upset?) Somewhat upset. (Effect on your life?) Some effect. It's made me angry that women are objects to men rather than persons.

Perhaps if nonabusive fathers, like mothers, were more aware of the prevalence of uncle-niece incest as well as the many other forms of incestuous abuse, they would be less likely to put their daughters at risk as Connie's father did.

The Reactions of Other Relatives

In all three of the cases to be presented next, a relative intervened to stop the sexual abuse. Jennifer was thirteen when her uncle, who was in his forties, tried to molest her when she was asleep. Her aunt responded after Jennifer called for her assistance.

> I was sleeping in my aunt's house in a hallway. One night my uncle got up. He was naked. He tried to get me to touch his penis, and he was trying to touch my vagina. *I called my aunt and that ended it.* Another time when he was drunk he tried to kiss me. I was sitting in a car and he came over and asked me for a kiss. (Upset?) Not very upset. (Effect on your life?) Some effect.

Hester was thirteen and her uncle was in his fifties when she was subjected to an experience almost identical to Jennifer's. Her grandmother came to her rescue; this happened once.

> My grandmother explained that you have to protect your honor. An uncle lived with us. He was single. He slept in the same room as me and my sister. One time he got up in the night, and he touched me. *I called my grandmother and he ran.* (Where did he touch you?) My legs. *My grandparents wanted to throw him out of the house.* (Did

he try anything else with you?) No, nothing else because he left the house. (What would you say he wanted?) Sexual relations. (Upset?) Somewhat upset. (Effect on your life?) A little. It didn't affect my life very much. If something had happened, then yes, it would have.

Hester discounted what her uncle did. Since her virginity was still intact, she considered that nothing happened.

Simply threatening to tell her grandparents proved to be a successful strategy in Hester's effort to prevent sexual abuse by a male first cousin. She was sixteen the one time her cousin tried to touch her sexually.

He tried to touch my breasts. I said, "I'm going to tell my grandparents." (Did anything else sexual happen with him?) No, because I didn't want it and *he was afraid of my grandparents.*

Geraldine was assisted by both a grandmother and an aunt. She was sixteen when her uncle, in his thirties, started sexually abusing her. The incidents occurred two to five times over a period of two years.

One time I was asleep when he came into my room and started to feel on me. Another time my cousins and I went to a drive-in. He [uncle] put a coat over my lap and started messing with me while I watched the movie. He tried to feel all over me, on my legs, under my pants, under my shirt. (Did he succeed?) No, not really. My cousins were in the backseat and I was too embarrassed to say anything, but I finally moved to the backseat. *(What ended it?) I told my grandmother and she told my aunt [his wife]. My grandmother told my aunt to tell him not to come around any more.*
(Upset?) Extremely upset. (Effect on your life?) Some effect. It makes me not trust men. I don't believe everything they say to me. (Which experience was most upsetting?) The one with my uncle.

Geraldine considered this sexual abuse more upsetting than a violent attempted rape in which her life was threatened by a stranger when she was twenty as well as a completed rape by a friend when she was seventeen.

Conclusion

About three-quarters of the cases in which the respondents mentioned that their mothers knew about the incestuous abuse involved less severe abuse in terms of the sex acts involved. In contrast, in 72 percent of the cases in which the respondents mentioned that their mothers did *not* know about it more severe abuse had occurred. (This association is significant at <0.05 level.) It is disturbing to realize, then, that the more severe cases were the ones most likely to remain secret.

Similarly, those cases of incestuous abuse in which the reaction of those who knew about it (not necessarily mothers) was unsupportive were more likely to be the more severe cases. Almost two-thirds (64 percent) of the unsupportive responses related to more severe incestuous abuse. In contrast, only 31 percent of the cases where the responses were supportive involved more severe incestuous abuse. (This relationship was significant at 0.05 level.)

Although the numbers are unreliably small, it is nevertheless suggestive that in six of the eight cases of incestuous abuse in which there was evidence of the victim being blamed, the abuse was more severe, and six of the nine cases where she was disbelieved were also at the more severe level.

Our survey data suggest, then, that when the incest perpetrator is a member of the nuclear family and when the abuse occurs at the more severe level, it is less likely to evoke a supportive response.

Our analysis of the response of mothers and other family members to the experiences of incest suffers from a serious omission: the perspectives of the family members themselves, particularly the mothers. One longs to ask them for their side of the story. Were their daughters correct in thinking that they knew about the incest in some cases and that they didn't know about it in others? How would Janet's or Olga's mother explain their lack of response to witnessing their husbands kiss or fondle their daughters in their presence? Were their husbands violent men of whom they were afraid? The possible questions seem endless.

The perspectives of the incest perpetrators are also missing from this book, but other books and articles focus on them. In contrast, there is little in the incest literature to help us to understand the mothers. As author Sarah Nelson (1982) points out, "If the victim is not considered guilty, the search for responsibility more often passes to her mother than to the male offender" (p. 53). Nelson also aptly observes that "mothers of incest victims often seem to be caught in a catch-22 and blamed for whatever they do—for conscious and unconscious behavior, for dependence and dominance, for promiscuity and frigidity . . ." (p. 53).

Chapter 24 will provide us with the perspectives of two mothers on their husbands' sexual abuse of their daughters.

24
Mothers of Incest Victims: Two Case Studies

Most children experience their mothers as the all-powerful representative of the adult world. The fact is, however, that her traditional role as the primary nurturer of her and her husband's children is intrinsic to her relatively powerless position both in her family and in society at large. A mother whose work entails caring for home and children earns no money, no health benefits, no insurance, and no pension. Her unpaid labor frees her husband to go out in the world and to obtain work with all these economic rewards and securities. The consequent power disparity between them means that when there is a conflict—for example, if she is distressed by the way her husband is behaving with their daughter—she confronts him from her one-down position, under threat of losing her own and her children's bread and butter. This is the economic reality under which traditional couples live. And even in families where the wife also has paid employment, she rarely earns enough to support her family alone. This is one reason why single mothers are the fastest-growing group of Americans who are living in poverty.

Karl Marx wrote much about the effects of economic disparities on the relationships of people in different social classes, but he overlooked the effects of these disparities on the husband-wife relationship. Unlike workers, many traditional wives live in isolated one-to-one relationships with the person who has power over them. They gain no strength through numbers comparable to hundreds of workers versus a handful of bosses; there are no trade unions for wives. Indeed, women have been socialized to want to live in these circumstances and frequently love the person who has power over them.

Most clinicians and researchers, as well as incest victims, evaluate the mothers' behavior without seeing it in its social and psychological context. Psychiatrist Judith Herman's analysis (1981) of father-daughter incest is unusual in that it combines an honest appraisal of the mothers' behavior with the necessary sociological perspective of it.

In this chapter the stories of two of our respondents who were mothers of incest victims will be presented. Their accounts provide us with unique access to these two mothers' perspectives on their husbands' sexual abuse of their daughters. We will also find out about these women's relationships with their husbands and their own histories of sexual abuse.

Ann Lucas

Ann Lucas was a thirty-year-old divorced white woman who was living alone with her two children at the time of the interview. She had never graduated from high school; she had married young and had a child when she was only sixteen years old. She had worked as a grocery clerk since leaving high school.

Ann was initially very suspicious about our study. She feared that one of the agencies to which she had applied for help in dealing with the incestuous abuse of her daughter had given out her address. But after investigating the study's authenticity and its sponsoring agency, she became very interested and involved. The interviewer judged her to be a "very willing" respondent. This is how Ann described what happened to her daughter.

There was a sexual relationship between my husband and one of my children. It went on for five years. It ended when my daughter told me because she reached an age where she felt that what was going on wasn't right. I got medical help from the local Medical Association of Psychiatry. (Who received services?) My daughter, myself, and her father—for a while. (What happened?) Sexual intercourse. (What was the age of your daughter?) It happened from when she was seven to twelve years old. (How old was your husband then?) He was twenty-five when it started.

He'd never been in any trouble as far as crime went. (Did he bother other people?) In retrospect, I started remembering other incidents I hadn't realized at the time might be like that—with other young girls. I found out about my daughter one and a half years ago.

(Was this ever reported to the police?) Yes. The juvenile child abuse center listed my daughter as being abused by him. But nothing happened to him because of it. He got no record for it.

Ann divorced her husband after she discovered that he was molesting their daughter.

Ann had been raped by her husband over twenty times (the maximum category used by our survey) in a period of nine years. Indeed, he had started raping her even before they married, when he was sixteen and she was thirteen years old.

There was no physical force, but there definitely was mental pressure. I played my part because of my insecurity. If I was a different person it might never have happened. He got me drunk with half a bottle of Seagram's 7. Then he took my virginity from me. I remember being in the kitchen and then waking up in the garage. He had undressed me and had sexual intercourse with me. (Vaginal intercourse?) Yes. (Did he ever use physical force?) One time. He was stronger than me and he just held me down.

(Verbal threats?) He threatened never to see me again if we didn't have sex. He said that he would leave me and no one would ever want me. He said that if I gave him too bad a time he'd call in a group of men, have them rape me, and take pictures to prove that I was an unfit mother. I never wanted sex with him then, so this went on for nine years until I desired him.

(What ended it?) I came into my own person. He was someone who was able to manipulate people and I was easily influenced by others. As long as I didn't realize I was being manipulated, it didn't end. After I had Gestalt therapy for four years, I started realizing things.

(Upset?) Extremely upset. (Effect on your life?) A great effect. I think it set up tremendous mental blocks in me. It left me with a very worthless attitude toward myself. I was more of an object than a person. It fed into my insecurities.

(Other physical violence?) He belted me in the mouth once, and I lost a front tooth. But basically he was a nonviolent person. I was with him seventeen years of my life. He did physical damage to me twice. The other time when wrestling with me he twisted my arm pretty badly. He sprained it. (Why did he hit you?) Because I was screaming at the top of my lungs about him and other women.

Ann said her husband was only violent when he was drunk. Her description of him as a basically nonviolent person seems inconsistent with his vicious threat to prove that she was an unfit mother.

Psychologists have often blamed the sexual abuse of daughters by fathers on their wives' "frigidity" and/or sexual rejection. Ann *had* sexually rejected her husband for the first nine years of their marriage, but she subsequently stopped doing so and he had stopped raping her. Within a couple of years following this change, however, her husband started sexually abusing their daughter. Perhaps he preferred an unwilling partner; perhaps he missed the sense of power he may have obtained by raping his wife—a sense of power that he could attain by having sex with his daughter over whom he was the supreme authority.

Whatever his motives for sexually abusing his daughter were, it seems clear that Ann's relationship with her husband was a very abusive one even prior to their marriage. What, then, was her history prior to this abusive relationship, which culminated in the incestuous abuse of her daughter?

Ann's first experience was a rather atypical form of sexual abuse, since it involved being spanked by her uncle. The issue of spanking as a covert form of sex is complicated because, perhaps even more so than with other behavior, those who do it are often unaware of its sexual element. (This is not to say that spanking necessarily includes a sexual element.) Ann was ten the one time her thirty-year-old uncle spanked her bare buttocks.

He was a policeman. When I look back on it I view it as sexual, but I didn't then. We were in a family group atmosphere and he was wrestling with me. I bit him; he reacted by pulling my pants and underpants down to spank me. The group [that witnessed this] was mostly male cousins and uncles. He took me over his knee and kept me there for what seemed like hours, and playfully spanked me. I cried and screamed and told him I hated him. He didn't touch my breasts or genitals—he did the reverse side—but I couldn't stop him. (Upset?) Very upset. (Effect on your life?) A little effect.

Ann's response to her uncle's spanking her was quite assertive: She cried and screamed and told him she hated him. But to no avail. Her sense of powerlessness during this incident comes through strongly. Two years later Ann was sexually assaulted twice—once by a first cousin and the other time by a friend. The incident with her first cousin occurred when she was twelve and he was seventeen.

We were swimming at my aunt's house and he kept trying to grab my breasts and pull my bathing suit off. He was terrible. He really shocked me. I got out of the pool and he threw me against a cement wall. He was a trip! I never expected that out of him. He told me that if I screamed, he'd hurt me. I told him no matter what he did to me, I'd tell his father. So he stopped. (Did he touch your breasts?) Yes he did, when in the swimming pool. (Did you report this to the police?) No. He works as a policeman now!

(Upset?) Extremely upset. (Effect on your life?) Some effect. It affected me along with all the other experiences. As a woman I feel I have to constantly be aware of the men that I'm around. It makes me suspicious of them.

Ann's next experience involved a friend who attempted to rape her on one occasion when she was twelve. He was approximately nineteen years old at the time.

We were sitting on a couch necking and he became very excited. He started to take his clothes off, then he threw me down on the ground. I screamed hysterically and he left. (Where did he touch you?) On my breasts. (What was he trying to do?) Rape me.

(Upset?) Extremely upset. I was petrified. (Effect on your life?) A great effect. At that age it taught me not to lay around and neck with someone, especially a

much older person. It educated me by showing me that men get very excited. I
think that even now I communicate to my girls about how men get somewhat more
excited than women, and I warn them to be aware of this and not to be alone with
men.

One year later, at thirteen years of age, Ann was molested by her
stepgrandfather, who was in his late fifties at the time. These incidents
occurred from six to ten times over a period of two years.

I think men can smell insecurities. It always occurred in situations with him
when I was alone. I think I was so afraid it just shined through. (Which time was
most upsetting?) The first time. He tried to put his hands down my blouse. That
happened off and on for a few years. (Did he actually do it?) Yes, at one time he
got into my blouse. He never forced me to do anything to him, but he forced a kiss
on me. (How?) He grabbed me by the back of the hair and pushed my head back
and kissed me. (On the mouth?) Yes. (What ended it?) We were in a group of
people. He touched my rear and I turned around and asked him very loudly what
he was doing. He never bothered me again. I exposed him and I guess that's why
it never happened again. (Did he have sexual relationships with other relatives?)
Not that I know of, but it wouldn't have surprised me. WAIT! There were other
girl cousins he had tried things with. They were my cousins—his granddaughters.
(Upset?) Extremely upset. (Effect on your life?) A little effect.

Since her stepgrandfather's sexual abuse of her continued over a two-
year period, it obviously overlapped with her future husband's abuse. Her
explanation of her repeated victimization illustrates a point emphasized in
chapter 11. "I think men can smell insecurities," she said. "I think I was
so afraid it just shined through." What this case unfortunately does not
illuminate is why Ann was so insecure and afraid. Was it a result of her
earlier victimizations? Or was some other factor responsible? This is a key
question for future research to address.

Nor did Ann's sexual assault experiences end with her husband's rapes.
Her twenty-year-old lover raped her when she was twenty-six—four
years before the interview.

I had a room downstairs. He rang the doorbell and one of my children let him
in. They knew him and so sent him in to talk to me. I was asleep at the time and
I woke up to him naked in my bed. He put his hand over my mouth and proceeded
to have sexual intercourse with me. We had been together voluntarily, but the
relationship wasn't such that it was okay for him to come in and do something like
that. He was drunk at the time.
  (Upset?) Very upset. (Effect on your life?) A great effect. It taught me to assert
myself, to scream or yell or somehow to get attention in a situation like that.

When asked which of her experiences had been the most upsetting, Ann
mentioned the incestuous abuse of her daughter. This was more distressing
to her than nine years of being raped by her husband. And in answer to

the question about whether there were any ways in which fear of sexual assault affected her behavior, Ann said yes and enumerated the following examples.

I have three girls and it has changed me totally. I'm very aware [of the possibility of sexual abuse]. I try not to set up situations that could make my children vulnerable to being raped. For example, my daughter had a babysitting job where a man was always around when she was there. I didn't know anything about him, so I stopped her from continuing to do the job. I don't have men over if I'm not going to be here, and I don't leave them alone with any of them. I keep the doors and windows locked, and I have two dogs for protection.

Ann described herself as "very worried" about her children becoming victims of sexual assault. All her concern for and precautions on behalf of them, however, had not prevented her daughter from being victimized by her husband. This experience seems to be quite common for incest victims. Why, one wonders, does the concern not translate into more effective protection for their daughters? This, too, is a matter for future research to illuminate.

Daphne Fulton

Daphne Fulton's second husband sexually abused her daughter.

Daphne was a forty-six-year-old divorced Latina woman who had been married twice and had raised seven children. She was living with four of her children at the time of the interview.

Daphne had attended college but had not graduated. She married her first husband when she was seventeen years old. She had worked outside the home about half the time after leaving college. At the time of the interview Daphne was working full time as a school administrator.

Daphne's second husband became violent toward her in the last two years of their marriage. The interviewer noted that Daphne became very upset when answering questions about her and her daughter's experiences of sexual assault: "She cried once and we had to stop for a while. I felt like I was treading on some very sensitive loaded areas of her life." This is how Daphne described what happened with her husband.

He tried to choke me to death when I saw him with my daughter once. He said it wasn't anything and to forgive him. He called me ignorant and alcoholic.

I used to beg him to go to bed with me, but all the while he was having something with my daughter. When I reproached him about it, that's when he started beating me.

I couldn't approach my daughter about it because she put him on a pedestal. Toward the end when I wouldn't want to come home, he slapped me around in front of the kids.

In this brief description, Daphne presents a picture that contradicts two stereotypes about the mother of father-daughter incest victims. The first stereotype is that mothers know when their daughters are being sexually abused but refuse to do anything about it, thereby colluding in the crime. Daphne, however, confronted her husband as soon as she realized what was going on, as a result of which he tried to choke her.

The second stereotype is that these wives sexually reject their husbands. Daphne was not sexually rejecting but sexually deprived, and assertive about her sexual desires: "I used to beg him to go to bed with me," she said.

Daphne alluded to one common element in cases of father-daughter incestuous abuse—the distance and/or hostility that this relationship creates between mother and daughter. Some daughters come to feel more anger at their mothers for not protecting them than they feel toward their fathers for abusing them.

In answer to the question: "Which of the experiences that have happened to you, would you now say was the *most* upsetting?" Daphne—like Ann—chose the experience with her second husband, including his sexual abuse of her daughter. Let us examine—as we did with Ann Lucas—what experiences of sexual victimization preceded Daphne's husband's abuse of her and her daughter.

Daphne's history of sexual abuse started when her stepfather first molested her at thirteen years old. She said that his abuse had occurred from six to ten times over a period of two years.

I lived with my mother. My stepfather used to come to my bed when no one else was at home. I used to tell him to leave me alone, and I would cry a lot. He would get into bed with me, then fondle and pet me. I was afraid of him; he was my mother's husband and I didn't know how to handle him. (Did he touch your breasts?) Yes. (And your genitals?) Yes. And he put his penis on top of me, though not all the way inside. I started to cry and said I was going to tell Mom, so he got up from my bed and left. I was afraid to go to bed at nights. I tried to avoid him. I wanted to stay with my brother. (Did anything else sexual occur with him?) He made me touch him. (Where?) His penis. Sometimes he bribed me; he gave me a nickel now and then.

(What ended it?) I told him I was going to tell my mother. (Upset?) Very upset, though I don't know if upset is the best word. I was confused and afraid. I didn't know anything about sex. (Effect on your life?) Some effect. I was afraid to talk to my mother. I felt guilty and that I had done something wrong. My mother never knew it; to this day she doesn't know. It frightened me for quite a while. I guess I stayed frightened until I ran off and got married.

Daphne's strategies had included avoidance, verbal protests (she told him to leave her alone), crying, threatening to tell her mother about the sexual abuse, and running away to get married. Though she said her threat to tell her mother proved effective, only after she left home did her fear of her stepfather subside.

One year later, when Daphne was fourteen, she was approached by a stranger whom she estimated to have been about fifty years old.

I was coming out of school and a man offered me candy if I would go with him. When we got to his room, he started grabbing me. I became scared and ran away. (Did he touch your breasts?) Yes. (And your genitals?) Yes. (Upset?) Very upset. (Effect on your life?) Some effect. I felt guilty for going off with somebody for some candy. I am feeling guilt about it right now.

Daphne's first husband started to rape her when she was twenty-one years old. He was twenty-four at the time. She said he raped her more than twenty times over a period of eleven years, and she gave identical figures for the frequency and duration of his other violence toward her.

He degraded me and slapped me around. He woke me up when I was asleep and forced me. He pushed me, held me down, and slapped me. That's why I liked being pregnant. He wouldn't hit me then. Otherwise, he would abuse and force me.

He was a jealous man. He always asked me dumb questions like why did I look at him and what did I think about other men. When I'd say something nice about a man, he would not say anything till we'd go to bed. I'd fall asleep and then he'd wake me and ask me all these questions while holding me down and making me look at him and touch him. He sat on me and forced himself inside me. [Daphne became very upset at this point. She started crying and the interview had to be stopped.] (Verbal threats?) He used them against the kids. He beat me and the kids up all the time. With the kids he would hit them with a stick or use a fork to pin their hands to the table until they bled. He did this especially to the boys.

(What ended it?) I tried to commit suicide. [Daphne again became very upset. She said she ended up in a mental hospital.] (Upset?) Extremely upset. (Effect on your life?) A great effect. I have a lot of bitterness. I can't look him in the face. I had to force him to pay child support. The kids love and respect him dearly and that bothers me more than anything else. He's now remarried and he's become a minister.

(Any other physical violence?) [Daphne was unwilling to answer this question. She was very upset and crying again at this point.]

Daphne disclosed further information about her husband's violence toward her in answer to the question: "Have you ever been upset by anyone trying to get you to do what they'd seen in pornographic pictures, movies or books?" "Yes," she replied, and then:

He forced me to go down on him. He said he'd been going to porno movies. He'd seen this and wanted me to do it. He also wanted to pour champagne in my vagina. I got beat up because I didn't want to do it. He pulled my hair and slapped me around. After that I went ahead and did it, but there was no feeling in it.

The last attack occurred by Daphne's husband when she was thirty-two years old—fourteen years before the interview. But she still could not talk about his abuse without crying repeatedly.

When Daphne was twenty-eight years of age a friend of her family tried to rape her. He was forty at the time.

It occurred during the time that I left the kids' father. He'd been drinking when he came over one night, and he tried to force me onto the couch. He said cruel things to me like that I was easy. He started pushing me and he twisted my arm because I wouldn't sit on his lap. Then he tried to rip off my nightgown. I screamed for my son and when he came, I told him to get this man out of the house. He was embarrassed when my son, who was only twelve, came in, so he left. (Did he touch your breasts?) Yes. (Your genitals?) No. (Did he try anything again?) No, but I was afraid he'd come again at any time of the night. I was a nervous wreck. (Did he use any verbal threats?) No, he just swore a lot and said that he knew what I was because I was single. He insulted me a lot.

(Upset?) Very upset. (Effect on your life?) Some effect. I don't trust friends. You think a guy is Jesus Christ, but he isn't.

Two years later, when Daphne was thirty, she was the victim of another attempted rape by a friend of her family. This would-be rapist was thirty-six years old.

We were at a convention and he came to my hotel room. I told him I didn't want to see him. He forced the door open, then he grabbed me, pushed me, and forced me onto the bed. I told him to leave me but he wouldn't. He pushed me on the bed and held me there, telling me all kinds of things like that he wanted me to make love with him. I told him I didn't want to. Then he got really forceful. (How?) I was already on the bed and he grabbed my arms and pinned me down. He tried to rub his penis all over me. It was a good fifteen- to twenty-minute struggle. (Did he touch your breasts and genitals?) Yes, with his penis. I was scared. We heard some people in the hall and I said I was going to scream to them, so he got up and left.

Later he said he hadn't meant it. He said he'd behave. But he didn't. He kept coming around the house. (Did he attack you again?) Well, that was the only time he was forceful. When he came around my house later, he would beg or make a lot of threats. (What kind of threats?) Actually, they were more like bribes. He'd say if I would have sex with him he'd give me a good job.

(Upset?) Extremely upset. (Effect on your life?) A great effect. I'm not trusting. I used to believe in people helping each other, the community, and the race. But it's a lot of bullshit. [Daphne was very upset at this point.]

Two years later, when Daphne was thirty-two, her twenty-eight-year-old lover forced anal intercourse and fellatio on her. This was the same year that her abusive marriage ended. She said these incidents occurred from six to ten times over a period of three months.

This was a real rough one for me. I got involved with him seriously. I really wanted him. It turned out to be real ugly in the end. I was trying to learn about sex, to do what he wanted. When he asked me to do things, I'd try, as difficult as they were for me, but there were times I just didn't want to, and I was afraid. He changed; toward the end he was real cruel to me. He tried all kinds of things with me. One New Year's Eve he was drinking and he bashed the hell out of me. He wanted to go up my rectum. I couldn't do it, it was too painful. I got upset. He put his penis in my rectum. I begged him not to. That's when he started hitting me. He beat me up and pulled me down the hall by the hair. I was screaming and asking for help. He turned wild, very wild. He slapped me, socked me all over, and when I fell on the floor he grabbed my hair and kicked me all over. He was very rough, biting me on my breasts. He left me in the hall crying. He went in the bedroom and slammed the door. About an hour later I left and walked home alone.

Another time he tried to force me to go down on him, but I couldn't do it. He'd hold me down on him and I couldn't breathe. (What ended it?) I walked away. I didn't want to see him again. Then I met my second husband.

(Upset?) Extremely upset. (Effect on your life?) Some effect. I was disappointed. I lacked trust. It turned me into a very bitter woman. I used to condemn a man before he even sat next to me. He'd say something nice, but I wouldn't believe it.

In summary: Daphne was sexually abused by her stepfather from the ages of thirteen to fifteen; she was molested by a much older stranger when she was fourteen; and she was raped and beaten by her first husband from the ages of twenty-one to thirty-two. The marital abuse ended with her attempting suicide and being admitted to a mental hospital. While she was twenty-eight and still married to her first husband, Daphne was the victim of an attempted rape by a friend of her family. This experience was repeated with another family friend when she was thirty. After her first marriage had ended, a lover with whom Daphne was seriously involved beat her up and forced her into having oral and anal sex. He sexually assaulted her from six to ten times over a period of three months. After this relationship broke up, Daphne met her second husband, who later sexually abused her daughter. He became violent toward her after she confronted him about the incest. His violent behavior occurred during the last two years of their marriage.

Conclusion

Ann Lucas and Daphne Fulton were both childhood incest victims; both of their daughters became incest victims. Ann and Daphne were victimized by many other men besides relatives; yet both reported that the incestuous abuse of their daughters was more distressing to them than any of their other experiences of rape and assault *or* their own experiences of incestuous abuse. This is some indication of how very different our picture of the mothers of incest victims might become if more of them were given the opportunity to speak and be heard.

It often appears that one way to discover the truth about incest is to consider what theories have become dogma and reverse them. Hence the realization that it is fathers who desire their daughters replaces the psychoanalytic dogma that small children sexually desire their parents. The belief that daughters often behave seductively toward their fathers conceals the fact that it is really the other way around. Such a reversal is also needed to better understand the role of the mother in the occurrence of father-daughter incest. For example, it is common to blame the weak or absent mother if her daughter is sexually abused by her father. The implicit assumption is that daughters must be chaperoned in their own homes in order to be safe, and any mother who does not realize this and is not able to be an effective protector is at fault.

But blaming the mother in this situation greatly misdirects the responsibility. What does it say about male behavior and sexuality if young girls are unsafe in their own homes with their own relatives without an adult female to protect them? It is the opportunistic, exploitive, and destructive behavior of the offending males that is the problem, as well as their gross lack of responsibility in the very relationships in which responsibility should be a primary feature—those with their family members.

Clearly some mothers are perpetrators along with the fathers, and others turn a blind eye to what is going on between their daughters and their husbands or sons. But some mothers are also victims of the incest between their husbands and their daughters. In cases of father-daughter incest, the mothers are placed in the profoundly painful and humiliating position of being rejected by their own mate for a younger female. In this culture it is a common enough situation for women beyond the age of forty to be rejected for a younger woman or girl. But what could be more excruciating than to have this occur in one's own home and to be preempted by one's own daughter? What could be more destructive to the relationship between mother and daughter?

It is commonly believed that father-daughter incest occurs only in families in which the mother and daughter have a poor relationship. This may be true; our survey data did not illuminate this issue. But what is often overlooked is that however the relationship between mother and daughter was before, father-daughter incest is likely to completely and permanently ruin it. There is always the possibility that a poor relationship between a mother and daughter may improve later in their lives. But father-daughter incest makes this much less likely to occur. The incestuous father is in a position to play mother and daughter off against each other. He is often so successful that many victims of father-daughter incest become and remain more angry with their mothers than with their fathers.

After disclosure of father-daughter incest, mothers have the extraordinarily difficult task of having to deal with their own feelings of pain and rage at having lost in the competition with a young girl—their daughter —while at the same time having to try to understand and accept their daughters' rage at them for what their husbands did. It is difficult to comprehend the pain and confusion of mothers who must handle being treated as perpetrators—both by the daughters and the culture at large— when they themselves have been victimized. The deep trauma that father-daughter incest usually causes mothers has been largely discounted.

In addition, we have seen that mothers who collude with father-daughter incest are often victims in a broader sense. They are frequently dependent on their husbands economically, and they are enmeshed in a family and culture that provides them with few ways out. Most of the forces that keep many battered women in their destructive marriages apply to other forms of abuse by husbands as well.

The family dynamics theory of incestuous abuse places the responsibility for incestuous abuse on all members of the family. This theory is only a slightly more sophisticated version of the old seductive child theory. What does it mean, for example, to consider a wife who doesn't want to have sex with her husband to be colluding in father-daughter incest? It means that wives are expected to have sex with their husbands no matter how selfishly he makes love, no matter how badly he treats them, no matter what their feelings are for each other. And what does it mean to accuse wives of colluding with their husbands' incest if they reject the traditional housewife role and their husbands then treat the daughters who play this role as substitute wives? It means a total acceptance of the patriarchal family as healthy and appropriate. It means that wives are supposed to sacrifice their lives in order to protect their daughters from their husbands. When we examine the assumptions on which the family dynamics theory of incest is based, it of course sounds ridiculous and unjust. But most people don't examine the assumptions.

25

Conclusion: Incest in the Lives of Girls and Women

Harmful Effects

The views of many researchers and clinicians who have expressed skepticism about the harmful effects of incestuous abuse have been quoted throughout this book, as well as the views of those who are convinced of its destructive impact. The skeptics often point out that most of the data cited to demonstrate harm comes from clinical samples. They quite rightly argue that these are very biased samples that don't represent the women who never seek treatment.

At last we have findings from a large-scale probability household sample on this important subject. This survey provides very strong evidence for the harmful effects of incest victimization. The chapters in part 3 considered the question of the trauma of incestuous abuse from many different angles. We noted that incest victims were significantly younger when they became mothers than women with no incest history; they were also more likely to be divorced or separated at the time of the interview, to have defected from their religion of upbringing, and to be subject to a whole range of further victimization experiences in their adult years. Not only did incest victims report considerable or extreme trauma as a result of incestuous abuse in the majority of cases, but those who reported the most extreme stress were different from the less traumatized victims in a number of ways: They were more likely to have a lower socioeconomic status, to have married, to be mothers, but also to have separated or divorced their husbands. In general, they were more likely to have lived the life of a traditional woman in terms of economic dependence as well as maternal and marital status. Finally, more incest victims than women with no history of incest had high scores on the nine-factor negative life experiences scale.

These chapters together provide strong evidence for the destructive effects of incestuous abuse in many cases. Our analysis also shows, however, that some incest victims report little distress and appear to suffer few if any of the long-term effects investigated by our survey. Although our analysis in chapter 10 illuminated some of the variables associated with trauma (the severity of the sexual abuse, the degree of force or violence involved, the frequency and duration of the attacks, the relative involved, the age disparity between the victim and the perpetrator, and the number of incest perpetrators who abused the child), further research is necessary to explore what factors facilitate a good recovery and what factors impede it.

Implications for Treatment and Prevention

Sound prevention and therapeutic strategies to combat and treat incestuous abuse must be based on sound knowledge of the true nature of incestuous abuse. One of the goals of this book has been to provide such knowledge.

The findings from our nonclinical sample reveal a much broader range of incestuous abuse than is usually found in clinical samples. These data, then, provide a more accurate picture of incestuous abuse of adult women in the population at large that can serve as a comparison group for clinical and other nonrandomly selected samples.

For example, the comparison of Judith Herman's clinical sample with our survey showed that the kinds of incest cases seen by therapists usually involve more force or violence, occur more frequently and over a longer duration, are more severe in terms of the sex acts involved, and more frequently involve fathers as well as multiple incest perpetrators than most of the victims in our study. All these factors were significantly related to the degree of trauma reported by our respondents. Although these findings are consistent with what most people might expect, the point is that our survey can provide a valuable comparison group for other researchers for whom obtaining a probability sample is not feasible.

Myths Dispelled

Our survey has dispelled many old myths about incest, as well as some new ones. For example:

- Only a decade ago experts were still citing the figure of one incest victim in every million children (e.g., Freedman, Kaplan, and Sadock 1975). Instead, extrapolating from our 16-percent prevalence rate, it is more likely that there are at least 160,000 victims of incestuous abuse per million female children and adolescents. For women aged eighteen to thirty-six years old, the prevalence of incestuous abuse increases in our study from 16 percent to 19 percent. For those interested in estimating the prevalence of incestuous abuse experienced by young women today, this 19 percent figure provides the more appropriate basis. Extrapolating from this figure, we would expect there to be at least 190,000 victims of incestuous abuse per million female children and adolescents.

  If we were to adjust our estimate for all the cases of repression and intentional nondisclosure, as well as all the cases missed because our household sample excluded some populations known to be very vulnerable to incestuous abuse (e.g., those in mental hospitals, prisons, half-way houses), our estimate would be much higher.

- Incestuous abuse of the girls at risk in our sample in each three-year period quadrupled from the early 1900s to 1973. This was also the case for extrafamilial child sexual abuse before fourteen years of age.
- Only 2 percent of all the experiences of incestuous abuse were ever reported to the police, and only 1 case resulted in a conviction.
- Only 2 percent of the cases of incestuous abuse in our survey were described as positive or neutral. This is particularly significant not only because our study was based on a probability sample, but because we asked respondents to tell us about all the experiences of sexual contact they may have had with relatives—whether wanted or not.
- In cases where some positive feelings or ambivalence were present, the trauma was often greater than when the experience was totally unwanted.
- There is a difference between childhood sexual trauma and child sexual abuse. Some incestuous or extrafamilial child sexual abuse may not be traumatic: This doesn't mean it's not abusive. On the other hand, not all experiences of sexual trauma at the hands of relatives are cases of sexual abuse.
- Middle-class girls reported just as much incestuous abuse as lower-class girls. When examining the total household income at the time of the onset of the incestuous abuse, upper-middle-class girls were, in fact, overrepresented among incest victims.
- White girls were victims of incest as often as Afro-American and Latina girls, while Asian girls were less frequently abused in this San Francisco sample.
- There was no relationship between being brought up in a rural setting and incestuous abuse for our respondents.
- Stepfather-daughter incest occurred seven times more frequently in proportion to the numbers of respondents reared by stepfathers than was the case for biological father-daughter incest.

- Sexual abuse by uncles was actually slightly more prevalent than father-daughter incest.
- Although father-daughter incestuous abuse was generally found to be most traumatic, incestuous abuse by other relatives was sometimes reported to be more disturbing.
- The severity of the sexual abuse in terms of the sex acts involved was found to be the best single predictor of the degree of trauma reported by the victim.
- The notion that brother-sister incest is often a reciprocal and mutual interaction was found to be a serious myth in most cases.
- Sexual abuse by relatives is often not repeated. It occurred only once in 43 percent of the 187 cases of incestuous abuse.
- Sexual abuse by nonblood relatives was found to be just as traumatic as sexual abuse by blood relatives—and sometimes more so.
- Incestuous abuse is not always perpetrated by adults. Just over a quarter (26 percent) of our cases involved perpetrators under eighteen years, and 15 percent of the incest perpetrators were less than five years older than their victims.
- Not only were female incest perpetrators very rare (only 5 percent of all the incest perpetrators), but they tended to be far less abusive than male perpetrators in terms of the frequency and severity of the sex acts, the amount of force used, and the age disparity between them and the victim.

Implications of Discounting Nonparental Incest

Karin Meiselman's otherwise useful book (1978) has been cited frequently for belittling most forms of nonfather-daughter incest. Yet she is one of the few researchers to even bother to analyze and speculate about non-paternal incest. Because father-daughter incest is more shocking and usually more traumatic than incestuous abuse by other relatives, there has been a tendency on the part of researchers, clinicians, and the population at large to belittle the other forms.

What Meiselman and others who share her perspective probably don't realize is that by belittling the many forms of nonparental incest, they are also belittling—if not condoning—adult-child sexual contact in general. For it would be absurd to argue that sexual contact with a grandfather or uncle would be *less* upsetting or disturbing than sexual contact with an elderly or middle-aged neighbor, family friend, or stranger.

Differences Between Incestuous Abuse and Extrafamilial Child Sexual Abuse

Some researchers and clinicians believe that it is not important to differentiate between sexual abuse by relatives outside the family and abuse by other trusted adults who are unrelated to the victim.* (Indeed, some people even extend the term "incest" to apply to sexual abuse by all trusted adults with whom the child has a relationship.) Although our survey data on extrafamilial child sexual abuse has not yet been analyzed to evaluate this hypothesis (this will be the next project pursued if funds are forthcoming), I doubt that it is true. We have seen repeatedly in the cases cited herein that the breaking of the incest taboo adds to the upset, shock, or disillusionment for many victims and that the incest taboo includes often very distant relatives.

In addition, discovery of sexual abuse by relatives may—if believed—jeopardize more significant or enduring relationships than is usually the case with sexual abuse by nonkin. For example, when the perpetrator is a grandfather, the way the abuse is handled usually has implications for the victim's parent's relationship with his or her offending parent; when the perpetrator is an uncle, this may affect the victim's parent's relationship with his or her abusive brother; and when the perpetrator is a brother-in-law, we have seen that the victim's relationship with her sister is often affected. Also, sexual abuse by these relatives might be discovered less frequently because the victim—realizing the conflict of loyalties involved—may be more reluctant to disclose such experiences. It may be remembered that we found in our study that the closer the kinship relationship, the more unsupportive were the responses of other people to known cases of incestuous abuse (see chapter 23 for a more detailed analysis of this finding). One way or another, the kinship relationship often has a significant impact on the way the sexual abuse is handled as well as the feelings about it.

People's kinship networks provide them with access to a group of people that they would not otherwise have access to. Kin are not usually treated as strangers even when they are strangers. When perpetrators commit acts of sexual abuse outside of their most intimate relationships, their relatives may become victims by virtue of this accessibility. Their belief in, and honoring of, the special bond of kinship may make girls and women particularly vulnerable to victimization by their relatives. Children in the kinship network of an adult who is sexually interested in children are

*L. Berliner. Personal communication, 1983. And D. Finkelhor. Personal communication, 1984.

probably more at risk of sexual abuse by him or her than other children who may have the equivalent amount of contact but be unrelated. Most children are taught to trust not only adults, but their relatives in particular. This trust can inhibit the child's rejection of sexual advances as well as her or his reluctance to report it.

Some Theoretical Implications

An examination of incestuous abuse by grandfathers, brothers, uncles, and other male and female relatives, in addition to fathers, also has important theoretical implications. For example, the most widely accepted distinction between types of sexual offenders against children, developed by psychologist Nicholas Groth (1982), distinguishes between regressed and fixated offenders. The regressed offender's primary sexual orientation is to his or her agemates; the sexual attraction to children is usually precipitated by stress and is frequently just occasional. Incest perpetrators are usually considered to belong to this category of offender (p. 217).

In contrast, the primary sexual orientation of the fixated offender is to children; it emerges at the onset of adolescence and is not precipitated by stress. The interest in children is persistent, the sexual offenses tend to be premeditated, and boys are often the preferred victims (1982, p. 216).

When incestuous fathers are the only perpetrators evaluated, this simple dichotomy of sex offenders may seem quite workable. But what sense does it make when applied to other relatives? Why would a man more likely be a regressed offender if he abuses his niece than a neighbor's child? Furthermore, we have seen that many of the incest perpetrators in our survey were known to sexually abuse other relatives. Although we did not ask our respondents whether the relative who sexually abused them had also abused nonrelatives, several respondents spontaneously mentioned that they had. Is it reasonable to consider a father who sexually abuses his daughter and a niece a regressed offender, but one who abuses his daughter as well as one or more of her friends a fixated offender? The more we learn about how often incest perpetrators sexually abuse more than one child, the more unsatisfactory this neat typology seems to be.

These same findings raise even more serious questions about the validity of the family-dynamics model for explaining incestuous abuse. According to this model, "Incest is a product of family pathology and, except on the rarest occasions, all family members contribute in some way to the pathology that breeds the incest" (de Young 1982, p. 9). Not only does this model remove responsibility for incestuous abuse from the perpetrator, but it ignores perpetrators outside the nuclear family. In addition, it ignores the fact that many incest perpetrators sexually abuse both relatives and non-relatives.

Rather than looking at family dynamics to explain incestuous abuse, we need to recognize that two of the major—but most neglected—causal factors in its occurrence, as well as in the occurrence of extrafamilial child sexual abuse, rape, and sexual harassment, are the way males are socialized to behave sexually and the power structure within which they act out this sexuality. The most glaring finding—and the one on which there is still considerable consensus—is that the vast majority of sexual assaults and sexual abuses of all kinds is perpetrated by males—adults, adolescents, and sometimes even by male children. As long as males are socialized with a predatory approach to obtaining sexual gratification, and as long as this is seen as so acceptable that to point it out is considered offensive, we will make little progress in our efforts to stop sexual assault, including incestuous abuse. As I pointed out in my book *Sexual Exploitation* (1984*b*), in which I dealt at length with the causes of child sexual abuse,

> the truth that must be faced is that this culture's notion of masculinity—particularly as it is applied to male sexuality—predisposes men to violence, to rape, to sexually harass, and to sexually abuse children. . . .
> If this culture considered it unmasculine for men to want sexual or romantic relationships with partners who are not their equals—partners who are younger, more innocent, vulnerable, less powerful, deferential, and uncritical—then the prevalence of child sexual abuse would also be likely to decline. (P. 290)

Freud may have been right in regarding incest as central in the development of young girls—but if so, he was right for the wrong reason. Incest may be central in the development of young girls because the maturation of every little girl may be affected by the incestuous urges—overt, covert, or repressed—that the males in their families often feel toward them. Only in a minority of cases are these wishes acted out. (Out of every one hundred girls, sixteen reported incestuous abuse in our study.) In many more cases the taboo is broken on a nonverbal level only. One form this takes is seductive behavior on the part of adults or older relatives. Judith Herman's study (1981) found that the negative effects of overt incestuous behavior by fathers was also evident to a lesser degree in the lives of daughters with seductive fathers.

Just as the source of incestuous feelings has been projected onto children, so has seductive behavior been projected onto young girls. It seems likely that this perception of young girls as seductive may be a rationalization for the desire of many fathers and other older male relatives to make sexual advances toward them. Even the widespread use of the word "se-duce" in this context is an offensive misnomer. It assumes a mutuality—if not initially, then once the child has submitted. But the notion that a father *could* seduce, rather than violate, his daughter is itself a myth. And the notion that some daughters seduce their fathers is a double myth.

My analysis, with its emphasis on the way male sexuality is socialized in this society, is at odds with a widely held view that incestuous abuse, as well as extrafamilial child sexual abuse, has nothing to do with sexual desire. Nicholas Groth and Ann Burgess (1977), for example, maintain that pedophiles are motivated by power and control issues, hostile and aggres-sive impulses, and affiliation needs, rather than by sexuality. Suzanne Sgroi (1982) likewise considers it a well-documented finding that sexual offend-ers against children "tend to engage in sexual behavior with children in the service of nonsexual needs, especially the need to feel powerful and in control" (pp. 1–2). She goes on to predict that "as long as we persist in treating child sexual abuse primarily as a *sexual problem* (which it is not), we will continue to intervene inappropriately in cases which come to our attention" (p. 2).

Many feminists have also extended their widely held view about rape as a violent rather than a sexual act to child sexual abuse. This perspective was expressed in the made-for-television movie, *Something About Amelia*. The clinician who was treating the incestuous father told his wife and daughter—as well as the nationwide audience—that the father's behavior had nothing to do with sex but was an expression of his need for intimacy.

What this analysis fails to recognize is that males are socialized to sexualize power, intimacy, and affection, and sometimes hatred and con-tempt as well. As Finkelhor (1984) points out: "Sex is always in the service of other needs. Just because it is infused with nonsexual motives does not make child sexual abuse different from other kinds of behavior we readily call 'sexual' " (p. 34).

Indeed, the research of Kurt Freund and associates (1972) suggests that normal male adults have a penile response to children sufficient to suggest the possibility that children could become "surrogate objects" when an adult partner is not available. Freund also found that female children elicited stronger penile responses in normal men than male children, and that they might therefore be more likely to be used as surrogates for adults. Less surprising is the fact documented by considerable research that sexual offenders against children—as distinct from "normals"—show a strong erotic response to children (Freund 1967). This research seems to contradict the view that acting out sexual feelings toward children has nothing or little to do with sexuality (Finkelhor 1984, pp. 33–35).

The view that child sexual assault should be seen as simply one more abuse on the continuum of violence against women is also not supported by our research (Lungen 1985). No violence accompanied 97 percent of the cases of incestuous abuse, and force or violence were used in only 35 percent of the cases. This suggests that incestuous abuse and nonsexual physical abuse of children are probably very separate phenomena, with very different causes and dynamics.

The fact that many mothers as well as fathers engage in nonsexual physical abuse of children provides further evidence for this thesis. Even though sociologist Mildred Pagelow maintains that "a careful reading of the available literature reveals that men are the primary [nonsexual] abusers of children" (1984, p. 191), there is no doubt that a much larger ratio of mothers to fathers physically abuse their children than is the case for child sexual abuse. This fact provides further evidence that the causes of child sexual abuse are significantly different from the causes of other forms of physical child abuse.

Conclusion

This study shows that incest affects the lives of a large percentage of girls and women in this culture. First, there are those who are affected by being directly sexually violated: 16 percent before the age of eighteen. This does not include the unknown number of girls and women who deny or repress their experiences. It does not include girls and women in institutions, like mental hospitals, prisons, drug programs, shelters, and halfway houses who were not included in our sample. It does not include women who live in the street. It does not include those who have committed suicide or been killed.

Second, there are the secondary victims, such as nonoffending mothers and siblings, who may not be sexually violated physically but who may often be greatly affected by the incestuous relationship. Siblings who are not incestuously abused often miss out on attention and what may seem to them to be special treats. A considerable amount of the perpetrator's energy is frequently directed toward the child or children he is sexually abusing. And if the incest secret is ever divulged, the other siblings have to deal with why they were not chosen. Perhaps the family dynamics theory of incestuous abuse should be transformed into a theory of impact rather than a theory of causation.

Third, there are the people who are close to those who are primary or secondary victims, either at the time of the sexual abuse or later in their lives. Given the traumatic impact of many experiences of incestuous abuse, the lovers, husbands, and intimate friends of victims are also likely to feel the effects.

Fourth, the experience is likely to affect the way incest victims rear their children, particularly the way they socialize them sexually. The other significant effects suggested by our study—plus many others that probably occur but which our study did not discover—will also have an impact on the ways in which these women rear their daughters, teach their students, treat their clients, and do whatever else they do in life. As Judith Herman (1981) so astutely pointed out: "Since much of psychoanalytic theory originated in the refusal to validate a common and central female experience, it is not surprising that Freud and his followers were never able to develop a satisfactory psychology of women" (p. 10). Jeffrey Masson makes the further insightful observation that Freud's refusal to come to terms with the reality of incest and other child sexual abuse makes his theory of the psychology of men equally unsatisfactory. For—among other things—it ignores the prevalence of men's desire and willingness to sexually abuse children.*

Our survey finding that it was the victims who actually ended the incestuous abuse in the greatest percentage of cases highlights the fact that prior to 1978—the year of our study—all this incestuous abuse was occurring under the noses of millions of adults who could or would not see it. The awesome burden of stopping the perpetrators, who are usually much older male adults, was largely left to the young female victims themselves. Now that we have a more accurate understanding of the true magnitude and impact of incestuous abuse, we must see that every conceivable effort is made to prevent the continuation of this grim but prevalent crime.

---

*J. Masson. Personal communication, 1985.

Appendix

Tables

To read these tables correctly, it is important to remember the following points:

- These tables compare all the major types of incest perpetrators investigated by our survey. Unless otherwise indicated, the significance levels reported for these tables refer to the entire table; they don't necessarily inform us about which of the within-table differences are statistically significant.
- In several tables, data on nonincest victims are included for the purposes of informal comparison only. The significance levels reported apply to the overall differences between incest perpetrators. Analyses of differences between incest victims and nonincest victims—including significance levels—were presented in chapters 8, 9, and 11.
- Women who were incestuously abused by more than one kind of relative—an uncle and a brother, for example—are counted in each category that applies. However, if they were abused more than once by the same kind of relative, only one of the experiences is counted. This policy leads to a certain amount of double counting, which is also reflected in the "total" columns. This explains why the total N for all incest perpetrators when there are no missing data is 176 rather than 152—the number of women who were incestuously abused in our sample. The alternative was to arbitrarily select a woman's experience with one kind of relative. We believe this would have resulted in a more serious distortion of our data and findings.

TABLE A–1

Victims' Degree of Upset by Type of Incest Perpetrator

Degree of Upset	Fathers (N = 43) (%)	Brothers (N = 25) (%)	Grandfathers (N = 10) (%)	Uncles (N = 48) (%)	First Cousins (N = 25) (%)	Other Males (N = 22) (%)	All Females (N = 8) (%)	Total (N = 181) (%)
Extremely	54	20	30	27	20	36	13	32
Very	16	28	0	21	28	18	25	20
Somewhat	21	24	20	25	40	36	25	27
Not very/not at all	9	28	50	27	12	9	38	20
Total	100	100	100	100	100	99	101	99

Missing observations: 6.
Significant at <0.05 level.

TABLE A–2

Long-term Effects by Type of Incest Perpetrator

Long-term Effects	Fathers (N = 43) (%)	Brothers (N = 25) (%)	Grandfathers (N = 10) (%)	Uncles (N = 48) (%)	First Cousins (N = 25) (%)	Other Males (N = 22) (%)	All Females (N = 8) (%)	Total (N = 181) (%)
Great	44	12	10	25	16	23	13	25
Some	33	44	40	19	20	14	25	27
A little	19	16	10	35	40	36	13	27
None	5	28	40	21	24	27	50	22
Total	101	100	100	100	100	100	101	101

Missing observations: 6.
Significant at <0.01 level.

TABLE A–3

Composite Measure of Trauma by Type of Incest Perpetrator

Degree of Trauma	Fathers (N = 43) (%)	Brothers (N = 19) (%)	Grandfathers (N = 10) (%)	Uncles (N = 46) (%)	First Cousins (N = 25) (%)	Other Males (N = 21) (%)	All Females (N = 8) (%)	Total (N = 172) (%)
Extreme or considerable	81	58	50	48	40	43	38	55
Some or none	19	42	50	52	60	57	63	45
Total	100	100	100	100	100	100	101	100

Missing observations: 15.
Significant at <0.01 level.

TABLE A–4

Composite Measure of Force or Violence by Type of Incest Perpetrator

Some Force or Violence Used	Fathers (N = 44) (%)	Brothers (N = 25) (%)	Grandfathers (N = 11) (%)	Uncles (N = 48) (%)	First Cousins (N = 27) (%)	Other Males (N = 22) (%)	All Females (N = 10) (%)	Total (N = 187) (%)
Yes	39	44	18	23	44	59	10	36
No	61	56	82	77	56	41	90	64
Total	100	100	100	100	100	100	100	100

Significant at <0.05 level.

TABLE A–5

Age Disparity Between Incest Perpetrators and Their Victims

Age Disparity (in years)	Fathers (N = 44) (%)	Brothers (N = 25) (%)	Grandfathers (N = 10) (%)	Uncles (N = 48) (%)	First Cousins (N = 25) (%)	Other Males (N = 22) (%)	All Females (N = 9) (%)	Total (N = 183) (%)
Less than 5 years	0	40	0	0	44	9	56	15
5–9 years	2	40	0	4	36	27	11	16
10–19 years	9	12	0	13	12	32	22	14
20–39 years	80	8	0	54	8	27	11	39
40 years and more	9	0	100	29	0	5	0	16
Total	100	100	100	100	100	100	100	100

Missing observations: 4.
Significant at <0.001 level.

TABLE A–6

Women Victimized by More Than One Relative by Type of Incest Perpetrator

Number Incest Perpetrators	Fathers (N = 42) (%)	Brothers (N = 19) (%)	Grandfathers (N = 11) (%)	Uncles (N = 46) (%)	First Cousins (N = 27) (%)	Other Males (N = 21) (%)	All Females (N = 10) (%)	Total (N = 176) (%)
One	83	74	46	76	63	71	70	73
More than one	17	26	55	24	37	29	30	27
Total	100	100	101	100	100	100	100	100

Missing observations: 11.
Not significant at <0.05 level.

TABLE A-7

Number of Sexual Assault Experiences Requiring Separate Questionnaires by Type of Incest Perpetrator

Number of Sexual Assault Experiences	Fathers (N = 42) (%)	Brothers (N = 19) (%)	Grandfathers (N = 11) (%)	Uncles (N = 46) (%)	First Cousins (N = 27) (%)	Other Males (N = 21) (%)	All Females (N = 10) (%)	Total (N = 176) (%)	Non-incest Victims (N = 778) (%)
None	0	0	0	0	0	0	0	0	51
One only	12	16	0	15	15	29	10	15	21
2–3	45	32	36	39	41	33	50	40	19
4–6	38	26	55	37	33	19	30	34	7
7–10	5	26	9	9	11	19	10	11	2
Total	100	100	100	100	100	100	100	100	100
Mean Number	3.6	4.2	4.5	3.7	3.9	3.9	3.6	3.8	1.2

Not significant at <0.05 level.

TABLE A-8

Rape and Other Victimization Experiences by Type of Incest Perpetrator

Type of Victimization Experiences	Fathers (N = 42) (%)	Brothers (N = 19) (%)	Grandfathers (N = 11) (%)	Uncles (N = 46) (%)	First Cousins (N = 27) (%)	Other Males (N = 21) (%)	All Females (N = 10) (%)	Total (N = 176) (%)	Non-incest Victims (N = 778) (%)
Victim of rape or attempted rape (excluding incestuous rape)	69	58	64	70	70	71	60	68	38
Percentage of married incest victims who were raped by husband	21	10	43	23	30	33	20	24	7
Percentage of married incest victims who were beaten by husband	43	50	57	39	30	53	40	42	18
Unwanted sexual experience with unrelated authority figure	60	58	82	41	41	52	50	52	27

None of these victimization rates for victims of different incest perpetrators are significantly different at <0.05 level.

TABLE A-9

Fear of Sexual Assault by Type of Incest Perpetrator

Fear of Sexual Assault	Fathers (N = 42) (%)	Brothers (N = 19) (%)	Grandfathers (N = 11) (%)	Uncles (N = 46) (%)	First Cousins (N = 27) (%)	Other Males (N = 21) (%)	All Females (N = 10) (%)	Total (N = 176) (%)	Non-incest Victims (N = 778) (%)
Afraid of sexual assault in childhood[a]	48	63	36	35	33	43	60	43	22
Somewhat or very afraid of sexual assault now[a]	67	79	73	52	70	67	60	65	66
Respondent believes she is likely to be sexually assaulted in future[b]	52	79	55	52	78	67	30	60	48
Respondent changes way of doing things because of fear of sexual assault[a]	79	84	91	83	85	71	90	82	76
Percentage women with children who worry child will be sexually assaulted[b]	78	80	83	78	86	92	67	81	63

[a]Not significant at <0.05 level.
[b]Significant at <0.05 level.

TABLE A-10

Composition of Family of Orientation of Incest Victims during Childhood by Type of Incest Perpetrator

Family of Orientation	Fathers (N = 42) (%)	Brothers (N = 19) (%)	Grandfathers (N = 11) (%)	Uncles (N = 46) (%)	First Cousins (N = 27) (%)	Other Males (N = 21) (%)	All Females (N = 10) (%)	Total (N = 176) (%)	Non-incest Victims (N = 778) (%)
Both biological or adoptive parents	64	74	64	74	78	76	80	72	81
Biological mother only	14	16	18	11	11	10	10	13	10
Biological mother and stepfather	17	5	18	0	4	10	0	7	3
Other	5	5	0	15	7	5	10	8	6
Total	100	100	100	100	100	101	100	100	100

Not significant at <0.05 level

TABLE A–11

Victims' Race and Ethnicity by Type of Incest Perpetrator

Race/Ethnicity	Fathers (N = 42) (%)	Brothers (N = 19) (%)	Grand-fathers (N = 11) (%)	Uncles (N = 46) (%)	First Cousins (N = 27) (%)	Other Males (N = 21) (%)	All Females (N = 10) (%)	Total (N = 176) %	Total N	All Survey Respondents (N = 930) %	All Survey Respondents N
White	71	79	100	70	59	57	60	69	122	61	563
Afro-American	10	11	0	13	0	10	0	8	14	10	90
Asian	0	11	0	2	11	5	20	5	9	8	70
Latina	10	0	0	9	15	10	0	8	14	7	66
Jewish	0	0	0	4	7	10	10	4	7	7	64
Filipina	0	0	0	0	0	5	0	1	1	4	41
Native American	7	0	0	2	0	5	0	3	5	1	11
Other	2	0	0	0	7	0	10	2	4	3	25
Total	100	101	100	100	99	102	100	100	176	101	930

Not significant at <0.05 level.

TABLE A–12

Social Class: Occupational Status of Fathers of Incest Victims by Type of Incest Perpetrator

Social Class	Fathers (N = 35) (%)	Brothers (N = 14) (%)	Grandfathers (N = 7) (%)	Uncles (N = 39) (%)	First Cousins (N = 22) (%)	Other Males (N = 19) (%)	All Females (N = 9) (%)	Total (N = 145) (%)	Non-incest Victims (N = 667) (%)
Upper middle	40	29	86	41	36	37	56	41	46
Middle	29	43	0	33	46	42	44	35	37
Lower	31	29	14	26	18	21	0	23	18
Total	100	101	100	100	100	100	100	99	101

Missing observations: 31 on incest victims; 111 on nonincest victims.
Not significant at <0.05 level.

TABLE A-13

Education of Incest Victims' Fathers by Type of Incest Perpetrator

Father's Education	Fathers (N = 34) (%)	Brothers (N = 16) (%)	Grandfathers (N = 8) (%)	Uncles (N = 37) (%)	First Cousins (N = 23) (%)	Other Males (N = 19) (%)	All Females (N = 9) (%)	Total (N = 146) (%)	Non-incest Victims (N = 628) (%)
Some college or more	38	25	50	35	39	21	11	33	39
High school graduate	29	31	13	32	35	37	33	32	32
Some high school or less	32	44	38	32	26	42	56	36	29
Total	99	100	101	99	100	100	100	101	100

Missing observations: 30 on incest victims; 150 on nonincest victims.
Not significant at <0.05 level.

TABLE A–14

Education of Incest Victims' Mothers by Type of Incest Perpetrator

Mothers' Education	Fathers (N = 39) (%)	Brothers (N = 19) (%)	Grandfathers (N = 10) (%)	Uncles (N = 39) (%)	First Cousins (N = 26) (%)	Other Males (N = 21) (%)	All Females (N = 10) (%)	Total (N = 164) (%)	Non-incest Victims (N = 707) (%)
Some college or more	18	32	30	18	27	14	10	21	27
High school graduate	67	42	60	56	39	43	50	52	42
Some high school or less	15	26	10	26	35	43	40	27	31
Total	100	100	100	100	101	100	100	100	100

Missing observations: 12 on incest victims; 71 on nonincest victims.
Not significant at <0.05 level.

TABLE A–15

Disparity in Respondents' Parents' Educational Levels by Type of Incest Perpetrator

Disparity in Parents' Education	Fathers (N = 33) (%)	Brothers (N = 16) (%)	Grandfathers (N = 8) (%)	Uncles (N = 34) (%)	First Cousins (N = 23) (%)	Other Males (N = 19) (%)	All Females (N = 9) (%)	Total (N = 142) (%)	Non-incest Victims (N = 602) (%)
Father had higher education	42	13	50	38	44	32	11	35	36
Equal level of education	27	63	25	38	48	47	67	42	46
Mother had higher education	30	25	25	24	9	21	22	23	18
Total	99	101	100	100	101	100	100	100	100

Missing observations: 34 on incest victims; 176 on nonincest victims.
Not significant at <0.05 level.

TABLE A-16

Amount of Time Mothers Worked Outside of Home During Daughters' Childhood Years by Type of Incest Perpetrator

Amount of Time Mothers Worked	Fathers (N = 41) (%)	Brothers (N = 19) (%)	Grand-fathers (N = 11) (%)	Uncles (N = 45) (%)	First Cousins (N = 27) (%)	Other Males (N = 21) (%)	All Females (N = 9) (%)	Total (N = 173) (%)	Non-incest Victims (N = 765) (%)	Survey Respondents %	Survey Respondents N
Most of time	29	26	0	20	22	33	33	24	19	20	181
Some of time	34	26	36	29	33	24	11	30	24	25	230
Didn't work	37	47	64	51	44	43	56	46	57	55	503
Total	100	99	100	100	99	100	100	100	100	100	914

Missing observations: 3 on incest victims; 13 on nonincest victims.
Not significant at <0.05 level.

TABLE A-17

Victims' Religious Upbringing by Type of Incest Perpetrator

Religious Upbringing	Fathers (N = 42) (%)	Brothers (N = 19) (%)	Grand-fathers (N = 11) (%)	Uncles (N = 46) (%)	First Cousins (N = 27) (%)	Other Males (N = 21) (%)	All Females (N = 10) (%)	Total (N = 176) (%)	Non-incest Victims (N = 778) (%)	Survey Respondents %	Survey Respondents N
Catholic	50	37	27	35	52	43	20	41	39	39	358
Protestant	36	53	55	50	22	38	70	43	40	41	380
Jewish	0	0	0	4	7	10	10	4	7	6	59
Other	7	0	0	4	7	10	0	5	7	7	61
None	7	11	18	7	11	0	0	7	8	7	69
Total	100	101	100	100	99	101	100	100	101	100	927

Missing observations: 3 on nonincest victims.
Not significant at <0.05 level.

TABLE A–18

Victims' Marital Status by Type of Incest Perpetrator

Marital Status	Fathers (N = 42) (%)	Brothers (N = 19) (%)	Grandfathers (N = 11) (%)	Uncles (N = 46) (%)	First Cousins (N = 27) (%)	Other Males (N = 21) (%)	All Females (N = 10) (%)	Total (N = 176) (%)	Non-incest Victims (N = 777) (%)
Never married	36	47	36	15	26	29	0	27	31
Married	17	26	36	44	44	52	50	36	40
Widowed	10	5	0	9	0	0	10	6	13
Divorced or separated	38	21	27	33	30	19	40	31	16
Total	101	99	99	101	100	100	100	100	100

Missing observations: 1 on nonincest victim.
Not significant at <0.05 level.
Note: When marital status is dichotomized into those who never married and those who married, the relationship becomes significant at <0.05 level.

TABLE A–19

Victims' Remarriage Rates by Type of Incest Perpetrator

Number of Marriages	Fathers (N = 27) (%)	Brothers (N = 10) (%)	Grandfathers (N = 7) (%)	Uncles (N = 39) (%)	First Cousins (N = 20) (%)	Other Males (N = 15) (%)	All Females (N = 10) (%)	Total (N = 128) (%)	Non-incest Victims (N = 539) (%)
Married more than once	44	10	57	33	5	20	20	28	25
Married once only	56	90	43	67	95	80	80	72	75
Total	100	100	100	100	100	100	100	100	100

Significant at <0.05 level.

TABLE A–20

Victims' Maternal Status by Type of Incest Perpetrator

Maternal Status	Fathers (N = 42) (%)	Brothers (N = 19) (%)	Grandfathers (N = 11) (%)	Uncles (N = 46) (%)	First Cousins (N = 27) (%)	Other Males (N = 21) (%)	All Females (N = 10) (%)	Total (N = 176) (%)	Non-incest Victims (N = 773) (%)
Raised 1 or more children	57	53	55	70	52	62	60	60	49
Raised no child	43	47	46	30	48	38	40	40	51
Total	100	100	101	100	100	100	100	100	100
Mean number children raised	.69	.68	.73	.93	.74	.90	1.0	.81	.65
Mean age at first childbearing	21.6	22.6	22.1	22.6	23.6	23.2	27.0	22.9	24.2

Missing observations: 5 on nonincest victims.
Not significant at <0.05 level.

TABLE A–21

Victims' Occupational Status by Type of Incest Perpetrator

Social Class	Fathers (N = 41) (%)	Brothers (N = 18) (%)	Grandfathers (N = 11) (%)	Uncles (N = 46) (%)	First Cousins (N = 26) (%)	Other Males (N = 20) (%)	All Females (N = 10) (%)	Total (N = 172) (%)	Non-incest Victims (N = 736) (%)
Upper middle class	34	28	55	15	23	35	20	27	29
Middle class	54	56	18	54	42	40	70	49	45
Lower class	12	17	27	30	35	25	10	23	26
Total	100	101	100	99	100	100	100	99	100

Missing observations: 4 on incest victims; 42 on nonincest victims.
Not significant at <0.05 level.

TABLE A–22

Victims' Educational Status by Type of Incest Perpetrator

Victims' Education	Fathers (N = 42) (%)	Brothers (N = 19) (%)	Grandfathers (N = 11) (%)	Uncles (N = 46) (%)	First Cousins (N = 27) (%)	Other Males (N = 21) (%)	All Females (N = 10) (%)	Total (N = 76) (%)	Non-incest Victims (N = 778) (%)
College graduate or more	31	21	55	20	30	33	40	29	31
Some college	33	47	27	41	30	33	30	36	27
High school graduate	21	21	0	30	30	19	30	24	25
Some high school or less	14	11	18	9	11	14	0	11	17
Total	99	100	100	100	101	99	100	100	100

Not significant at <0.05 level.

TABLE A–23

Victims' Total Household Income in 1977 by Type of Incest Perpetrator

Total Household Income	Fathers (N = 39) (%)	Brothers (N = 18) (%)	Grandfathers (N = 11) (%)	Uncles (N = 44) (%)	First Cousins (N = 26) (%)	Other Males (N = 19) (%)	All Females (N = 8) (%)	Total (N = 165) (%)	Non-incest Victims (N = 741) (%)
Less than $7,500	41	44	27	32	27	26	0	32	34
$7,500–$14,999	33	39	36	32	39	32	38	35	33
$15,000 or more	26	17	36	36	35	42	63	33	33
Total	100	100	99	100	101	100	101	100	100

Missing observations: 11 on incest victims; 37 on nonincest victims.
Not significant at <0.05 level.

TABLE A-24

Victims' Religious Defection by Type of Incest Perpetrator[a]

Religious Defection	Fathers (N = 39)	Brothers (N = 17)	Grandfathers (N = 9)	Uncles (N = 43)	First Cousins (N = 24)	Other Males (N = 21)	All Females (N = 10)	Total (N = 163)	Non-incest Victims (N = 715)
Still prefer religion of upbringing	14	6	2	21	11	14	4	72	463
Rejected religion of upbringing	25	11	7	22	13	7	6	91	252
Rate of religious defection (%)[d]	64[b]	65[b]	78[b]	51[c]	54[c]	21	60	56[b]	35

[a]Respondents who were reared with no religion are excluded from these calculations.
[b]The defection rate is significantly different at <0.01 level for the victims of particular incest perpetrators when compared with women who have no history of incest.
[c]The same as [b] except the significance level is <0.05.
[d]The defection rate was calculated by dividing row 2 (number of respondents rejecting religion of upbringing) by total N for perpetrator group.
Not significant at <0.05 level.

TABLE A–25

Period Rates for Incestuous Abuse and Extrafamilial Child Sexual Abuse for Three-year Age Groupings (Calculations for Figure 5–1)

	Number Girls at Risk of Sexual Abuse Before 18	Incestuous Abuse Before 18 Years		Number Girls at Risk of Sexual Abuse Before 14	Extrafamilial Abuse Before 14 Years	
		#	%		#	%
1908 and before	88	1	1.1	82	3	3.7
1909–1911	114	1	.9	109	4	3.7
1912–1914	142	2	1.4	127	5	3.9
1915–1917	166	1	.6	147	7	4.8
1918–1920	184	2	1.1	159	6	3.8
1921–1923	196	3	1.5	151	6	4.0
1924–1926	193	3	1.6	151	8	5.3
1927–1929	188	5	2.7	142	4	2.8
1930–1932	196	3	1.5	146	3	2.1
1933–1935	196	4	2.0	154	6	3.9
1936–1938	188	2	1.1	149	8	5.4
1939–1941	184	8	4.3	140	7	5.0
1942–1944	194	6	3.1	154	7	4.5
1945–1947	227	11	4.8	179	14	7.8
1948–1950	274	7	2.6	234	11	4.7
1951–1953	333	10	3.0	301	10	3.3
1954–1956	414	15	3.6	372	14	3.8
1957–1959	442	18	4.1	399	13	3.3
1960–1962	444	27	6.1	374	27	7.2
1963–1965	396	11	2.8	285	21	7.4
1966–1968	310	12	3.9	182	15	8.2
1969–1971	216	9	4.2	77	10	13.0
1972–1974	110	5	4.5	25	4	16.0

TABLE A-26

Cohort Rates of Incestuous Abuse of Females 17 Years and Younger
(Only Victims' First Experiences are Included)
(Calculations for Figure 5–2)

Cohort 1, Age 60+, born 1918 and earlier, $N = 218$, 17 cases of incestuous abuse

Age at Onset x	Incest Cases/ Women at Risk	qx	lx	dx	%	Abuse by Age
0–4	2/218	.009	1000	9	.9	5
5–9	2/216	.009	991	9	1.8	10
10–14	7/214	.033	982	32	5.1	15
15–17	6/207	.029	950	28	8.0	18

Cohort 2, Age 50–59, born 1919–1928, $N = 103$, 12 cases of incestuous abuse

Age at Onset x	Incest Cases/ Women at Risk	qx	lx	dx	%	Abuse by Age
0–4	0/103	.000	1000	0	0	5
5–9	2/103	.019	1000	19	1.9	10
10–14	7/101	.069	981	68	8.8	15
15–17	3/94	.032	913	29	12.0	18

Cohort 3, Age 40–49, born 1929–1938, $N = 101$, 21 cases of incestuous abuse

Age at Onset x	Incest Cases/ Women at Risk	qx	lx	dx	%	Abuse by Age
0–4	2/101	.020	1000	20	2.0	5
6–9	5/99	.051	980	50	7.1	10
10–14	10/94	.106	931	99	17.7	15
15–17	4/84	.048	832	40	22.5	18

Cohort 4, Age 30–39, born 1939–1948, $N = 198$, 46 cases of incestuous abuse

Age at Onset x	Incest Cases/ Women at Risk	qx	lx	dx	%	Abuse by Age
0–4	6/198	.030	1000	30	3.0	5
5–9	7/192	.036	970	35	6.6	10
10–14	24/185	.130	935	122	19.6	15
15–17	9/161	.056	813	46	25.2	18

Cohort 5, Age 18–29, born 1949–1960, $N = 310$, 52 cases of incestuous abuse

Age at Onset x	Incest Cases/ Women at Risk	qx	lx	dx	%	Abuse by Age
0–4	1/310	.003	1000	3	.3	5
5–9	19/309	.061	997	61	6.4	10
10–14	20/290	.069	936	65	13.3	15
15–17	12/270	.044	871	38	17.7	18

Total $N = 148$ (four cases were known to have occurred before the victim turned eighteen, but more precise information on her age was missing).

References

Allen, C. V. 1980. *Daddy's girl.* New York: Wyndham Books.

American Humane Association. 1981. *National Study on Child Neglect and Abuse Reporting.* Denver, Colo.: American Humane Association.

Anderson, S. C., Bach, C. M., and Griffith, S. 1981. "Psychosocial sequelae in intrafamilial victims of sexual assault and abuse." Paper presented at the Third International Conference on Child Abuse and Neglect, Amsterdam, The Netherlands.

Armstrong, L. 1978. *Kiss daddy goodnight.* New York: Hawthorn Press.

———. 1983. *The home front: Notes from the family war zone.* New York: McGraw-Hill.

Badgley, R. F. 1984. *Sexual offences against children,* vol. 1–2. Ottawa, Canada: Canadian Government Publishing Centre.

Bagley, C. 1985. *Child sexual abuse within the family: An account of studies 1978–1984.* Calgary, Canada: University of Calgary Press.

Bagley, C., and Ramsay, R. 1985. "Disrupted childhood and vulnerability to sexual assault: Long-term sequels with implications for counselling." Paper presented at the Conference on Counselling the Sexual Abuse Survivor, Winnipeg.

Bank, S. P., and Kahn, M. 1982. *The sibling bond.* New York: Basic Books.

Bass, E., and Thornton, L., eds. 1983. *I never told anyone: Writings by women survivors of child sexual abuse.* New York: Harper & Row.

Bell, A. P., and Weinberg, M. S. 1978. *Homosexualities: A study of diversity among men and women.* New York: Simon and Schuster.

Bell, A. P. and Weinberg, M. S. 1981. *Sexual preference: Its development among men and women.* Bloomington, Ind: Indiana University Press.

Benward, J., and Densen-Gerber, J. 1975. "Incest as a causative factor in antisocial behavior: An exploratory study." *Contemporary Drug Problems* 4 (Fall): 323–340.

Beserra, S. S., Jewel, N. M., and Matthews, M. W. 1973. *Sex code of California: A compendium.* Sausalito, Calif: Graphic Arts of Marin.

Brady, K. 1979. *Father's days: A true story of incest.* New York: Seaview Books.

Breines, W., and Gordon, L. 1983. "The new scholarship on family violence." *Signs: Journal of Women in Culture and Society* 8 (3): 490–531.

Briere, J. 1984. "The effects of childhood sexual abuse on later psychological functioning: Defining a post-sexual-abuse syndrome." Paper presented at the Third National Conference on Sexual Victimization of Children, Children's Hospital National Medical Center, Washington, D.C.

Browne, A., and Finkelhor, D. 1986. "The impact of child sexual abuse: A review of the research." *Psychological Bulletin* 99 (1).

Brownmiller, S. 1975. *Against our will: Men, women and rape.* New York: Simon and Schuster.

Burgess, A. W. 1984. *Child pornography and sex rings.* Lexington, Mass.: D.C. Heath.

Burgess, A. W., Groth, A. N., Holmstrom, L. L., and Sgroi, S. M. 1978. *Sexual assault of children and adolescents.* Lexington, Mass.: Lexington Books.

Burgess, A. W., Groth, A. N., and McCausland, M. 1981. "Child sex initiation rings." *American Journal of Orthopsychiatry* 51: 110–118.

Butler, S. 1978. *Conspiracy of silence: The trauma of incest.* San Francisco: New Glide Publications.

Carnes, P. 1983. *The sexual addiction.* Minneapolis: CompCare Publications.

Cole, R. 1984. "Freudianism and its malcontents." *Boston Globe,* 27 May.

Constantine, L., and Martinson, F. 1981. *Children and sex: New findings and new perspectives.* Boston: Little, Brown.

Courtois, C. A. 1979. "The incest experience and its aftermath." *Victimology: An International Journal* 4 (4): 337–347.

DeFrancis, V. 1969. *Protecting the child victim of sex crimes committed by adults.* Denver, Colo.: The American Humane Association, Children's Division.

DeLora, J., and Warren, C. 1977. *Understanding sexual interaction.* Boston: Houghton Mifflin.
DeMott, B. 1980. "The pro-incest lobby." *Psychology Today* (March): 11–16.
Densen-Gerber, J., and Hutchinson, S. F. 1978. "Medical-legal and societal problems involving children—child prostitution, child pornography and drug-related abuse: Recommended legislation," in *The maltreatment of children,* ed. S. M. Smith. Baltimore: University Park Press.
de Young, M. 1982. *The sexual victimization of children.* Jefferson, N.C.: McFarland.
———. 1985. *Incest: An annotated bibliography.* Jefferson, N.C.: McFarland.
Donnerstein, E. 1984. "Pornography: Its effect on violence against women," in *Pornography and sexual aggression,* eds. N. M. Malamuth and E. Donnerstein, pp. 53–81. New York: Academic Press.
Durfee, M. 1984. Unpublished memo citing statistics gathered by the Los Angeles County Department of Health Services, Calif.
Faller, K. C. 1984. "Sexual abuse by caretakers." Typescript.
Ferracuti, F. 1972. "Incest between father and daughter," in *Sexual behaviors,* ed. H. L. P. Resnick and M. E. Wolfgang, pp. 169–183. Boston: Little, Brown.
Finkelhor, D. 1979. *Sexually victimized children.* New York: Free Press.
———. 1980. "Sex among siblings." *Archives of Sexual Behavior* 10: 171–194.
———. 1984. *Child sexual abuse: New theory and research.* New York: Free Press.
Finkelhor, D., and Baron, L. 1985. "Risk factors for childhood sexual abuse: A review of the evidence." Typescript.
Finkelhor, D., and Browne, A. 1985. "The traumatic impact of child sexual abuse: A conceptualization." *American Journal of Orthopsychiatry* 55 (4): 530–541.
Finkelhor, D., and Hotaling, G. 1984. "Sexual abuse in the national incidence study of child abuse and neglect." *Child Abuse and Neglect: The International Journal* 8: 22–33.
Finkelhor, D., and Redfield, D. 1984. "How the public defines sexual abuse," in *Child sexual abuse: New theory and research,* by D. Finkelhor, pp. 107–133. New York: Free Press.
Ford, C. S., and Beach, F. A. 1951. *Patterns of sexual behavior.* New York: Harper & Row.
Forward, S., and Buck, C. 1978. *Betrayal of innocence: Incest and its devastation.* New York: Penguin.
Fox, R. 1980. *The red lamp of incest.* New York: E. P. Dutton.
Freedman, A. M., Kaplan, H. I., and Sadock, B. J., eds. 1975. *Comprehensive textbook of psychiatry,* 2nd ed. Baltimore: Williams & Wilkins.
Freund, K. 1967. "Erotic preference in pedophilia." *Behavioral Research and Therapy* 5: 339–348.
Freund, K., McKnight, C. K., Longevin, R., and Cibiri, S. 1972. "The female child as surrogate object." *Archives of Sexual Behavior* 2: 119–133.
Frieze, Irene. 1983. "Investigating the causes and consequences of marital rape," *Signs: Journal of Women in Culture and Society* 8 (3): 532–553.
Fromuth, M. E. 1983. "The long term psychological impact of childhood sexual abuse." Ph.D. doctoral diss., Auburn University, Auburn, Alabama.
Gagnon, J. 1965. "Female child victims of sex offenses." *Social Problems* 13: 176–192.
Giaretto, H. 1982. *Integrated treatment of child sexual abuse.* Palo Alto, Calif.: Science and Behavior Books.
Giles-Sims, J., and Finkelhor, D. 1984. "Child abuse in stepfamilies," *Family Relations* 33 (3): 407–413.
Goodwin, J., Cormier, L., and Owen, J. 1983. "Grandfather-granddaughter incest: A trigenerational view." *Child Abuse and Neglect: The International Journal* 7 (2): 163–170.
Groth, A. N. 1979. *Men who rape: The psychology of the offender.* New York: Plenum Press.
———. 1982. "The incest offender," in *Handbook of clinical intervention in child sexual abuse,* ed. S. M. Sgroi, pp. 215–239. Lexington, Mass.: Lexington Books.
Groth, A. N., and Burgess, A. W. 1977. "Motivational intent in the sexual assault of children." *Criminal Justice and Behavior* 4 (3): 253–264.
Henderson, J. 1983. "Is incest harmful?" *Canadian Journal of Psychiatry* 28 (February): 34–39.
Herman, J. 1981. *Father-daughter incest.* Cambridge, Mass.: Harvard University Press.
Herman, J., Russell, D., and Trocki, K. 1985. "Recovery from incestuous abuse in childhood." Paper presented at the Annual Meeting of the American Psychiatric Association, Dallas, Texas.
Herman, J., and Schatzow, E. 1985. "Recovery and verification of memories of childhood sexual trauma." Typescript.
Hill, E. 1985. *The family secret: A personal account of incest.* Santa Barbara, Calif.: Capra Press.
Hite, S. 1976. *The Hite report: A nationwide study of female sexuality.* New York: Dell.

————. 1981. *The Hite report on male sexuality.* New York: Knopf.

Howells, K. 1981. "Adult sexual interest in children: Considerations relevant to theories of aetiology," in *Adult sexual interest in children,* ed. M. Cook and K. Howells, pp. 55–94. New York: Academic Press.

James, J., and Meyerding, J. 1977. "Early sexual experience as a factor in prostitution." *Archives of Sexual Behavior* 7 (1): 31–42.

Janoff-Bulman, B., and Frieze, I. H. 1983. "A theoretical perspective for understanding reactions to victimization." *Journal of Social Issues* 39 (2): 1–17.

Janus, S. 1981. *The death of innocence: How our children are endangered by the new sexual freedom.* New York: William Morrow.

Justice, B., and Justice, R. 1979. *The broken taboo: Sex in the family.* New York: Human Sciences Press.

Katz, S., and Mazur, M. A. 1979. *Understanding the rape victim: A synthesis of research findings.* New York: John Wiley & Sons.

Kendrick, W. 1984. "Not just another oedipal drama: The unsinkable Sigmund Freud." *Voice Literary Supplement* (June): 12–16.

Kercher, G., and McShane, M. 1984. "The prevalence of child sexual abuse victimization in an adult sample of Texas residents." *Child Abuse and Neglect: The International Journal* 8: 495–501.

Kilpatrick, D. G., and Amick, A. E. 1984. "Intrafamilial and extrafamilial sexual assault: Results of a random community survey." Paper presented at the Second National Family Violence Research Conference, Durham, New Hampshire.

Kinsey, A. C., Pomeroy, W. B., and Martin, C. E. 1948. *Sexual behavior in the human male.* Philadelphia: W. B. Saunders.

Kinsey, A. C., Pomeroy, W. B., Martin, C. E., and Gebhard, P. H. 1953. *Sexual behavior in the human female.* Philadelphia: W. B. Saunders.

Kubler-Ross, E. 1984. Public lecture on child sexual abuse in Berkeley, Calif. (May 29).

Landis, J. T. 1956. "Experience of 500 children with adult's sexual deviance." *Psychiatric Quarterly Supplement* 30: 91–109.

Lewis, I. A. 1985. Unpublished memo. *Los Angeles Times* Poll No. 98 (July).

Lukianowicz, N. 1972. "Paternal incest." *British Journal of Psychiatry* 120: 301–313.

Lungen, A. 1985. "Sexual abuse in the continuum of violence against women." Paper presented at Conference on Counselling the Sexual Abuse Survivor, Winnipeg.

MacFarlane, K. 1978. "Sexual abuse of children," in *The victimization of women,* eds. J. R. Chapman and M. Gates, pp. 301–313. Beverly Hills, Calif: Sage Publications.

McNaron, T., and Morgan, Y., eds. 1982. *Voices in the night: Women speaking about incest.* Minneapolis: Cleis Press.

Maisch, H. 1972. *Incest.* New York: Stein & Day.

Malamuth, N. M. 1984. "Aggression against women: Cultural and individual causes," in *Pornography and sexual aggression,* eds. N. M. Malamuth and E. Donnerstein, pp. 19–52. New York: Academic Press.

Malamuth, N. M., and Donnerstein, E., eds. 1984. *Pornography and sexual aggression.* New York: Academic Press.

Malcolm, J. 1984. *In the Freud archives.* New York: Knopf.

Masson, J. M. 1984. *The assault on truth: Freud's suppression of the seduction theory.* New York: Farrar, Straus & Giroux.

Masters, W. H., and Johnson, V. E. (1966). *Human sexual response.* Boston: Little, Brown.

Meiselman, K. C. 1978. *Incest.* San Francisco: Jossey-Bass.

Miller, A. 1984. *Thou shalt not be aware: Society's betrayal of the child.* New York: Farrar, Straus & Giroux.

Morris, M. 1982. *If I should die before I wake.* Los Angeles: J. P. Tarcher.

Mrazek, P. 1981. "The nature of incest: A review of contributing factors," in *Sexually abused children and their families,* eds. P. Mrazek and C. H. Kempe, pp. 97–107. New York: Pergamon Press.

Mrazek, P., and Bentovim, A. 1981. "Incest and the dysfunctional family system," in *Sexually abused children and their families,* eds. P. Mrazek and C. H. Kempe, pp. 167–177. New York: Pergamon Press.

Mrazek, P., and Kempe, C. H., eds. 1981. *Sexually abused children and their families.* New York: Pergamon Press.

National Center on Child Abuse and Neglect (NCCAN). 1981. *Study findings: National study of the incidence and severity of child abuse and neglect.* Washington D.C.: U.S. Department of Health and Human Services.

National Study on Child Neglect and Abuse Reporting. 1980. *National analysis of official child neglect and abuse reporting (1978).* Washington D.C.: U.S. Department of Health and Human Services.

————. 1981. *National analysis of official child neglect and abuse reporting (1979).* Washington D.C.: U.S. Department of Health and Human Services.

Nelson, S. 1982. *Incest: Fact and myth.* Edinburgh, Scotland: Stramullion.

Nobile, P. 1977. "Incest: The last taboo." *Penthouse* (December): 117–118, 126, 157–158.

Pagelow, M. D. 1984. *Family violence.* New York: Praeger.

Peters, S. D. 1984. "The relationship between childhood sexual victimization and adult depression among Afro-American and white women." Ph.D. diss., University of California, Los Angeles.

Peters, S., Wyatt, G., and Finkelhor, D. In press, 1986. "The prevalence of child sexual abuse: Reviewing the evidence." In *Child sexual abuse: A research handbook,* by David Finkelhor.

Phelan, P. 1981. "The process of incest: A cultural analysis." Ph.D. diss., Stanford University.

Plummer, K. 1981. "Pedophilia, constructing a sociological baseline," in *Adult sexual interest in children,* eds. M. Cook and K. Howells, pp. 221–250. New York: Academic Press.

Pomeroy, W. B. 1976. "A new look at incest." *Forum* (November): 9–13.

Ramey, J. 1979. "Dealing with the last taboo." *Siecus Report VII* 5: 1–2, 6–7.

Renvoize, J. 1982. *Incest: A family pattern.* London: Routledge & Kegan Paul.

Robinson, P. 1984. "The rape of Sigmund Freud." *New Republic* (March 12): 29–33.

The report of the commission on obscenity and pornography. 1970. Washington, D.C.: U.S. Government Printing Office.

Rush, F. 1974. "The sexual abuse of children: A feminist point of view," in *Rape: The first sourcebook for women,* eds. N. Connell and C. Wilson, pp. 64–75. New York: New American Library.

————. 1977. "The Freudian cover-up." *Chrysalis* 1: 31–45.

————. 1980. *The best kept secret: Sexual abuse of children.* Englewood Cliffs, N.J.: Prentice-Hall.

Russell, D. E. H. 1975. *The politics of rape: The victim's perspective.* New York: Stein & Day.

————. 1982. *Rape in marriage.* New York: Macmillan.

————. 1983. "The incidence and prevalence of intrafamilial and extrafamilial sexual abuse of female children." *Child Abuse and Neglect: The International Journal* 7 (2): 133–146.

————. 1984a. "The prevalence and seriousness of incestuous abuse: Stepfathers vs. biological fathers." *Child Abuse and Neglect: The International Journal* 8 (1): 15–22.

————. 1984b. *Sexual exploitation: Rape, child sexual abuse, and workplace harassment.* Beverly Hills, Calif.: Sage Publications.

Russell, D. E. H., and Trocki, K. 1985. "The impact of pornography on women." Testimony presented to the Attorney General's Commission on Pornography Hearings, Texas, September 11.

Rycroft, C. 1984. "A case of hysteria." *New York Review of Books* (April 12).

Sapp, A. D., and Carter, D. L. 1978. *Child abuse in Texas: A descriptive study of Texas residents' attitudes.* Huntsville, Texas: University Graphic Arts Dept.

Seidner, A., and Calhoun, K. S. 1984. "Childhood sexual abuse: Factors related to differential adult adjustment." Paper presented at the Second National Conference for Family Violence Researchers, Durham, New Hampshire.

Sgroi, S. M., ed. 1982. *Handbook of clinical intervention in child sexual abuse.* Lexington, Mass.: Lexington Books.

Silbert, M., and Pines, A. 1981. "Sexual child abuse as an antecedent to prostitution." *Child Abuse and Neglect: The International Journal* 5: 407–411.

Sim, M. 1974. *Guide to psychiatry,* 3rd ed. London: Churchill Livingstone.

Steinem, G. 1977. "Pornography—not sex but the obscene use of power." *Ms.* (August): 43–44.

Summit, R. 1983. "The child abuse accommodation syndrome." *Child Abuse and Neglect: The International Journal* 7 (2): 177–193.

Thorman, G. 1983. *Incestuous families.* Springfield, Ill.: Charles C. Thomas.

Tufts New England Medical Center, Division of Child Psychiatry. 1984. "Sexually exploited children: Service and research project." Final report for the Office of Juvenile Justice and Delinquency Prevention. Washington, D.C.: U.S. Department of Justice.

Ward, E. 1985. *Father-daughter rape.* New York: Grove Press.

Weinberg, S. K. 1976, orig. pub. 1955. *Incest Behavior,* rev. ed. Secaucus, N.J.: Citadel Press.

Wyatt, G. E. 1984. "The aftermath of child sexual abuse: The victims' experience." Typescript.

————. 1985. "The sexual abuse of Afro-American and white women in childhood." *Child Abuse and Neglect: The International Journal.* 9: 507–519.

Wyatt, G., and Peters, S. In press, 1986*a.* "Methodological considerations in research on the prevalence of child sexual abuse." *Child Abuse and Neglect: The International Journal.*

————. 1986*b.* "Issues in the definition of child sexual abuse in prevalence research."

Yates, A. 1978. *Sex without shame.* New York: William Morrow.

Zillmann, D., and Bryant, J. 1984. "Effects of massive exposure to pornography," in *Pornography and sexual aggression,* eds. N. M. Malamuth and E. Donnerstein., pp. 115–141. New York: Academic Press.

Index